# NETWORK PROGRAMMING WITH GO

# NETWORK PROGRAMMING WITH GO

## Code Secure and Reliable Network Services from Scratch

### Adam Woodbeck

**no starch press**

San Francisco

**NETWORK PROGRAMMING WITH GO.** © 2021 by Adam Woodbeck

Printed in the United States of America

First printing

24 23 22 21    1 2 3 4 5 6 7 8 9

ISBN-13: 978-1-7185-0088-4 (print)
ISBN-13: 978-1-7185-0089-1 (ebook)

Publisher: William Pollock
Executive Editor: Barbara Yien
Production Editor: Kate Kaminski
Developmental Editor: Frances Saux
Cover Illustration: Gina Redman
Interior Design: Octopod Studios
Technical Reviewer: Jeremy Bowers
Copyeditor: Sharon Wilkey
Compositor: Jeff Lytle, Happenstance Type-O-Rama
Proofreader: Paula L. Fleming

For information on book distributors or translations, please contact No Starch Press, Inc. directly:
No Starch Press, Inc.
245 8th Street, San Francisco, CA 94103
phone: 1-415-863-9900; info@nostarch.com
www.nostarch.com

Library of Congress Control Number: 2020943331

For my wife, Mandy, and my children,
Benjamin and Lilyanna

## About the Author

Adam Woodbeck is a senior software engineer at Barracuda Networks, where he implemented a distributed cloud environment in Go to supplant the previous cloud infrastructure, profoundly increasing its scalability and performance. He's since served as the architect for many network-based services in Go.

## About the Technical Reviewer

Jeremy Bowers is a distinguished software architect in the Office of CTO at Barracuda Networks. Equipped with many years of lead developer experience at Barracuda and security startups, especially in network engineering, Jeremy has successfully designed and implemented services that efficiently serve hundreds of thousands of customers worldwide. He holds a bachelor's and a master's degree in computer science from Michigan State University.

# BRIEF CONTENTS

# CONTENTS IN DETAIL

# PART II: SOCKET-LEVEL PROGRAMMING  43

## 3
## RELIABLE TCP DATA STREAMS  45

## 4
## SENDING TCP DATA  73

## 5
## UNRELIABLE UDP COMMUNICATION  105

# 6
# ENSURING UDP RELIABILITY 119

# 7
# UNIX DOMAIN SOCKETS 141

# PART III: APPLICATION-LEVEL PROGRAMMING 163

# 8
# WRITING HTTP CLIENTS 165

# 9
# BUILDING HTTP SERVICES         187

# 10
# CADDY: A CONTEMPORARY WEB SERVER         217

# 14
# MOVING TO THE CLOUD 329

# ACKNOWLEDGMENTS

I've never played in a rock band, but I imagine writing this book is a bit like that. I may have been the singer-songwriter, but this book would have been noticeably inferior had it not been for the exceptional talents and support of the following people.

Jeremy Bowers is one of the most talented engineers and enjoyable human beings I've had the pleasure of knowing. The depth and breadth of his knowledge considerably eased my impostor syndrome, knowing that he staked his reputation and likely his career on the success of this book. He reviewed every paragraph and line of code to ensure their coherence and accuracy. But as with any large pull request, the responsibility for any bugs lies with me, and despite Jeremy's best efforts, I've been known to write some profoundly clever bugs. Thank you, Jeremy, for contributing your technical expertise to this book.

I don't know how much editing my writing required compared to the average author, but judging by the red markup on my drafts, Frances Saux is a saint. She shepherded me through this process and was an outstanding advocate for the reader. I could rely on her to keep my writing conversational and ask pointed questions that prompted me to elaborate on topics I take for granted. Thank you, Frances, for your patience and consistency throughout the writing process. This book certainly wouldn't be the same without your extensive efforts.

I would also like to thank Bill Pollock for giving this book his blessing; Barbara Yien for supervising it; Sharon Wilkey and Kate Kaminski for their copyediting and production expertise, respectively; Paula Fleming for proofreading; Derek Yee for the book's cover and interior design; Gina Redman for the cover illustration; and Matt Holt for reviewing Chapter 10 for technical accuracy.

Most of all, I'd like to thank my wife, Amandalyn; my son, Benjamin; and my daughter, Lilyanna. As with any extracurricular endeavor, the research and writing process consumed a lot of our family time. But I'm thankful for your patience while I strived to find a balance that worked for our family during this undertaking. Your love and support allowed me to step outside my comfort zone. Hopefully, my example will encourage you to do the same.

# INTRODUCTION

With the advent of the internet came an ever-increasing demand for network engineers and developers. Today, personal computers, tablets, phones, televisions, watches, gaming systems, vehicles, common household items, and even doorbells communicate over the internet. Network programming makes all this possible. And *secure* network programming makes it trustworthy, driving increasing numbers of people to adopt these services. This book will teach you how to write contemporary network software using Go's asynchronous features.

Google created the Go programming language in 2007 to increase the productivity of developers working with large code bases. Since then, Go has earned a reputation as a fast, efficient, and safe language for the development and deployment of software at some of the largest companies in the world. Go is easy to learn and has a rich standard library, well suited for taking advantage of multicore, networked systems.

This book details the basics of network programming with an emphasis on security. You will learn socket-level programming including TCP, UDP, and Unix sockets, interact with application-level protocols like HTTPS and HTTP/2, serialize data with formats like Gob, JSON, XML, and protocol buffers, perform authentication and authorization for your network services, create streams and asynchronous data transfers, write gRPC microservices, perform structured logging and instrumentation, and deploy your applications to the cloud.

At the end of our journey, you should feel comfortable using Go, its standard library, and popular third-party packages to design and implement secure network applications and microservices. Every chapter uses best practices and includes nuggets of wisdom that will help you avoid potential pitfalls.

## Who This Book Is For

If you'd like to learn how to securely share data over a network using standard protocols, all the while writing Go code that is stable, secure, and effective, this book is for you.

The target reader is a security-conscious developer or system administrator who wishes to take a deep dive into network programming and has a working knowledge of Go and Go's module support. That said, the first few chapters introduce basic networking concepts, so networking newcomers are welcome.

Staying abreast of contemporary protocols, standards, and best practices when designing and developing network applications can be difficult. That's why, as you work through this book, you'll be given increased responsibility. You'll also be introduced to tools and tech that will make your workload manageable.

## Installing Go

To follow along with the code in this book, install the latest stable version of Go available at *https://golang.org/*. For most programs in this book, you'll need at least Go 1.12. That said, certain programs in this book are compatible with only Go 1.14 or newer. The book calls out the use of this code.

Keep in mind that the Go version available in your operating system's package manager may be several versions behind the latest stable version.

# Recommended Development Environments

The code samples in this book are mostly compatible with Windows 10, Windows Subsystem for Linux, macOS Catalina, and contemporary Linux distributions, such as Ubuntu 20.04, Fedora 32, and Manjaro 20.1. The book calls out any code samples that are incompatible with any of those operating systems.

Some command line utilities used to test network services, such as curl or nmap, may not be part of your operating system's standard installation. You may need to install some of these command line utilities by using a package manager compatible with your operating system, such as Homebrew at *https://brew.sh/* for macOS or Chocolatey at *https://chocolatey.org/* for Windows 10. Contemporary Linux operating systems should include newer binaries in their package managers that will allow you to work through the code examples.

# What's in This Book

This book is divided into four parts. In the first, you'll learn the foundational networking knowledge you'll need to understand before you begin writing network software.

**Chapter 1: An Overview of Networked Systems** introduces computer network organization models and the concepts of bandwidth, latency, network layers, and data encapsulation.

**Chapter 2: Resource Location and Traffic Routing** teaches you how human-readable names identify network resources, how devices locate network resources using their addresses, and how traffic gets routed between nodes on a network.

Part II of this book will put your new networking knowledge to use and teach you how to write programs that communicate using TCP, UDP, and Unix sockets. These protocols allow different devices to exchange data over a network and are fundamental to most network software you'll encounter or write.

**Chapter 3: Reliable TCP Data Streams** takes a deeper dive into the Transmission Control Protocol's handshake process, as well as its packet sequence numbering, acknowledgments, retransmissions, and other features that ensure reliable data transmission. You will use Go to establish and communicate over TCP sessions.

**Chapter 4: Sending TCP Data** details several programming techniques for transmitting data over a network using TCP, proxying data between network connections, monitoring network traffic, and avoiding common connection-handling bugs.

**Chapter 5: Unreliable UDP Communication** introduces you to the User Datagram Protocol, contrasting it with TCP. You'll learn how the difference between the two translates to your code and when to use UDP in your network applications. You'll write code that exchanges data with services using UDP.

**Chapter 6: Ensuring UDP Reliability** walks you through a practical example of performing reliable data transfers over a network using UDP.

**Chapter 7: Unix Domain Sockets** shows you how to efficiently exchange data between network services running on the same node using file-based communication.

The book's third part teaches you about application-level protocols such as HTTP and HTTP/2. You'll learn how to build applications that securely interact with servers, clients, and APIs over a network using TLS.

**Chapter 8: Writing HTTP Clients** uses Go's excellent HTTP client to send requests to, and receive resources from, servers over the World Wide Web.

**Chapter 9: Building HTTP Services** demonstrates how to use handlers, middleware, and multiplexers to build capable HTTP-based applications with little code.

**Chapter 10: Caddy: A Contemporary Web Server** introduces you to a contemporary web server named Caddy that offers security, performance, and extensibility through modules and configuration adapters.

**Chapter 11: Securing Communications with TLS** gives you the tools to incorporate authentication and encryption into your applications using TLS, including mutual authentication between a client and a server.

Part IV shows you how to serialize data into formats suitable for exchange over a network; gain insight into your services; and deploy your code to Amazon Web Services, Google Cloud, and Microsoft Azure.

**Chapter 12: Data Serialization** discusses how to exchange data between applications that use different platforms and languages. You'll write programs that serialize and deserialize data using Gob, JSON, and protocol buffers and communicate using gRPC.

**Chapter 13: Logging and Metrics** introduces tools that provide insight into how your services are working, allowing you to proactively address potential problems and recover from failures.

**Chapter 14: Moving to the Cloud** discusses how to develop and deploy a serverless application on Amazon Web Services, Google Cloud, and Microsoft Azure.

# PART I

## NETWORK ARCHITECTURE

# 1

## AN OVERVIEW OF NETWORKED SYSTEMS

*[handwritten: ✦ nodes - devices or connectors on a network]*

In the digital age, an increasing number of devices communicate over computer networks. A *computer network* is a connection between two or more devices, or *nodes,* that allows each node to share data. These connections aren't inherently reliable or secure. Thankfully, Go's standard library and its rich ecosystem are well suited for writing secure, reliable network applications.

This chapter will give you the foundational knowledge needed for this book's exercises. You'll learn about the structure of networks and how networks use protocols to communicate.

## Choosing a Network Topology

The organization of nodes in a network is called its *topology*. A network's topology can be as simple as a single connection between two nodes or as

*[handwritten: topology]*

complex as a layout of nodes that don't share a direct connection but are nonetheless able to exchange data. That's generally the case for connections between your computer and nodes on the internet. Topology types fall into six basic categories: point-to-point, daisy chain, bus, ring, star, and mesh.

In the simplest network, *point-to-point*, two nodes share a single connection (Figure 1-1). This type of network connection is uncommon, though it is useful when direct communication is required between two nodes.

Point-to-point

Figure 1-1: A direct connection between two nodes

A series of point-to-point connections creates a *daisy chain*. In the daisy chain in Figure 1-2, traffic from node C, destined for node F, must traverse nodes D and E. Intermediate nodes between an origin node and a destination node are commonly known as *hops*. You are unlikely to encounter this topology in a modern network.

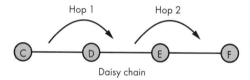

Daisy chain

Figure 1-2: Point-to-point segments joined in a daisy chain

*Bus* topology nodes share a common network link. Wired bus networks aren't common, but this type of topology drives wireless networks. The nodes on a wired network see all the traffic and selectively ignore or accept it, depending on whether the traffic is intended for them. When node H sends traffic to node L in the bus diagram in Figure 1-3, nodes I, J, K, and M receive the traffic but ignore it. Only node L accepts the data because it's the intended recipient. Although wireless clients can see each other's traffic, traffic is usually encrypted.

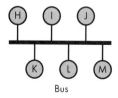

Bus

Figure 1-3: Nodes connected in a bus topology

A *ring* topology, which was used in some fiber-optic network deployments, is a closed loop in which data travels in a single direction. In Figure 1-4, for example, node N could send a message destined for node R by way of nodes O, P, and Q. Nodes O, P, and Q retransmit the message until it reaches node R. If node P fails to retransmit the message, it will never reach its destination. Because of this design, the slowest node can limit the speed at which data travels. Assuming traffic travels clockwise and node Q is the slowest, node Q slows traffic sent from node O to node N. However, traffic sent from node N to node O is not limited by node Q's slow speed since that traffic does not traverse node Q.

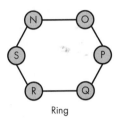

Ring

Figure 1-4: Nodes arranged
in a ring, with traffic traveling
in a single direction

In a *star* topology, a central node has individual point-to-point connections to all other nodes. You will likely encounter this network topology in wired networks. The central node, as shown in Figure 1-5, is often a *network switch*, which is a device that accepts data from the origin nodes and retransmits data to the destination nodes, like a postal service. Adding nodes is a simple matter of connecting them to the switch. Data can traverse only a single hop within this topology.

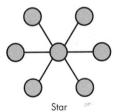

Star

Figure 1-5: Nodes connected to
a central node, which handles
traffic between nodes

Every node in a fully connected *mesh* network has a direct connection to every other node (Figure 1-6). This topology eliminates single points of failure because the failure of a single node doesn't affect traffic between any other nodes on the network. On the other hand, costs and complexity increase as the number of nodes increases, making this topology untenable for large-scale networks. This is another topology you may encounter only in larger wireless networks.

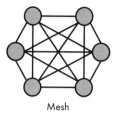

Mesh

*Figure 1-6: Interconnected
nodes in a mesh network*

You can also create a hybrid network topology by combining two or more basic topologies. Real-world networks are rarely composed of just one network topology. Rather, you are likely to encounter hybrid topologies. Figure 1-7 shows two examples. The *star-ring* hybrid network is a series of ring networks connected to a central node. The *star-bus* hybrid network is a hierarchical topology formed by the combination of bus and star network topologies.

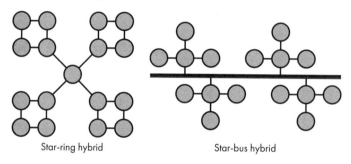

Star-ring hybrid                    Star-bus hybrid

*Figure 1-7: The star-ring and star-bus hybrid topologies*

Hybrid topologies are meant to improve reliability, scalability, and flexibility by taking advantage of each topology's strengths and by limiting the disadvantages of each topology to individual network segments.

For example, the failure of the central node in the *star-ring* hybrid in Figure 1-7 would affect inter-ring communication only. Each ring network would continue to function normally despite its isolation from the other rings. The failure of a single node in a ring would be much easier to diagnose in a star-ring hybrid network than in a single large ring network. Also, the outage would affect only a subset of the overall network.

## Bandwidth vs. Latency

Network *bandwidth* is the amount of data we can send over a network connection in an interval of time. If your internet connection is advertised as

*100Mbps download,* that means your internet connection should theoretically be able to transfer up to 100 megabits every second from your internet service provider (ISP) to your modem.

ISPs inundate us with advertisements about the amount of bandwidth they offer, so much so that it's easy for us to fixate on bandwidth and equate it with the speed of the connection. However, faster doesn't always mean greater performance. It may seem counterintuitive, but a lower-bandwidth network connection may seem to have better performance than a higher-bandwidth network connection because of one characteristic: latency.

Network *latency* is a measure of the time that passes between sending a network resource request and receiving a response. An example of latency is the delay that occurs between clicking a link on a website and the site's rendering the resulting page. You've probably experienced the frustration of clicking a link that fails to load before your web browser gives up on ever receiving a reply from the server. This happens when the latency is greater than the maximum amount of time your browser will wait for a reply.

High latency can negatively impact the user experience, lead to attacks that make your service inaccessible to its users, and drive users away from your software or service. The importance of managing latency in network software is often underappreciated by software developers. Don't fall into the trap of thinking that bandwidth is all that matters for optimal network performance.

A website's latency comes from several sources: the network latency between the client and server, the time it takes to retrieve data from a data store, the time it takes to compile dynamic content on the server side, and the time it takes for the web browser to render the page. If a user clicks a link and the page takes too long to render, the user likely won't stick around for the results, and the latency will drive traffic away from your application. Keeping latency to a minimum while writing network software, be it web applications or application-programming interfaces, will pay dividends by improving the user experience and your application's ranking in popular search engines.

You can address the most common sources of latency in several ways. First, you can reduce both the distance and the number of hops between users and your service by using a content delivery network (CDN) or cloud infrastructure to locate your service near your users. Optimizing the request and response sizes will further reduce latency. Incorporating a caching strategy in your network applications can have dramatic effects on performance. Finally, taking advantage of Go's concurrency to minimize server-side blocking of the response can help. We'll focus on this in the later chapters of this book.

## The Open Systems Interconnection Reference Model

In the 1970s, as computer networks became increasingly complex, researchers created the *Open Systems Interconnection (OSI) reference model* to

" OSI "

*Protocols*

standardize networking. The OSI reference model serves as a framework for the development of and communication about protocols. *Protocols* are rules and procedures that determine the format and order of data sent over a network. For example, communication using the *Transmission Control Protocol (TCP)* requires the recipient of a message to reply with an acknowledgment of receipt. Otherwise, TCP may retransmit the message.

Although OSI is less relevant today than it once was, it's still important to be familiar with it so you'll understand common concepts, such as lower-level networking and routing, especially with respect to the involved hardware.

## The Hierarchal Layers of the OSI Reference Model

The OSI reference model divides all network activities into a strict hierarchy composed of seven layers. Visual representations of the OSI reference model, like the one in Figure 1-8, arrange the layers into a stack, with Layer 7 at the top and Layer 1 at the bottom.

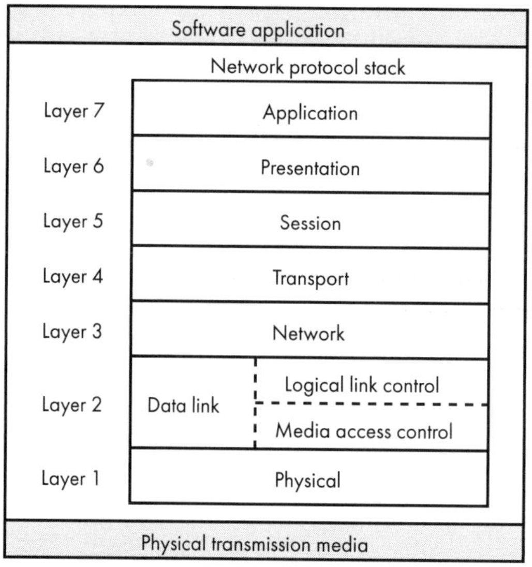

| | | Software application | |
|---|---|---|---|
| | | Network protocol stack | |
| Layer 7 | | Application | |
| Layer 6 | | Presentation | |
| Layer 5 | | Session | |
| Layer 4 | | Transport | |
| Layer 3 | | Network | |
| Layer 2 | Data link | Logical link control | |
| | | Media access control | |
| Layer 1 | | Physical | |
| | | Physical transmission media | |

*Figure 1-8: Seven layers of the OSI reference model*

It's easy to interpret these layer designations as independent units of code. Rather, they describe abstractions we ascribe to parts of our software. For example, there is no *Layer 7* library you can incorporate into your software. But you can say that the software you wrote implements a service at Layer 7. The seven layers of the OSI model are as follows:

**Layer 7—application layer** Your network applications and libraries most often interact with the application layer, which is responsible for identifying hosts and retrieving resources. Web browsers, Skype, and bit torrent clients are examples of Layer 7 applications.

**Layer 6—presentation layer**  The presentation layer prepares data for the network layer when that data is moving down the stack, and it presents data to the application layer when that data moves up the stack. Encryption, decryption, and data encoding are examples of Layer 6 functions.

**Layer 5—session layer**  The session layer manages the connection life cycle between nodes on a network. It's responsible for establishing the connection, managing connection time-outs, coordinating the mode of operation, and terminating the connection. Some Layer 7 protocols rely on services provided by Layer 5.

**Layer 4—transport layer**  The transport layer controls and coordinates the transfer of data between two nodes while maintaining the reliability of the transfer. Maintaining the reliability of the transfer includes correcting errors, controlling the speed of data transfer, chunking or segmenting the data, retransmitting missing data, and acknowledging received data. Often protocols in this layer might retransmit data if the recipient doesn't acknowledge receipt of the data.

**Layer 3—network layer**  The network layer is responsible for transmitting data between nodes. It allows you to send data to a network address without having a direct point-to-point connection to the remote node. OSI does not require protocols in this layer to provide reliable transport or report transmission errors to the sender. The network layer is home to network management protocols involved in routing, addressing, multicasting, and traffic control. The next chapter covers these topics.

**Layer 2—data link layer**  The data link layer handles data transfers between two directly connected nodes. For example, the data link layer facilitates data transfer from a computer to a switch and from the switch to another computer. Protocols in this layer identify and attempt to correct errors on the physical layer.

The data link layer's retransmission and flow control functions are dependent on the underlying physical medium. For example, Ethernet does not retransmit incorrect data, whereas wireless does. This is because bit errors on Ethernet networks are infrequent, whereas they're common over wireless. Protocols further up the network protocol stack can ensure that the data transmission is reliable if this layer doesn't do so, though generally with less efficiency.

**Layer 1—physical layer**  The physical layer converts bits from the network stack to electrical, optic, or radio signals suitable for the underlying physical medium and from the physical medium back into bits. This layer controls the bit rate. The bit rate is the data speed limit. A gigabit per second bit rate means data can travel at a maximum of 1 billion bits per second between the origin and destination.

A common confusion when discussing network transmission rates is using bytes per second instead of bits per second. We count the number of zeros and ones, or *bits*, we can transfer per second. Therefore, network transmission rates are measured in bits per second. We use bytes per second when discussing the amount of data transferred.

If your ISP advertises a 100Mbps download rate, that doesn't mean you can download a 100MB file in one second. Rather, it may take closer to eight seconds under ideal network conditions. It's appropriate to say we can transfer a maximum of 12.5MB per second over the 100Mbps connection.

## Sending Traffic by Using Data Encapsulation

*Encapsulation* is a method of hiding implementation details or making only relevant details available to the recipient. Think of encapsulation as being like a package you send through the postal service. We could say that the envelope encapsulates its contents. In doing so, it may include the destination address or other crucial details used by the next leg of its journey. The actual contents of your package are irrelevant; only the details on the package are important for transport.

As data travels down the stack, it's encapsulated by the layer below. We typically call the data traveling down the stack a *payload*, although you might see it referred to as a *message body*. The literature uses the term *service data unit (SDU)*. For example, the transport layer encapsulates payloads from the session layer, which in turn encapsulates payloads from the presentation layer. When the payload moves up the stack, each layer strips the header information from the previous stack.

Even protocols that operate in a single OSI layer use data encapsulation. Take version 1 of the *HyperText Transfer Protocol (HTTP/1)*, for example, a Layer 7 protocol that both the client and the server use to exchange web content. HTTP defines a complete message, including header information, that the client sends from its Layer 7 to the server's Layer 7; the network stack delivers the client's request to the HTTP server application. The HTTP server application initiates a response to its network stack, which creates a Layer 7 payload and sends it back to the client's Layer 7 application (Figure 1-9).

Communication between the client and the server on the same layer is called *horizontal communication,* a term that makes it sound like a single-layer protocol on the client directly communicates with its counterpart on the server. In fact, in horizontal communication, data must travel all the way down the client's stack, then back up the server's stack.

For example, Figure 1-10 shows how an HTTP request traverses the stack.

Generally, a payload travels down the client's network stack, over physical media to the server, and up the server's network stack to its corresponding layer. The result is that data sent from one layer at the origin node arrives at the same layer on the destination node. The server's response takes the same path in the opposite direction. On the client's side, Layer 6 receives Layer 7's payload, then encapsulates the payload with a header to create Layer 6's payload. Layer 5 receives Layer 6's payload, adds its own header, and sends its payload on to Layer 4, where we're introduced to our first transmission protocol: TCP.

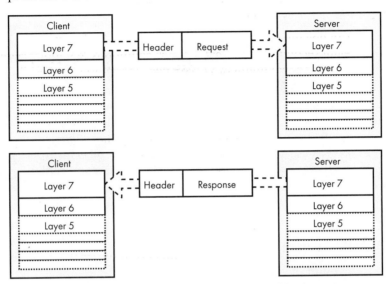

Figure 1-9: Horizontal communication from the client to the server and back

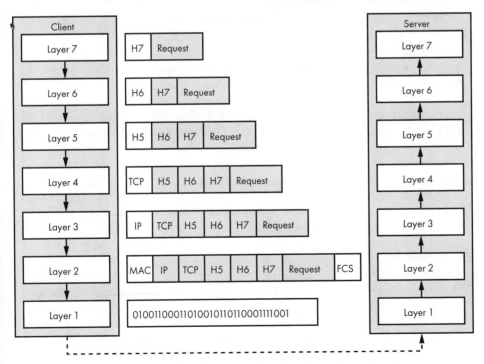

Figure 1-10: An HTTP request traveling from Layer 7 on the client to Layer 7 on the server

TCP is a Layer 4 protocol whose payloads are also known as *segments* or *datagrams*. TCP accepts Layer 5's payload and adds its header before sending the segment on to Layer 3. The *Internet Protocol (IP)* at Layer 3 receives the TCP segment and encapsulates it with a header to create Layer 3's payload, which is known as a *packet*. Layer 2 accepts the packet and adds a header and a footer, creating its payload, called a *frame*. Layer 2's header translates the recipient's IP address into a *media access control (MAC)* address, which is a unique identifier assigned to the node's network interface. Its footer contains a *frame check sequence (FCS)*, which is a checksum to facilitate error detection. Layer 1 receives Layer 2's payload in the form of bits and sends the bits to the server.

The server's Layer 1 receives the bits, converts them to a frame, and sends the frame up to Layer 2. Layer 2 strips its header and footer from the frame and passes the packet up to Layer 3. The process of reversing each layer's encapsulation continues up the stack until the payload reaches Layer 7. Finally, the HTTP server receives the client's request from the network stack.

## The TCP/IP Model

Around the same time as researchers were developing the OSI reference model, the Defense Advanced Research Projects Agency (DARPA), an agency of the US Department of Defense, spearheaded a parallel effort to develop protocols. This effort resulted in a set of protocols we now call the *TCP/IP model*. The project's impact on the US military, and subsequently the world's communications, was profound. The TCP/IP model reached critical mass when Microsoft incorporated it into Windows 95 in the early 1990s. Today, TCP/IP is ubiquitous in computer networking, and it's the protocol stack we'll use in this book.

TCP/IP—named for the Transmission Control Protocol and the Internet Protocol—facilitated networks designed using the *end-to-end principle*, whereby each network segment includes only enough functionality to properly transmit and route bits; all other functionality belongs to the endpoints, or the sender and receiver's network stacks. Contrast this with modern cellular networks, where more of the network functionality must be provided by the network between cell phones to allow for a cell phone connection to jump from tower to tower without disconnecting its phone call. The TCP/IP specification recommends that implementations be robust; they should send well-formed packets yet accept any packet whose intention is clear, regardless of whether the packet adheres to technical specifications.

Like the OSI reference model, TCP/IP relies on layer encapsulation to abstract functionality. It consists of four named layers: the application, transport, internet, and link layers. TCP/IP's application and link layers generalize their OSI counterparts, as shown in Figure 1-11.

| Software application | | |
|---|---|---|
| TCP/IP | OSI | |
| Application | Application | |
| | Presentation | |
| | Session | |
| Transport | Transport | |
| Internet/network | Network | |
| Link | Data link | |
| | Physical | |
| Physical transmission media | | |

*Figure 1-11: The four-layer TCP/IP model compared to the seven-layer OSI reference model*

The TCP/IP model simplifies OSI's application, presentation, and session layers into a single application layer, primarily because TCP/IP's protocols frequently cross boundaries of OSI Layers 5 through 7. Likewise, OSI's data link and physical layers correspond to TCP/IP's link layer. TCP/IP's and OSI's transport and network layers share a one-to-one relationship.

This simplification exists because researchers developed prototype implementations first and then formally standardized their final implementation, resulting in a model geared toward practical use. On the other hand, committees spent considerable time devising the OSI reference model to address a wide range of requirements before anyone created an implementation, leading to the model's increased complexity.

### The Application Layer

Like OSI's application layer, the TCP/IP model's *application layer* interacts directly with software applications. Most of the software we write uses protocols in this layer, and when your web browser retrieves a web page, it reads from this layer of the stack.

You'll notice that the TCP/IP application layer encompasses three OSI layers. This is because TCP/IP doesn't define specific presentation or session functions. Instead, the specific application protocol implementations concern themselves with those details. As you'll see, some TCP/IP application layer protocols would be hard-pressed to fit neatly into a single upper layer of the OSI model, because they have functionality that spans more than one OSI layer.

Common TCP/IP application layer protocols include HTTP, the *File Transfer Protocol (FTP)* for file transfers between nodes, and the *Simple Mail Transfer Protocol (SMTP)* for sending email to mail servers. The

*Dynamic Host Configuration Protocol (DHCP)* and the *Domain Name System (DNS)* also function in the application layer. DHCP and DNS provide the addressing and name resolution services, respectively, that allow other application layer protocols to operate. HTTP, FTP, and SMTP are examples of protocol implementations that provide the presentation or session functionality in TCP/IP's application layer. We'll discuss these protocols in later chapters.

## The Transport Layer

*Transport layer* protocols handle the transfer of data between two nodes, like OSI's Layer 4. These protocols can help ensure *data integrity* by making sure that all data sent from the origin completely and correctly makes its way to the destination. Keep in mind that data integrity doesn't mean the destination will receive all segments we send through the transport layer. There are just too many causes of packet loss over a network. It does mean that TCP specifically will make sure the data received by the destination is in the correct order, without duplicate data or missing data.

The primary transport layer protocols you'll use in this book are TCP and the *User Datagram Protocol (UDP)*. As mentioned in "Sending Traffic by Using Data Encapsulation" on page 10, this layer handles segments, or datagrams.

**NOTE**     *TCP also overlaps a bit with OSI's Layer 5, because TCP includes session-handling capabilities that would otherwise fall under the scope of OSI's session layer. But, for our purposes, it's okay to generalize the transport layer as representing OSI's Layer 4.*

Most of our network applications rely on the transport layer protocols to handle the error correction, flow control, retransmission, and transport acknowledgment of each segment. However, the TCP/IP model doesn't require every transport layer protocol to fulfill each of those elements. UDP is one such example. If your application requires the use of UDP for maximal throughput, the onus is on you to implement some sort of error-checking or session management, since UDP provides neither.

## The Internet Layer

The *internet layer* is responsible for routing packets of data from the upper layers between the origin node and the destination node, often over multiple networks with heterogeneous physical media. It has the same functions as OSI's Layer 3 network layer. (Some sources may refer to TCP/IP's internet layer as the *network layer*.)

*Internet Protocol version 4 (IPv4)*, *Internet Protocol version 6 (IPv6)*, *Border Gateway Protocol (BGP)*, *Internet Control Message Protocol (ICMP)*, *Internet Group Management Protocol (IGMP)*, and the *Internet Protocol Security (IPsec)* suite, among others, provide host identification and routing to TCP/IP's internet layer. We will cover these protocols in the next chapter, when we discuss host addressing and routing. For now, know that this layer plays an integral role in ensuring that the data we send reaches its destination, no matter the complexity between the origin and destination.

### The Link Layer

The *link layer*, which corresponds to Layers 1 and 2 of the OSI reference model, is the interface between the core TCP/IP protocols and the physical media.

The link layer's *Address Resolution Protocol (ARP)* translates a node's IP address to the MAC address of its network interface. The link layer embeds the MAC address in each frame's header before passing the frame on to the physical network. We'll discuss MAC addresses and their routing significance in the next chapter.

Not all TCP/IP implementations include link layer protocols. Older readers may remember the joys of connecting to the internet over phone lines using analog modems. Analog modems made serial connections to ISPs. These serial connections didn't include link layer support via the serial driver or modem. Instead, they required the use of link layer protocols, such as the *Serial Line Internet Protocol (SLIP)* or the *Point-to-Point Protocol (PPP)*, to fill the void. Those that do not implement a link layer typically rely on the underlying network hardware and device drivers to pick up the slack. The TCP/IP implementations over Ethernet, wireless, and fiber-optic networks we'll use in this book rely on device drivers or network hardware to fulfill the link layer portion of their TCP/IP stack.

## What You've Learned

In this chapter, you learned about common network topologies and how to combine those topologies to maximize their advantages and minimize their disadvantages. You also learned about the OSI and TCP/IP reference models, their layering, and data encapsulation. You should feel comfortable with the order of each layer and how data moves from one layer to the next. Finally, you learned about each layer's function and the role it plays in sending and receiving data between nodes on a network.

This chapter's goal was to give you enough networking knowledge to make sense of the next chapter. However, it's important that you explore these topics in greater depth, because comprehensive knowledge of networking principles and architectures can help you devise better algorithms. I'll suggest additional reading for each of the major topics covered in this chapter to get you started. I also recommend you revisit this chapter after working through some of the examples in this book.

The OSI reference model is available for reading online at *https://www .itu.int/rec/T-REC-X.200-199407-I/en/.* Two Requests for Comments (RFCs)—detailed publications meant to describe internet technologies—outline the TCP/IP reference model: RFC 1122 and RFC 1123 (*https://tools.ietf.org/html/ rfc1122/* and *https://tools.ietf.org/html/rfc1123/*). RFC 1122 covers the lower three layers of the TCP/IP model, whereas RFC 1123 describes the application layer and support protocols, such as DNS. If you'd like a more comprehensive reference for the TCP/IP model, you'd be hard-pressed to do better than *The TCP/IP Guide* by Charles M. Kozierok (No Starch Press, 2005).

Network latency has plagued countless network applications and spawned an industry. Some CDN providers write prolifically on the topic of latency and interesting issues they've encountered while improving their offerings. CDN blogs that provide insightful posts include the Cloudflare Blog (*https://blog.cloudflare.com/*), the KeyCDN Blog (*https://www.keycdn.com/blog/*), and the Fastly Blog (*https://www.fastly.com/blog/*). If you're purely interested in learning more about latency and its sources, consider "Latency (engineering)" on Wikipedia (*https://en.wikipedia.org/wiki/Latency_(engineering)*) and Cloudflare's glossary (*https://www.cloudflare.com/learning/performance/glossary/what-is-latency/*) as starting points.

# 2

## RESOURCE LOCATION AND
## TRAFFIC ROUTING

To write effective network programs, you need to understand how to use human-readable names to identify nodes on the internet, how those names are translated into addresses for network devices to use, and how traffic makes its way between nodes on the internet, even if they're on opposite sides of the planet. This chapter covers those topics and more.

We'll first have a look at how IP addresses identify hosts on a network. Then we'll discuss *routing*, or sending traffic between network hosts that aren't directly connected, and cover some common routing protocols. Finally, we'll discuss *domain name resolution* (the process of translating human-readable names to IP addresses), potential privacy implications of DNS, and the solutions to overcome those privacy concerns.

You'll need to understand these topics to provide comprehensive network services and locate the resources used by your services, such as third-party application programming interfaces (APIs). This information should

*API's*
*3rd party*
*application*
*program*
*interfaces*

also help you debug inevitable network outages or performance issues your code may encounter. For example, say you provide a service that integrates the Google Maps API to provide interactive maps and navigation. Your service would need to properly locate the API endpoint and route traffic to it. Or your service may need to store archives in an Amazon Simple Storage Service (S3) bucket via the Amazon S3 API. In each example, name resolution and routing play an integral role.

## The Internet Protocol

The *Internet Protocol (IP)* is a set of rules that dictate the format of data sent over a network—specifically, the internet. *IP addresses* identify nodes on a network at the internet layer of the TCP/IP stack, and you use them to facilitate communication between nodes.

IP addresses function in the same way as postal addresses; nodes send packets to other nodes by addressing packets to the destination node's IP address. Just as it's customary to include a return address on postal mail, packet headers include the IP address of the origin node as well. Some protocols require an acknowledgment of successful delivery, and the destination node can use the origin node's IP address to send the delivery confirmation.

Two versions of IP addresses are in public use: IPv4 and IPv6. This chapter covers both.

## IPv4 Addressing

*IPv4* is the fourth version of the Internet Protocol. It was the first IP version in use on the internet's precursor, ARPANET, in 1983, and the predominant version in use today. IPv4 addresses are 32-bit numbers arranged in four groups of 8 bits (called *octets*) separated by decimal points.

**NOTE** *RFCs use the term* octet *as a disambiguation of the term* byte, *because a byte's storage size has historically been platform dependent.*

The total range of 32-bit numbers limits us to just over four billion possible IPv4 addresses. Figure 2-1 shows the binary and decimal representation of an IPv4 address.

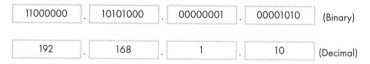

*Figure 2-1: Four 8-bit octets representing an IPv4 address in both binary and decimal formats*

The first line of Figure 2-1 illustrates an IPv4 address in binary form. The second line is the IPv4 address's decimal equivalent. We usually write IPv4 addresses in the more readable decimal format when displaying them or when using them in code. We will use their binary representation when we're discussing network addressing later in this section.

## Network and Host IDs

The 32 bits that compose an IPv4 address represent two components: a network ID and a host ID. The *network ID* informs the network devices responsible for shuttling packets toward their destination about the next appropriate hop in the transmission. These devices are called *routers*. Routers are like the mail carrier of a network, in that they accept data from a device, examine the network ID of the destination address, and determine where the data needs to be sent to reach its destination. You can think of the network ID as a mailing address's ZIP (or postal) code.

Once the data reaches the destination network, the router uses the *host ID* to deliver the data to the specific recipient. The host ID is like your street address. In other words, a network ID identifies a group of nodes whose address is part of the same network. We'll see what network and host IDs look like later in this chapter, but Figure 2-2 shows IPv4 addresses sharing the same network ID.

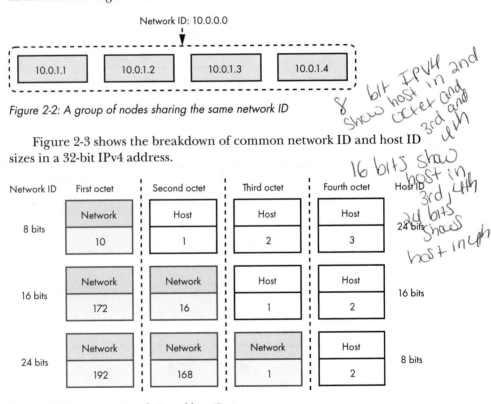

Figure 2-2: A group of nodes sharing the same network ID

Figure 2-3 shows the breakdown of common network ID and host ID sizes in a 32-bit IPv4 address.

Figure 2-3: Common network ID and host ID sizes

The network ID portion of an IPv4 address always starts with the leftmost bit, and its size is determined by the size of the network it belongs to. The remaining bits designate the host ID. For example, the first 8 bits of the IPv4 address represent the network ID in an 8-bit network, and the remaining 24 bits represent the host ID.

Figure 2-4 shows the IP address 192.168.156.97 divided into its network ID and host ID. This IP address is part of a 16-bit network. This tells us that the first 16 bits form the network ID and the remaining 16 bits form the host ID.

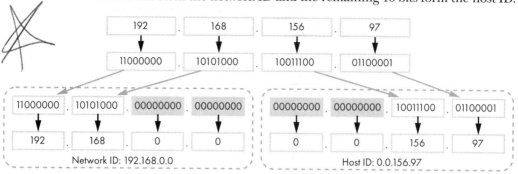

Figure 2-4: Deriving the network ID and the host ID from an IPv4 address in a 16-bit network

To derive the network ID for this example, you take the first 16 bits and append zeros for the remaining bits to produce the 32-bit network ID of 192.168.0.0. You prepend zeroed bits to the last 16 bits, resulting in the 32-bit host ID of 0.0.156.97.

## Subdividing IPv4 Addresses into Subnets

IPv4's network and host IDs allow you to *subdivide*, or partition, the more than four billion IPv4 addresses into smaller groups to keep the network secure and easier to manage. All IP addresses in these smaller networks, called *subnets,* share the same network ID but have unique host IDs. The size of the network dictates the number of host IDs and, therefore, the number of individual IP addresses in the network.

Identifying individual networks allows you to control the flow of information between networks. For example, you could split your network into a subnet meant for public services and another for private services. You could then allow external traffic to reach your public services while preventing external traffic from reaching your private network. As another example, your bank provides services such as online banking, customer support, and mobile banking. These are public services that you interact with after successful authentication. But you don't have access to the bank's internal network, where its systems manage electronic transfers, balance ledgers, serve internal email, and so on. These services are restricted to the bank's employees via the private network.

### Allocating Networks with CIDR

You allocate networks using a method known as *Classless Inter-Domain Routing (CIDR)*. In CIDR, you indicate the number of bits in the network ID by appending a *network prefix* to each IP address, consisting of a forward slash and an integer. Though it's appended to the end of the IP address, you call it a *prefix* rather than a *suffix* because it indicates how many of the IP address's most significant bits, or prefixed bits, constitute the network ID. For example, you'd write the IP address 192.168.156.97 from Figure 2-4 as 192.168.156.97/16 in CIDR notation, indicating that it belongs to a 16-bit network and that the network ID is the first 16 bits of the IP address.

From there, you can derive the network IP address by applying a subnet mask. Subnet masks encode the CIDR network prefix in its decimal representation. They are applied to an IP address using a bitwise AND to derive the network ID.

Table 2-1 details the most common CIDR network prefixes, the corresponding subnet mask, the available networks for each network prefix, and the number of usable hosts in each network.

**Table 2-1:** CIDR Network Prefix Lengths and Their Corresponding Subnet Masks

| CIDR network prefix length | Subnet mask | Available networks | Usable hosts per network |
|---|---|---|---|
| 8 | 255.0.0.0 | 1 | 16,777,214 |
| 9 | 255.128.0.0 | 2 | 8,388,606 |
| 10 | 255.192.0.0 | 4 | 4,194,302 |
| 11 | 255.224.0.0 | 8 | 2,097,150 |
| 12 | 255.240.0.0 | 16 | 1,048,574 |
| 13 | 255.248.0.0 | 32 | 524,286 |
| 14 | 255.252.0.0 | 64 | 262,142 |
| 15 | 255.254.0.0 | 128 | 131,070 |
| 16 | 255.255.0.0 | 256 | 65,534 |
| 17 | 255.255.128.0 | 512 | 32,766 |
| 18 | 255.255.192.0 | 1,024 | 16,382 |
| 19 | 255.255.224.0 | 2,048 | 8,190 |
| 20 | 255.255.240.0 | 4,096 | 4,094 |
| 21 | 255.255.248.0 | 8,192 | 2,046 |
| 22 | 255.255.252.0 | 16,384 | 1,022 |
| 23 | 255.255.254.0 | 32,768 | 510 |
| 24 | 255.255.255.0 | 65,536 | 254 |
| 25 | 255.255.255.128 | 131,072 | 126 |
| 26 | 255.255.255.192 | 262,144 | 62 |
| 27 | 255.255.255.224 | 524,288 | 30 |
| 28 | 255.255.255.240 | 1,048,576 | 14 |
| 29 | 255.255.255.248 | 2,097,152 | 6 |
| 30 | 255.255.255.252 | 4,194,304 | 2 |

You may have noticed that the number of usable hosts per network is two less than expected in each row because each network has two special addresses. The first IP address in the network is the network address, and the last IP address is the broadcast address. (We'll cover broadcast addresses a bit later in this chapter.) Take 192.168.0.0/16, for example. The first IP address in the network is 192.168.0.0. This is the network address. The last IP address in the network is 192.168.255.255, which is the broadcast address. For now, understand that you do not assign the network IP address or the broadcast IP address to a host's network interface. These special IP addresses are used for routing data between networks and broadcasting, respectively.

The 31- and 32-bit network prefixes are purposefully absent from Table 2-1, largely because they are beyond the scope of this book. If you're curious about 31-bit network prefixes, RFC 3021 covers their application. A 32-bit network prefix signifies a single-host network. For example, 192.168.1.1/32 represents a subnetwork of one node with the address 192.168.1.1.

### Allocating Networks That Don't Break at an Octet Boundary

Some network prefixes don't break at an octet boundary. For example, Figure 2-5 derives the network ID and host ID of 192.168.156.97 in a 19-bit network. The full IP address in CIDR notation is 192.168.156.97/19.

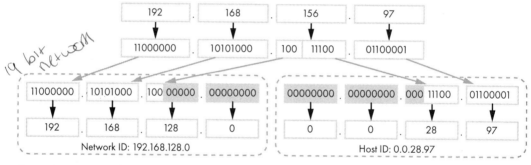

Figure 2-5: Deriving the network ID and the host ID from the IPv4 address in a 19-bit network

In this case, since the network prefix isn't a multiple of 8 bits, an octet's bits are split between the network ID and host ID. The 19-bit network example in Figure 2-5 results in the network ID of 192.168.128.0 and the host ID of 0.0.28.97, where the network ID borrows 3 bits from the third octet, leaving 13 bits for the host ID.

Appending a zeroed host ID to the network ID results in the network address. In a comparable manner, appending a host ID in which all its bits are 1 to the network ID derives the broadcast address. But the third octet's equaling 156 can be a little confusing. Let's focus on just the third octet. The third octet of the network ID is 1000 0000. The third octet of the host ID of all ones is 0001 1111 (the first 3 bits are part of the network ID, remember). If we append the network ID's third octet to the host ID's third octet, the result is 1001 1111, which is the decimal 156.

### Private Address Spaces and Localhost

RFC 1918 details the private address spaces of 10.0.0.0/8, 172.16.0.0/12, and 192.168.0.0/16 for use in local networks. Universities, corporations, governments, and residential networks can use these subnets for local addressing.

In addition, each host has the 127.0.0.0/8 subnet designated as its local subnet. Addresses in this subnet are local to the host and simply called *localhost*. Even if your computer is not on a network, it should still have an address on the 127.0.0.0/8 subnet, most likely 127.0.0.1.

## Ports and Socket Addresses

If your computer were able to communicate over the network with only one node at a time, that wouldn't provide a very efficient or pleasant experience. It would become annoying if your streaming music stopped every time you clicked a link in your web browser because the browser needed to interrupt the stream to retrieve the requested web page. Thankfully, TCP and UDP allow us to multiplex data transmissions by using *ports*.

The operating system uses ports to uniquely identify data transmission between nodes for the purposes of multiplexing the outgoing application data and demultiplexing the incoming data back to the proper application. The combination of an IP address and a port number is a *socket address*, typically written in the format *address:port*.

Ports are 16-bit unsigned integers. Port numbers 0 to 1023 are well-known ports assigned to common services by the *Internet Assigned Numbers Authority (IANA)*. The IANA is a private US nonprofit organization that globally allocates IP addresses and port numbers. For example, HTTP uses port 80. Port 443 is the HTTPS port. SSH servers typically listen on port 22. (These well-known ports are guidelines. An HTTP server may listen to any port, not just port 80.)

Despite these ports being well-known, there is no restriction on which ports services may use. For example, an administrator who wants to obscure a service from attackers expecting it on port 22 may configure an SSH server to listen on port 22422. The IANA designates ports 1024 to 49151 as semi-reserved for lesser common services. Ports 49152 to 65535 are ephemeral ports meant for client socket addresses as recommended by the IANA. (The port range used for client socket addresses is operating-system dependent.)

A common example of port usage is the interaction between your web browser and a web server. Your web browser opens a socket with the operating system, which assigns an address to the socket. Your web browser sends a request through the socket to port 80 on the web server. The web server sends its response to the socket address corresponding to the socket your web browser is monitoring. Your operating system receives the response and passes it onto your web browser through the socket. Your web browser's socket address and the web server's socket address (server IP and port 80) uniquely identify this transaction. This allows your operating system to properly demultiplex the response and pass it along to the right application (that is, your web browser).

## Network Address Translation

The four billion IPv4 addresses may seem like a lot until you consider there will be an estimated 24.6 billion Internet of Things (IoT) devices by 2025, according to the Ericsson Mobility Report of June 2020 (*https://www.ericsson .com/en/mobility-report/reports/june-2020/iot-connections-outlook/*). In fact, we've already run out of unreserved IPv4 addresses. The IANA allocated the last IPv4 address block on January 31, 2011.

One way to address the IPv4 shortage is by using *network address translation (NAT)*, a process that allows numerous nodes to share the same public IPv4 address. It requires a device, such as a firewall, load balancer, or router that can keep track of incoming and outgoing traffic and properly route incoming traffic to the correct node.

Figure 2-6 illustrates the NAT process between nodes on a private network and the internet.

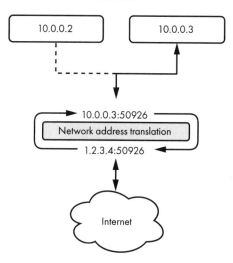

*Figure 2-6: Network address translation between a private network and the internet*

In Figure 2-6, a NAT-capable device receives a connection from the client socket address 10.0.0.3:50926 destined for a host on the internet. First, the NAT device opens its own connection to the destination host using its public IP 1.2.3.4, preserving the client's socket address port. Its socket address for this transaction is 1.2.3.4:50926. If a client is already using port 50926, the NAT device chooses a random port for its socket address. Then, the NAT device sends the request to the destination host and receives the response on its 1.2.3.4:50926 socket. The NAT device knows which client receives the response because it translates its socket address to the client socket address that established the connection. Finally, the client receives the destination host's response from the NAT device.

The important thing to remember with network address translation is that a node's private IPv4 address behind a NAT device is not visible or directly accessible to other nodes outside the network address–translated network segment. If you're writing a service that needs to provide a public address for its clients, you may not be able to rely on your node's private IPv4 address if it's behind a NAT device. Hosts outside the NAT device's private network cannot establish incoming connections. Only clients in the private network may establish connections through the NAT device. Instead, your service must rely on the NAT device's properly forwarding a port from its public IP to a socket address on your node.

### Unicasting, Multicasting, and Broadcasting

Sending packets from one IP address to another IP address is known as *unicast addressing*. But TCP/IP's internet layer supports IP *multicasting*, or sending a single message to a group of nodes. You can think of it as an opt-in mailing list, such as a newspaper subscription.

From a network programming perspective, multicasting is simple. Routers and switches typically replicate the message for us, as shown in Figure 2-7. We'll discuss multicasting later in this book.

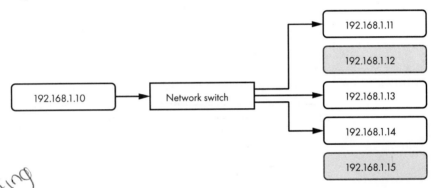

Figure 2-7: The 192.168.1.10 node sending a packet to a subset of network addresses

*Broadcasting* is the ability to concurrently deliver a message to all IP addresses in a network. To do this, nodes on a network send packets to the *broadcast address* of a subnet. A network switch or router then propagates the packets out to all IPv4 addresses in the subnet (Figure 2-8).

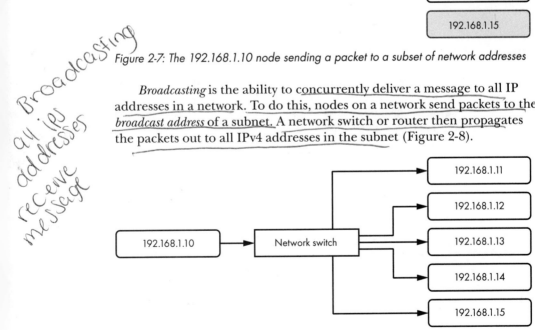

Figure 2-8: The 192.168.1.10 node sending a packet to all addresses on its subnet

Unlike multicasting, the nodes in the subnet don't first need to opt in to receiving broadcast messages. If the node at 192.168.1.10 in Figure 2-8 sends a packet to the broadcast address of its subnet, the network switch will deliver a copy of that packet to the other five IPv4 addresses in the same subnet.

### Resolving the MAC Address to a Physical Network Connection

Recall from Chapter 1 that every network interface has a MAC address uniquely identifying the node's physical connection to the network. The MAC address is relevant to only the local network, so routers cannot use a MAC address to route data across network boundaries. Instead, they can route traffic across network boundaries by using an IPv4 address. Once a packet reaches the local network of a destination node, the router sends the data to the destination node's MAC address and, finally, to the destination node's physical network connection.

The *Address Resolution Protocol (ARP)*, detailed in RFC 826 (*https://tools.ietf .org/html/rfc826/*), finds the appropriate MAC address for a given IP address— a process called *resolving* the MAC address. Nodes maintain ARP tables that map an IPv4 address to a MAC address. If a node does not have an entry in its ARP table for a destination IPv4 address, the node will send a request to the local network's broadcast address asking, "Who has this IPv4 address? Please send me your MAC address. Oh, and here is my MAC address." The destination node will receive the ARP request and respond with an ARP reply to the originating node. The originating node will then send the data to the destination node's MAC address. Nodes on the network privy to this conversation will typically update their ARP tables with the values.

## IPv6 Addressing

Another solution to the IPv4 shortage is to migrate to the next generation of IP addressing, IPv6. *IPv6 addresses* are 128-bit numbers arranged in eight colon-separated groups of 16 bits, or *hextets*. There are more than 340 unde-cillion ($2^{128}$) IPv6 addresses.

### Writing IPv6 Addresses

In binary form, IPv6 addresses are a bit ridiculous to write. In the interest of legibility and compactness, we write IPv6 addresses with lowercase hexa-decimal values instead.

**NOTE**  *IPv6 hexadecimal values are case-insensitive. However, the Internet Engineering Task Force (IETF) recommends using lowercase values.*

A hexadecimal (hex) digit represents 4 bits, or a *nibble*, of an IPv6 address. For example, we'd represent the two nibbles 1111 1111 in their hexadecimal equivalent of ff. Figure 2-9 illustrates the same IPv6 address in binary and hex.

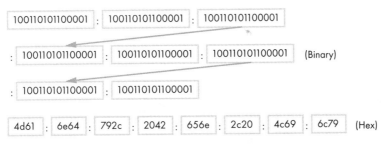

| 100110101100001 | : | 100110101100001 | : | 100110101100001 | |
| :---: | :---: | :---: | :---: | :---: | :---: |
| : | 100110101100001 | : | 100110101100001 | : | 100110101100001 | (Binary) |
| : | 100110101100001 | : | 100110101100001 | |

| 4d61 | : | 6e64 | : | 792c | : | 2042 | : | 656e | : | 2c20 | : | 4c69 | : | 6c79 | (Hex) |

Figure 2-9: Binary and hex representations of the same IPv6 address

Even though hexadecimal IPv6 addresses are a bit more succinct than their binary equivalent, we still have some techniques available to us to simplify them a bit more.

### Simplifying IPv6 Addresses

An IPv6 address looks something like this: fd00:4700:0010:0000:0000: 0000:6814:d103. That's quite a bit harder to remember than an IPv4 address. Thankfully, you can improve the IPv6 address's presentation to make it more readable by following a few rules.

First, you can remove all leading zeros in each hextet. This simplifies your address without changing its value. It now looks like this: fd00:4700:10:0:0:0:6814:d103. Better, but still long.

Second, you can replace the leftmost group of consecutive, zero-value hextets with double colons, producing the shorter fd00:4700:10::6814:d103. If your address has more than one group of consecutive zero-value hextets, you can remove only the leftmost group. Otherwise, it's impossible for routers to accurately determine the number of hextets to insert when repopulating the full address from its compressed representation. For example, fd00:4700: 0000:0000:ef81:0000:6814:d103 rewrites to fd00:4700::ef81:0:6814:d103. The best you could do with the sixth hextet is to remove the leading zeros.

### IPv6 Network and Host Addresses

Like IPv4 addresses, IPv6 addresses have a network address and a host address. IPv6's host address is commonly known as the *interface ID*. The network and host addresses are both 64 bits, as shown in Figure 2-10. The first 48 bits of the network address are known as the *global routing prefix (GRP)*, and the last 16 bits of the network address are called the *subnet ID*. The 48-bit GRP is used for globally subdividing the IPv6 address space and routing traffic between these groups. The subnet ID is used to further subdivide each GRP-unique network into site-specific networks. If you run a large ISP, you are assigned one or more GRP-unique blocks of IPv6 addresses. You can then use the subnet ID in each network to further subdivide your allocated IPv6 addresses to your customers.

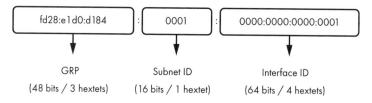

| fd28:e1d0:d184 | : | 0001 | : | 0000:0000:0000:0001 |

GRP

(48 bits / 3 hextets)

Subnet ID

(16 bits / 1 hextet)

Interface ID

(64 bits / 4 hextets)

*Figure 2-10: IPv6 global routing prefix, subnet ID, and interface ID*

The GRP gets determined for you when you request a block of IPv6 addresses from your ISP. IANA assigns the first hextet of the GRP to a regional internet registry (an organization that handles the allocation of addresses for a global region). The regional internet registry then assigns the second GRP hextet to an ISP. The ISP finally assigns the third GRP hextet before assigning a 48-bit subnet of IPv6 addresses to you.

**NOTE** *For more information on the allocation of IPv6 addresses, see IANA's "IPv6 Global Unicast Address Assignments" document at* https://www.iana.org/assignments/ipv6-unicast-address-assignments/ipv6-unicast-address-assignments.xml.

The first hextet of an IPv6 address gives you a clue to its use. Addresses beginning with the prefix 2000::/3 are meant for global use, meaning every node on the internet will have an IPv6 address starting with 2 or 3 in the first hex. The prefix fc00::/7 designates a unique local address like the 127.0.0.0/8 subnet in IPv4.

**NOTE** *IANA's "Internet Protocol Version 6 Address Space" document at* https://www.iana.org/assignments/ipv6-address-space/ipv6-address-space.xhtml *provides more details.*

Let's assume your ISP assigned the 2600:fe56:7891::/48 netblock to you. Your 16-bit subnet ID allows you to further subdivide your netblock into a maximum of 65,536 ($2^{16}$) subnets. Each of those subnets supports over 18 quintillion ($2^{64}$) hosts. If you assign 1 to the subnet as shown in Figure 2-10, you'd write the full network address as 2600:fe56:7891:1::/64 after removing leading zeros and compressing zero value hextets. Further subnetting your netblock may look like this: 2600:fe56:7891:**2**::/64, 2600:fe56:7891:**3**::/64, 2600:fe56:7891:**4**::/64.

## IPv6 Address Categories

IPv6 addresses are divided into three categories: anycast, multicast, and unicast. Notice there is no broadcast type, as in IPv4. As you'll see, anycast and multicast addresses fulfill that role in IPv6.

### Unicast Addresses

A *unicast* IPv6 address uniquely identifies a node. If an originating node sends a message to a unicast address, only the node with that address will receive the message, as shown in Figure 2-11.

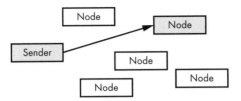

*Figure 2-11: Sending to a unicast address*

## Multicast Addresses

*Multicast* addresses represent a group of nodes. Whereas IPv4 broadcast addresses will propagate a message out to all addresses on the network, multicast addresses will simultaneously deliver a message to a subset of network addresses, not necessarily all of them, as shown in Figure 2-12.

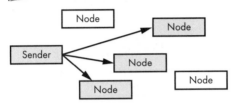

*Figure 2-12: Sending to a multicast address*

 Multicast addresses use the prefix ff00::/8.

## Anycast Addresses

Remember that IPv4 addresses must be unique per network segment, or network communication issues can occur. But IPv6 includes support for multiple nodes using the same network address. An *anycast* address represents a group of nodes listening to the same address. A message sent to an anycast address goes to the nearest node listening to the address. Figure 2-13 represents a group of nodes listening to the same address, where the nearest node to the sender receives the message. The sender could transmit to any of the nodes represented by the dotted lines, but sends to the nearest node (solid line).

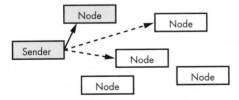

*Figure 2-13: Sending to an anycast address*

The nearest node isn't always the most physically close node. It is up to the router to determine which node receives the message, usually the node with the least latency between the origin and the destination. Aside from reducing latency, anycast addressing increases redundancy and can geolocate services.

Sending traffic around the world takes a noticeable amount of time, to the point that the closer you are to a service provider's servers, the better performance you'll experience. Geolocating services across the internet is a common method of placing servers geographically close to users to make sure performance is optimal for all users across the globe. It's unlikely you access servers across an ocean when streaming Netflix. Instead, Netflix geolocates servers close to you so that your experience is ideal.

### Advantages of IPv6 over IPv4

Aside from the ridiculously large address space, IPv6 has inherent advantages over IPv4, particularly with regard to efficiency, autoconfiguration, and security.

#### Simplified Header Format for More Efficient Routing

The IPv6 header is an improvement over the IPv4 header. The IPv4 header contains mandatory yet rarely used fields. IPv6 makes these fields optional. The IPv6 header is extensible, in that functionality can be added without breaking backward compatibility. In addition, the IPv6 header is designed for improved efficiency and reduced complexity over the IPv4 header.

IPv6 also lessens the loads on routers and other hops by ensuring that headers require minimal processing, eliminating the need for checksum calculation at every hop.

#### Stateless Address Autoconfiguration

Administrators manually assign IPv4 addresses to each node on a network or rely on a service to dynamically assign addresses. Nodes using IPv6 can automatically configure or derive their IPv6 addresses through *stateless address autoconfiguration (SLAAC)* to reduce administrative overhead.

When connected to an IPv6 network, a node can solicit the router for its network address parameters using the *Neighbor Discovery Protocol (NDP)*. NDP leverages the Internet Control Message Protocol, discussed later in this chapter, for router solicitation. It performs the same duties as IPv4's ARP. Once the node receives a reply from the router with the 64-bit network address, the node can derive the 64-bit host portion of its IPv6 address on its own using the 48-bit MAC address assigned to its network interface. The node appends the 16-bit hex FFFE to the first three octets of the MAC address known as the *originally unique identifier (OUI)*. To this, the node appends the remaining three octets of the MAC address, the network interface controller (NIC) identifier. The result is a unique 64-bit interface ID, as shown in Figure 2-14. SLAAC works only in the presence of a router that can respond with router advertisement packets. *Router advertisement packets* contain information clients need to automatically configure their IPv6 address, including the 64-bit network address.

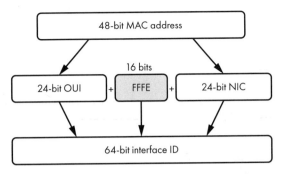

Figure 2-14: Deriving the interface ID from the MAC address

If you value your privacy, the method SLAAC uses to derive a unique interface ID should concern you. No matter which network your device is on, SLAAC will make sure the host portion of your IPv6 address contains your NIC's MAC address. The MAC address is a unique fingerprint that betrays the hardware you use and allows anyone to track your online activity. Thankfully, many people raised these concerns, and SLAAC gained privacy extensions (*https://tools.ietf.org/html/rfc4941/*), which randomize the interface ID. Because of this randomization, it's possible for more than one node on a network to generate the same interface ID. Thankfully, the NDP will automatically detect and fix any duplicate interface ID for you.

### Native IPsec Support

IPv6 has native support for *IPsec,* a technology that allows multiple nodes to dynamically create secure connections between each other, ensuring that traffic is encrypted.

**NOTE** *RFC 6434 made IPsec optional for IPv6 implementations.*

## The Internet Control Message Protocol

The Internet Protocol relies on the *Internet Control Message Protocol (ICMP)* to give it feedback about the local network. ICMP can inform you of network problems, unreachable nodes or networks, local network configuration, proper traffic routes, and network time-outs. Both IPv4 and IPv6 have their own ICMP implementations, designated ICMPv4 and ICMPv6, respectively.

Network events often result in ICMP response messages. For instance, if you attempt to send data to an unreachable node, a router will typically respond with an ICMP *destination unreachable* message informing you that your data couldn't reach the destination node. A node may become unreachable if it runs out of resources and can no longer respond to incoming data or if data cannot route to the node. Disconnecting a node from a network will immediately make it unreachable.

Routers use ICMP to help inform you of better routes to your destination node. If you send data to a router that isn't the appropriate or best

*ICMP echo request also called a "ping" and pong = your ICMP reply*

*time-to-live value dictates maximum hops before it expires*

*intermediate nodes*

*network stack*

router to handle traffic for your destination, it may reply with an ICMP *redirect* message after forwarding your data onto the correct router. The ICMP redirect message is the router's way of telling you to send your data to the appropriate router in the future.

You can determine whether a node is online and reachable by using an ICMP *echo* request (also called a *ping*). If the destination is reachable and receives your ping, it will reply with its own ICMP *echo reply* message (also called a *pong*). If the destination isn't reachable, the router will respond with a destination unreachable message.

ICMP can also notify you when data reaches the end of its life before delivery. Every IP packet has a *time-to-live* value that dictates the maximum number of hops the packet can take before its lifetime expires. The packet's time-to-live value is a counter and decrements by one for every hop it takes. You will receive an ICMP *time exceeded* message if the packet you sent doesn't reach its destination by the time its time-to-live value reaches zero.

IPv6's NDP relies heavily on ICMP router solicitation messages to properly configure a node's NIC.

## Internet Traffic Routing

Now that you know a bit about internet protocol addressing, let's explore how packets make their way across the internet from one node to another using those addresses. In Chapter 1, we discussed how data travels down the network stack of the originating node, across a physical medium, and up the stack of the destination node. But in most cases, nodes won't have a direct connection, so they'll have to make use of intermediate nodes to transfer data. Figure 2-15 shows that process.

The intermediate nodes (Nodes 1 and 2 in Figure 2-15) are typically routers or firewalls that control the path data takes from one node to the other. *Firewalls* control the flow of traffic in and out of a network, primarily to secure networks behind the firewall.

No matter what type of node they are, intermediate nodes have a network stack associated with each network interface. In Figure 2-15, Node 1 receives data on its incoming network interface. The data climbs the stack to Layer 3, where it's handed off to the outgoing network interface's stack. The data then makes its way to Node 2's incoming network interface before ultimately being routed to the server.

The incoming and outgoing network interfaces in Node 1 and Node 2 may send data over different media types using IPv4, so they must use encapsulation to isolate the implementation details of each media type from the data being sent. Let's assume Node 1 receives data from the client over a wireless network and it sends data to Node 2 over an Ethernet connection. Node 1's incoming Layer 1 knows how to convert the radio signals from the wireless network into bits. Layer 1 sends the bits up to Layer 2. Layer 2 converts the bits to a frame and extracts the packet and sends it up to Layer 3.

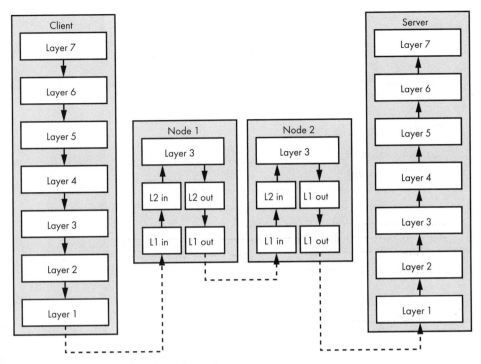

Figure 2-15: Routing packets through two hops

Layer 3 on both the incoming and outgoing NICs speak IPv4, which routes the packet between the two interface network stacks. The outgoing NIC's Layer 2 receives the packet from its Layer 3 and encapsulates it before sending the frame onto its Layer 1 as bits. The outgoing Layer 1 converts the bits into electric signals suitable for transmission over Ethernet. The data in transport from the client's Layer 7 never changed despite the data's traversing multiple nodes over different media on its way to the destination server.

## Routing Protocols

The routing overview in Figure 2-15 makes the process look easy, but the routing process relies on a symphony of protocols to make sure each packet reaches its destination no matter the physical medium traversed or network outages along the way. Routing protocols have their own criteria for determining the best path between nodes. Some protocols determine a route's efficiency based on hop count. Some may use bandwidth. Others may use more complicated means to determine which route is the most efficient.

Routing protocols are either internal or external depending on whether they route packets within an autonomous system or outside of one. An *autonomous system* is an organization that manages one or more networks. An ISP is an example of an autonomous system. Each autonomous system is assigned an autonomous system number (ASN), as outlined in RFC 1930 (*https://tools.ietf.org/html/rfc1930/*). This ASN is used to broadcast an ISP's network information to other autonomous systems using an external routing protocol. An *external routing protocol* routes data between autonomous systems. The only routing protocol we'll cover is BGP since it is the glue of the internet, binding all ASN-assigned ISPs together. You don't need to understand BGP in depth, but being familiar with it can help you better debug network issues related to your code and improve your code's resiliency.

### The Border Gateway Protocol

The *Border Gateway Protocol (BGP)* allows ASN-assigned ISPs to exchange routing information. BGP relies on trust between ISPs. That is, if an ISP says it manages a specific network and all traffic destined for that network should be sent to it, the other ISPs trust this claim and send traffic accordingly. As a result, BGP misconfigurations, or *route leaks*, often result in very public network outages.

In 2008, Pakistan Telecommunications Company effectively took down YouTube worldwide after the Pakistani Ministry of Communications demanded the country block *youtube.com* in protest of a YouTube video. Pakistan Telecom used BGP to send all requests destined for YouTube to a null route, a route that drops all data without notification to the sender. But Pakistan Telecom accidentally leaked its BGP route to the world instead of restricting it to the country. Other ISPs trusted the update and null routed YouTube requests from their clients, making *youtube.com* inaccessible for two hours all over the world.

In 2012, Google's services were rerouted through Indonesia for 27 minutes when the ISP Moratel shared a BGP route directing all Google traffic to Moratel's network as if Moratel was now hosting Google's network infrastructure. There was speculation at the time that the route leakage was malicious, but Moratel blamed a hardware failure.

BGP usually makes news only when something goes wrong. Other times, it plays the silent hero, serving a significant role in mitigating distributed denial-of-service (DDOS) attacks. In a *DDOS attack*, a malicious actor directs traffic from thousands of compromised nodes to a victim node with the aim of overwhelming the victim and consuming all its bandwidth, effectively denying service to legitimate clients. Companies that specialize in mitigating DDOS attacks use BGP to reroute all traffic destined for the victim node to their AS networks, filter out the malicious traffic from the legitimate traffic, and route the sanitized traffic back to the victim, nullifying the effects of the attack.

## Name and Address Resolution

The *Domain Name System (DNS)* is a way of matching IP addresses to *domain names*, which are the names we enter in an address bar when we want to visit websites. Although the internet protocol uses IP addresses to locate hosts, domain names (like *google.com*) are easier for humans to understand and remember. If I gave you the IP address 172.217.6.14 to visit, you wouldn't know who owned that IP address or what I was directing you to visit. But if

I gave you *google.com* instead, you'd know exactly where I was sending you. DNS allows you to remember a hostname instead of its IP address in the same way that your smartphone's contact list frees you from having to memorize all those phone numbers.

All domains are children of a *top-level domain*, such as *.com*, *.net*, *.org*, and so on. Take *nostarch.com*, for instance. No Starch Press registered the *nostarch* domain on the *.com* top-level domain from a registrar with the authority from IANA to register *.com* domains. No Starch Press now has the exclusive authority to manage DNS records for *nostarch.com* and publish records on its DNS server. This includes the ability for No Starch Press to publish *subdomains*—a subdivision of a domain—under its domain. For example, *maps.google.com* is a subdomain of *google.com*. A longer example is *sub3.sub2.sub1.domain.com*, where *sub3* is a subdomain under *sub2.sub1.domain.com*, *sub2* is subdomain under *sub1.domain.com*, and *sub1* is a subdomain under *domain.com*.

If you enter https://nostarch.com in your web browser, your computer will consult its configured *domain name resolver*, a server that knows how to retrieve the answer to your query. The resolver will start by asking one of the 13 IANA-maintained root name servers for the IP address of *nostarch.com*. The root name server will examine the top-level domain of the domain you requested and give your resolver the address of the *.com* name server. Your resolver will then ask the *.com* name server for *nostarch.com*'s IP address, which will examine the domain portion and direct your resolver to ask No Starch Press's name server. Finally, your resolver will ask No Starch Press's name server and receive the IP address that corresponds to *nostarch.com*. Your web browser will establish a connection to this IP address, retrieve the web page, and render it for you. This hierarchical journey of domain resolution allows you to zero in on a specific web server, and all you had to know was the domain name. No Starch Press is free to move its servers to a different ISP with new IP addresses, and yet you'll still be able to visit its website by using *nostarch.com*.

## Domain Name Resource Records

Domain name servers maintain *resource records* for the domains they serve. Resource records contain domain-specific information, used to satisfy domain name queries, like IP addresses, mail server hostnames, mail-handling rules, and authentication tokens. There are many resource records, but this section focuses on only the most common ones: address records, start-of-authority records, name server records, canonical name records, mail exchange records, pointer records, and text records.

NOTE    *For more details on types of resource records, see Wikipedia's entry at* https://en.wikipedia.org/wiki/List_of_DNS_record_types.

Our exploration of each resource record will use a utility called *dig* to query domain name servers. This utility may be available on your operating system, but in case you don't have dig installed, you can use the G Suite Toolbox Dig utility (*https://toolbox.googleapps.com/apps/dig/*) in a web browser and receive similar output. All domain names you'll see are *fully qualified*, which means they end in a period, displaying the domain's entire hierarchy from the root zone. The *root zone* is the top DNS namespace.

Dig's default output includes a bit of data relevant to your query but irrelevant to your study of its output. Therefore, I've elected to snip out header and footer information in dig's output in each example to follow. Also please be aware that the specific output in this book is a snapshot from when I executed each query. It may look different when you execute these commands.

### The Address Record

The *Address (A) record* is the most common record you'll query. An A record will resolve to one or more IPv4 addresses. When your computer asks its resolver to retrieve the IP address for *nostarch.com*, the resolver ultimately asks the domain name server for the *nostarch.com* Address (A) resource record. Listing 2-1 shows the question and answer sections when you query for the *google.com* A record.

```
$ dig google.com. a
-- snip --
❶ ;QUESTION
❷ google.com. ❸IN ❹A
❺ ;ANSWER
❻ google.com. ❼299 IN A ❽172.217.4.46
-- snip --
```

*Listing 2-1: DNS answer of the* google.com *A resource record*

Each section in a DNS reply begins with a header ❶, prefixed with a semicolon to indicate that the line is a comment rather than code to be processed. Within the question section, you ask the domain name server for the domain name *google.com* ❷ with the class IN ❸, which indicates that this record is internet related. You also use A to ask for the A record ❹ specifically.

In the Answer section ❺, the domain name server resolves the *google .com* A record to six IPv4 addresses. The first field of each returned line is the domain name ❻ you queried. The second field is the TTL value ❼ for the record. The *TTL value* tells domain name resolvers how long to cache or remember the record, and it lets you know how long you have until the cached record expires. When you request a DNS record, the domain name resolver will first check its cache. If the answer is in its cache, it will simply return the cached answer instead of asking the domain name server for the answer. This improves domain name resolution performance for records that are unlikely to change frequently. In this example, the record will expire in 299 seconds. The last field is the IPv4 address ❽. Your web browser could use any one of the six IPv4 addresses to establish a connection to *google.com*.

The AAAA resource record is the IPv6 equivalent of the A record.

*SOA authoritative or admin records of a domain. mandatory*

## The Start of Authority Record

The *Start of Authority (SOA) record* contains authoritative and administrative details about the domain, as shown in Listing 2-2. All domains must have an SOA record.

```
$ dig google.com. soa
-- snip --
;QUESTION
google.com. IN SOA
;ANSWER
google.com. 59 IN SOA ❶ns1.google.com. ❷dns-admin.google.com. ❸248440550
900 900 1800 60
-- snip --
```

*email*

Listing 2-2: DNS answer of the google.com SOA resource record

The first four fields of an SOA record are the same as those found in an A record. The SOA record also includes the primary name server ❶, the administrator's email address ❷, and fields ❸ used by secondary name servers outside the scope of this book. Domain name servers primarily consume SOA records. However, the email address is useful if you wish to contact the domain's administrator.

**NOTE** *The administrator's email address is encoded as a name, with the at sign (@) replaced by a period.* ✗

## The Name Server Record

*NS name server records*

The *Name Server (NS) record* returns the authoritative name servers for the domain name. *Authoritative name servers* are the name servers able to provide answers for the domain name. NS records will include the primary name server from the SOA record and any secondary name servers answering DNS queries for the domain. Listing 2-3 is an example of the NS records for *google.com*.

```
$ dig google.com. ns
-- snip --
;QUESTION
google.com. IN NS
;ANSWER
google.com. 21599 IN NS ❶ns1.google.com.
google.com. 21599 IN NS ns2.google.com.
google.com. 21599 IN NS ns3.google.com.
google.com. 21599 IN NS ns4.google.com.
-- snip --
```

Listing 2-3: DNS answer of the google.com NS resource records

Like the CNAME record, discussed next, the NS record will return a fully qualified domain name ❶, not an IP address.

## The Canonical Name Record

The *Canonical Name (CNAME) record* points one domain at another. Listing 2-4 shows a CNAME record response. CNAME records can make administration a bit easier. For example, you can create one named *mail.yourdomain.com* and direct it to Gmail's login page. This not only is easier for your users to remember but also gives you the flexibility of pointing the CNAME at another email provider in the future without having to inform your users.

```
$ dig mail.google.com. a
-- snip --
;QUESTION
mail.google.com. IN A
;ANSWER
❶ mail.google.com. 21599 IN CNAME ❷googlemail.l.google.com.
googlemail.l.google.com. 299 IN A 172.217.3.229
-- snip --
```

*Listing 2-4: DNS answer of the* mail.google.com *CNAME resource record*

Notice that you ask the domain name server for the A record of the subdomain *mail.google.com*. But in this case, you receive a CNAME instead. This tells you that *googlemail.l.google.com* ❷ is the canonical name for *mail .google.com* ❶. Thankfully, you receive the A record for *googlemail.l.google.com* with the response, alleviating you from having to make a second query. You now know your destination IP address is 172.217.3.229. Google's domain name server was able to return both the CNAME answer and the corresponding Address answer in the same reply because it is an authority for the CNAME answer's domain name as well. Otherwise, you would expect only the CNAME answer and would then need to make a second query to resolve the CNAME answer's IP address.

## The Mail Exchange Record

The *Mail Exchange (MX) record* specifies the mail server hostnames that should be contacted when sending email to recipients at the domain. Remote mail servers will query the MX records for the domain portion of a recipient's email address to determine which servers should receive mail for the recipient. Listing 2-5 shows the response a mail server will receive.

```
$ dig google.com. mx
-- snip --
;QUESTION
google.com. IN MX
;ANSWER
google.com. 599 IN MX ❶10 aspmx.l.google.com.
google.com. 599 IN MX 50 alt4.aspmx.l.google.com.
google.com. 599 IN MX 30 alt2.aspmx.l.google.com.
google.com. 599 IN MX 20 alt1.aspmx.l.google.com.
google.com. 599 IN MX 40 alt3.aspmx.l.google.com.
-- snip --
```

*Listing 2-5: DNS answer of the* google.com *MX resource records*

In addition to the domain name, TTL value, and record type, MX records contain the *priority field* ❶, which rates the priority of each mail server. The lower the number, the higher the priority of the mail server. Mail servers attempt to deliver emails to the mail server with the highest priority, then resort to the mail servers with the next highest priority if necessary. If more than one mail server shares the same priority, the mail server will pick one at random.

### The Pointer Record

The *Pointer (PTR) record* allows you to perform a reverse lookup by accepting an IP address and returning its corresponding domain name. Listing 2-6 shows the reverse lookup for 8.8.4.4.

```
$ dig 4.4.8.8.in-addr.arpa. ptr
-- snip --
;QUESTION
❶ 4.4.8.8.in-addr.arpa. IN PTR
;ANSWER
4.4.8.8.in-addr.arpa. 21599 IN PTR ❷google-public-dns-b.google.com.
-- snip --
```

*Listing 2-6: DNS answer of the 8.8.4.4 PTR resource record*

To perform the query, you ask the domain name server for the IPv4 address in reverse order ❶ with the special domain *in-addr.arpa* appended because the reverse DNS records are all under the *.arpa* top-level domain. For example, querying the pointer record for the IP 1.2.3.4 means you need to ask for *4.3.2.1.in-addr.arpa*. The query in Listing 2-6 tells you that the IPv4 address 8.8.4.4 reverses to the domain name *google-public-dns-b.google.com* ❷. If you were performing a reverse lookup of an IPv6 address, you'd append the special domain *ip6.arpa* to the reversed IPv6 address as you did for the IPv4 address.

**NOTE** *See Wikipedia for more information on reverse DNS lookup:* https://en.wikipedia .org/wiki/Reverse_DNS_lookup.

### The Text Record

The *Text (TXT) record* allows the domain owner to return arbitrary text. These records can contain values that prove domain ownership, values that remote mail servers can use to authorize email, and entries to specify which IP addresses may send mail on behalf of the domain, among other uses. Listing 2-7 shows the text records associated with *google.com*.

```
$ dig google.com. txt
-- snip --
;QUESTION
google.com. IN TXT
;ANSWER
```

```
google.com. 299 IN TXT
    ❶ "facebook-domain-verification=22rm551cu4k0ab0bxsw536t1ds4h95"
google.com. 299 IN TXT "docusign=05958488-4752-4ef2-95eb-aa7ba8a3bd0e"
google.com. 299 IN TXT ❷ "v=spf1 include:_spf.google.com ~all"
google.com. 299 IN TXT
    "globalsign-smime-dv=CDYX+XFHUw2wml6/Gb8+59BsH31KzUr6c1l2BPvqKX8="
-- snip --
```

*Listing 2-7: DNS answer of the google.com TXT resource records*

The domain queries and answers should start to look familiar by now. The last field in a TXT record is a string of the TXT record value ❶. In this example, the field has a Facebook verification key, which proves to Facebook that Google's corporate Facebook account is who they say they are and has the authority to make changes to Google's content on Facebook. It also contains *Sender Policy Framework* rules ❷, which inform remote mail servers which IP addresses may deliver email on Google's behalf.

**NOTE** *The Facebook for Developers site has more information about domain verification at https://developers.facebook.com/docs/sharing/domain-verification/.*

## Multicast DNS

*Multicast DNS (mDNS)* is a protocol that facilitates name resolution over a local area network (LAN) in the absence of a DNS server. When a node wants to resolve a domain name to an IP address, it will send a request to an IP multicast group. Nodes listening to the group receive the query, and the node with the requested domain name responds to the IP multicast group with its IP address. You may have used mDNS the last time you searched for and configured a network printer on your computer.

## Privacy and Security Considerations of DNS Queries

DNS traffic is typically unencrypted when it traverses the internet. A potential exception occurs if you're connected to a virtual private network (VPN) and are careful to make sure all DNS traffic passes through its encrypted tunnel. Because of DNS's unencrypted transport, unscrupulous ISPs or intermediate providers may glean sensitive information in your DNS queries and share those details with third parties. You can make a point of visiting HTTPS-only websites, but your DNS queries may betray your otherwise secure browsing habits and allow the DNS server's administrators to glean the sites you visit.

Security is also a concern with plaintext DNS traffic. An attacker could convince your web browser to visit a malicious website by inserting a response to your DNS query. Considering the difficulty of pulling off such an attack, it's not an attack you're likely to experience, but it's concerning nonetheless. Since DNS servers often cache responses, this attack usually takes place between your device and the DNS server it's configured to use. RFC 7626 (*https://tools.ietf.org/html/rfc7626/*) covers these topics in more detail.

## Domain Name System Security Extensions

Generally, you can ensure the authenticity of data sent over a network in two ways: authenticating the content and authenticating the channel. *Domain Name System Security Extensions (DNSSEC)* is a method to prevent the covert modification of DNS responses in transit by using digital signatures to authenticate the response. DNSSEC ensures the authenticity of data by authenticating the content. DNS servers cryptographically sign the resource records they serve and make those signatures available to you. You can then validate the responses from authoritative DNS servers against the signatures to make sure the responses aren't fraudulent.

DNSSEC doesn't address privacy concerns. DNSSEC queries still traverse the network unencrypted, allowing for passive observation.

## DNS over TLS

DNS over TLS (DoT), detailed in RFC 7858 (*https://tools.ietf.org/html/rfc7858/*), addresses both security and privacy concerns by using *Transport Layer Security (TLS)* to establish an encrypted connection between the client and its DNS server. TLS is a common protocol used to provide cryptographically secure communication between nodes on a network. Using TLS, DNS requests and responses are fully encrypted in transit, making it impossible for an attacker to eavesdrop on or manipulate responses. DoT ensures the authenticity of data by authenticating the channel. It does not need to rely on cryptographic signatures like DNSSEC because the entire conversation between the DNS server and the client is encrypted.

DoT uses a different network port than does regular DNS traffic.

## DNS over HTTPS

*DNS over HTTPS (DoH)*, detailed in RFC 8484 (*https://tools.ietf.org/html/rfc8484/*) aims to address DNS security and privacy concerns while using a heavily used TCP port. Like DoT, DoH sends data over an encrypted connection, authenticating the channel. DoH uses a common port and maps DNS requests and responses to HTTP requests and responses. Queries over HTTP can take advantage of all HTTP features, such as caching, compression, proxying, and redirection.

# What You've Learned

We covered a lot of ground in this chapter. You learned about IP addressing, starting with the basics of IPv4 multicasting, broadcasting, TCP and UDP ports, socket addresses, network address translation, and ARP. You then learned about IPv6, its address categories, and its advantages over IPv4.

You learned about the major network-routing protocols, ICMP and DNS. I'll again recommend the *TCP/IP Guide* by Charles M. Kozierok (No Starch Press, 2005) for its extensive coverage of the topics in this chapter.

# PART II

## SOCKET-LEVEL PROGRAMMING

# 3

## RELIABLE TCP DATA STREAMS

TCP allows you to reliably stream data between nodes on a network. This chapter takes a deeper dive into the protocol, focusing on the aspects directly influenced by the code we'll write to establish TCP connections and transmit data over those connections. This knowledge should help you debug network-related issues in your programs.

We'll start by covering the TCP handshake process, its sequence numbers, acknowledgments, retransmissions, and other features. Next, we'll implement the steps of a TCP session in Go, from dialing, listening, and accepting to the session termination. Then, we'll discuss time-outs and temporary errors, how to detect them, and how to use them to keep our users happy. Finally, we'll cover the early detection of unreliable network connections. Go's standard library allows you to write robust TCP-based networking applications. But it doesn't hold your hand. If you aren't mindful of managing incoming data or properly closing connections, you'll experience insidious bugs in your programs.

## What Makes TCP Reliable?

TCP is reliable because it overcomes the effects of packet loss or receiving packets out of order. *Packet loss* occurs when data fails to reach its destination—typically because of data transmission errors (such as wireless network interference) or network congestion. *Network congestion* happens when nodes attempt to send more data over a network connection than the connection can handle, causing the nodes to discard the excess packets. For example, you can't send data at a rate of 1 gigabit per second (Gbps) over a 10 megabit-per-second (Mbps) connection. The 10Mbps connection quickly becomes saturated, and nodes involved in the flow of the data drop the excess data.

TCP adapts its data transfer rate to make sure it transmits data as fast as possible while keeping dropped packets to a minimum, even if the network conditions change—for example, the Wi-Fi signal fades, or the destination node becomes overwhelmed with data. This process, called *flow control*, does its best to make up for the deficiencies of the underlying network media. TCP cannot send good data over a bad network and is at the mercy of the network hardware.

TCP also keeps track of received packets and retransmits unacknowledged packets, as necessary. Recipients can also receive packets out of sequence if, for example, data is rerouted in transit. Remember from Chapter 2 that routing protocols use metrics to determine how to route packets. These metrics may change as network conditions change. There is no guarantee that all packets you send take the same route for the duration of the TCP session. Thankfully, TCP organizes unordered packets and processes them in sequence.

Together with flow control and retransmission, these properties allow TCP to overcome packet loss and facilitate the delivery of data to the recipient. As a result, TCP eliminates the need for you to concern yourself with these errors. You are free to focus on the data you send and receive.

## Working with TCP Sessions

A *TCP session* allows you to deliver a stream of data of any size to a recipient and receive confirmation that the recipient received the data. This saves you from the inefficiency of sending a large amount of data across a network, only to find out at the end of the transmission that the recipient didn't receive it.

Much like the occasional head nod that people use to indicate they're listening to someone speaking, streaming allows you to receive feedback from the recipient while the transfer is taking place so that you can correct any errors in real time. In fact, you can think of a TCP session as you would a conversation between two nodes. It starts with a greeting, progresses into the conversation, and concludes with a farewell.

As we discuss the specifics of TCP, I want you to understand that Go takes care of the implementation details for you. Your code will take advantage of the net package's interfaces when working with TCP connections.

## Establishing a Session with the TCP Handshake

A TCP connection uses a three-way handshake to introduce the client to the server and the server to the client. The handshake creates an established TCP session over which the client and server exchange data. Figure 3-1 illustrates the three messages sent in the handshake process.

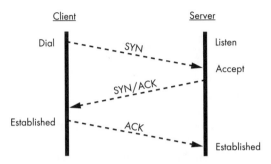

Figure 3-1: The three-way handshake process leading to
an established TCP session

Before it can establish a TCP session, the server must listen for incoming connections. (I use the terms *server* and *client* in this chapter to refer to the listening node and dialing node, respectively. TCP itself doesn't have a concept of a client and server, but an established session between two nodes, whereby one node reaches out to another node to establish the session.)

As the first step of the handshake, the client sends a packet with the *synchronize (SYN) flag* to the server. This SYN packet informs the server of the client's capabilities and preferred window settings for the rest of the conversation. We'll discuss the receive window shortly. Next, the server responds with its own packet, with both the *acknowledgment (ACK)* and SYN flags set. The ACK flag tells the client that the server acknowledges receipt of the client's SYN packet. The server's SYN packet tells the client what settings it's agreed to for the duration of the conversation. Finally, the client replies with an ACK packet to acknowledge the server's SYN packet, completing the three-way handshake.

Completion of the three-way handshake process establishes the TCP session, and nodes may then exchange data. The TCP session remains idle until either side has data to transmit. Unmanaged and lengthy idle TCP sessions may result in wasteful consumption of memory. We'll cover techniques for managing idle connections in your code later in this chapter.

When you initiate a connection in your code, Go will return either a connection object or an error. If you receive a connection object, the TCP handshake succeeded. You do not need to manage the handshake yourself.

## Acknowledging Receipt of Packets by Using Their Sequence Numbers

Each TCP packet contains a *sequence number,* which the receiver uses to acknowledge receipt of each packet and properly order the packets for presentation to your Go application (Figure 3-2).

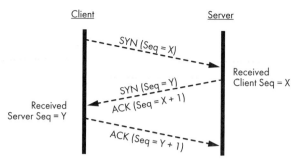

*Figure 3-2: Client and server exchanging sequence numbers*

The client's operating system determines the initial sequence number (X in Figure 3-2) and sends it to the server in the client's SYN packet during the handshake. The server acknowledges receipt of the packet by including this sequence number in its ACK packet to the client. Likewise, the server shares its generated sequence number Y in its SYN packet to the client. The client replies with its ACK to the server.

An ACK packet uses the sequence number to tell the sender, "I've received all packets up to and including the packet with this sequence number." One ACK packet can acknowledge the receipt of one or more packets from the sender. The sender uses the sequence number in the ACK packet to determine whether it needs to retransmit any packets. For example, if a sender transmits a bunch of packets with sequence numbers up through 100 but then receives an ACK from the receiver with sequence number 90, the sender knows it needs to retransmit packets from sequence numbers 91 to 100.

While writing and debugging network programs, it's often necessary to view the traffic your code sends and receives. To capture and inspect TCP packets, I strongly recommend you familiarize yourself with Wireshark (*https://www.wireshark.org/*). This program will go a long way toward helping you understand how your code influences the data sent over the network. To learn more, see *Practical Packet Analysis*, 3rd Edition, by Chris Sanders (No Starch, 2017).

If you view your application's network traffic in Wireshark, you may notice *selective acknowledgments (SACKs)*. These are ACK packets used to acknowledge the receipt of a *subset* of sent packets. For example, let's assume the sender transmitted a hundred packets but only packets 1 to 59 and 81 to 100 made it to the receiver. The receiver could send a SACK to inform the sender what subset of packets it received.

Here again, Go handles the low-level details. Your code will not need to concern itself with sequence numbers and acknowledgments.

### Receive Buffers and Window Sizes

Since TCP allows a single ACK packet to acknowledge the receipt of more than one incoming packet, the receiver must advertise to the sender how much space it has available in its receive buffer before it sends an acknowledgment. A *receive buffer* is a block of memory reserved for incoming data on a network connection. The receive buffer allows the node to accept a certain amount of data from the network without requiring an application to immediately read the data. Both the client and the server maintain their own per-connection receive buffer. When your Go code reads data from a network connection object, it reads the data from the connection's receive buffer.

ACK packets include a particularly important piece of information: the *window size,* which is the number of bytes the sender can transmit to the receiver without requiring an acknowledgment. If the client sends an ACK packet to the server with a window size of 24,537, the server knows it can send 24,537 bytes to the client before expecting the client to send another ACK packet. A window size of zero indicates that the receiver's buffer is full and can no longer receive additional data. We'll discuss this scenario a bit later in this chapter.

Both the client and the server keep track of each other's window size and do their best to completely fill each other's receive buffers. This method— of receiving the window size in an ACK packet, sending data, receiving an updated window size in the next ACK, and then sending more data—is known as a *sliding window,* as shown in Figure 3-3. Each side of the connection offers up a window of data that can it can receive at any one time.

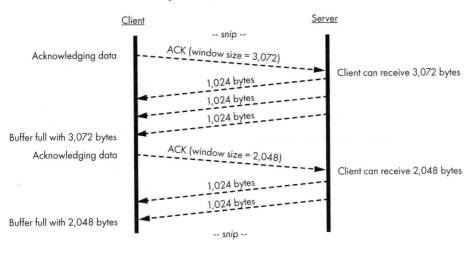

Figure 3-3: A client's ACKs advertising the amount of data it can receive

In this snippet of communication, the client sends an ACK for previously received data. This ACK includes a window size of 3,072 bytes. The server now knows that it can send up to 3,072 bytes before it requires an ACK from the client. The server sends three packets with 1,024 bytes each to fill the client's receive buffer. The client then sends another ACK with an updated window size of 2,048 bytes. This means that the application running on the client read 2,048 bytes from the receive buffer before the client sent its acknowledgment to the server. The server then sends two more packets of 1,024 bytes to fill the client's receive buffer and waits for another ACK.

Here again, all you need to concern yourself with is reading and writing to the connection object Go gives you when you establish a TCP connection. If something goes wrong, Go will surely let you know by returning an error.

## Gracefully Terminating TCP Sessions

Like the handshake process, gracefully terminating a TCP session involves exchanging a sequence of packets. Either side of the connection may initiate the termination sequence by sending a *finish (FIN)* packet. In Figure 3-4, the client initiates the termination by sending a FIN packet to the server.

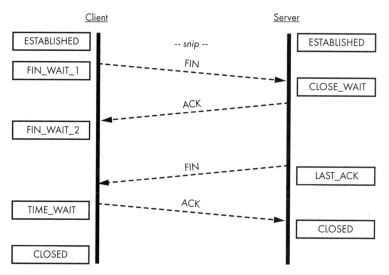

Figure 3-4: The client initiates a TCP session termination with the server.

The client's connection state changes from ESTABLISHED to FIN _WAIT_1, which indicates the client is in the process of tearing down the connection from its end and is waiting for the server's acknowledgment. The server acknowledges the client's FIN and changes its connection state from ESTABLISHED to CLOSE_WAIT. The server sends its own FIN packet, changing its state to LAST_ACK, indicating it's waiting for a final acknowledgment from the client. The client acknowledges the server's FIN and enters a TIME_WAIT state, whose purpose is to allow the client's final ACK packet to reach the server. The client waits for twice the maximum segment lifetime (the segment lifetime arbitrarily defaults to two minutes, per RFC 793, but your operating system may allow you to tweak this value), then changes its connection state to CLOSED without any further input required from the server. The *maximum segment lifetime* is the duration a TCP segment can remain in transit before the sender considers it abandoned. Upon receiving the client's last ACK packet, the server immediately changes its connection state to CLOSED, fully terminating the TCP session.

Like the initial handshake, Go handles the details of the TCP connection teardown process when you close a connection object.

RST
reset
packet

### Handling Less Graceful Terminations

Not all connections politely terminate. In some cases, the application that opened a TCP connection may crash or abruptly stop running for some reason. When this happens, the TCP connection is immediately closed. Any packets sent from the other side of the former connection will prompt the closed side of the connection to return a *reset (RST) packet*. The RST packet informs the sender that the receiver's side of the connection closed and will no longer accept data. The sender should close its side of the connection knowing the receiver ignored any packets it did not acknowledge.

Intermediate nodes, such as firewalls, can send RST packets to each node in a connection, effectively terminating the socket from the middle.

## Establishing a TCP Connection by Using Go's Standard Library

The net package in Go's standard library includes good support for creating TCP-based servers and clients capable of connecting to those servers. Even so, it's your responsibility to make sure you handle the connection appropriately. Your software should be attentive to incoming data and always strive to gracefully shut down the connection. Let's write a TCP server that can listen for incoming TCP connections, initiate connections from a client, accept and asynchronously handle each connection, exchange data, and terminate the connection.

### Binding, Listening for, and Accepting Connections

To create a TCP server capable of listening for incoming connections (called a *listener*), use the net.Listen function. This function will return an object that implements the net.Listener interface. Listing 3-1 shows the creation of a listener.

```
package ch03

import (
    "net"
    "testing"
)

func TestListener(t *testing.T) {
  ❶listener, err := net.Listen("❷tcp", "❸127.0.0.1:0")
    if err != nil {
        t.Fatal(err)
    }
❹   defer func() { _ = listener.Close() }()

    t.Logf("bound to %q", ❺listener.Addr())
}
```

*Listing 3-1: Creating a listener on 127.0.0.1 using a random port (listen_test.go)*

The net.Listen function accepts a network type ❷ and an IP address and port separated by a colon ❸. The function returns a net.Listener interface ❶ and an error interface. If the function returns successfully, the listener is bound to the specified IP address and port. *Binding* means that the operating system has exclusively assigned the port on the given IP address to the listener. The operating system allows no other processes to listen for incoming traffic on bound ports. If you attempt to bind a listener to a currently bound port, net.Listen will return an error.

You can choose to leave the IP address and port parameters empty. If the port is zero or empty, Go will randomly assign a port number to your listener. You can retrieve the listener's address by calling its Addr method ❺. Likewise, if you omit the IP address, your listener will be bound to all unicast and anycast IP addresses on the system. Omitting both the IP address and port, or passing in a colon for the second argument to net.Listen, will cause your listener to bind to all unicast and anycast IP addresses using a random port.

In most cases, you should use tcp as the network type for net.Listener's first argument. You can restrict the listener to just IPv4 addresses by passing in tcp4 or exclusively bind to IPv6 addresses by passing in tcp6.

You should always be diligent about closing your listener gracefully by calling its Close method ❹, often in a defer if it makes sense for your code. Granted, this is a test case, and Go will tear down the listener when the test completes, but it's good practice nonetheless. Failure to close the listener may lead to memory leaks or deadlocks in your code, because calls to the listener's Accept method may block indefinitely. Closing the listener immediately unblocks calls to the Accept method.

Listing 3-2 demonstrates how a listener can accept incoming TCP connections.

```
❶   for {
❷       conn, err := ❸listener.Accept()
        if err != nil {
            return err
        }

❹       go func(c net.Conn) {
❺           defer c.Close()

            // Your code would handle the connection here.
        }(conn)
    }
```

*Listing 3-2: Accepting and handling incoming TCP connection requests*

Unless you want to accept only a single incoming connection, you need to use a for loop ❶ so your server will accept each incoming connection, handle it in a goroutine, and loop back around, ready to accept the next connection. Serially accepting connections is perfectly acceptable and efficient, but beyond that point, you should use a goroutine to handle each connection. You could certainly write serialized code after accepting a connection if your use case demands it, but it would be woefully inefficient and fail to take advantage of Go's strengths. We start the for loop by calling the listener's Accept method ❷. This method will block until the listener detects an incoming connection and completes the TCP handshake process between the client and the server. The call returns a net.Conn interface ❸ and an error. If the handshake failed or the listener closed, for example, the error interface would be non-nil.

The connection interface's underlying type is a pointer to a net.TCPConn object because you're accepting TCP connections. The connection interface represents the server's side of the TCP connection. In most cases, net.Conn provides all methods you'll need for general interactions with the client. However, the net.TCPConn object provides additional functionality we'll cover in Chapter 4 should you require more control.

To concurrently handle client connections, you spin off a goroutine to asynchronously handle each connection ❹ so your listener can ready itself for the next incoming connection. Then you call the connection's Close method ❺ before the goroutine exits to gracefully terminate the connections by sending a FIN packet to the server.

### Establishing a Connection with a Server

From the client's side, Go's standard library net package makes reaching out and establishing a connection with a server a simple matter. Listing 3-3 is a test that demonstrates the process of initiating a TCP connection with a server listening to 127.0.0.1 on a random port.

```
package ch03

import (
    "io"
    "net"
    "testing"
)

func TestDial(t *testing.T) {
    // Create a listener on a random port.
    listener, err := net.Listen("tcp", "127.0.0.1:")
    if err != nil {
        t.Fatal(err)
    }

    done := make(chan struct{})
❶   go func() {
        defer func() { done <- struct{}{} }()

        for {
            conn, err := ❷listener.Accept()
            if err != nil {
                t.Log(err)
                return
            }
```

```
❸   go func(c net.Conn) {
         defer func() {
             c.Close()
             done <- struct{}{}
         }()

         buf := make([]byte, 1024)
         for {
             n, err := ❹c.Read(buf)
             if err != nil {
                 if err != io.EOF {
                     t.Error(err)
                 }
                 return
             }

             t.Logf("received: %q", buf[:n])
         }
     }(conn)
     }
   }()

   ❺conn, err := net.Dial("❻tcp", ❼listener.Addr().String())
   if err != nil {
       t.Fatal(err)
   }

❽  conn.Close()
   <-done
❾  listener.Close()
   <-done
}
```

*Listing 3-3: Establishing a connection to 127.0.0.1 (dial_test.go)*

You start by creating a listener on the IP address 127.0.0.1, which the client will connect to. You omit the port number altogether, so Go will randomly pick an available port for you. Then, you spin off the listener in a goroutine ❶ so you can work with the client's side of the connection later in the test. The listener's goroutine contains code like Listing 3-2's for accepting incoming TCP connections in a loop, spinning off each connection into its own goroutine. (We often call this goroutine a *handler.* I'll explain the implementation details of the handler shortly, but it will read up to 1024 bytes from the socket at a time and log what it received.)

The standard library's net.Dial function is like the net.Listen function in that it accepts a network ❻ like tcp and an IP address and port combination ❼— in this case, the IP address and port of the listener to which it's trying to connect. You can use a hostname in place of an IP address and a service name, like *http*, in place of a port number. If a hostname resolves to more than one IP address, Go will attempt a connection to each one in order until a connection succeeds or all IP addresses have been exhausted. Since IPv6 addresses include colon delimiters, you must enclose an IPv6 address in square brackets. For example, `"[2001:ed27::1]:https"` specifies port 443 at the IPv6 address 2001:ed27::1. `Dial` returns a connection object ❺ and an error interface value.

Now that you've established a successful connection to the listener, you initiate a graceful termination of the connection from the client's side ❽. After receiving the FIN packet, the `Read` method ❹ returns the io.EOF error, indicating to the listener's code that you closed your side of the connection. The connection's handler ❸ exits, calling the connection's `Close` method on the way out. This sends a FIN packet to your connection, completing the graceful termination of the TCP session.

Finally, you close the listener ❾. The listener's `Accept` method ❷ immediately unblocks and returns an error. This error isn't necessarily a failure, so you simply log it and move on. It doesn't cause your test to fail. The listener's goroutine ❶ exits, and the test completes.

## Understanding Time-outs and Temporary Errors

In a perfect world, your connection attempts will immediately succeed, and all read and write attempts will never fail. But you need to hope for the best and prepare for the worst. You need a way to determine whether an error is temporary or something that warrants termination of the connection altogether. The error interface doesn't provide enough information to make that determination. Thankfully, Go's net package provides more insight if you know how to use it.

Errors returned from functions and methods in the net package typically implement the net.Error interface, which includes two notable methods: `Timeout` and `Temporary`. The `Timeout` method returns true on Unix-based operating systems and Windows if the operating system tells Go that the resource is temporarily unavailable, the call would block, or the connection timed out. We'll touch on time-outs and how you can use them to your advantage a bit later in this chapter. The `Temporary` method returns true if the error's `Timeout` function returns true, the function call was interrupted, or there are too many open files on the system, usually because you've exceeded the operating system's resource limit.

Since the functions and methods in the net package return the more general error interface, you'll see the code in this chapter use type assertions to verify you received a net.Error, as in Listing 3-4.

```
if nErr, ok := err.(net.Error); ok && !nErr.Temporary() { return err }
```

*Listing 3-4: Asserting a net.Error to check whether the error was temporary*

Robust network code won't rely exclusively on the error interface. Rather, it will readily use net.Error's methods, or even dive in further and assert the underlying net.OpError struct, which contains more details about the connection, such as the operation that caused the error, the network type, the source address, and more. I encourage you to read the net.OpError documentation (available at *https://golang.org/pkg/net/#OpError/*) to learn more about specific errors beyond what the net.Error interface provides.

## Timing Out a Connection Attempt with the DialTimeout Function

Using the `Dial` function has one potential problem: you are at the mercy of the operating system to time out each connection attempt. For example, if you use the `Dial` function in an interactive application and your operating system times out connection attempts after two hours, your application's user may not want to wait that long, much less give your app a five-star rating.

To keep your applications predictable and your users happy, it'd be better to control time-outs yourself. For example, you may want to initiate a connection to a low-latency service that responds quickly if it's available. If the service isn't responding, you'll want to time out quickly and move onto the next service.

One solution is to explicitly define a per-connection time-out duration and use the `DialTimeout` function instead. Listing 3-5 implements this solution.

```
package ch03

import (
    "net"
    "syscall"
    "testing"
    "time"
)

func ❶DialTimeout(network, address string, timeout time.Duration,
) (net.Conn, error) {
    d := net.Dialer{
    ❷   Control: func(_, addr string, _ syscall.RawConn) error {
            return &net.DNSError{
                Err:         "connection timed out",
                Name:        addr,
                Server:      "127.0.0.1",
                IsTimeout:   true,
                IsTemporary: true,
            }
        },
        Timeout: timeout,
    }
    return d.Dial(network, address)
}

func TestDialTimeout(t *testing.T) {
    c, err := DialTimeout("tcp", "10.0.0.1:http", ❸5*time.Second)
    if err == nil {
        c.Close()
        t.Fatal("connection did not time out")
    }
    nErr, ok := ❹err.(net.Error)
    if !ok {
        t.Fatal(err)
    }
```

```
    if ❺!nErr.Timeout() {
        t.Fatal("error is not a timeout")
    }
}
```

*Listing 3-5: Specifying a time-out duration when initiating a TCP connection (dial_timeout_test.go)*

Since the net.DialTimeout function ❶ does not give you control of its net.Dialer to mock the dialer's output, you're using our own implementation that matches the signature. Your DialTimeout function overrides the Control function ❷ of the net.Dialer to return an error. You're mocking a DNS time-out error.

Unlike the net.Dial function, the DialTimeout function includes an additional argument, the time-out duration ❸. Since the time-out duration is five seconds in this case, the connection attempt will time out if a connection isn't successful within five seconds. In this test, you dial 10.0.0.0, which is a non-routable IP address, meaning your connection attempt assuredly times out. For the test to pass, you need to first use a type assertion to verify you've received a net.Error ❹ before you can check its Timeout method ❺.

If you dial a host that resolves to multiple IP addresses, Go starts a connection race between each IP address, giving the primary IP address a head start. The first connection to succeed persists, and the remaining contenders cancel their connection attempts. If all connections fail or time out, net.DialTimeout returns an error.

### Using a Context with a Deadline to Time Out a Connection

A more contemporary solution to timing out a connection attempt is to use a context from the standard library's context package. A *context* is an object that you can use to send cancellation signals to your asynchronous processes. It also allows you to send a cancellation signal after it reaches a deadline or after its timer expires.

All cancellable contexts have a corresponding cancel function returned upon instantiation. The cancel function offers increased flexibility since you can optionally cancel the context before the context reaches its deadline. You could also pass along its cancel function to hand off cancellation control to other bits of your code. For example, you could monitor for specific signals from your operating system, such as the one sent to your application when a user presses the CTRL-C key combination, to gracefully abort connection attempts and tear down existing connections before terminating your application.

Listing 3-6 illustrates a test that accomplishes the same functionality as DialTimeout, using context instead.

```
package ch03

import (
    "context"
    "net"
    "syscall"
```

```
    "testing"
    "time"
)

func TestDialContext(t *testing.T) {
❶  dl := time.Now().Add(5 * time.Second)
❷  ctx, cancel := context.WithDeadline(context.Background(), dl)
❸  defer cancel()

    var d net.Dialer // DialContext is a method on a Dialer
    d.Control = ❹func(_, _ string, _ syscall.RawConn) error {
        // Sleep long enough to reach the context's deadline.
        time.Sleep(5*time.Second + time.Millisecond)
        return nil
    }
    conn, err := d.DialContext(❺ctx, "tcp", "10.0.0.0:80")
    if err == nil {
        conn.Close()
        t.Fatal("connection did not time out")
    }
    nErr, ok := err.(net.Error)
    if !ok {
        t.Error(err)
    } else {
        if !nErr.Timeout() {
            t.Errorf("error is not a timeout: %v", err)
        }
    }
❻  if ctx.Err() != context.DeadlineExceeded {
        t.Errorf("expected deadline exceeded; actual: %v", ctx.Err())
    }
}
```

*Listing 3-6: Using a context with a deadline to time out the connection attempt
(dial_context_test.go)*

Before you make a connection attempt, you create the context with
a deadline of five seconds into the future ❶, after which the context will
automatically cancel. Next, you create the context and its cancel function by
using the context.WithDeadline function ❷, setting the deadline in the process. It's good practice to defer the cancel function ❸ to make sure the context is garbage collected as soon as possible. Then, you override the dialer's
Control function ❹ to delay the connection just long enough to make sure
you exceed the context's deadline. Finally, you pass in the context as the
first argument to the DialContext function ❺. The sanity check ❻ at the end
of the test makes sure that reaching the deadline canceled the context, not
an erroneous call to cancel.

As with DialTimeout, if a host resolves to multiple IP addresses, Go starts
a connection race between each IP address, giving the primary IP address
a head start. The first connection to succeed persists, and the remaining
contenders cancel their connection attempts. If all connections fail or the
context reaches its deadline, net.Dialer.DialContext returns an error.

## Aborting a Connection by Canceling the Context

Another advantage to using a context is the cancel function itself. You can use it to cancel the connection attempt on demand, without specifying a deadline, as shown in Listing 3-7.

```
package ch03

import (
    "context"
    "net"
    "syscall"
    "testing"
    "time"
)

func TestDialContextCancel(t *testing.T) {
    ctx, cancel := ❶context.WithCancel(context.Background())
    sync := make(chan struct{})

❷  go func() {
        defer func() { sync <- struct{}{} }()

        var d net.Dialer
        d.Control = func(_, _ string, _ syscall.RawConn) error {
            time.Sleep(time.Second)
            return nil
        }
        conn, err := d.DialContext(ctx, "tcp", "10.0.0.1:80")
        if err != nil {
            t.Log(err)
            return
        }

        conn.Close()
        t.Error("connection did not time out")
    }()

❸  cancel()
    <-sync

    if ctx.Err() != ❹context.Canceled {
        t.Errorf("expected canceled context; actual: %q", ctx.Err())
    }
}
```

*Listing 3-7: Directly canceling the context to abort the connection attempt (dial_cancel_test.go)*

Instead of creating a context with a deadline and waiting for the deadline to abort the connection attempt, you use context.WithCancel to return a context and a function to cancel the context ❶. Since you're manually canceling the context, you create a closure and spin it off in a goroutine to handle the connection attempt ❷. Once the dialer is attempting to connect to and handshake with the remote node, you call the cancel function ❸ to cancel the context. This causes the DialContext method to immediately return with a non-nil error, exiting the goroutine. You can check the context's Err method to make sure the call to cancel was what resulted in the canceled context, as opposed to a deadline in Listing 3-6. In this case, the context's Err method should return a context.Canceled error ❹.

## Canceling Multiple Dialers

You can pass the same context to multiple DialContext calls and cancel all the calls at the same time by executing the context's cancel function. For example, let's assume you need to retrieve a resource via TCP that is on several servers. You can asynchronously dial each server, passing each dialer the same context. You can then abort the remaining dialers after you receive a response from one of the servers.

In Listing 3-8, you pass the same context to multiple dialers. When you receive the first response, you cancel the context and abort the remaining dialers.

```
package ch03

import (
    "context"
    "net"
    "sync"
    "testing"
    "time"
)

func TestDialContextCancelFanOut(t *testing.T) {
❶   ctx, cancel := context.WithDeadline(
        context.Background(),
        time.Now().Add(10*time.Second),
    )

    listener, err := net.Listen("tcp", "127.0.0.1:")
    if err != nil {
        t.Fatal(err)
    }
    defer listener.Close()

❷   go func() {
            // Only accepting a single connection.
            conn, err := listener.Accept()
            if err == nil {
                conn.Close()
            }
    }()

❸   dial := func(ctx context.Context, address string, response chan int,
            id int, wg *sync.WaitGroup) {
            defer wg.Done()

            var d net.Dialer
```

```
        c, err := d.DialContext(ctx, "tcp", address)
        if err != nil {
            return
        }
        c.Close()

        select {
        case <-ctx.Done():
        case response <- id:
        }
    }

    res := make(chan int)
    var wg sync.WaitGroup

❹  for i := 0; i < 10; i++ {
        wg.Add(1)
        go dial(ctx, listener.Addr().String(), res, i+1, &wg)
    }

❺  response := <-res
    cancel()
    wg.Wait()
    close(res)

    if ctx.Err() != ❻context.Canceled {
        t.Errorf("expected canceled context; actual: %s",
            ctx.Err(),
        )
    }

    t.Logf("dialer %d retrieved the resource", response)
}
```

*Listing 3-8: Canceling all outstanding dialers after receiving the first response
(dial_fanout_test.go)*

You create a context by using context.WithDeadline ❶ because you want
to have three potential results when checking the context's Err method:
context.Canceled, context.DeadlineExceeded, or nil. You expect Err will return
the context.Canceled error, since your test aborts the dialers with a call to the
cancel function.

First, you need a listener. This listener accepts a single connection and
closes it after the successful handshake ❷. Next, you create your dialers. Since
you're spinning up multiple dialers, it makes sense to abstract the dialing code
to its own function ❸. This anonymous function dials out to the given address
by using DialContext. If it succeeds, it sends the dialer's ID across the response
channel, provided you haven't yet canceled the context. You spin up multiple
dialers by calling dial in separate goroutines using a for loop ❹. If dial blocks
on the call to DialContext because another dialer won the race, you cancel the
context, either by way of the cancel function or the deadline, causing the dial
function to exit early. You use a wait group to make sure the test doesn't proceed until all dial goroutines terminate after you cancel the context.

Once the goroutines are running, one will win the race and make a successful connection to the listener. You receive the winning dialer's ID on the res channel ❺, then abort the losing dialers by canceling the context. At this point, the call to wg.Wait blocks until the aborted dialer goroutines return. Finally, you make sure it was your call to cancel that caused the cancelation of the context ❻. Calling cancel does not guarantee that Err will return context.Canceled. The deadline can cancel the context, at which point calls to cancel become a no-op and Err will return context.DeadlineExceeded. In practice, the distinction may not matter to you, but it's there if you need it.

## Implementing Deadlines

Go's network connection objects allow you to include deadlines for both read and write operations. Deadlines allow you to control how long network connections can remain idle, where no packets traverse the connection. You can control the Read deadline by using the SetReadDeadline method on the connection object, control the Write deadline by using the SetWriteDeadline method, or both by using the SetDeadline method. When a connection reaches its read deadline, all currently blocked and future calls to a network connection's Read method immediately return a time-out error. Likewise, a network connection's Write method returns a time-out error when the connection reaches its write deadline.

Go's network connections don't set any deadline for reading and writing operations by default, meaning your network connections may remain idle for a long time. This could prevent you from detecting network failures, like an unplugged cable, in a timely manner, because it's tougher to detect network issues between two nodes when no traffic is in flight.

The server in Listing 3-9 implements a deadline on its connection object.

```
package ch03

import (
    "io"
    "net"
    "testing"
    "time"
)

func TestDeadline(t *testing.T) {
    sync := make(chan struct{})

    listener, err := net.Listen("tcp", "127.0.0.1:")
    if err != nil {
        t.Fatal(err)
    }

    go func() {
        conn, err := listener.Accept()
        if err != nil {
            t.Log(err)
            return
```

*(margin handwriting: SetreadDeadline, SetwriteDeadline, SetDeadline)*

```
    }
    defer func() {
        conn.Close()
        close(sync) // read from sync shouldn't block due to early return
    }()

❶  err = conn.SetDeadline(time.Now().Add(5 * time.Second))
    if err != nil {
        t.Error(err)
        return
    }

    buf := make([]byte, 1)
    _, err = conn.Read(buf) // blocked until remote node sends data
    nErr, ok := err.(net.Error)
    if !ok || ❷!nErr.Timeout() {
        t.Errorf("expected timeout error; actual: %v", err)
    }

    sync <- struct{}{}

❸  err = conn.SetDeadline(time.Now().Add(5 * time.Second))
    if err != nil {
        t.Error(err)
        return
    }

    _, err = conn.Read(buf)
    if err != nil {
        t.Error(err)
    }
}()

    conn, err := net.Dial("tcp", listener.Addr().String())
    if err != nil {
        t.Fatal(err)
    }
    defer conn.Close()

    <-sync
    _, err = conn.Write([]byte("1"))
    if err != nil {
        t.Fatal(err)
    }

    buf := make([]byte, 1)
    _, err = conn.Read(buf) // blocked until remote node sends data
    if err != ❹io.EOF {
        t.Errorf("expected server termination; actual: %v", err)
    }
}
```

*Listing 3-9: A server-enforced deadline terminates the network connection (deadline_test.go).*

Once the server accepts the client's TCP connection, you set the connection's read deadline ❶. Since the client won't send data, the call to Read will block until the connection exceeds the read deadline. After five seconds, Read returns an error, which you verify is a time-out ❷. Any future reads to the connection object will immediately result in another time-out error. However, you can restore the functionality of the connection object by pushing the deadline forward again ❸. After you've done this, a second call to Read succeeds. The server closes its end of the network connection, which initiates the termination process with the client. The client, currently blocked on its Read call, returns io.EOF ❹ when the network connection closes.

We typically use deadlines to provide a window of time during which the remote node can send data over the network connection. When you read data from the remote node, you push the deadline forward. The remote node sends more data, and you push the deadline forward again, and so on. If you don't hear from the remote node in the allotted time, you can assume that either the remote node is gone and you never received its FIN or that it is idle.

## Implementing a Heartbeat

For long-running network connections that may experience extended idle periods at the application level, it's wise to implement a heartbeat between nodes to advance the deadline. This allows you to quickly identify network issues and promptly reestablish a connection as opposed to waiting to detect the network error when your application goes to transmit data. In this way, you can help make sure your application always has a good network connection when it needs it.

For our purposes, a heartbeat is a message sent to the remote side with the intention of eliciting a reply, which we can use to advance the deadline of our network connection. Nodes send these messages at a regular interval, like a heartbeat. Not only is this method portable over various operating systems, but it also makes sure the application using the network connection is responding, since the application implements the heartbeat. Also, this technique tends to play well with firewalls that may block TCP keepalives. We'll discuss keepalives in Chapter 4.

To start, you'll need a bit of code you can run in a goroutine to ping at regular intervals. You don't want to needlessly ping the remote node when you recently received data from it, so you need a way to reset the ping timer. Listing 3-10 is a simple implementation from a file named *ping.go* that meets those requirements.

I use *ping* and *pong* messages in my heartbeat examples, where the reception of a ping message—the challenge—tells the receiver it should reply with a pong message—the response. The challenge and response messages are arbitrary. You could use anything you want to here, provided the remote node knows your intention is to elicit its reply.

```
package ch03

import (
```

```
        "context"
        "io"
        "time"
    )

    const defaultPingInterval = 30 * time.Second

    func Pinger(ctx context.Context, w io.Writer, reset <-chan time.Duration) {
        var interval time.Duration
        select {
        case <-ctx.Done():
            return
❶      case interval = <-reset: // pulled initial interval off reset channel
        default:
        }
        if interval <= 0 {
            interval = defaultPingInterval
        }

❷      timer := time.NewTimer(interval)
        defer func() {
            if !timer.Stop() {
                <-timer.C
            }
        }()

        for {
            select {
❸          case <-ctx.Done():
                return
❹          case newInterval := <-reset:
                if !timer.Stop() {
                    <-timer.C
                }
                if newInterval > 0 {
                    interval = newInterval
                }
❺          case <-timer.C:
                if _, err := w.Write([]byte("ping")); err != nil {
                    // track and act on consecutive timeouts here
                    return
                }
            }

❻          _ = timer.Reset(interval)
        }
    }
```

*Listing 3-10: A function that pings a network connection at a regular interval (ping.go)*

The Pinger function writes ping messages to a given writer at regular intervals. Because it's meant to run in a goroutine, Pinger accepts a context as its first argument so you can terminate it and prevent it from leaking. Its remaining arguments include an io.Writer interface and a channel to signal a timer reset. You create a buffered channel and put a duration on it to set the timer's initial interval ❶. If the interval isn't greater than zero, you use the default ping interval.

You initialize the timer to the interval ❷ and set up a deferred call to drain the timer's channel to avoid leaking it, if necessary. The endless for loop contains a select statement, where you block until one of three things happens: the context is canceled, a signal to reset the timer is received, or the timer expires. If the context is canceled ❸, the function returns, and no further pings will be sent. If the code selects the reset channel ❹, you shouldn't send a ping, and the timer resets ❻ before iterating on the select statement again.

If the timer expires ❺, you write a ping message to the writer, and the timer resets before the next iteration. If you wanted, you could use this case to keep track of any consecutive time-outs that occur while writing to the writer. To do this, you could pass in the context's cancel function and call it here if you reach a threshold of consecutive time-outs.

Listing 3-11 illustrates how to use the Pinger function introduced in Listing 3-10 by giving it a writer and running it in a goroutine. You can then read pings from the reader at the expected intervals and reset the ping timer with different intervals.

```go
package ch03

import (
    "context"
    "fmt"
    "io"
    "time"
)

func ExamplePinger() {
    ctx, cancel := context.WithCancel(context.Background())
    r, w := io.Pipe() // in lieu of net.Conn
    done := make(chan struct{})
❶  resetTimer := make(chan time.Duration, 1)
    resetTimer <- time.Second // initial ping interval

    go func() {
        Pinger(ctx, w, resetTimer)
        close(done)
    }()

    receivePing := func(d time.Duration, r io.Reader) {
        if d >= 0 {
            fmt.Printf("resetting timer (%s)\n", d)
            resetTimer <- d
        }

        now := time.Now()
        buf := make([]byte, 1024)
        n, err := r.Read(buf)
```

```
        if err != nil {
            fmt.Println(err)
        }

        fmt.Printf("received %q (%s)\n",
            buf[:n], time.Since(now).Round(100*time.Millisecond))
    }

❷  for i, v := range []int64{0, 200, 300, 0, -1, -1, -1} {
        fmt.Printf("Run %d:\n", i+1)
        receivePing(time.Duration(v)*time.Millisecond, r)
    }

    cancel()
    <-done // ensures the pinger exits after canceling the context

    // Output:
❸  // Run 1:
    // resetting timer (0s)
    // received "ping" (1s)
❹  // Run 2:
    // resetting timer (200ms)
    // received "ping" (200ms)
❺  // Run 3:
    // resetting timer (300ms)
    // received "ping" (300ms)
❻  // Run 4:
    // resetting timer (0s)
    // received "ping" (300ms)
❼  // Run 5:
    // received "ping" (300ms)
    // Run 6:
    // received "ping" (300ms)
    // Run 7:
    // received "ping" (300ms)

}
```

*Listing 3-11: Testing the pinger and resetting its ping timer interval (ping_example_test.go)*

In this example, you create a buffered channel ❶ that you'll use to signal a reset of the Pinger's timer. You put an initial ping interval of one second on the resetTimer channel before passing the channel to the Pinger function. You'll use this duration to initialize the Pinger's timer and dictate when to write the ping message to the writer.

You run through a series of millisecond durations in a loop ❷, passing each to the receivePing function. This function resets the ping timer to the given duration and then waits to receive the ping message on the given reader. Finally, it prints to stdout the time it takes to receive the ping message. Go checks stdout against the expected output in the example.

During the first iteration ❸, you pass in a duration of zero, which tells the Pinger to reset its timer by using the previous duration—one second in this example. As expected, the reader receives the ping message after one second. The second iteration ❹ resets the ping timer to 200 ms. Once this expires, the reader receives the ping message. The third run resets the ping timer to 300 ms ❺, and the ping arrives at the 300 ms mark.

You pass in a zero duration for run 4 ❻, preserving the 300 ms ping timer from the previous run. I find the technique of using zero durations to mean "use the previous timer duration" useful because I do not need to keep track of the initial ping timer duration. I can simply initialize the timer with the duration I want to use for the remainder of the TCP session and reset the timer by passing in a zero duration every time I need to pre-empt the transmission of the next ping message. Changing the ping timer duration in the future involves the modification of a single line as opposed to every place I send on the resetTimer channel.

Runs 5 to 7 ❼ simply listen for incoming pings without resetting the ping timer. As expected, the reader receives a ping at 300 ms intervals for the last three runs.

With Listing 3-10 saved to a file named *ping.go* and Listing 3-11 saved to a file named *ping_example_test.go*, you can run the example by executing the following:

```
$ go test ping.go ping_example_test.go
```

### Advancing the Deadline by Using the Heartbeat

Each side of a network connection could use a Pinger to advance its deadline if the other side becomes idle, whereas the previous examples showed only a single side using a Pinger. When either node receives data on the network connection, its ping timer should reset to stop the delivery of an unnecessary ping. Listing 3-12 is a new file named *ping_test.go* that shows how you can use incoming messages to advance the deadline.

```
package ch03

import (
    "context"
    "io"
    "net"
    "testing"
    "time"
)

func TestPingerAdvanceDeadline(t *testing.T) {
    done := make(chan struct{})
    listener, err := net.Listen("tcp", "127.0.0.1:")
    if err != nil {
        t.Fatal(err)
    }

    begin := time.Now()
    go func() {
        defer func() { close(done) }()
```

```
        conn, err := listener.Accept()
        if err != nil {
            t.Log(err)
            return
        }
        ctx, cancel := context.WithCancel(context.Background())
        defer func() {
            cancel()
            conn.Close()
        }()

        resetTimer := make(chan time.Duration, 1)
        resetTimer <- time.Second
        go Pinger(ctx, conn, resetTimer)

        err = conn.SetDeadline(time.Now().Add(❶5 * time.Second))
        if err != nil {
            t.Error(err)
            return
        }

        buf := make([]byte, 1024)
        for {
            n, err := conn.Read(buf)
            if err != nil {
                return
            }
            t.Logf("[%s] %s",
                time.Since(begin).Truncate(time.Second), buf[:n])

    ❷    resetTimer <- 0
            err = ❸conn.SetDeadline(time.Now().Add(5 * time.Second))
            if err != nil {
                t.Error(err)
                return
            }
        }
    }()

    conn, err := net.Dial("tcp", listener.Addr().String())
    if err != nil {
        t.Fatal(err)
    }
    defer conn.Close()

    buf := make([]byte, 1024)
❹  for i := 0; i < 4; i++ { // read up to four pings
        n, err := conn.Read(buf)
        if err != nil {
            t.Fatal(err)
        }
        t.Logf("[%s] %s", time.Since(begin).Truncate(time.Second), buf[:n])
    }
    _, err = ❺conn.Write([]byte("PONG!!!")) // should reset the ping timer
    if err != nil {
```

```
            t.Fatal(err)
    }
❻  for i := 0; i < 4; i++ { // read up to four more pings
        n, err := conn.Read(buf)
        if err != nil {
            if err != io.EOF {
                t.Fatal(err)
            }
            break
        }
        t.Logf("[%s] %s", time.Since(begin).Truncate(time.Second), buf[:n])
    }
    <-done
    end := time.Since(begin).Truncate(time.Second)
    t.Logf("[%s] done", end)
    if end != ❼9*time.Second {
        t.Fatalf("expected EOF at 9 seconds; actual %s", end)
    }
}
```

*Listing 3-12: Receiving data advances the deadline (ping_test.go)*

You start a listener that accepts a connection, spins off a Pinger set to
ping every second, and sets the initial deadline to five seconds ❶. From
a client's perspective, it receives four pings followed by an io.EOF when
the server reaches its deadline and terminates its side of the connection.
However, a client can advance the server's deadline by sending the server
data ❺ before the server reaches its deadline.

If the server reads data from its connection, it can be confident the
network connection is still good. Therefore, it can inform the Pinger to
reset ❷ its timer and push the connection's deadline forward ❸. To
preempt the termination of the socket, the client listens for four ping
messages ❹ from the server before sending an emphatic pong message ❺.
This should buy the client five more seconds until the server reaches its
deadline. The client reads four more pings ❻ and then waits for the inevitable. You check that a total of nine seconds ❼ has elapsed by the time the
server terminates the connection, indicating the client's pong successfully
triggered the reset of the ping timer.

In practice, this method of advancing the ping timer cuts down on the
consumption of bandwidth by unnecessary pings. There is rarely a need to
challenge the remote side of a network connection if you just received data
on the connection.

The strings "ping" and "pong" are arbitrary. You could use smaller payloads,
such as a single byte, for the same purpose, provided both sides of the network
connection agree upon what values constitute a ping and a pong.

## What You've Learned

We covered a lot of ground in this chapter. We started with a dive into TCP's handshake, sequences, and acknowledgments, the sliding window, and connection terminations. Then, we covered the process of establishing TCP connections using Go's standard library. We talked about temporary errors, time-outs, listening for incoming connections, and dialing remote services. Finally, we covered techniques to help you detect and timely correct network integrity issues.

I strongly recommend picking up *Practical Packet Analysis* by Chris Sanders (No Starch Press, 2017) and installing Wireshark. Manipulating your network code and seeing how it affects TCP traffic in Wireshark is a fantastic way to gain a deeper understanding of both TCP and Go's networking packages. The next chapter covers sending and receiving data over TCP connections. Wireshark will help you gain a deeper understanding of data you send, including each payload's effects on the sliding window. Familiarizing yourself with it now will pay dividends.

# 4

## SENDING TCP DATA

Now that you know how to properly establish
and gracefully terminate TCP connections
in Go, it's time to put that knowledge to use
by transmitting data. This chapter covers various
techniques for sending and receiving data over a network using TCP.

We'll talk about the most common methods of reading data from network connections. You'll create a simple messaging protocol that allows you
to transmit dynamically sized payloads between nodes. You'll then explore
the networking possibilities afforded by the net.Conn interface. The chapter
concludes with a deeper dive into the TCPConn object and insidious TCP networking problems that Go developers may experience.

## Using the net.Conn Interface

Most of the network code in this book uses Go's net.Conn interface whenever possible, because it provides the functionality we need for most cases. You can write powerful network code using the net.Conn interface without having to assert its underlying type, ensuring your code is compatible across operating systems and allowing you to write more robust tests. (You will learn how to access net.Conn's underlying type to use its more advanced methods later in this chapter.) The methods available on net.Conn cover most use cases.

The two most useful net.Conn methods are Read and Write. These methods implement the io.Reader and io.Writer interfaces, respectively, which are ubiquitous in the Go standard library and ecosystem. As a result, you can leverage the vast amounts of code written for those interfaces to create incredibly powerful network applications.

You use net.Conn's Close method to close the network connection. This method will return nil if the connection successfully closed or an error otherwise. The SetReadDeadline and SetWriteDeadline methods, which accept a time.Time object, set the absolute time after which reads and writes on the network connection will return an error. The SetDeadline method sets both the read and write deadlines at the same time. As discussed in "Implementing Deadlines" on page 62, deadlines allow you to control how long a network connection may remain idle and allow for timely detection of network connectivity problems.

## Sending and Receiving Data

Reading data from a network connection and writing data to it is no different from reading and writing to a file object, since net.Conn implements the io.ReadWriteCloser interface used to read and write to files. In this section, you'll first learn how to read data into a fixed-size buffer. Next, you'll learn how to use bufio.Scanner to read data from a network connection until it encounters a specific delimiter. You'll then explore TLV, an encoding method that enables you to define a basic protocol to dynamically allocate buffers for varying payload sizes. Finally, you'll see how to handle errors when reading from and writing to network connections.

### Reading Data into a Fixed Buffer

TCP connections in Go implement the io.Reader interface, which allows you to read data from the network connection. To read data from a network connection, you need to provide a buffer for the network connection's Read method to fill.

The Read method will populate the buffer to its capacity if there is enough data in the connection's receive buffer. If there are fewer bytes in the receive buffer than the capacity of the buffer you provide, Read will populate the given buffer with the data and return instead of waiting for more data to arrive. In other words, Read is not guaranteed to fill your buffer to capacity before it returns. Listing 4-1 demonstrates the process of reading data from a network connection into a byte slice.

```go
package main

import (
    "crypto/rand"
    "io"
    "net"
    "testing"
)

func TestReadIntoBuffer(t *testing.T) {
❶    payload := make([]byte, 1<<24) // 16 MB
    _, err := rand.Read(payload)    // generate a random payload
    if err != nil {
        t.Fatal(err)
    }

    listener, err := net.Listen("tcp", "127.0.0.1:")
    if err != nil {
        t.Fatal(err)
    }

    go func() {
        conn, err := listener.Accept()
        if err != nil {
            t.Log(err)
            return
        }
        defer conn.Close()

❷        _, err = conn.Write(payload)
        if err != nil {
            t.Error(err)
        }
    }()

    conn, err := net.Dial("tcp", listener.Addr().String())
    if err != nil {
        t.Fatal(err)
    }

    buf := make([]byte, ❸1<<19) // 512 KB

    for {
❹        n, err := conn.Read(buf)
        if err != nil {
            if err != io.EOF {
                t.Error(err)
            }
            break
```

```
        }

        t.Logf("read %d bytes", n) // buf[:n] is the data read from conn
    }

    conn.Close()
}
```

*Listing 4-1: Receiving data over a network connection (read_test.go)*

You need something for the client to read, so you create a 16MB payload of random data ❶—more data than the client can read in its chosen buffer size of 512KB ❸ so that it will make at least a few iterations around its for loop. It's perfectly acceptable to use a larger buffer or a smaller payload and read the entirety of the payload in a single call to Read. Go correctly processes the data regardless of the payload and receive buffer sizes.

You then spin up the listener and create a goroutine to listen for incoming connections. Once accepted, the server writes the entire payload to the network connection ❷. The client then reads up to the first 512KB from the connection ❹ before continuing around the loop. The client continues to read up to 512KB at a time until either an error occurs or the client reads the entire 16MB payload.

## Delimited Reading by Using a Scanner

Reading data from a network connection by using the method I just showed means your code needs to make sense of the data it receives. Since TCP is a stream-oriented protocol, a client can receive a stream of bytes across many packets. Unlike sentences, binary data doesn't include inherent punctuation that tells you where one message starts and stops.

If, for example, your code is reading a series of email messages from a server, your code will have to inspect each byte for delimiters indicating the boundaries of each message in the stream of bytes. Alternatively, your client may have an established protocol with the server whereby the server sends a fixed number of bytes to indicate the payload size the server will send next. Your code can then use this size to create an appropriate buffer for the payload. You'll see an example of this technique a little later in this chapter.

However, if you choose to use a delimiter to indicate the end of one message and the beginning of another, writing code to handle edge cases isn't so simple. For example, you may read 1KB of data from a single Read on the network connection and find that it contains two delimiters. This indicates that you have two complete messages, but you don't have enough information about the chunk of data following the second delimiter to know whether it is also a complete message. If you read another 1KB of data and find no delimiters, you can conclude that this entire block of data is a continuation of the last message in the previous 1KB you read. But what if you read 1KB of nothing but delimiters?

If this is starting to sound a bit complex, it's because you must account for data across multiple Read calls and handle any errors along the way.

*delimited data?*

Anytime you're tempted to roll your own solution to such a problem, check the standard library to see if a tried-and-true implementation already exists. In this case, bufio.Scanner does what you need.

The bufio.Scanner is a convenient bit of code in Go's standard library that allows you to read delimited data. The Scanner accepts an io.Reader as its input. Since net.Conn has a Read method that implements the io.Reader interface, you can use the Scanner to easily read delimited data from a network connection. Listing 4-2 sets up a listener to serve up delimited data for later parsing by bufio.Scanner.

```
package main

import (
    "bufio"
    "net"
    "reflect"
    "testing"
)

const ❶payload = "The bigger the interface, the weaker the abstraction."

func TestScanner(t *testing.T) {
    listener, err := net.Listen("tcp", "127.0.0.1:")
    if err != nil {
        t.Fatal(err)
    }

    go func() {
        conn, err := listener.Accept()
        if err != nil {
            t.Error(err)
            return
        }
        defer conn.Close()

        _, err = conn.Write([]byte(payload))
        if err != nil {
            t.Error(err)
        }
    }()
```
--snip--

*Listing 4-2: Creating a test to serve up a constant payload (scanner_test.go)*

This listener should look familiar by now. All it's meant to do is serve up the payload ❶. Listing 4-3 uses bufio.Scanner to read a string from the network, splitting each chunk by whitespace.

--snip--

```
    conn, err := net.Dial("tcp", listener.Addr().String())
    if err != nil {
```

```
            t.Fatal(err)
        }
        defer conn.Close()

❶  scanner := bufio.NewScanner(conn)
        scanner.Split(bufio.ScanWords)

        var words []string

❷  for scanner.Scan() {
            words = append(words, ❸scanner.Text())
        }

        err = scanner.Err()
        if err != nil {
            t.Error(err)
        }

        expected := []string{"The", "bigger", "the", "interface,", "the",
            "weaker", "the", "abstraction."}

        if !reflect.DeepEqual(words, expected) {
            t.Fatal("inaccurate scanned word list")
        }
❹  t.Logf("Scanned words: %#v", words)
    }
```

*Listing 4-3: Using bufio.Scanner to read whitespace-delimited text from the network (scanner_test.go)*

Since you know you're reading a string from the server, you start by creating a bufio.Scanner that reads from the network connection ❶. By default, the scanner will split data read from the network connection when it encounters a newline character (\n) in the stream of data. Instead, you elect to have the scanner delimit the input at the end of each word by using bufio.ScanWords, which will split the data when it encounters a word border, such as whitespace or sentence-terminating punctuation.

You keep reading data from the scanner as long as it tells you it's read data from the connection ❷. Every call to Scan can result in multiple calls to the network connection's Read method until the scanner finds its delimiter or reads an error from the connection. It hides the complexity of searching for a delimiter across one or more reads from the network connection and returning the resulting messages.

The call to the scanner's Text method returns the chunk of data as a string—a single word and adjacent punctuation, in this case—that it just read from the network connection ❸. The code continues to iterate around the for loop until the scanner receives an io.EOF or other error from the network connection. If it's the latter, the scanner's Err method will return a non-nil error. You can view the scanned words ❹ by adding the -v flag to the go test command.

## Dynamically Allocating the Buffer Size

You can read data of variable length from a network connection, provided that both the sender and receiver have agreed on a protocol for doing so. The *type-length-value (TLV)* encoding scheme is a good option. TLV encoding uses a fixed number of bytes to represent the type of data, a fixed number of bytes to represent the value size, and a variable number of bytes to represent the value itself. Our implementation uses a 5-byte header: 1 byte for the type and 4 bytes for the length. The TLV encoding scheme allows you to send a type as a series of bytes to a remote node and constitute the same type on the remote node from the series of bytes.

Listing 4-4 defines the types that our TLV encoding protocol will accept.

```go
package main

import (
    "bytes"
    "encoding/binary"
    "errors"
    "fmt"
    "io"
)

const (
 ❶ BinaryType uint8 = iota + 1
 ❷ StringType

 ❸ MaxPayloadSize uint32 = 10 << 20 // 10 MB
)

var ErrMaxPayloadSize = errors.New("maximum payload size exceeded")

type ❹Payload interface {
    fmt.Stringer
    io.ReaderFrom
    io.WriterTo
    Bytes() []byte
}
```

*Listing 4-4: The message struct implements a simple protocol (types.go).*

You start by creating constants to represent each type you will define. In this example, you will create a BinaryType ❶ and a StringType ❷. After digesting the implementation details of each type, you should be able to create types that fit your needs. For security purposes that we'll discuss in just a moment, you must define a maximum payload size ❸.

You also define an interface named Payload ❹ that describes the methods each type must implement. Each type must have the following methods: Bytes, String, ReadFrom, and WriteTo. The io.ReaderFrom and io.WriterTo interfaces allow your types to read from readers and write to writers, respectively. You have some flexibility in this regard. You could just as easily make the

Payload implement the encoding.BinaryMarshaler interface to marshal itself to a byte slice and the encoding.BinaryUnmarshaler interface to unmarshal itself from a byte slice. But the byte slice is one level removed from the network connection, so you'll keep the Payload interface as is. Besides, you'll use the binary encoding interfaces in the next chapter.

You now have the foundation built to create TLV-based types. Listing 4-5 details the first type, Binary.

```
--snip--

type ❶Binary []byte

func (m Binary) ❷Bytes() []byte  { return m }
func (m Binary) ❸String() string { return string(m) }

func (m Binary) ❹WriteTo(w io.Writer) (int64, error) {
    err := ❺binary.Write(w, binary.BigEndian, BinaryType) // 1-byte type
    if err != nil {
        return 0, err
    }
    var n int64 = 1

    err = ❻binary.Write(w, binary.BigEndian, uint32(len(m))) // 4-byte size
    if err != nil {
        return n, err
    }
    n += 4

    o, err := ❼w.Write(m) // payload

    return n + int64(o), err
}
```

*Listing 4-5: Creating the Binary type (types.go)*

The Binary type ❶ is a byte slice; therefore, its Bytes method ❷ simply returns itself. Its String method ❸ casts itself as a string before returning. The WriteTo method accepts an io.Writer and returns the number of bytes written to the writer and an error interface ❹. The WriteTo method first writes the 1-byte type to the writer ❺. It then writes the 4-byte length of the Binary to the writer ❻. Finally, it writes the Binary value itself ❼.

Listing 4-6 rounds out the Binary type with its ReadFrom method.

```
--snip--

func (m *Binary) ReadFrom(r io.Reader) (int64, error) {
    var typ uint8
    err := ❶binary.Read(r, binary.BigEndian, &typ) // 1-byte type
    if err != nil {
        return 0, err
    }
    var n int64 = 1
    if typ != ❷BinaryType {
```

```
        return n, errors.New("invalid Binary")
    }

    var size uint32
    err = ❸binary.Read(r, binary.BigEndian, &size) // 4-byte size
    if err != nil {
        return n, err
    }
    n += 4
❹ if size > MaxPayloadSize {
        return n, ErrMaxPayloadSize
    }

❺ *m = make([]byte, size)
    o, err := ❻r.Read(*m) // payload

    return n + int64(o), err
}
```

*Listing 4-6: Completing the Binary type's implementation (types.go)*

The ReadFrom method reads ❶ 1 byte from the reader into the typ variable. It next verifies ❷ that the type is BinaryType before proceeding. Then it reads ❸ the next 4 bytes into the size variable, which sizes the new Binary byte slice ❺. Finally, it populates the Binary byte slice ❻.

Notice that you enforce a maximum payload size ❹. This is because the 4-byte integer you use to designate the payload size has a maximum value of 4,294,967,295, indicating a payload of over 4GB. With such a large payload size, it would be easy for a malicious actor to perform a denial-of-service attack that exhausts all the available random access memory (RAM) on your computer. Keeping the maximum payload size reasonable makes memory exhaustion attacks harder to execute.

Listing 4-7 introduces the String type, which, like Binary, implements the Payload interface.

```
--snip--

type String string

func (m String) ❶Bytes() []byte  { return []byte(m) }
func (m String) ❷String() string { return string(m) }

func (m String) ❸WriteTo(w io.Writer) (int64, error) {
    err := ❹binary.Write(w, binary.BigEndian, StringType) // 1-byte type
    if err != nil {
        return 0, err
    }
    var n int64 = 1

    err = binary.Write(w, binary.BigEndian, uint32(len(m))) // 4-byte size
    if err != nil {
        return n, err
    }
}
```

```
    n += 4

    o, err := ❺w.Write([]byte(m)) // payload

    return n + int64(o), err
}
```

*Listing 4-7: Creating the String type (types.go)*

The String implementation's Bytes method ❶ casts the String to a byte slice. The String method ❷ casts the String type to its base type, string. The String type's WriteTo method ❸ is like Binary's WriteTo method except the first byte written ❹ is the StringType and it casts the String to a byte slice before writing it to the writer ❺.

Listing 4-8 finishes up the String type's Payload implementation.

```
--snip--

func (m *String) ReadFrom(r io.Reader) (int64, error) {
    var typ uint8
    err := binary.Read(r, binary.BigEndian, &typ) // 1-byte type
    if err != nil {
        return 0, err
    }
    var n int64 = 1
    if typ != ❶StringType {
        return n, errors.New("invalid String")
    }

    var size uint32
    err = binary.Read(r, binary.BigEndian, &size) // 4-byte size
    if err != nil {
        return n, err
    }
    n += 4

    buf := make([]byte, size)
    o, err := r.Read(buf) // payload
    if err != nil {
        return n, err
    }
❷ *m = String(buf)

    return n + int64(o), nil
}
```

*Listing 4-8: Completing the String type's implementation (types.go)*

Here, too, String's ReadFrom method is like Binary's ReadFrom method, with two exceptions. First, the method compares the typ variable against the StringType ❶ before proceeding. Second, the method casts the value read from the reader to a String ❷.

All that's left to implement is a way to read arbitrary data from a network connection and use it to constitute one of our two types. For that, we turn to Listing 4-9.

```
--snip--

func ❶decode(r io.Reader) (Payload, error) {
    var typ uint8
    err := ❷binary.Read(r, binary.BigEndian, &typ)
    if err != nil {
        return nil, err
    }

❸   var payload Payload

    switch ❹typ {
    case BinaryType:
        payload = new(Binary)
    case StringType:
        payload = new(String)
    default:
        return nil, errors.New("unknown type")
    }

    _, err = payload.ReadFrom(
      ❺ io.MultiReader(bytes.NewReader([]byte{typ}), r))
    if err != nil {
        return nil, err
    }

    return payload, nil
}
```

*Listing 4-9: Decoding bytes from a reader into a Binary or String type (types.go)*

The decode function ❶ accepts an io.Reader and returns a Payload interface and an error interface. If decode cannot decode the bytes read from the reader into a Binary or String type, it will return an error along with a nil Payload.

You must first read a byte from the reader ❷ to determine the type and create a payload variable ❸ to hold the decoded type. If the type you read from the reader is an expected type constant ❹, you assign the corresponding type to the payload variable.

You now have enough information to finish decoding the binary data from the reader into the payload variable by using its ReadFrom method. But you have a problem here. You cannot simply pass the reader to the ReadFrom method. You've already read a byte from it corresponding to the type, yet the ReadFrom method expects the first byte it reads to be the type as well. Thankfully, the io package has a helpful function you can use: MultiReader. We cover io.MultiReader in more detail later in this chapter, but here you use it to concatenate the byte you've already read with the reader ❺. From the ReadFrom method's perspective, it will read the bytes in the sequence it expects.

Although the use of io.MultiReader shows you how to inject bytes back into a reader, it isn't optimal in this use case. The proper fix is to remove each type's need to read the first byte in its ReadFrom method. Then, the ReadFrom method would read only the 4-byte size and the payload, eliminating the need to inject the type byte back into the reader before passing it on to ReadFrom. As an exercise, I recommend you refactor the code to eliminate the need for io.MultiReader.

Let's see the decode function in action in the form of a test. Listing 4-10 illustrates how you can send your two distinct types over a network connection and properly decode them back into their original type on the receiver's end.

```go
package main

import (
    "bytes"
    "encoding/binary"
    "net"
    "reflect"
    "testing"
)

func TestPayloads(t *testing.T) {
    b1 := ❶Binary("Clear is better than clever.")
    b2 := Binary("Don't panic.")
    s1 := ❷String("Errors are values.")
    payloads := ❸[]Payload{&b1, &s1, &b2}

    listener, err := net.Listen("tcp", "127.0.0.1:")
    if err != nil {
        t.Fatal(err)
    }

    go func() {
        conn, err := listener.Accept()
        if err != nil {
            t.Error(err)
            return
        }
        defer conn.Close()

        for _, p := range payloads {
            _, err = ❹p.WriteTo(conn)
            if err != nil {
                t.Error(err)
                break
            }
        }
    }()
```

--snip--

*Listing 4-10: Creating the TestPayloads test (types_test.go)*

Your test should first create at least one of each type. You create two Binary types ❶ and one String type ❷. Next, you create a slice of Payload interfaces and add pointers to the Binary and String types you created ❸. You then create a listener that will accept a connection and write each type in the payloads slice to it ❹.

This is a good start. Let's finish up the client side of the test in Listing 4-11.

```
--snip--

    conn, err := ❶net.Dial("tcp", listener.Addr().String())
    if err != nil {
        t.Fatal(err)
    }
    defer conn.Close()

    for i := 0; i < len(payloads); i++ {
        actual, err := ❷decode(conn)
        if err != nil {
            t.Fatal(err)
        }

❸     if expected := payloads[i]; !reflect.DeepEqual(expected, actual) {
            t.Errorf("value mismatch: %v != %v", expected, actual)
            continue
        }

❹     t.Logf("[%T] %[1]q", actual)
    }
}
```

*Listing 4-11: Completing the TestPayloads test (types_test.go)*

You know how many types to expect in the payloads slice, so you initiate a connection to the listener ❶ and attempt to decode each one ❷. Finally, your test compares the type you decoded with the type the server sent ❸. If there's any discrepancy with the variable type or its contents, the test fails. You can run the test with the -v flag to see the type and its value ❹.

Let's make sure the Binary type enforces the maximum payload size in Listing 4-12.

```
--snip--

func TestMaxPayloadSize(t *testing.T) {
    buf := new(bytes.Buffer)
    err := buf.WriteByte(BinaryType)
    if err != nil {
        t.Fatal(err)
    }

    err = binary.Write(buf, binary.BigEndian, ❶uint32(1<<30)) // 1 GB
    if err != nil {
```

```
        t.Fatal(err)
    }

    var b Binary
    _, err = b.ReadFrom(buf)
❷ if err != ErrMaxPayloadSize {
        t.Fatalf("expected ErrMaxPayloadSize; actual: %v", err)
    }
}
```

*Listing 4-12: Testing the maximum payload size (types_test.go)*

This test starts with the creation of a bytes.Buffer containing the
BinaryType byte and a 4-byte, unsigned integer indicating the payload is
1GB ❶. When this buffer is passed to the Binary type's ReadFrom method,
you receive the ErrMaxPayloadSize error in return ❷. The test cases in
Listings 4-10 and 4-11 should cover the use case of a payload that is less
than the maximum size, but I encourage you to modify this test to make
sure that's the case.

### Handling Errors While Reading and Writing Data

Unlike writing to file objects, writing to network connections can be unreliable, especially if your network connection is spotty. Files don't often return
errors while you're writing to them, but the receiver on the other end of a
network connection may abruptly disconnect before you write your entire
payload.

Not all errors returned when reading from or writing to a network connection are permanent. The connection can recover from some errors. For
example, writing data to a network connection where adverse network conditions delay the receiver's ACK packets, and where your connection times
out while waiting to receive them, can result in a temporary error. This can
occur if someone temporarily unplugs a network cable between you and
the receiver. In that case, the network connection is still active, and you
can either attempt to recover from the error or gracefully terminate your
end of the connection.

Listing 4-13 illustrates how to check for temporary errors while writing
data to a network connection.

```
var (
    err error
    n int
    i = 7 // maximum number of retries
)

❶ for ; i > 0; i-- {
    n, err = ❷conn.Write(❸[]byte("hello world"))
    if err != nil {
        if nErr, ok := ❹err.(net.Error); ok && ❺nErr.Temporary() {
            log.Println("temporary error:", nErr)
```

```
                time.Sleep(10 * time.Second)
                continue
            }
        ❻   return err
        }
        break
    }

    if i == 0 {
        return errors.New("temporary write failure threshold exceeded")
    }

    log.Printf("wrote %d bytes to %s\n", n, conn.RemoteAddr())
```

*Listing 4-13: Sending the string "hello world" over the connection*

Since you might receive a transient error when writing to a network connection, you might need to retry a write operation. One way to account for this is to encapsulate the code in a for loop ❶. This makes it easy to retry the write operation, if necessary.

To write to the connection, you pass a byte slice ❸ to the connection's Write method ❷ as you would to any other io.Writer. This returns the number of bytes written and an error interface. If the error interface is not nil, you check whether the error implements the net.Error interface by using a type assertion ❹ and check whether the error is temporary ❺. If the net.Error's Temporary method returns true, the code makes another write attempt by iterating around the for loop. If the error is permanent, the code returns the error ❻. A successful write breaks out of the loop.

# Creating Robust Network Applications by Using the io Package

In addition to interfaces common in Go code, such as io.Reader and io.Writer, the io package provides several useful functions and utilities that make the creation of robust network applications easy. In this section, you'll learn how to use the io.Copy, io.MultiWriter, and io.TeeReader functions to proxy data between connections, log network traffic, and ping hosts when firewalls attempt to keep you from doing so.

## Proxying Data Between Connections

One of the most useful functions from the io package, the io.Copy function reads data from an io.Reader and writes it to an io.Writer. This is useful for creating a *proxy*, which, in this context, is an intermediary that transfers data between two nodes. Since net.Conn includes both io.Reader and io.Writer interfaces, and io.Copy writes whatever it reads from an io.Reader to an io.Writer, you can easily create a proxy between network connections, such

as the one you define in the proxyConn function in Listing 4-14. This function copies any data sent from the source node to the destination node,
and vice versa.

```go
package main

import (
    "io"
    "net"
)

func proxyConn(source, destination string) error {
    connSource, err := ❶net.Dial("tcp", source)
    if err != nil {
        return err
    }
    defer connSource.Close()

    connDestination, err := ❷net.Dial("tcp", destination)
    if err != nil {
        return err
    }
    defer connDestination.Close()

    // connDestination replies to connSource
❸   go func() { _, _ = io.Copy(connSource, connDestination) }()

    // connSource messages to connDestination
❹   _, err = io.Copy(connDestination, connSource)

    return err
}
```

*Listing 4-14: Proxying data between two network connections (proxy_conn.go)*

The io.Copy function does all the heavy input/output (I/O) lifting for
you. It takes an io.Writer as its first argument and an io.Reader as its second
argument. It then writes, to the writer, everything it reads from the reader
until the reader returns an io.EOF, or, alternately, either the reader or writer
returns an error. The io.Copy function returns an error only if a non-io.EOF
error occurred during the copy, because io.EOF means it has read all the
data from the reader.

You start by creating a connection to the source node ❶ and a connection to the destination node ❷. Next, you run io.Copy in a goroutine, reading from connDestination and writing to connSource ❸ to handle any replies.
You don't need to worry about leaking this goroutine, since io.Copy will
return when either connection is closed. Then, you make another call to
io.Copy, reading from connSource and writing to connDestination ❹. Once this
call returns and the function returns, each connection's Close method runs,

which causes io.Copy to return, terminating its goroutine ❸. As a result, the data is proxied between network connections as if they had a direct connection to one another.

*Since Go version 1.11, if you use io.Copy or io.CopyN when the source and destination are both \*net.TCPConn objects, the data never enters the user space on Linux, thereby causing the data transfer to occur more efficiently. Think of it as the Linux kernel reading from one socket and writing to the other without the data needing to interact directly with your Go code. io.CopyN functions like io.Copy except it copies up to n bytes. We'll use io.CopyN in the next chapter.*

Listing 4-15 illustrates how to use a slight variation of the proxyConn function. Whereas Listing 4-14's proxyConn function established network connections and proxied traffic between them, Listing 4-15's proxy function proxies data between an io.Reader and an io.Writer, making it applicable to more than just network connections and much easier to test.

```
package main

import (
    "io"
    "net"
    "sync"
    "testing"
)

❶ func proxy(from io.Reader, to io.Writer) error {
    fromWriter, fromIsWriter := from.(io.Writer)
    toReader, toIsReader := to.(io.Reader)

    if toIsReader && fromIsWriter {
        // Send replies since "from" and "to" implement the
        // necessary interfaces.
        go func() { _, _ = io.Copy(fromWriter, toReader) }()
    }

    _, err := io.Copy(to, from)

    return err
}
```

*Listing 4-15: Proxy data between a reader and writer (proxy_test.go)*

This proxy function ❶ is a bit more useful in that it accepts the ubiquitous io.Reader and io.Writer interfaces instead of net.Conn. Because of this change, you could proxy data from a network connection to os.Stdout, \*bytes.Buffer, \*os.File, or any number of objects that implement the io.Writer interface. Likewise, you could read bytes from any object that implements the io.Reader interface and send them to the writer. This implementation of proxy supports replies if the *from* reader implements the io.Writer interface and the *to* writer implements the io.Reader interface.

Listing 4-16 creates a test to make sure the proxy functions as you expect.

```go
func TestProxy(t *testing.T) {
    var wg sync.WaitGroup

    // server listens for a "ping" message and responds with a
    // "pong" message. All other messages are echoed back to the client.
❶   server, err := net.Listen("tcp", "127.0.0.1:")
    if err != nil {
        t.Fatal(err)
    }

    wg.Add(1)

    go func() {
        defer wg.Done()

        for {
            conn, err := server.Accept()
            if err != nil {
                return
            }

            go func(c net.Conn) {
                defer c.Close()

                for {
                    buf := make([]byte, 1024)
                    n, err := c.Read(buf)
                    if err != nil {
                        if err != io.EOF {
                            t.Error(err)
                        }

                        return
                    }

                    switch msg := string(buf[:n]); msg {
                    case "ping":
                        _, err = c.Write([]byte("pong"))
                    default:
                        _, err = c.Write(buf[:n])
                    }

                    if err != nil {
                        if err != io.EOF {
                            t.Error(err)
                        }

                        return
                    }
                }
            }(conn)
        }
    }
```

```
    }()

--snip--
```

*Listing 4-16: Creating the listener (proxy_test.go)*

You start by initializing a server ❶ that listens for incoming connections. It reads bytes from each connection, replies with the string "pong"
when it receives the string "ping," and echoes any other message it receives.
Listing 4-17 continues the test implementation.

```
--snip--

    // proxyServer proxies messages from client connections to the
    // destinationServer. Replies from the destinationServer are proxied
    // back to the clients.
❶ proxyServer, err := net.Listen("tcp", "127.0.0.1:")
    if err != nil {
        t.Fatal(err)
    }

    wg.Add(1)

    go func() {
        defer wg.Done()

        for {
            conn, err := ❷proxyServer.Accept()
            if err != nil {
                return
            }

            go func(from net.Conn) {
                defer from.Close()

                to, err := ❸net.Dial("tcp",
                    server.Addr().String())
                if err != nil {
                    t.Error(err)
                    return
                }

                defer to.Close()

                err = ❹proxy(from, to)
                if err != nil && err != io.EOF {
                    t.Error(err)
                }
            }(conn)
        }
    }()

--snip--
```

*Listing 4-17: Set up the proxy between the client and server (proxy_test.go)*

You then set up a proxy server ❶ that handles the message passing between the client and the destination server. The proxy server listens for incoming client connections. Once a client connection accepts ❷, the proxy establishes a connection to the destination server ❸ and starts proxying messages ❹. Since the proxy server passes two net.Conn objects to proxy, and net.Conn implements the io.ReadWriter interface, the server proxies replies automatically. Then io.Copy writes to the Write method of the destination net.Conn everything it reads from the Read method of the origin net.Conn, and vice versa for replies from the destination to the origin.

Listing 4-18 implements the client portion of the test.

```
--snip--
    conn, err := net.Dial("tcp", proxyServer.Addr().String())
    if err != nil {
        t.Fatal(err)
    }

❶  msgs := []struct{ Message, Reply string }{
        {"ping", "pong"},
        {"pong", "pong"},
        {"echo", "echo"},
        {"ping", "pong"},
    }

    for i, m := range msgs {
        _, err = conn.Write([]byte(m.Message))
        if err != nil {
            t.Fatal(err)
        }

        buf := make([]byte, 1024)

        n, err := conn.Read(buf)
        if err != nil {
            t.Fatal(err)
        }

        actual := string(buf[:n])
        t.Logf("%q -> proxy -> %q", m.Message, actual)

        if actual != m.Reply {
            t.Errorf("%d: expected reply: %q; actual: %q",
                i, m.Reply, actual)
        }
    }

    _ = conn.Close()
    _ = proxyServer.Close()
    _ = server.Close()
```

```
    wg.Wait()
}
```

*Listing 4-18: Proxying data from an upstream server to a downstream server
(proxy_test.go)*

You run the proxy through a series of tests ❶ to verify that your ping
messages result in pong replies and that the destination echoes anything
else you send. The output should look like the following:

```
$ go test ❶-race -v proxy_test.go
=== RUN    TestProxy
--- PASS: TestProxy (0.00s)
    proxy_test.go:138: "ping" -> proxy -> "pong"
    proxy_test.go:138: "pong" -> proxy -> "pong"
    proxy_test.go:138: "echo" -> proxy -> "echo"
    proxy_test.go:138: "ping" -> proxy -> "pong"
PASS
ok      command-line-arguments  1.018s
```

I'm in the habit of running my tests with the -race flag ❶ to enable the
race detector. The race detector can help alert you to data races that need
your attention. Although not necessary for this test, enabling it is a good
habit.

## Monitoring a Network Connection

The io package includes useful tools that allow you to do more with
network data than just send and receive it using connection objects. For
example, you could use io.MultiWriter to write a single payload to multiple
network connections. You could also use io.TeeReader to log data read
from a network connection. Listing 4-19 gives an example of using the
io.TeeReader and io.MultiWriter to log all network traffic on a TCP listener.

```
package main

import (
    "io"
    "log"
    "net"
    "os"
)

// Monitor embeds a log.Logger meant for logging network traffic.
type Monitor struct {
    *log.Logger
}

// Write implements the io.Writer interface.
func (m *Monitor) ❶Write(p []byte) (int, error) {
    return len(p), m.Output(2, string(p))
}
```

```
func ExampleMonitor() {
❷  monitor := &Monitor{Logger: log.New(os.Stdout, "monitor: ", 0)}

    listener, err := net.Listen("tcp", "127.0.0.1:")
    if err != nil {
        monitor.Fatal(err)
    }

    done := make(chan struct{})

    go func() {
        defer close(done)

        conn, err := listener.Accept()
        if err != nil {
            return
        }
        defer conn.Close()

        b := make([]byte, 1024)
❸      r := io.TeeReader(conn, monitor)

        n, err := r.Read(b)
        if err != nil && err != io.EOF {
            monitor.Println(err)
            return
        }

❹      w := io.MultiWriter(conn, monitor)

        _, err = w.Write(b[:n]) // echo the message
        if err != nil && err != io.EOF {
            monitor.Println(err)
            return
        }
    }()

--snip--
```

Listing 4-19: Using io.TeeReader and io.MultiWriter to capture a network connection's input and output (monitor_test.go)

You create a new struct named Monitor that embeds a log.Logger for the purposes of logging the server's network traffic. Since the io.TeeReader and the io.MultiWriter expect an io.Writer, the monitor implements the io.Writer interface ❶.

You start by creating an instance of Monitor ❷ that writes to os.Stdout. You use the monitor in conjunction with the connection object in an io.TeeReader ❸. This results in an io.Reader that will read from the network connection and write all input to the monitor before passing along the input to the caller. Likewise, you log server output by creating an io.MultiWriter ❹, writing to the network connection and the monitor.

Listing 4-20 details the client portion of the example and its output.

```
--snip--
    conn, err := net.Dial("tcp", listener.Addr().String())
    if err != nil {
        monitor.Fatal(err)
    }

    _, err = ❶conn.Write([]byte("Test\n"))
    if err != nil {
        monitor.Fatal(err)
    }

    _ = conn.Close()
    <-done

    // ❷Output:
    // monitor: Test
    // monitor: Test
}
```

*Listing 4-20: The client implementation and example output (monitor_test.go)*

When you send the message Test\n ❶, it's logged to os.Stdout twice ❷: once when you read the message from the connection, and again when you echo the message back to the client. If you want to get fancy, you could decorate the log entries to differentiate between incoming and outgoing data. One way to do this would be to create an object that implements the io.Writer interface and embeds the monitor. When its Write method is called, it prepends the data with the prefix before passing the data along to the monitor's Write method.

Although using the io.TeeReader and the io.MultiWriter in this fashion is powerful, it isn't without a few caveats. First, both the io.TeeReader and the io.MultiWriter will block while writing to your writer. Your writer will add latency to the network connection, so be mindful not to block too long. Second, an error returned by your writer will cause the io.TeeReader or io.MultiWriter to return an error as well, halting the flow of network data. If you don't want your use of these objects to potentially interrupt network data flow, I strongly recommend you implement a reader that always returns a nil error and logs its underlying error in a manner that's actionable.

For example, you can modify Monitor's Write method to always return a nil error:

```
func (m *Monitor) Write(p []byte) (int, error) {
    err := m.Output(2, string(p))
    if err != nil {
        log.Println(err) // use the log package's default Logger
    }

    return len(p), nil
}
```

The `Monitor` attempts to write the byte slice to its embedded logger. Failing that, it writes the error to the `log` package's default logger and returns a `nil` error to `io.TeeReader` and `io.MultiWriter` in Listing 4-19 so as not to interrupt the flow of data.

## Pinging a Host in ICMP-Filtered Environments

In "The Internet Control Message Protocol" on page 31, you learned that ICMP is a protocol that gives you feedback about local network conditions. One of its most common uses is to determine whether a host is online by issuing a ping request and receiving a pong reply from the host. Most operating systems have a built-in ping command that sends an ICMP echo request to a destination IP address. Once the host responds with an ICMP echo reply, `ping` prints the duration between sending the ping and receiving the pong.

Unfortunately, many internet hosts filter or block ICMP echo replies. If a host filters pongs, the `ping` erroneously reports that the remote system is unavailable. One technique you can use instead is to establish a TCP connection with the remote host. If you know that the host listens for incoming TCP connections on a specific port, you can use this knowledge to confirm that the host is available, because you can establish a TCP connection only if the host is up and completes the handshake process.

Listing 4-21 shows a small application that reports the time it takes to establish a TCP connection with a host on a specific port.

```
package main

import (
    "flag"
    "fmt"
    "net"
    "os"
    "time"
)

❶ var (
    count    = flag.Int("c", 3, "number of pings: <= 0 means forever")
    interval = flag.Duration("i", time.Second, "interval between pings")
    timeout  = flag.Duration("W", 5*time.Second, "time to wait for a reply")
)

func init() {
    flag.Usage = func() {
        fmt.Printf("Usage: %s [options] host:port\nOptions:\n", os.Args[0])
        flag.PrintDefaults()
    }
}

--snip--
```

Listing 4-21: The command line flags for the ping command (ping.go)

This example starts by defining a few command line options ❶ that mimic a subset of the functionality provided by the ping command on Linux.

Listing 4-22 adds the main function.

```
--snip--

func main() {
    flag.Parse()

    if flag.NArg() != 1 {
        fmt.Print("host:port is required\n\n")
        flag.Usage()
        os.Exit(1)
    }

    target := flag.Arg(0)
    fmt.Println("PING", target)

    if *count <= 0 {
        fmt.Println("CTRL+C to stop.")
    }

    msg := 0

    for (*count <= 0) || (msg < *count) {
        msg++
        fmt.Print(msg, " ")

        start := time.Now()
    ❶ c, err := net.DialTimeout("tcp", target, *timeout)
    ❷ dur := time.Since(start)

        if err != nil {
            fmt.Printf("fail in %s: %v\n", dur, err)
            if nErr, ok := err.(net.Error); !ok || ❸!nErr.Temporary() {
                os.Exit(1)
            }
        } else {
            _ = c.Close()
            fmt.Println(dur)
        }

        time.Sleep(*interval)
    }
}
```

Listing 4-22: Reporting the time to establish a TCP socket to a given host and port (ping.go)

You attempt to establish a connection to a remote host's TCP port ❶, setting a reasonable time-out duration if the remote host doesn't respond. You keep track of the time it takes to complete the TCP handshake and consider this duration ❷ the ping interval between your host and the remote host. If you encounter a temporary error (for example, a time-out), you'll continue trying, and you'll exit if the error is permanent ❸. This is handy if you restart a TCP service and want to monitor its progress in restarting. Initially, the code in Listing 4-22 will report time-out errors, but it will eventually start printing valid results when the service is again listening on the specific port.

It's important to understand that system admins could consider the code in Listing 4-22 abusive, especially if you specify a large ping count. That's because you aren't simply asking the remote host to send an echo reply using ICMP. Instead, you're rapidly establishing and tearing down a TCP connection with every interval. Establishing a TCP connection has more overhead than an ICMP echo request and response. I recommend that you use this method only when intermediate firewalls filter ICMP echo messages and, even then, with the permission of the system admin.

## Exploring Go's TCPConn Object

For most use cases, the net.Conn interface will provide adequate functionality and the best cross-platform support for TCP sessions between nodes. But accessing the underlying net.TCPConn object allows fine-grained control over the TCP network connection should you need to do such things as modify the read and write buffers, enable keepalive messages, or change the behavior of pending data upon closing the connection. The net.TCPConn object is the concrete object that implements the net.Conn interface. Keep in mind that not all the following functionality may be available on your target operating system.

The easiest way to retrieve the net.TCPConn object is by using a type assertion. This works for connections where the underlying network is TCP:

```
tcpConn, ok := conn.(*net.TCPConn)
```

On the server side, you can use the AcceptTCP method on a net .TCPListener, as shown in Listing 4-23, to retrieve the net.TCPConn object.

```
addr, err := net.ResolveTCPAddr("tcp", "127.0.0.1:")
if err != nil {
    return err
}

listener, err := net.ListenTCP("tcp", addr)
if err != nil {
    return err
}

tcpConn, err := listener.AcceptTCP()
```

*Listing 4-23: Retrieving net.TCPConn from the listener*

On the client side, use the net.DialTCP function, as shown in Listing 4-24.

```
addr, err := net.ResolveTCPAddr("tcp", "www.google.com:http")
if err != nil {
    return err
}

tcpConn, err := net.DialTCP("tcp", nil, addr)
```

Listing 4-24: Using DialTCP to retrieve a net.TCPConn object

The next few sections cover useful methods on net.TCPConn that are unavailable on net.Conn. Some of these methods may not be available on your target operating system or may have hard limits imposed by the operating system. My advice is to use the following methods only when necessary. Altering these settings on the connection object from the operating system defaults may lead to network behavior that's difficult to debug. For example, shrinking the read buffer on a network connection may lead to unexpected zero window issues unexplained by checking the operating system's default read buffer value.

## Controlling Keepalive Messages

A *keepalive* is a message sent over a network connection to check the connection's integrity by prompting an acknowledgment of the message from the receiver. After an operating system–specified number of unacknowledged keepalive messages, the operating system will close the connection.

The operating system configuration dictates whether a connection uses keepalives for TCP sessions by default. If you need to enable keepalives on a net.TCPConn object, pass true to its SetKeepAlive method:

```
err := tcpConn.SetKeepAlive(true)
```

You also have control over how often the connection sends keepalive messages using the SetKeepAlivePeriod method. This method accepts a time .Duration that dictates the keepalive message interval:

```
err := tcpConn.SetKeepAlivePeriod(time.Minute)
```

Using deadlines advanced by a heartbeat is usually the better method for detecting network problems. As mentioned earlier in this chapter, deadlines provide better cross-platform support, traverse firewalls better, and make sure your application is actively managing the network connection.

## Handling Pending Data on Close

By default, if you've written data to net.Conn but the data has yet to be sent to or acknowledged by the receiver and you close the network connection, your operating system will complete the delivery in the background. If you don't want this behavior, the net.TCPConn object's SetLinger method allows you to tweak it:

```
err := tcpConn.SetLinger(-1) // anything < 0 uses the default behavior
```

With the linger disabled, it is possible that the server may receive the last portion of data you send along with your FIN when you close your connection. Since your call to conn.Close doesn't block, you have no way of knowing whether the server received the data you just sent prior to your FIN. It's possible the data sat in the server's receive buffer and then the server crashed, taking your unacknowledged data and FIN with it. Lingering on the connection to give the server time to acknowledge the data may seem tempting. But this won't solve your problem if the server crashes, as in the example. Also, some developers may argue that using linger for this purpose is a code smell. Your application should instead verify that the server received all data before tearing down its connection if this last bit of unacknowledged data is a concern.

If you wish to abruptly discard all unsent data and ignore acknowledgments of sent data upon closing the network connection, set the connection's linger to zero:

```
err := tcpConn.SetLinger(0) // immediately discard unsent data on close
```

Setting linger to zero will cause your connection to send an RST packet when your code calls your connection's Close method, aborting the connection and bypassing the normal teardown procedures.

If you're looking for a happy medium and your operating system supports it, you can pass a positive integer $n$ to SetLinger. Your operating system will attempt to complete delivery of all outstanding data up to $n$ seconds, after which point your operating system will discard any unsent or unacknowledged data:

```
err := tcpConn.SetLinger(10) // discard unsent data after 10 seconds
```

If you feel compelled to modify your connection's linger value, please read up on how your operating system handles lingering on network connections. When in doubt, use the default value.

## Overriding Default Receive and Send Buffers

Your operating system assigns read and write buffers to each network connection you create in your code. For most cases, those values should be enough. But in the event you want greater control over the read or write buffer sizes, you can tweak their value, as demonstrated in Listing 4-25.

```
if err := tcpConn.SetReadBuffer(212992); err != nil {
    return err
}
```

```
if err := tcpConn.SetWriteBuffer(212992); err != nil {
    return err
}
```

*Listing 4-25: Setting read and write buffer sizes on a TCP connection*

The SetReadBuffer method accepts an integer representing the connection's read buffer size in bytes. Likewise, the SetWriteBuffer method accepts an integer and sets the write buffer size in bytes on the connection. Keep in mind that you can't exceed your operating system's maximum value for either buffer size.

# Solving Common Go TCP Network Problems

Go doesn't hold your hand when working with TCP network connections. As such, it's possible to introduce bugs in your code that manifest as network errors. This section presents two common TCP networking issues: zero window errors and sockets stuck in the CLOSE_WAIT state.

## Zero Window Errors

We spent a bit of time in "Receive Buffers and Window Sizes" on page 48 discussing TCP's sliding window and how the window size tells the sender how much data the receiver can accept before the next acknowledgment. A common workflow when reading from a network connection is to read some data from the connection, handle the data, read more data from the connection, handle it, and so on.

But what happens if you don't read data from a network connection quickly enough? Eventually, the sender may fill the receiver's receive buffer, resulting in a zero-window state. The receiver will not be able to receive data until the application reads data from the buffer. This most often happens when the handling of data read from a network connection blocks and the code never makes its way around to reading from the socket again, as shown in Listing 4-26.

```
buf := make([]byte, 1024)

for {
❶   n, err := conn.Read(buf)
    if err != nil {
        return err
    }

❷   handle(buf[:n]) // BLOCKS!
}
```

*Listing 4-26: Handling received data blocks preventing iteration around the loop*

Reading data from the network connection ❶ frees up receive buffer space. If the code blocks for an appreciable amount of time while handling the received data ❷, the receive buffer may fill up. A full receive buffer isn't necessarily bad. Zeroing the window is a way to *throttle*, or slow, the flow of data from the sender by creating backpressure on the sender. But if it's unintended or prolonged, a zero window may indicate a bug in your code.

### Sockets Stuck in the CLOSE_WAIT State

In "Gracefully Terminating TCP Sessions" on page 50, I mentioned that the server side of a TCP network connection will enter the CLOSE_WAIT state after it receives and acknowledges the FIN packet from the client. If you see TCP sockets on your server that persist in the CLOSE_WAIT state, it's likely your code is neglecting to properly call the Close method on its network connections, as in Listing 4-27.

```
for {
    conn, err := listener.Accept()
    if err != nil {
        return err
    }

❶  go func(c net.Conn) { // we never call c.Close() before returning!
        buf := make([]byte, 1024)

        for {
            n, err := c.Read(buf)
            if err != nil {
❷              return
            }

            handle(buf[:n])
        }
    }(conn)
}
```

*Listing 4-27: Returning from a connection-handling goroutine without properly closing the connection*

The listener handles each connection in its own goroutine ❶. However, the goroutine fails to call the connection's Close method before fully returning from the goroutine ❷. Even a temporary error will cause the goroutine to return. And because you never close the connection, this will leave the TCP socket in the CLOSE_WAIT state. If the server attempted to send anything other than a FIN packet to the client, the client would respond with an RST packet, abruptly tearing down the connection. The solution is to make sure to defer a call to the connection's Close method soon after creating the goroutine ❶.

## What You've Learned

In this chapter, you first learned several methods of reading data from and writing data to a network connection, including the type-length-value encoding scheme. You built on this knowledge and learned an efficient way to proxy data between network connections. Next, you used a few io tools to monitor network traffic. Then, you used your knowledge of TCP handshakes to ping remote hosts in environments where ICMP echo requests and replies are filtered. Finally, the chapter wrapped up by covering the more platform-specific, yet powerful, methods provided by the net.TCPConn object and a few common connection-handling bugs.

# 5

## UNRELIABLE UDP COMMUNICATION

Although most networking applications take advantage of TCP's reliability and flow control, the less popular User Datagram Protocol (UDP) is nonetheless an important part of the TCP/IP stack. UDP is a simple protocol with minimal features. Some applications do not require TCP's feature set and session overhead. Those applications, like domain name resolution services, opt to use UDP instead.

This chapter starts by comparing UDP to TCP, focusing on scenarios where UDP may be a better choice over TCP. Then, you'll learn how to send and receive UDP packets in Go. Finally, you'll learn why it's best to limit the size of UDP packets you send across a network and how to determine an optimal packet size.

# Using UDP: Simple and Unreliable

UDP is unreliable because it does not include many of the mechanisms that make TCP so trustworthy. It provides little more than a socket address (an IP address and port). In fact, the protocol is so simple that RFC 768 describes the entire thing in about three pages. Unlike TCP, UDP does not provide session support or even confirm that the destination is accessible; it simply makes a best-effort attempt to deliver the packet. Recipients do not automatically acknowledge UDP packets, so UDP has no inherent delivery confirmation. UDP does not manage congestion, control data flow, or retransmit packets. Lastly, UDP does not guarantee that the destination receives packets in the order they originate. UDP is simply a conduit between applications and the IP layer. This simplicity is what makes UDP fast and attractive for some applications.

UDP has a few strengths over TCP. Whereas TCP must establish a session with each individual node in a group before it can transmit data, UDP can send a single packet to a group of nodes without duplicating the packet, a process known as *multicasting*. UDP is also capable of broadcasting packets to all members of a subnet since it doesn't need to establish a session between each node.

UDP is ideal when missing packets aren't detrimental to overall communication because the most recently received packets can take the place of earlier, dropped packets. Weather data is a good example of this. If you're tracking a tornado in your area by streaming weather data to your phone, you aren't as concerned about dropped packets indicating the tornado's location two minutes ago if you've received packets giving you the tornado's current location.

You should consider using UDP in your application if it doesn't require all the features TCP provides. For most network applications, TCP is the right protocol choice. But UDP is an option if its speed and simplicity better fit your use case and the reliability trade-offs aren't detrimental.

UDP's packet structure consists of an 8-byte header and a payload. The header contains 2 bytes for the source port, 2 bytes for the destination port, 2 bytes for the packet length in bytes, and a 2-byte checksum. The minimum packet length is 8 bytes to account for the header and an empty payload. Figure 5-1 illustrates the organization of a UDP packet.

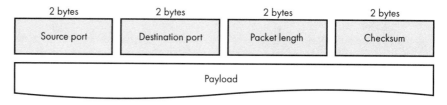

*Figure 5-1: UDP packet header and payload*

Although the maximum packet length is 65,535 bytes, application layer protocols often limit the packet length to avoid fragmentation, which we discuss in "Avoiding Fragmentation" on page 115.

## Sending and Receiving UDP Data

When it comes to sending and receiving data, UDP is uncivilized compared to TCP. For example, let's assume your neighbor baked you a pie and wants to give it to you. Using TCP to communicate is like your neighbor shouting a greeting from her window (her socket address) to your open window (your socket address). You hear her greeting and return a greeting of your own (the TCP handshake). Your neighbor then delivers your pie. You accept it and thankfully acknowledge the pie (the data transfer). You then both exchange farewells and go about your business (the termination). By contrast, using UDP to communicate is like your neighbor abruptly throwing the pie at your window, whether it's open or not, and awaiting no confirmation that you received it.

The section "Using the net.Conn Interface" on page 74 introduced the net.Conn interface for handling stream-oriented connections, such as TCP, between a client and a server. But this interface isn't ideal for UDP connections because UDP is not a stream-oriented protocol. UDP does not maintain a session or involve a handshake process like TCP. UDP does not have the concept of acknowledgments, retransmissions, or flow control.

Instead, UDP primarily relies on the packet-oriented net.PacketConn interface. We'll discuss a use case for net.Conn with UDP later in this chapter, but net.PacketConn is the better choice for most UDP applications.

### Using a UDP Echo Server

Sending and receiving UDP packets is a nearly identical process to sending and receiving TCP packets. But since UDP doesn't have session support, you must be able to handle an additional return value, the sender's address, when reading data from the connection object, as shown in Listing 5-1's UDP echo server implementation.

```
package echo

import (
    "context"
    "net"
)

func echoServerUDP(❶ctx context.Context, addr string) (net.Addr, error) {
    s, err := ❷net.ListenPacket("udp", addr)
    if err != nil {
        return nil, fmt.Errorf("binding to udp %s: %w", addr, err)
    }

❸ go func() {
        go func() {
        ❹ <-ctx.Done()
            _ = s.Close()
        }()

        buf := make([]byte, 1024)
```

```
      for {
          n, ❺clientAddr, err := ❻s.ReadFrom(buf) // client to server
          if err != nil {
              return
          }

          _, err = ❼s.WriteTo(buf[:n], ❽clientAddr) // server to client
          if err != nil {
              return
          }
      }
  }()

  return s.LocalAddr(), nil
}
```

*Listing 5-1: A simple UDP echo server implementation (echo.go)*

This code allows you to spin up a UDP server that will echo any UDP packets it receives to the sender. You'll make use of this code quite a bit in this chapter, so it behooves you to understand what's happening here.

The function receives a context ❶ to allow cancellation of the echo server by the caller and a string address in the familiar *host:port* format. It returns a net.Addr interface and an error interface. The caller uses the net.Addr interface to address messages to the echo server. The returned error interface is not nil if anything goes wrong while instantiating the echo server.

You create a UDP connection for your server with a call to net .ListenPacket ❷, which returns a net.PacketConn interface and an error interface. The net.ListenPacket function is analogous to the net.Listen function you used to create a TCP listener in Chapters 3 and 4, except net.ListenPacket exclusively returns a net.PacketConn interface.

A goroutine manages the asynchronous echoing of messages by your echo server ❸. A second goroutine blocks on the context's Done channel ❹. Once the caller cancels the context, receiving on the Done channel unblocks and the server is closed, tearing down both this goroutine and the parent goroutine ❸.

To read from the UDP connection, you pass a byte slice to the ReadFrom method ❻. This returns the number of bytes read, the sender's address, and an error interface. Notice there is no Accept method on your UDP connection as there is with the TCP-based listeners in the previous chapters. This is because UDP doesn't use a handshake process. Here, you simply create a UDP connection listening to a UDP port and read any incoming messages. Since you don't have the luxury of a proper introduction and an established session, you rely on the returned address ❺ to determine which node sent you the message.

To write a UDP packet, you pass a byte slice and a destination address ❽ to the connection's WriteTo method ❼. The WriteTo method returns the number of bytes written and an error interface. Just as with reading data, you need to tell the WriteTo method where to send the packet, because you do not have an established session with a remote node. In Listing 5-1, you write the message to the original sender. But you could just as easily forward the message onto another node using your existing UDP connection object. You do not have to establish a new UDP connection object to forward on the message as you would if you were using TCP.

## Receiving Data from the Echo Server

Now that you are familiar with the UDP-based echo server, let's have a look at some client code that interacts with the echo server. Listing 5-2 shows a simple interaction with the echo server.

```
package echo

import (
    "bytes"
    "context"
    "net"
    "testing"
)

func TestEchoServerUDP(t *testing.T) {
    ctx, cancel := context.WithCancel(context.Background())
 ❶  serverAddr, err := echoServerUDP(ctx, "127.0.0.1:")
    if err != nil {
        t.Fatal(err)
    }
    defer cancel()

 ❷  client, err := net.ListenPacket("udp", "127.0.0.1:")
    if err != nil {
        t.Fatal(err)
    }
    defer func() { _ = client.Close() }()

    msg := []byte("ping")
    _, err = ❸client.WriteTo(msg, serverAddr)
    if err != nil {
        t.Fatal(err)
    }

    buf := make([]byte, 1024)
    n, ❹addr, err := ❺client.ReadFrom(buf)
    if err != nil {
        t.Fatal(err)
    }

    if addr.String() != serverAddr.String() {
        t.Fatalf("received reply from %q instead of %q", addr, serverAddr)
    }
```

```
        if !bytes.Equal(msg, buf[:n]) {
            t.Errorf("expected reply %q; actual reply %q", msg, buf[:n])
        }
    }
}
```

*Listing 5-2: Sending UDP packets to the echo server and receiving replies (echo_test.go)*

You pass along a context and the address string to the echoServer function and receive the server's address ❶ object. You defer a call to the context's cancel function, which signals the server to exit and close its goroutines. In a real-world application, using a context for cancellation of long-running processes is useful to make sure you aren't leaking resources like memory or unnecessarily keeping files open.

You instantiate the client's net.PacketConn ❷ in the same way that you instantiated the echo server's net.PacketConn. The net.ListenPacket function creates the connection object for both the client and the server. Here, too, you need to tell the client where to send its message with each invocation of its WriteTo method ❸. After sending the message to the echo server, the client should immediately receive a message via its ReadFrom method ❺. You can examine the address ❹ returned by the ReadFrom method to confirm that the echo server sent the message.

It's important to note that the test in Listing 5-2 can fail under certain circumstances. Even though you're reading packets from and writing packets to a computer's local network stack, the packets are still subject to all of the conditions that make UDP unreliable over inter-node networks. For example, full send or receive buffers, or the lack of available RAM, can result in dropped packets; large UDP packets may be subject to fragmentation (discussed later in this chapter); and operating systems using multiple threads to deliver UDP packets may deliver the packets out of order.

## Every UDP Connection Is a Listener

Recall from Chapter 3 that Go's net package distinguishes between a TCP connection object (TCPConn) and a TCP listener (TCPListener). The TCP listener is what accepts the connection and returns an object that represents the listener's side of the connection so that the listener can then send a message to the client.

There is no UDP equivalent of the TCPListener because UDP lacks sessions. This means your code has a bit more accounting to do when it receives packets. You need to verify the sender's address, because you can no longer trust that all incoming packets to a connection object are from the same sender.

The next few listings are part of a test that a single UDP connection object can receive packets from more than one sender. Listing 5-3 spins up an echo server and a client for the test.

```
package echo

import (
    "bytes"
    "context"
    "net"
    "testing"
)

func TestListenPacketUDP(t *testing.T) {
    ctx, cancel := context.WithCancel(context.Background())
❶  serverAddr, err := echoServerUDP(ctx, "127.0.0.1:")
    if err != nil {
        t.Fatal(err)
    }
    defer cancel()

❷  client, err := net.ListenPacket("udp", "127.0.0.1:")
    if err != nil {
        t.Fatal(err)
    }
    defer func() { _ = client.Close() }()
```

Listing 5-3: Creating an echo server and client (listen_packet_test.go)

You start by creating the echo server ❶ and client connection ❷.
Listing 5-4 adds a second network connection to interact with the client.

```
--snip--

❶  interloper, err := net.ListenPacket("udp", "127.0.0.1:")
    if err != nil {
        t.Fatal(err)
    }

    interrupt := []byte("pardon me")
❷  n, err := interloper.WriteTo(interrupt, client.LocalAddr())
    if err != nil {
        t.Fatal(err)
    }
    _ = interloper.Close()

    if l := len(interrupt); l != n {
        t.Fatalf("wrote %d bytes of %d", n, l)
    }
}
```

Listing 5-4: Adding an interloper and interrupting the client with a message
(listen_packet_test.go)

You then create a new UDP connection ❶ meant to interlope on the client and echo server and interrupt the client ❷. This message should queue
up in the client's receive buffer.

The client sends its ping message to the echo server and reconciles the replies in Listing 5-5.

```
--snip--

    ping := []byte("ping")
    _, err = ❶client.WriteTo(ping, serverAddr)
    if err != nil {
        t.Fatal(err)
    }

    buf := make([]byte, 1024)
    n, addr, err := ❷client.ReadFrom(buf)
    if err != nil {
        t.Fatal(err)
    }

    if !bytes.Equal(❸interrupt, buf[:n]) {
        t.Errorf("expected reply %q; actual reply %q", interrupt, buf[:n])
    }

    if addr.String() != interloper.LocalAddr().String() {
        t.Errorf("expected message from %q; actual sender is %q",
            interloper.LocalAddr(), addr)
    }

    n, addr, err = client.ReadFrom(buf)
    if err != nil {
        t.Fatal(err)
    }

    if !bytes.Equal(❹ping, buf[:n]) {
        t.Errorf("expected reply %q; actual reply %q", ping, buf[:n])
    }

❺   if addr.String() != serverAddr.String() {
        t.Errorf("expected message from %q; actual sender is %q",
            serverAddr, addr)
    }
}
```

*Listing 5-5: Receiving UDP packets from multiple senders at once (listen_packet_test.go)*

Meanwhile, the client writes a ping message to the echo server ❶ and promptly reads an incoming message ❷. What's unique about the UDP client connection is it first reads the interruption message from the interloping connection ❸ and then the reply from the echo server ❹. Were this a TCP connection, the client would have never received the interloper's message. As such, your code should always verify the sender of each packet it reads by evaluating the second return value ❺ from the ReadFrom method, the sender's address.

## Using net.Conn in UDP

You can establish a UDP connection that implements the net.Conn interface
so that your code behaves indistinguishably from a TCP net.Conn. You do so
by passing udp as the first argument to the net.Dial function used in the preceding two chapters. Using net.Conn with your UDP-based connections can
prevent interlopers from sending you messages and eliminate the need to
check the sender's address on every reply you receive.

Listing 5-6 creates the UDP-based net.Conn and demonstrates how net.Conn
encapsulates the implementation details of UDP to emulate a stream-oriented
network connection.

```
package echo

import (
    "bytes"
    "context"
    "net"
    "testing"
    "time"
)

func TestDialUDP(t *testing.T) {
    ctx, cancel := context.WithCancel(context.Background())
 ❶ serverAddr, err := echoServerUDP(ctx, "127.0.0.1:")
    if err != nil {
        t.Fatal(err)
    }
    defer cancel()

    client, err := ❷net.Dial("udp", serverAddr.String())
    if err != nil {
        t.Fatal(err)
    }
    defer func() { _ = client.Close() }()
```

*Listing 5-6: Creating an echo server and client (dial_test.go)*

The client side of a connection can leverage the stream-oriented functionality of net.Conn over UDP, but the UDP listener must still use net.PacketConn.
You spawn an instance of the echo server ❶ for the purpose of sending a reply
to the client. You then dial the echo server over UDP by passing udp as the first
argument to net.Dial ❷. Unlike TCP, the echo server receives no traffic upon
calling net.Dial because no handshake is necessary.

Listing 5-7 interrupts the client by sending a message to it before the
echo server sends its reply.

```
--snip--

    interloper, err := net.ListenPacket("udp", "127.0.0.1:")
    if err != nil {
        t.Fatal(err)
    }
```

```
    interrupt := []byte("pardon me")
❶ n, err := interloper.WriteTo(interrupt, client.LocalAddr())
    if err != nil {
        t.Fatal(err)
    }
    _ = interloper.Close()

    if l := len(interrupt); l != n {
        t.Fatalf("wrote %d bytes of %d", n, l)
    }
```

*Listing 5-7: Interrupting the client (dial_test.go)*

Just as in Listing 5-4, you send a message to the client from an interloping connection ❶.

Listing 5-8 details the difference between a UDP connection using net.Conn and one using net.PacketConn, as in Listing 5-5.

```
--snip--

    ping := []byte("ping")
    _, err = ❶client.Write(ping)
    if err != nil {
        t.Fatal(err)
    }

    buf := make([]byte, 1024)
    n, err = ❷client.Read(buf)
    if err != nil {
        t.Fatal(err)
    }

    if !bytes.Equal(ping, buf[:n]) {
        t.Errorf("expected reply %q; actual reply %q", ping, buf[:n])
    }

    err = ❸client.SetDeadline(time.Now().Add(time.Second))
    if err != nil {
        t.Fatal(err)
    }

    _, err = ❹client.Read(buf)
    if err == nil {
        t.Fatal("unexpected packet")
    }
}
```

*Listing 5-8: Using net.Conn to manage UDP traffic (dial_test.go)*

The client sends a ping message to the echo server by using net.Conn's Write method ❶. The net.Conn client will write its messages to the address specified in the net.Dial call. You do not need to specify a destination address for every packet you send using the client connection. Likewise, you read packets using the client's Read method ❷. The client reads packets only from the sender address specified in the net.Dial call, as you would expect using a stream-oriented connection object. The client never reads the message sent by the interloping connection. To make sure, you set an ample deadline ❸ and attempt to read another message ❹.

For your purposes, using net.Conn over net.PacketConn may make your UDP connection code cleaner. Just be aware of the trade-offs. Using net.Conn with UDP does not offer the same functionality as you would expect when using net.Conn with TCP. For example, a UDP-based net.Conn's Write method will not return an error if the destination failed to receive the packet. The onus is still on your application code to confirm delivery when using UDP.

## Avoiding Fragmentation

*Fragmentation* is a Layer 3 IP process of splitting a packet into smaller pieces suitable for efficient transmission over a network. All network media have packet size limitations known as the *maximum transmission unit (MTU)*. Packets larger than the medium's maximum transmission unit require fragmentation so that each fragment is less than or equal to the medium's MTU before nodes pass them over the medium. Once the fragments reach their destination, the operating system reassembles each packet and presents the packet to your application.

But fragments can corrupt or fail to reach their destination for one reason or another. This is a significant consideration if you're using UDP because, unlike TCP, UDP does not gracefully recover from missing or corrupt data. If an operating system fails to receive even a single fragment, the sender must retransmit the entire UDP packet. As you can imagine, retransmitting large packets is woefully inefficient. Although there are numerous approaches to mitigating the effects of fragmentation, we'll attempt to avoid it altogether. We'll focus on a straightforward way to identify the MTU between your computer and a destination node, and then use those results to inform your choice of payload size to avoid fragmentation.

You can use the ping command to determine the MTU between your computer and a destination node. The ping command allows you to send an ICMP packet of a specific size with a flag set to inform nodes not to fragment it. If the packet reaches a node that needs to fragment the packet because of its size, the node will see the *do not fragment* flag and respond with an ICMP message informing you that the packet is too large.

The following example sends these pings over Ethernet, which has a minimum MTU of 46 bytes and a maximum MTU of 1,500 bytes, per its specification. If any hop between your computer and its destination has an MTU of less than 1,500 bytes, your packet will fragment. Let's confirm that with the ping command on Linux (Listing 5-9).

```
$ ping -M ❶do -s ❷1500 1.1.1.1
PING 1.1.1.1 (1.1.1.1) 1500(❸1528) bytes of data.
ping: sendmsg: ❹Message too long
```

*Listing 5-9: Pinging 1.1.1.1 with a payload size of 1,500 bytes on Linux*

You set the -M flag ❶ to do, which sets the prohibit fragmentation option, and set the -s flag ❷ to 1500, which sets a payload of 1,500 bytes. Since you aren't accounting for the packet's header size, this should exceed the Ethernet MTU. As expected, you get a notification that the packet needs fragmentation ❹. You also see that the total packet size is 1,528 bytes ❸. The extra 28 bytes is the sum of the 8-byte ICMP header and the 20-byte IP header. Any payload you specify should account for the overall header size as well.

As you can see, you never received a reply from 1.1.1.1 in Listing 5-9 because the packet you sent was too big to traverse each hop without requiring fragmentation. Instead, the ping command informed you that your message was too long.

Let's try again and subtract 28 bytes from the payload (Listing 5-10).

```
$ ping -M do -s 1472 1.1.1.1
PING 1.1.1.1 (1.1.1.1) 1472(1500) bytes of data.
1480 bytes from 1.1.1.1: icmp_seq=1 ttl=59 time=11.8 ms
```

Listing 5-10: Pinging 1.1.1.1 with a payload size of 1472 bytes on Linux

That's more like it. You confirmed that the MTU between this computer and 1.1.1.1 over the internet is set to 1,500 bytes. This is the maximum packet size you can send on the network before it will require fragmentation. Thankfully, the UDP header is also 8 bytes, so the ping command gives accurate results despite using ICMP. Accounting for the headers, your maximum UDP payload size is 1,472 bytes to avoid fragmentation.

The equivalent ping command on Windows is the following:

```
C:\>ping -f -l 1500 1.1.1.1
```

The -f flag instructs nodes to not fragment the packet, and the -l flag sets the packet size to the given integer in bytes.

On macOS, the ping command looks like this:

```
$ ping -D -s 1500 1.1.1.1
```

The -D flag sets the no fragmentation flag, and the -s flag specifies the payload size.

Keep in mind that the MTU from your computer may differ from the examples in this chapter because of MTU settings either on your network or between your computer and the destination you choose to ping. I recommend you experiment with the ping command to determine the MTU from your computer to various hosts on the internet and see if you find any differences.

# What You've Learned

UDP is a minimalistic, datagram-based protocol that favors speed over reliability by eschewing many of TCP's flow control and reliability features. UDP is ideal when speed and simplicity are required and the potential for data loss is acceptable, such as with live video streaming.

Since UDP is not session based, there is no concept of a UDP listener that accepts a connection after establishing a session. Rather, you create a network connection by using net.ListenPacket, which returns a net.PacketConn interface. Your code can then read any incoming messages, or datagrams, from the net.PacketConn interface since every net.PacketConn listens for incoming messages.

Fragmentation is a serious consideration when using UDP. It's important to avoid fragmentation of your UDP packets whenever possible to help ensure delivery. The ping command can help you derive the appropriate maximum transmission unit between your computer and your destination network. Since ICMP packet headers used by the ping command are the same size as UDP headers, you can use that knowledge to easily determine the payload size threshold at which fragmentation will occur. Aside from managing fragmentation by appropriately sizing your payloads, your code must manage acknowledgments and retransmissions to ensure reliability.

# 6

## ENSURING UDP RELIABILITY

Chapter 5 introduced basic network applications using UDP and demonstrated the flexibility of Go's net package and interfaces for writing portable code. This chapter picks up where the last one left off to introduce one method of ensuring reliability when communicating over UDP.

This chapter starts by introducing an application protocol built on top of UDP. We'll cover a subset of types used by this protocol and demonstrate how they are used to reliably transfer data. We'll then implement a server that allows clients to download files using the application protocol. Finally, we'll download a file from our server and verify its integrity.

## Reliable File Transfers Using TFTP

As discussed in the preceding chapter, UDP is inherently unreliable. That means it's your application's job to make the UDP connection reliable.

Since we spent the last chapter covering UDP and how it's best used in situations that require a subset of TCP features, it's only appropriate that we look at an example of such an application-level protocol.

The *Trivial File Transfer Protocol (TFTP)* is an example of an application protocol that ensures reliable data transfers over UDP. It allows two nodes to transfer files over UDP by implementing a subset of the features that make TCP reliable. A TFTP server implements ordered packet delivery, acknowledgments, and retransmissions. To distill this example down to the essential bits, your server allows clients to download binary data only. It does not support uploads, American Standard Code for Information Interchange (ASCII) transfers, or some of the later additions to TFTP specified outside RFC 1350. Your server expediently serves the same file, no matter what file the client requests, in the name of simplicity.

Please keep in mind that TFTP is not appropriate for secure file transmission. Though it adds reliability to UDP connections, it does not support encryption or authentication. If your application requires communication over UDP, you may want to use WireGuard (*https://github.com/WireGuard/wireguard-go/*), an application that allows for secure communication over UDP.

The next few sections will implement a read-only TFTP server to teach you the basics of adding reliability to UDP. By *read-only*, I mean your server will allow clients to only download files, not upload them. You will start by defining the subset of constants and types your TFTP server supports. You will encapsulate as much of the type-related logic in each type's methods. You'll then implement the TFTP server portion of the code that will interact with clients and use the types we define to facilitate reliable file transfers.

## TFTP Types

Your TFTP server will accept read requests from the client, send data packets, transmit error packets, and accept acknowledgments from the client. To do this, you must define a few types in your code to represent client requests, transmitted data, acknowledgments, and errors. Listing 6-1 outlines key types used to cap packet sizes, identify operations, and codify various errors.

```
package tftp

import (
    "bytes"
    "encoding/binary"
    "errors"
    "io"
    "strings"
)

const (
    DatagramSize = ❶516 // the maximum supported datagram size
    BlockSize = ❷DatagramSize - 4 // the DatagramSize minus a 4-byte header
)
```

❸ type OpCode uint16

```
const (
    OpRRQ OpCode = iota + 1
    _                     // no WRQ support
    OpData
    OpAck
    OpErr
)
```

❹ type ErrCode uint16

```
const (
    ErrUnknown ErrCode = iota
    ErrNotFound
    ErrAccessViolation
    ErrDiskFull
    ErrIllegalOp
    ErrUnknownID
    ErrFileExists
    ErrNoUser
)
```

*Listing 6-1: Types and codes used by the TFTP server (types.go)*

TFTP limits datagram packets to 516 bytes or fewer to avoid fragmentation. You define two constants to enforce the datagram size limit ❶ and the maximum data block size ❷. The maximum block size is the datagram size minus a 4-byte header. The first 2 bytes of a TFTP packet's header is an operation code ❸.

Each operation code is a 2-byte, unsigned integer. Your server supports four operations: a read request (RRQ), a data operation, an acknowledgment, and an error. Since your server is read-only, you skip the write request (WRQ) definition.

As with the operation codes, you define a series of unsigned 16-bit integer error codes ❹ per the RFC. Although you don't use all error codes in your server since it allows only downloads, a client could return these error codes in lieu of an acknowledgment packet.

The following sections detail the types that implement your server's four supported operations.

### Read Requests

The server receives a *read request* packet when the client wants to download a file. The server must then respond with either a data packet or an error packet, both of which you'll look at in the next few sections. Either packet serves as an acknowledgment to the client that the server received the read request. If the client does not receive a data or error packet, it may retransmit the read request until the server responds or the client gives up.

Figure 6-1 illustrates the structure of a read request packet.

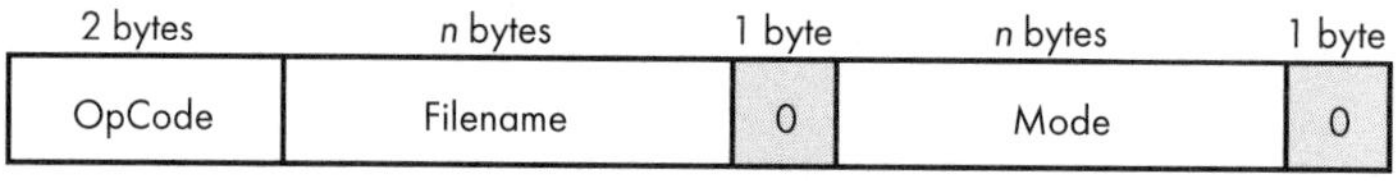

| 2 bytes | n bytes | 1 byte | n bytes | 1 byte |
|---------|---------|--------|---------|--------|
| OpCode | Filename | 0 | Mode | 0 |

*Figure 6-1: Read request packet structure*

The read request packet consists of a 2-byte operation code, a filename, a null byte, a mode, and a trailing null byte. An *operation code* is an integer that is unique to each of your operation types. Each type's operation code corresponds to the integer detailed in RFC 1350. For example, a read request's operation code is 1. The filename and mode are strings of varying lengths. The mode indicates to the server how it should send the file: netascii or octet. If a client requests a file using the *netascii* mode, the client must convert the file to match its own line-ending format. For our purposes, you will accept only the *octet* mode, which tells the server to send the file in a binary format, or as is.

Listing 6-2 is a continuation of Listing 6-1. Here, you define the read request and its method that allows the server to marshal the request into a slice of bytes in preparation for writing to a network connection.

```
--snip--

❶ type ReadReq struct {
      Filename string
      Mode     string
  }

  // Although not used by our server, a client would make use of this method.
  func (q ReadReq) MarshalBinary() ([]byte, error) {
      mode := "octet"
      if q.Mode != "" {
          mode = q.Mode
      }

      // operation code + filename + 0 byte + mode + 0 byte
      cap := 2 + 2 + len(q.Filename) + 1 + len(q.Mode) + 1

      b := new(bytes.Buffer)
      b.Grow(cap)

      err := ❷binary.Write(b, binary.BigEndian, OpRRQ) // write operation code
      if err != nil {
          return nil, err
      }

      _, err = b.WriteString(q.Filename) // write filename
      if err != nil {
          return nil, err
      }

      err = ❸b.WriteByte(0) // write 0 byte
      if err != nil {
```

```
        return nil, err
    }

    _, err = b.WriteString(mode) // write mode
    if err != nil {
        return nil, err
    }

    err = ❸b.WriteByte(0) // write 0 byte
    if err != nil {
        return nil, err
    }

    return b.Bytes(), nil
}
```

*Listing 6-2: Read request and its binary marshaling method (types.go continued)*

The struct representing your read request ❶ needs to keep track of the filename and the mode. You insert the operation code ❷ and null bytes ❸ into the buffer while marshaling the packet to a byte slice.

Listing 6-3 continues where Listing 6-2 left off and rounds out the read request's implementation by defining a method that allows the server to unmarshal a read request from a byte slice, typically read from a network connection with a client.

```
--snip--

func (q *ReadReq) ❶UnmarshalBinary(p []byte) error {
    r := bytes.NewBuffer(p)

    var code OpCode

    err := ❷binary.Read(r, binary.BigEndian, &code) // read operation code
    if err != nil {
        return err
    }

    if code != OpRRQ {
        return errors.New("invalid RRQ")
    }

    q.Filename, err = ❸r.ReadString(0) // read filename
    if err != nil {
        return errors.New("invalid RRQ")
    }

    q.Filename = ❹strings.TrimRight(q.Filename, "\x00") // remove the 0-byte
    if len(q.Filename) == 0 {
        return errors.New("invalid RRQ")
    }

    q.Mode, err = ↑.ReadString(0) // read mode
    if err != nil {
```

```
        return errors.New("invalid RRQ")
    }

    q.Mode = strings.TrimRight(q.Mode, "\x00") // remove the 0-byte
    if len(q.Mode) == 0 {
        return errors.New("invalid RRQ")
    }

    actual := strings.ToLower(q.Mode) // enforce octet mode
    if actual != "octet" {
        return errors.New("only binary transfers supported")
    }

    return nil
}
```

*Listing 6-3: Read request type implementation (types.go continued)*

Your TFTP server's read request, data, acknowledgment, and error packets all implement the encoding.BinaryMarshaler and encoding.BinaryUnmarshaler
interfaces. These methods allow your types to marshal themselves to a
binary format suitable for transmission over the network and from network
bytes back into the original types. For example, the read request type can
marshal itself into a byte slice that matches the read request format showed
in Figure 6-1 by using its MarshalBinary method from Listing 6-2. Likewise,
it can constitute itself from a byte slice read from the network using its
UnmarshalBinary method ❶. Although your server does not send a read
request and make use of its MarshalBinary method, I encourage you to write a
TFTP client that will marshal a read request to its binary form as you progress through this chapter. I leave it as an exercise for you to implement.

The UnmarshalBinary method returns nil only if the given byte slice
matches the read request format. If you are unsure of whether a given byte
slice is a read request, you can pass the byte slice to this method and make
that determination based on the return value. You will see this in action
when you look at the server code.

The UnmarshalBinary method reads in the first 2 bytes ❷ and confirms
the operation code is that of a read request. It then reads all bytes up to the
first null byte ❸ and strips the null byte delimiter ❹. The resulting string
of bytes represents the filename. Similarly, you read in the mode, returning nil if everything is as expected. The server can then use the populated
ReadReq to retrieve the requested file for the client.

## Data Packets

Clients receive *data packets* in response to their read requests, provided the
server was able to retrieve the requested file. The server sends the file in a
series of data packets, each of which has an assigned block number, starting
at 1 and incrementing with every subsequent data packet. The block number allows the client to properly order the received data and account for
duplicates.

All data packets have a payload of 512 bytes except for the last packet. The client continues to read data packets until it receives a data packet whose payload is less than 512 bytes, indicating the end of the transmission. At any point, the client can return an error packet in place of an acknowledgment, and the server can return an error packet instead of a data packet. An error packet immediately terminates the transfer.

Figure 6-2 shows the format of a data packet.

| 2 bytes | 2 bytes | n bytes |
|---------|---------|---------|
| OpCode | Block # | Payload |

*Figure 6-2: Data packet structure*

Like the read request packet, the data packet's first 2 bytes contain its operation code. The next 2 bytes represent the block number. The remaining bytes, up to 512, are the payload.

The server requires an acknowledgment from the client after each data packet. If the server does not receive a timely acknowledgment or an error from the client, the server will retry the transmission until it receives a reply or exhausts its number of retries. Figure 6-3 illustrates the initial communication between a client downloading a file from a TFTP server.

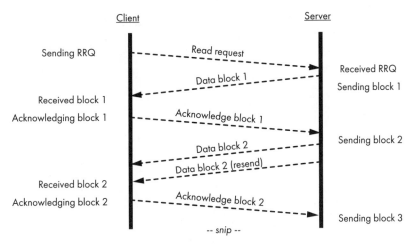

*Figure 6-3: Downloading a file by using the Trivial File Transfer Protocol*

Once the client has sent the initial read request packet, the server responds with the first block of data. Next, the client acknowledges receipt of block 1. The server receives the acknowledgment and replies with the second block of data. But in this contrived example, the server does not receive a timely reply from the client, so it resends block 2. The client receives block 2 and sends its acknowledgment. This back-and-forth continues until the server sends the last block with a payload of fewer than 512 bytes.

Listing 6-4 details the data type that is used for the actual data transfer.

```
--snip--
```

❶ ```go
type Data struct {
    Block   uint16
    Payload io.Reader
}
```

❷ ```go
func (d *Data) MarshalBinary() ([]byte, error) {
    b := new(bytes.Buffer)
    b.Grow(DatagramSize)

    d.Block++ // block numbers increment from 1

    err := binary.Write(b, binary.BigEndian, OpData) // write operation code
    if err != nil {
        return nil, err
    }

    err = binary.Write(b, binary.BigEndian, d.Block) // write block number
    if err != nil {
        return nil, err
    }

    // write up to BlockSize worth of bytes
    _, err = ❸io.CopyN(b, d.Payload, BlockSize)
    if err != nil && err != io.EOF {
        return nil, err
    }

    return b.Bytes(), nil
}
```

Listing 6-4: Data type and its binary marshaling method (types.go continued)

The Data struct ❶ keeps track of the current block number and the data source. In this case, your payload is an io.Reader instead of a byte slice, the reasoning being that an io.Reader allows greater flexibility about where you retrieve the payload. You could just as easily use an *os.File object to read a file from the filesystem as you could use a net.Conn to read the data from another network connection. The io.Reader interface gives you options that a simple byte slice doesn't. You're relying on the reader to keep track of the bytes left to read, eliminating a lot of code you'd otherwise have to write.

Every call to MarshalBinary ❷ will return 516 bytes per call at most by relying on the io.CopyN function ❸ and the BlockSize constant. Since you want MarshalBinary to modify the state, you need to use a pointer receiver. The intention is that the server can keep calling this method to get sequential blocks of data, each with an increasing block number, from the io.Reader until it exhausts the reader. Just like the client, the server needs to monitor the packet size returned by this method. When the packet size is less than 516 bytes, the server knows it received the last packet and should stop calling MarshalBinary. You'll see this in action in the server code later in this chapter.

You may have recognized the potential for an integer overflow of the 16-bit, unsigned block number. If you send a payload larger than about 33.5MB (65,535 × 512 bytes), the block number will overflow back to 0. Your server will happily continue sending data packets, but the client may not be as graceful handling the overflow. You should consider mitigating overflow risks by limiting the file size the TFTP server will support so as not to trigger the overflow, recognizing that an overflow can occur and determining whether it is acceptable to the client, or using a different protocol altogether.

Listing 6-5 finishes up the data type implementation with its binary unmarshaling method. This method follows the code in Listing 6-4.

```
--snip--

func (d *Data) UnmarshalBinary(p []byte) error {
❶ if l := len(p); l < 4 || l > DatagramSize {
        return errors.New("invalid DATA")
    }

    var opcode

    err := ❷binary.Read(bytes.NewReader(p[:2]), binary.BigEndian, &opcode)
    if err != nil || opcode != OpData {
        return errors.New("invalid DATA")
    }

    err = ❸binary.Read(bytes.NewReader(p[2:4]), binary.BigEndian, &d.Block)
    if err != nil {
        return errors.New("invalid DATA")
    }

    d.Payload = ❹bytes.NewBuffer(p[4:])

    return nil
}
```

Listing 6-5: Data type implementation (types.go continued)

To unmarshal data, you perform an initial sanity check ❶ to determine whether the packet size is within the expected bounds, making it worth reading the remaining bytes. You then read the operation code ❷ and check it, then the block number ❸. Finally, you stuff the remaining bytes into a new buffer ❹ and assign it to the Payload field.

The client uses the block number to send a corresponding acknowledgment to the server and to properly order this block of data among the other received blocks of data.

## Acknowledgments

*Acknowledgment packets* are only 4 bytes long, as shown in Figure 6-4.

| 2 bytes | 2 bytes |
|---------|---------|
| OpCode | Block # |

*Figure 6-4: Acknowledgment packet structure*

As in the other types, the first 2 bytes represent the operation code. The final 2 bytes contain the number of the acknowledged block.

Listing 6-6 shows the entire implementation of the acknowledgment type, which follows Listing 6-5's code.

```go
--snip--

❶ type Ack uint16

func (a Ack) MarshalBinary() ([]byte, error) {
    cap := 2 + 2 // operation code + block number

    b := new(bytes.Buffer)
    b.Grow(cap)

    err := binary.Write(b, binary.BigEndian, OpAck) // write operation code
    if err != nil {
        return nil, err
    }

    err = binary.Write(b, binary.BigEndian, a) // write block number
    if err != nil {
        return nil, err
    }

    return b.Bytes(), nil
}

func (a *Ack) UnmarshalBinary(p []byte) error {
    var code OpCode

    r := bytes.NewReader(p)

    err := binary.Read(r, binary.BigEndian, &code) // read operation code
    if err != nil {
        return err
    }

    if code != OpAck {
        return errors.New("invalid ACK")
    }
```

```
        return binary.Read(r, binary.BigEndian, a) // read block number
}
```

*Listing 6-6: Acknowledgment type implementation (types.go continued)*

You represent an acknowledgment packet by using a 16-bit, unsigned integer ❶. This integer is set to the acknowledged block number. The MarshalBinary and UnmarshalBinary methods should look familiar by this point. They handle marshaling the operation code and block number to a byte slice and populating an Ack object from bytes read from the network, respectively.

## Handling Errors

In TFTP, clients and servers convey errors by using an *error packet*, illustrated in Figure 6-5.

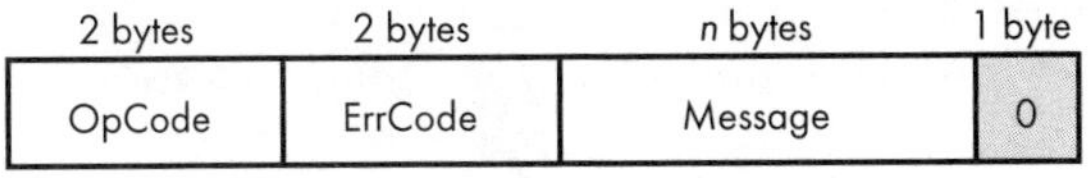

| 2 bytes | 2 bytes | n bytes | 1 byte |
|---------|---------|---------|--------|
| OpCode  | ErrCode | Message | 0      |

*Figure 6-5: Error packet structure*

Error packets consist of a 2-byte operation code, a 2-byte error code, an error message of variable length, and a terminating null byte.

Listing 6-7 details the error type and its binary marshal method, a continuation of Listing 6-6.

```
--snip--

❶ type Err struct {
        Error    ErrCode
        Message string
}

func (e Err) MarshalBinary() ([]byte, error) {
        // operation code + error code + message + 0 byte
        cap := 2 + 2 + len(e.Message) + 1

        b := new(bytes.Buffer)
        b.Grow(cap)

        err := binary.Write(b, binary.BigEndian, OpErr) // write operation code
        if err != nil {
                return nil, err
        }

        err = binary.Write(b, binary.BigEndian, e.Error) // write error code
        if err != nil {
                return nil, err
        }

        _, err = b.WriteString(e.Message) // write message
        if err != nil {
```

```
            return nil, err
    }

    err = b.WriteByte(0) // write 0 byte
    if err != nil {
        return nil, err
    }

    return b.Bytes(), nil
}
```

*Listing 6-7: Error type used for conveying errors between the client and server (types.go continued)*

Like the read request, the error type ❶ contains the minimum data required to craft an error packet: an error code and an error message. The MarshalBinary method populates a bytes buffer following the byte sequence detailed in Figure 6-5.

Listing 6-8 completes the error type implementation with its binary unmarshaler method. This code is appended to the code in Listing 6-7.

```
--snip--

func (e *Err) UnmarshalBinary(p []byte) error {
    r := bytes.NewBuffer(p)

    var code OpCode

    err := ❶binary.Read(r, binary.BigEndian, &code) // read operation code
    if err != nil {
        return err
    }

    if code != OpErr {
        return errors.New("invalid ERROR")
    }

    err = ❷binary.Read(r, binary.BigEndian, &e.Error) // read error message
    if err != nil {
        return err
    }

    e.Message, err = ❸r.ReadString(0)
    e.Message = ❹strings.TrimRight(e.Message, "\x00") // remove the 0-byte

    return err
}
```

*Listing 6-8: Error type's binary unmarshaler implementation (types.go continued)*

The UnmarshalBinary method is quite simple in that it reads and verifies the operation code ❶, consumes the error code ❷ and error message ❸, and strips the trailing null byte ❹.

# The TFTP Server

Now you'll write the server code, which will use the types you defined to interact with TFTP clients.

## Writing the Server Code

Listing 6-9 describes your server type and the methods that allow it to serve incoming requests. The fact that your packet types implement the encoding .BinaryMarshaler and encoding.BinaryUnmarshaler interfaces means that your server code can act as a conduit between the network interface and these types, leading to simpler code. All your server must concern itself with is transferring byte slices between your types and the network connection. The logic in the type interfaces takes care of the rest.

```
package tftp

import (
    "bytes"
    "errors"
    "fmt"
    "log"
    "net"
    "time"
)

type Server struct {
❶   Payload []byte // the payload served for all read requests
❷   Retries uint8 // the number of times to retry a failed transmission
❸   Timeout time.Duration // the duration to wait for an acknowledgment
}

func (s Server) ListenAndServe(addr string) error {
    conn, err := net.ListenPacket("udp", addr)
    if err != nil {
        return err
    }
    defer func() { _ = conn.Close() }()

    log.Printf("Listening on %s ...\n", conn.LocalAddr())

    return s.Serve(conn)
}

func (s *Server) ❹ Serve(conn net.PacketConn) error {
    if conn == nil {
        return errors.New("nil connection")
    }

    if s.Payload == nil {
        return errors.New("payload is required")
    }
```

```
    if s.Retries == 0 {
        s.Retries = 10
    }

    if s.Timeout == 0 {
        s.Timeout = 6 * time.Second
    }

    var rrq ReadReq

    for {
        buf := make([]byte, DatagramSize)

        _, addr, err := conn.ReadFrom(buf)
        if err != nil {
            return err
        }

        err = ❺rrq.UnmarshalBinary(buf)
        if err != nil {
            log.Printf("[%s] bad request: %v", addr, err)
            continue
        }

      ❻ go s.handle(addr.String(), rrq)
    }
}
```

*Listing 6-9: Server type implementation (server.go)*

Our server maintains a payload ❶ that it returns for every read request, a record of the number of times to attempt packet delivery ❷, and a time-out duration between each attempt ❸. The server's Serve method accepts a net.PacketConn and uses it to read incoming requests ❹. Closing the network connection will cause the method to return.

The server reads up to 516 bytes from its connection and attempts to unmarshal the bytes to a ReadReq object ❺. Since your server is read-only, it's interested only in servicing read requests. If the data read from the connection is a read request, the server passes it along to a handler method in a goroutine ❻. We'll define that next.

### Handling Read Requests

The handler (Listing 6-10) accepts read requests from the client and replies with the server's payload. It uses the features you built into your TFTP server's type system to improve the reliability of the data transfer over UDP. The handler sends one data packet and waits for an acknowledgment from the client before sending another data packet. It also attempts to retransmit the current data packet when it fails to receive a timely reply from the client.

```
❶ func (s Server) handle(clientAddr string, rrq ReadReq) {
      log.Printf("[%s] requested file: %s", clientAddr, rrq.Filename)

      conn, err := ❷net.Dial("udp", clientAddr)
      if err != nil {
          log.Printf("[%s] dial: %v", clientAddr, err)
          return
      }
      defer func() { _ = conn.Close() }()

      var (
          ackPkt  Ack
          errPkt  Err
          dataPkt = ❸Data{Payload: bytes.NewReader(s.Payload)}
          buf     = make([]byte, DatagramSize)
      )

NEXTPACKET:
  ❹ for n := DatagramSize; n == DatagramSize; {
          data, err := dataPkt.MarshalBinary()
          if err != nil {
              log.Printf("[%s] preparing data packet: %v", clientAddr, err)
              return
          }

      RETRY:
        ❺ for i := s.Retries; i > 0; i-- {
            ❻ n, err = conn.Write(data) // send the data packet
              if err != nil {
                  log.Printf("[%s] write: %v", clientAddr, err)
                  return
              }

              // wait for the client's ACK packet
              _ = conn.SetReadDeadline(time.Now().Add(s.Timeout))

              _, err = conn.Read(buf)
              if err != nil {
                  if nErr, ok := err.(net.Error); ok && nErr.Timeout() {
                      continue RETRY
                  }

                  log.Printf("[%s] waiting for ACK: %v", clientAddr, err)
                  return
              }

              switch {
              case ackPkt.UnmarshalBinary(buf) == nil:
                ❼ if uint16(ackPkt) == dataPkt.Block {
                      // received ACK; send next data packet
                      continue NEXTPACKET
```

```
            }
        case errPkt.UnmarshalBinary(buf) == nil:
            log.Printf("[%s] received error: %v",
                clientAddr, errPkt.Message)
            return
        default:
            log.Printf("[%s] bad packet", clientAddr)
        }
    }

    log.Printf("[%s] exhausted retries", clientAddr)
    return
}

log.Printf("[%s] sent %d blocks", clientAddr, dataPkt.Block)
}
```

*Listing 6-10: Handling read requests (server.go continued)*

This handler is a method ❶ on your Server type that accepts a client address and a read request. It's defined as a method because you need access to the Server's fields. You then initiate a connection with the client by using net.Dial ❷. The resulting UDP connection object created with net.Dial, if you remember, will read only packets from the client, freeing you from having to check the sender address on every Read call. You prepare a data object ❸ by using the server's payload, then enter a for loop to send each data packet ❹. This for loop will continue looping as long as the data packet size is equal to 516 bytes.

After marshaling the data object to a byte slice, you enter the for loop ❺ meant to resend the data packet until you either exhaust the number of retries or successfully deliver the data packet. Writing the data packet to the network connection ❻ updates the n loop variable with the number of bytes sent. If this value is 516 bytes, you iterate again when control passes back to the for loop ❹ labeled NEXTPACKET. If this value is less than 516 bytes, you break out of the loop.

Before you determine whether the transfer is complete, you must first verify that the client successfully received the last data packet. You read bytes from the client and attempt to unmarshal them into an Ack object or Err object. If you successfully unmarshal them into an Err object, you know the client returned an error, so you should log that fact and return early. An early return from this handler means the transmission terminated short of sending the entire payload. For our purposes, this is unrecoverable. The client would need to re-request the file to initiate another transfer.

If you successfully unmarshal the bytes into an Ack object, you can then check the object's Block value to determine whether it matches the block number of the current data packet ❼. If so, you iterate around the for loop ❹ and send the next packet. If not, you iterate around the inner for loop ❺ and resend the current data packet.

### Starting the Server

To start your TFTP server, you need to give the server two things: a file (its payload) and an address on which to listen for incoming requests (Listing 6-11).

```
package main

import (
    "flag"
    "io/ioutil"
    "log"

    "github.com/awoodbeck/gnp/ch06/tftp"
)

var (
    address = flag.String("a", "127.0.0.1:69", "listen address")
    payload = flag.String("p", "payload.svg", "file to serve to clients")
)

func main() {
    flag.Parse()

    p, err := ❶ioutil.ReadFile(*payload)
    if err != nil {
        log.Fatal(err)
    }

    s := ❷tftp.Server{Payload: p}
  ❸ log.Fatal(s.ListenAndServe(*address))
}
```

Listing 6-11: Command line TFTP server implementation (tftp.go)

Once you've read the file ❶ that your TFTP server will serve into a byte slice, you instantiate the server and assign the byte slice to the server's Payload field ❷. The last step is calling its ListenAndServe method to establish the UDP connection on which it will listen for requests. The ListenAndServe method ❸ calls the server's Serve method for you, which listens on the network connection for incoming requests. The server will continue to run until you terminate it with a CTRL-C on the command line.

## Downloading Files over UDP

Now let's try to download a file from the server you just wrote. First, you need to make sure you have a TFTP client installed. Windows has a native TFTP client that you can install through the Programs and Features section of the Control Panel by clicking the Turn Windows features on or off link. Select the **TFTP Client** checkbox and click the **OK** button to install it. Most

Linux distributions have a TFTP client available for installation through the distribution's package manager, and macOS has a TFTP client installed by default.

This example uses Windows 10. Start by running the TFTP server by running the code in Listing 6-11 in a terminal:

```
Microsoft Windows [Version 10.0.18362.449]
(c) 2019 Microsoft Corporation. All rights reserved.

C:\Users\User\gnp\ch06\tftp\tftp>go run tftp.go
2006/01/02 15:04:05 Listening on 127.0.0.1:69 ...
```

The server should bind to UDP port 69 on 127.0.0.1 by default. Port 69 is a privileged port, and you may need root permissions on Linux. You may need to first build the binary by using go build tftp.go and then run the resulting binary by using the sudo command to bind to port 69: sudo ./tftp. The TFTP server should log a message to standard output that indicates it's listening.

From a separate terminal, execute the TFTP client, making sure to pass the -i argument to tell the server you wish to initiate a binary (octet) transfer. Remember, your TFTP server doesn't care what the source filename is because it returns the same payload regardless of the requested filename. You'll use *test.svg* in this example:

```
Microsoft Windows [Version 10.0.18362.449]
(c) 2019 Microsoft Corporation. All rights reserved.

C:\Users\User>tftp -i 127.0.0.1 GET test.svg
Transfer successful: 75352 bytes in 1 second(s), 75352 bytes/s
```

Almost immediately upon pressing ENTER, the client should report the transfer was successful. The TFTP server's terminal should show its progress as well:

```
Microsoft Windows [Version 10.0.18362.449]
(c) 2019 Microsoft Corporation. All rights reserved.

C:\Users\User\gnp\ch06\tftp\tftp>go run tftp.go
2006/01/02 15:04:05 Listening on 127.0.0.1:69 ...
2006/01/02 15:04:05 [127.0.0.1:57944] requested file: test.svg
2006/01/02 15:04:05 [127.0.0.1:57944] sent 148 blocks
```

You can confirm that the downloaded file is the same as the payload provided to the TFTP server by comparing *test.svg*'s checksum with the checksum of the server's *payload.svg*. A *checksum* is a calculated value used to verify the integrity of a file. If two files are identical, they will have equivalent checksums. Linux and macOS both have various command line utilities for generating checksums, but you'll use a pure Go implementation, as shown in Listing 6-12.

```
package main

import (
    "crypto/sha512"
    "flag"
    "fmt"
    "io/ioutil"
    "os"
)

func init() {
    flag.Usage = func() {
        fmt.Printf("Usage: %s file...\n", os.Args[0])
        flag.PrintDefaults()
    }
}

func main() {
    flag.Parse()
    for _, file := range ❶flag.Args() {
        fmt.Printf("%s  %s\n", checksum(file), file)
    }
}

func checksum(file string) string {
    b, err := ❷ioutil.ReadFile(file)
    if err != nil {
        return err.Error()
    }

    return fmt.Sprintf("%x", ❸sha512.Sum512_256(b))
}
```

*Listing 6-12: Generating SHA512/256 checksums for given command line arguments (sha512-256sum.go)*

This bit of code will accept one or more file paths as command line arguments ❶ and generate SHA512/256 checksums ❸ from their contents ❷.

A SHA512/256 checksum is a SHA512 checksum truncated to 256 bits. Calculating SHA512 on a 64-bit machine is faster than calculating a SHA256 checksum, because the SHA512 computation uses 64-bit words, whereas SHA256 uses 32-bit words. By truncating SHA512 to 256 bits, you eliminate a length extension hashing attack that SHA512 is vulnerable to by itself. SHA512/256 isn't necessary here since you're not using the checksum beyond verifying the integrity of a file, but you should be familiar with it, and it should be on your short list of hashing algorithms.

You can use the code from Listing 6-12 in Listing 6-13 to verify that the file you downloaded (*test.svg*) is identical to the file the server sent (*payload.svg*).

You'll continue to use Windows as your target platform, but the code will work on Linux and macOS without changes:

```
Microsoft Windows [Version 10.0.18362.449]
(c) 2019 Microsoft Corporation. All rights reserved.

C:\Users\User\dev\gnp\ch06>go build sha512-256sum\sha512-256sum.go

C:\Users\User\dev\gnp\ch06>sha512-256sum \Users\User\test.svg

\Users\User\test.svg =>
❶ 3f5794c522e83b827054183658ce63cb701dc49f4e59335f08b5c79c56873969

C:\Users\User\dev\gnp\ch06>sha512-256sum tftp\tftp\payload.svg

tftp\tftp\payload.svg =>
❷ 3f5794c522e83b827054183658ce63cb701dc49f4e59335f08b5c79c56873969
```

*Listing 6-13: Generating SHA512/256 checksums for test.svg and payload.svg*

As you can see, the *test.svg* checksum ❶ is equal to the *payload.svg* checksum ❷.

In this case, the *test.svg* file is an image of a gopher from Egon Elbre's excellent *gophers* repository on GitHub (*https://github.com/egonelbre/gophers/*). If you opened the file in a web browser, you'd see the image in Figure 6-6.

Although you transferred the payload over localhost and don't expect data loss or corruption, the client and server still acknowledged every data packet, ensuring the proper delivery of the payload.

*Figure 6-6: Downloaded payload from the TFTP server*

# What You've Learned

UDP can be made reliable at the application level, as evident by the Trivial File Transfer Protocol. TFTP uses a combination of data packet sequence numbers and acknowledgments to ensure that the client and server agree on all transferred data, redelivering packets as necessary.

Liberal use of Go's binary marshaling and unmarshaling interfaces allow you to implement types that make communication using TFTP straightforward. Each TFTP type meant for delivery over UDP implements the encoding .BinaryMarshaler interface to marshal its data into a format suitable for writing to a network connection. Likewise, each type you expect to read from a network connection should implement the encoding.BinaryUnmarshaler interface. Successfully unmarshaling binary data to your custom type allows you to determine what binary data was received and that it is correct.

# 7

## UNIX DOMAIN SOCKETS

So far in this book, we've discussed communications between nodes on a network. But not all network programming occurs exclusively between separate nodes. Your applications may sometimes need to communicate with services, such as a database, hosted on the same node.

One way to connect your application to a database running on the same system would be to send data to the node's IP address or localhost address—commonly 127.0.0.1—and the database's port number. However, there's another way: using Unix domain sockets. The *Unix domain socket* is a communication method that uses the filesystem to determine a packet's destination address, allowing services running on the same node to exchange data with one another, a process known as *inter-process communication (IPC)*.

This chapter first defines exactly what Unix domain sockets are and how you can control read and write access to them. Next, you'll explore the three types of Unix domain sockets available through Go's net package and write a simple echo server in each of them. Finally, you'll write a service that uses Unix domain sockets to authenticate clients based on their user and group ID information.

**NOTE**  *Not all operating systems support the three types of Unix domain sockets. This chapter uses build constraints and special filename suffixes to identify the target platforms for each code listing.*

## What Are Unix Domain Sockets?

In Chapter 2, I defined a network socket as an IP address and port number. Socket addressing allows individual services on the same node, at the same IP address, to listen for incoming traffic. To illustrate the importance of socket addressing, just imagine how inefficient having a single phone line at a large corporation would be. If you wanted to speak to someone, you'd best hope the phone wasn't already in use. That's why, to alleviate the congestion, most corporations assign an extension number to each employee. This allows you to contact the person you want to speak to by dialing the company's phone number (which is like the node's IP address) followed by the employee's extension (which is like the port number). Just as phone numbers and extensions allow you to individually call every single person at a corporation, the IP address and port number of a socket address allow you to communicate with every single service listening to each socket address on a node.

Unix domain sockets apply the socket-addressing principle to the filesystem: each Unix domain socket has an associated file on the filesystem, which corresponds to a network socket's IP address and port number. You can communicate with a service listening to the socket by reading from and writing to this file. Likewise, you can leverage the filesystem's ownership and permissions to control read and write access to the socket. Unix domain sockets increase efficiency by bypassing the operating system's network stack, eliminating the overhead of traffic routing. For the same reasons, you won't need to worry about fragmentation or packet ordering when using Unix domain sockets. If you choose to forgo Unix domain sockets and exclusively use network sockets when communicating with local services (for example, to connect your application to a local database, a memory cache, and so on), you ignore significant security advantages and performance gains.

Though this system brings distinct advantages, it comes with a caveat: Unix domain sockets are local to the node using them, so you cannot use them to communicate with other nodes, as you can with network sockets. Therefore, Unix domain sockets may not be a good fit if you anticipate moving a service to another node or require maximum portability for your application. To maintain communication, you'd have to first migrate to a network socket.

# Binding to Unix Domain Socket Files

A Unix domain socket file is created when your code attempts to bind to an unused Unix domain socket address by using the net.Listen, net.ListenUnix, or net.ListenPacket functions. If the socket file for that address already exists, the operating system will return an error indicating that the address is in use. In most cases, simply removing the existing Unix domain socket file is enough to clear up the error. However, you should first make sure that the socket file exists not because a process is currently using that address but because you didn't properly clean up the file from a defunct process.

If you wish to reuse a socket file, use the net package's FileListener function to bind to an existing socket file. This function is beyond the scope of this book, but I encourage you to read its documentation.

## Changing a Socket File's Ownership and Permissions

Once a service binds to the socket file, you can use Go's os package to modify the file's ownership and read/write permissions. Specifically, the os.Chown function allows you to modify the user and group that owns the file. Windows does not support this function, though this function is supported on Windows Subsystem for Linux (WSL), Linux, and macOS, among others outside the scope of this book. We'll look at the lines of code that change file ownership and permissions now but cover them in context later in this chapter.

The following line instructs the operating system to update the user and group ownership of the given file:

```
err := os.Chown("/path/to/socket/file", ❶-1, ❷100)
```

The os.Chown function accepts three arguments: the path to a file, the user ID of the owner ❶, and the group ID of the owner ❷. A user or group ID of -1 tells Go you want to maintain the current user or group ID. In this example, you want to maintain the socket file's current user ID but set its group ID to 100, which here is assumed to be a valid group ID in the */etc/group* file.

Go's os/user package includes functions to help you translate between user and group names and IDs. For example, this line of code uses the LookupGroup function to find the group ID for the *users* group:

```
grp, err := user.LookupGroup("users")
```

Provided user.LookupGroup did not return an error, the grp variable's Gid field contains the group ID for the *users* group.

The os.Chmod function changes the file's mode and the numeric notation of Unix-compatible permission bits. These bits inform the operating system of the file's mode, the file's user read/write/execute permissions, the file's group read/write/execute permissions, and the read/write/execute permissions for any user not in the file's group:

```
err := os.Chmod("/path/to/socket/file", os.ModeSocket|0660)
```

The os.Chmod function accepts a file path and an os.FileMode, which represents the file mode, the user permissions, the group permissions, and non-group user permissions. Since you're dealing with a socket file, you should always set the os.ModeSocket mode on the file. You do that using a bitwise OR between the os.ModeSocket and the numeric file permission notation. Here, you're passing the octal 0660, which gives the user and group read and write access but prevents anyone outside the group from reading or writing to the socket. You can read more about os.FileMode in Go's documentation at *https://golang.org/pkg/os/#FileMode* and familiarize yourself with filesystem permissions numeric notation at *https://en.wikipedia.org/wiki/File_system_permissions#Numeric_notation*.

## Understanding Unix Domain Socket Types

There are three types of Unix domain sockets: *streaming sockets*, which operate like TCP; *datagram sockets*, which operate like UDP; and *sequence packet sockets*, which combine elements of both. Go designates these types as unix, unixgram, and unixpacket, respectively. In this section, we'll write echo servers that work with each of these types.

The net.Conn interface allows you to write code once and use it across multiple network types. It abstracts many of the differences between the network sockets used by TCP and UDP and Unix domain sockets, which means that you can take code written for communication over TCP, for example, and use it over a Unix domain socket by simply changing the address and network type.

### The unix Streaming Socket

The streaming Unix domain socket works like TCP without the overhead associated with TCP's acknowledgments, checksums, flow control, and so on. The operating system is responsible for implementing the streaming inter-process communication over Unix domain sockets in lieu of TCP.

To illustrate this type of Unix domain socket, let's write a function that creates a generic stream-based echo server (Listing 7-1). You'll be able to use this function with any streaming network type. That means you can use it to create a TCP connection to a different node, but you'll also be able to use it with the unix type to communicate with a Unix socket address.

**NOTE**    *Linux, macOS, and Windows all support the unix network type.*

---

```
package echo

import (
    "context"
    "net"
)

func ❶streamingEchoServer(ctx context.Context, network string,
```

```
    addr string) (net.Addr, error) {
    s, err := ❷net.Listen(network, addr)
    if err != nil {
        return nil, err
    }
}
```

*Listing 7-1: Creating the streaming echo server function (echo.go)*

The streamingEchoServer function ❶ accepts a string representing a stream-based network and a string representing an address and returns an address object and an error interface. You should recognize these arguments and return types from earlier in the book.

Since you've made the echo server a bit more generic by accepting a context, a network string, and an address string, you can pass it any stream-based network type, such as tcp, unix, or unixpacket. The address would then need to correspond to the network type. The context is used for signaling the server to close. If the network type is tcp, the address string must be an IP address and port combination, such as 127.0.0.1:80. If the network type is unix or unixpacket, the address must be the path to a nonexistent file. The socket file will be created when the echo server binds to it ❷. Then the server will start listening for incoming connections.

Listing 7-2 completes the streaming echo server implementation.

```
--snip--

    go func() {
        go func() {
            ❶<-ctx.Done()
            _ = s.Close()
        }()

        for {
            conn, err := ❷s.Accept()
            if err != nil {
                return
            }

            go func() {
                defer func() { _ = conn.Close() }()

                for {
                    buf := make([]byte, 1024)
                    n, err := ❸conn.Read(buf)
                    if err != nil {
                        return
                    }

                    _, err = ❹conn.Write(buf[:n])
                    if err != nil {
                        return
                    }
                }
            }()
        }
    }()
```

```
        }
    }()

    return s.Addr(), nil
}
```

*Listing 7-2: A stream-based echo server (echo.go)*

A listener created with either net.Listen or net.ListenUnix will auto-matically remove the socket file when the listener exits. You can modify this behavior with net.UnixListener's SetUnlinkOnClose method, though the default is ideal for most use cases. Unix domain socket files created with net.ListenPacket won't be automatically removed when the listener exits, as you'll see a little later in this chapter.

As before, you spin off the echo server in its own goroutine so it can asyn-chronously accept connections. Once the server accepts a connection ❷, you start a goroutine to echo incoming messages. Since you're using the net.Conn interface, you can use its Read ❸ and Write ❹ methods to communicate with the client no matter whether the server is communicating over a network socket or a Unix domain socket. Once the caller cancels the context ❶, the server closes.

Listing 7-3 tests the streaming echo server over a Unix domain socket using the unix network type.

```
package echo

import (
    "bytes"
    "context"
    "fmt"
    "io/ioutil"
    "net"
    "os"
    "path/filepath"
    "testing"
)

func TestEchoServerUnix(t *testing.T) {
    dir, err := ❶ioutil.TempDir("", "echo_unix")
    if err != nil {
        t.Fatal(err)
    }
    defer func() {
        if rErr := ❷os.RemoveAll(dir); rErr != nil {
            t.Error(rErr)
        }
    }()

    ctx, cancel := context.WithCancel(context.Background())
❸   socket := filepath.Join(dir, fmt.Sprintf("%d.sock", os.Getpid()))
    rAddr, err := streamingEchoServer(ctx, "unix", socket)
    if err != nil {
```

```
        t.Fatal(err)
    }

    err = ❹os.Chmod(socket, os.ModeSocket|0666)
    if err != nil {
        t.Fatal(err)
    }
```

*Listing 7-3: Setting up an echo server test over a unix domain socket (echo_test.go)*

You create a subdirectory in your operating system's temporary directory named *echo_unix* ❶ that will contain the echo server's socket file. The
deferred call to os.RemoveAll cleans up after the server ❷ by removing your
temporary subdirectory when the test completes. You pass a socket file
named *#.sock* ❸, where *#* is the server's process ID, saved in the temporary
subdirectory (*/tmp/echo_unix/123.sock*) to the streamingEchoServer function.
Finally, you make sure everyone has read and write access to the socket ❹.

Listing 7-4 makes a connection to the streaming echo server and sends
a test.

```
--snip--

    conn, err := net.Dial("unix", ❶rAddr.String())
    if err != nil {
        t.Fatal(err)
    }
    defer func() { _ = conn.Close() }()

    msg := []byte("ping")
❷ for i := 0; i < 3; i++ { // write 3 "ping" messages
        _, err = conn.Write(msg)
        if err != nil {
            t.Fatal(err)
        }
    }

    buf := make([]byte, 1024)
    n, err := ❸conn.Read(buf) // read once from the server
    if err != nil {
        t.Fatal(err)
    }

    expected := ❹bytes.Repeat(msg, 3)
    if !bytes.Equal(expected, buf[:n]) {
        t.Fatalf("expected reply %q; actual reply %q", expected,
            buf[:n])
    }

    _ = closer.Close()
    <-done
}
```

*Listing 7-4: Streaming data over a Unix domain socket (echo_test.go)*

You dial the server by using the familiar net.Dial function. It accepts the unix network type and the server's address, which is the full path to the Unix domain socket file ❶.

You write three ping messages to the echo server before reading the first response ❷. The reasoning for sending three separate pings will be clear when you explore the unixpacket type later in this chapter. When you read the first response ❸ with a buffer large enough to store the three messages you just sent, you receive all three ping messages ❹ in a single read as the string pingpingping. Remember, a stream-based connection does not delineate messages. The onus is on you to determine where one message stops and another one starts when you read a series of bytes from the server.

### The unixgram Datagram Socket

Next let's create an echo server that will communicate using datagram-based network types, such as udp and unixgram. Whether you're communicating over UDP or a unixgram socket, the server you'll write looks essentially the same. The difference is, you will need to clean up the socket file with a unixgram listener, as you'll see in Listing 7-5.

NOTE    *Windows and Windows Subsystem for Linux do not support unixgram domain sockets.*

```
--snip--

func datagramEchoServer(ctx context.Context, network string,
    addr string) (net.Addr, error) {
    s, err := ❶net.ListenPacket(network, addr)
    if err != nil {
        return nil, err
    }

    go func() {
        go func() {
            <-ctx.Done()
            _ = s.Close()
            if network == "unixgram" {
                _ = ❷os.Remove(addr)
            }
        }()

        buf := make([]byte, 1024)
        for {
            n, clientAddr, err := s.ReadFrom(buf)
            if err != nil {
                return
            }

            _, err = s.WriteTo(buf[:n], clientAddr)
            if err != nil {
                return
```

```
            }
        }
    }()

    return s.LocalAddr(), nil
}
```

*Listing 7-5: A datagram-based echo server (echo.go)*

You call net.ListenPacket ❶, which returns a net.PacketConn. As mentioned earlier in this chapter, since you don't use net.Listen or net.ListenUnix to create the listener, Go won't clean up the socket file for you when your server is done with it. You must make sure you remove the socket file yourself, ❷ or subsequent attempts to bind to the existing socket file will fail.

Since the unixgram network type doesn't work on Windows, Listing 7-6 uses a build constraint to make sure this code does not run on Windows and then imports the necessary packages.

```
// +build darwin linux

package echo

import (
    "bytes"
    "context"
    "fmt"
    "io/ioutil"
    "net"
    "os"
    "path/filepath"
    "testing"
)
```

*Listing 7-6: Building constraints and imports for macOS and Linux (echo_posix_test.go)*

The build constraint tells Go to include this code only if it's running on a macOS or Linux operating system. Granted, Go supports other operating systems, many of which may offer unixgram support, that are outside the scope of this book. This build constraint does not take those other operating systems into account, and I encourage you to test this code on your target operating system.

With the build constraint in place, you can add the test in Listing 7-7.

```
--snip--

func TestEchoServerUnixDatagram(t *testing.T) {
    dir, err := ioutil.TempDir("", "echo_unixgram")
    if err != nil {
        t.Fatal(err)
    }
    defer func() {
        if rErr := os.RemoveAll(dir); rErr != nil {
            t.Error(rErr)
```

```
    }
}()

ctx, cancel := context.WithCancel(context.Background())
❶ sSocket := filepath.Join(dir, fmt.Sprintf("s%d.sock", os.Getpid()))
serverAddr, err := datagramEchoServer(ctx, "unixgram", sSocket)
if err != nil {
    t.Fatal(err)
}
defer cancel()

err = os.Chmod(sSocket, os.ModeSocket|0622)
if err != nil {
    t.Fatal(err)
}
```

*Listing 7-7: Instantiating the datagram-based echo server (echo_posix_test.go)*

Just as with UDP connections, both the server and the client must bind to an address so they can send and receive datagrams. The server has its own socket file ❶ that is separate from the client's socket file in Listing 7-8.

```
--snip--

❶ cSocket := filepath.Join(dir, fmt.Sprintf("c%d.sock", os.Getpid()))
client, err := net.ListenPacket("unixgram", cSocket)
if err != nil {
    t.Fatal(err)
}
❷ defer func() { _ = client.Close() }()

err = ❸os.Chmod(cSocket, os.ModeSocket|0622)
if err != nil {
    t.Fatal(err)
}
```

*Listing 7-8: Instantiating the datagram-based client (echo_posix_test.go)*

The call to os.Remove in Listing 7-5's datagramEchoServer function cleans up the socket file when the server closes. The client has some additional housecleaning, so you make the client clean up its own socket file ❶ when it's done listening to it. Thankfully, this is taken care of for you by the call to os.RemoveAll to remove your temporary subdirectory in Listing 7-7. Otherwise, you would need to add a call to os.Remove to remove the client's socket file in the defer ❷. Also, the server should be able to write to the client's socket file as well as its own socket file, or the server won't be able to reply to messages. In this example, you set very permissive permissions so all users can write to the socket ❸.

Now that the server and client are instantiated, Listing 7-9 tests the difference between a streaming echo server and a datagram echo server.

```
--snip--

    msg := []byte("ping")
    for i := 0; i < 3; i++ { // write 3 "ping" messages
        _, err = ❶client.WriteTo(msg, serverAddr)
        if err != nil {
            t.Fatal(err)
        }
    }

    buf := make([]byte, 1024)
    for i := 0; i < 3; i++ { // read 3 "ping" messages
        n, addr, err := ❷client.ReadFrom(buf)
        if err != nil {
            t.Fatal(err)
        }

        if addr.String() != serverAddr.String() {
            t.Fatalf("received reply from %q instead of %q",
                addr, serverAddr)
        }

        if !bytes.Equal(msg, buf[:n]) {
            t.Fatalf("expected reply %q; actual reply %q", msg,
                buf[:n])
        }
    }
}
```

*Listing 7-9: Using unixgram sockets to echo messages (echo_posix_test.go)*

You write three ping messages to the server ❶ before reading the first datagram. You then perform three reads ❷ with a buffer large enough to fit all three ping messages. As expected, unixgram sockets maintain the delineation between messages; you sent three messages and read three replies. Compare this to the unix socket type in Listings 7-3 and 7-4, where you sent three messages and received all three replies with a single read from the connection.

### The unixpacket Sequence Packet Socket

The *sequence packet socket* type is a hybrid that combines the session-oriented connections and reliability of TCP with the clearly delineated datagrams of UDP. However, sequence packet sockets discard unrequested data in each datagram. If you read 32 bytes of a 50-byte datagram, for example, the operating system discards the 18 unrequested bytes.

Of the three Unix domain socket types, unixpacket enjoys the least cross-platform support. Coupled with unixpacket's hybrid behavior and discarding of unrequested data, unix or unixgram are better suited for most applications. You are unlikely to find sequence packet sockets in use over the internet. It was largely used in old X.25 telecommunication networks, some types of financial transactions, and AX.25 used in amateur radio.

The test code in Listing 7-10 sets up a demonstration of unixpacket sockets.

NOTE *Windows, WSL, and macOS do not support unixpacket domain sockets.*

```
package echo

import (
    "bytes"
    "context"
    "fmt"
    "io/ioutil"
    "net"
    "os"
    "path/filepath"
    "testing"
)

func TestEchoServerUnixPacket(t *testing.T) {
    dir, err := ioutil.TempDir("", "echo_unixpacket")
    if err != nil {
        t.Fatal(err)
    }
    defer func() {
        if rErr := os.RemoveAll(dir); rErr != nil {
            t.Error(rErr)
        }
    }()

    ctx, cancel := context.WithCancel(context.Background())
    socket := filepath.Join(dir, fmt.Sprintf("%d.sock", os.Getpid()))
    rAddr, err := streamingEchoServer(ctx, "unixpacket", socket)
    if err != nil {
        t.Fatal(err)
    }
    defer cancel()

    err = os.Chmod(socket, os.ModeSocket|0666)
    if err != nil {
        t.Fatal(err)
    }
```

*Listing 7-10: Instantiating a packet-based streaming echo server (echo_linux_test.go)*

Notice first that you save this code in a file called *echo_linux_test.go*. The *_linux_test.go* suffix is a build constraint informing Go that it should include this file only when tests are invoked on Linux.

Listing 7-11 dials the echo server and sends a series of ping messages.

```
--snip--

    conn, err := ❶ net.Dial("unixpacket", rAddr.String())
    if err != nil {
```

```
        t.Fatal(err)
    }
    defer func() { _ = conn.Close() }()

    msg := []byte("ping")
❷ for i := 0; i < 3; i++ { // write 3 "ping" messages
        _, err = conn.Write(msg)
        if err != nil {
            t.Fatal(err)
        }
    }

    buf := make([]byte, 1024)
❸ for i := 0; i < 3; i++ { // read 3 times from the server
        n, err := conn.Read(buf)
        if err != nil {
            t.Fatal(err)
        }

        if !bytes.Equal(msg, buf[:n]) {
            t.Errorf("expected reply %q; actual reply %q", msg, buf[:n])
        }
    }
}
```

*Listing 7-11: Using a unixpacket socket to echo messages (echo_linux_test.go)*

Since unixpacket is session oriented, you use net.Dial ❶ to initiate a connection with the server. You do not simply write to the server's address, as you would if the network type were datagram based.

You can see the distinction between the unix and unixpacket socket types by writing three ping messages to the server ❷ before reading the first reply. Whereas a unix socket type would return all three ping messages with a single read, unixpacket acts just like other datagram-based network types and returns one message for each read operation ❸.

Listing 7-12 illustrates how unixpacket discards unrequested data in each datagram.

```
--snip--

    for i := 0; i < 3; i++ { // write 3 more "ping" messages
        _, err = conn.Write(msg)
        if err != nil {
            t.Fatal(err)
        }
    }

❶ buf = make([]byte, 2)    // only read the first 2 bytes of each reply
    for i := 0; i < 3; i++ { // read 3 times from the server
        n, err := conn.Read(buf)
        if err != nil {
            t.Fatal(err)
        }
    }

    if !bytes.Equal(❷msg[:2], buf[:n]) {
```

```
                                t.Errorf("expected reply %q; actual reply %q", msg[:2],
                                    buf[:n])
                        }
                }
        }
```

*Listing 7-12: Discarding unread bytes (echo_linux_test.go)*

This time around, you reduce your buffer size to 2 bytes ❶ and read the first 2 bytes of each datagram. If you were using a streaming network type like tcp or unix, you would expect to read pi for the first read and ng for the second read. But unixpacket discards the ng portion of the ping message because you requested only the first 2 bytes—pi. Therefore, you make sure you're receiving only the first 2 bytes of the datagram with each read ❷.

# Writing a Service That Authenticates Clients

On Linux systems, Unix domain sockets allow you to glean details about the process on the other end of a socket—your peer—by receiving the credentials from your peer's operating system. You can use this information to authenticate your peer on the other side of the Unix domain socket and deny access if the peer's credentials don't meet your criteria. For instance, if the user *davefromaccounting* connects to your administrative service through a Unix domain socket, the peer credentials might indicate that you should deny access; Dave should be crunching numbers, not sending bits to your administrative service.

You can create a service that allows connections only from specific users or any user in a specific group found in the */etc/groups* file. Each named group in the */etc/groups* file has a corresponding group ID number. When a client connects to your Unix domain socket, you can request the peer credentials and compare the client's group ID in the peer credentials to the group ID of any allowed groups. If the client's group ID matches one of the allowed group IDs, you can consider the client authenticated. Go's standard library has useful support for working with Linux groups, which you'll use in "Writing the Service" on page 156.

## Requesting Peer Credentials

The process of requesting peer credentials isn't exactly straightforward. You cannot simply request the peer credentials from the connection object itself. Rather, you need to use the golang.org/x/sys/unix package to request peer credentials from the operating system, which you can retrieve using the following command:

```
go get -u golang.org/x/sys/unix
```

Listing 7-13 shows a function that accepts a Unix domain socket connection and denies access if the peer isn't a member of specific groups.

*The code in Listings 7-13 through 7-16 works on Linux systems only.*

```go
package auth

import (
    "log"
    "net"
    "golang.org/x/sys/unix"
)

func Allowed(conn *net.UnixConn, groups map[string]struct{}) bool {
    if conn == nil || groups == nil || len(groups) == 0 {
        return false
    }

    file, _ := ❶conn.File()
    defer func(){ _ = file.Close() }()

    var (
        err    error
        ucred *unix.Ucred
    )

    for {
        ucred, err = ❷unix.GetsockoptUcred(int(❸file.Fd()), unix.SOL_SOCKET,
            unix.SO_PEERCRED)
        if err == unix.EINTR {
            continue // syscall interrupted, try again
        }
        if err != nil {
            log.Println(err)
            return false
        }

        break
    }

    u, err := ❹user.LookupId(string(ucred.Uid))
    if err != nil {
        log.Println(err)
        return false
    }

    gids, err := ❺u.GroupIds()
    if err != nil {
        log.Println(err)
        return false
    }

    for _, gid := range gids {
        if _, ok := ❻groups[gid]; ok {
```

```
                return true
        }
    }

    return false
}
```

*Listing 7-13: Retrieving the peer credentials for a socket connection (creds/auth/allowed_ linux.go)*

To retrieve the peer's Unix credentials, you first grab the underlying file object from net.UnixConn ❶, the object that represents your side of the Unix domain socket connection. It's analogous to net.TCPConn of a TCP connection in Go. Since you need to extract the file descriptor details from the connection, you cannot simply rely on the net.Conn interface that you receive from the listener's Accept method. Instead, your Allowed function requires the caller to pass in a pointer to the underlying net.UnixConn object, typically returned from the listener's AcceptUnix method. You'll see this method in action in the next section.

You can then pass the file object's descriptor ❸, the protocol-level unix .SOL_SOCKET, and the option name unix.SO_PEERCRED to the unix.GetsockoptUcred function ❷. Retrieving socket options from the Linux kernel requires that you specify both the option you want and the level at which the option resides. The unix.SOL_SOCKET tells the Linux kernel you want a socket-level option, as opposed to, for example, unix.SOL_TCP, which indicates TCP-level options. The unix.SO_PEERCRED constant tells the Linux kernel that you want the peer credentials option. If the Linux kernel finds the peer credentials option at the Unix domain socket level, unix.GetsockoptUcred returns a pointer to a valid unix.Ucred object.

The unix.Ucred object contains the peer's process, user, and group IDs. You pass the peer's user ID to the user.LookupId function ❹. If successful, you then retrieve a list of group IDs from the user object ❺. The user can belong to more than one group, and you want to consider each one for access. Finally, you check each group ID against a map of allowed groups ❻. If any one of the peer's group IDs is in your map, you return true, allowing the peer to connect.

This example is largely didactic. You can achieve similar results by assigning group ownership to the socket file, as we discussed in "Changing a Socket File's Ownership and Permissions" on page 143. However, knowledge of group membership could be used for access control and other security decisions within your application.

## Writing the Service

Let's now use this function in a service that you can run from the command line. This service will accept one or more group names found in the Linux operating system's */etc/group* file as arguments on the command line and begin listening to a Unix domain socket file. The service will allow clients to connect only if they are a member of one of the groups specified on the command line. Clients can then make a Unix domain socket connection to the service. The service will retrieve the peer credentials of the client and either allow the client to remain connected, if the client is a member of one of the allowed groups, or immediately disconnect the unauthorized client. The service doesn't do anything beyond authenticating the client's group ID.

In Listing 7-14, you specify the imports you'll need and create a meaningful usage message for the service.

```
package main

import (
    "flag"
    "fmt"
    "log"
    "net"
    "os"
    "os/signal"
    "os/user"
    "path/filepath"

    "github.com/awoodbeck/gnp/ch07/creds/auth"
)

func init() {
    flag.Usage = func() {
        _, _ = fmt.Fprintf(flag.CommandLine.Output(),
            "Usage:\n\t%s ❶<group names>\n", filepath.Base(os.Args[0]))
        flag.PrintDefaults()
    }
}
```

Listing 7-14: Expecting group names on the command line (creds/creds.go)

Our application expects a series of group names as arguments ❶. You'll add the group ID for each group name to the map of allowed groups. The code in Listing 7-15 parses these group names.

```
--snip--

func parseGroupNames(args []string) map[string]struct{} {
    groups := make(map[string]struct{})

    for _, arg := range args {
        grp, err := ❶user.LookupGroup(arg)
        if err != nil {
            log.Println(err)
            continue
        }

        groups[❷grp.Gid] = struct{}{}
    }

    return groups
}
```

Listing 7-15: Parsing group names into group IDs (creds/creds.go)

The `parseGroupNames` function accepts a string slice of group names, retrieves the group information for each group name ❶, and inserts each group ID into the groups map ❷.

Listing 7-16 ties the last few listings together into a service that you can connect to from the command line.

```
--snip--

func main() {
    flag.Parse()

    groups := parseGroupNames(flag.Args())
    socket := filepath.Join(os.TempDir(), "creds.sock")
    addr, err := net.ResolveUnixAddr("unix", socket)
    if err != nil {
        log.Fatal(err)
    }

    s, err := net.ListenUnix("unix", addr)
    if err != nil {
        log.Fatal(err)
    }

    c := make(chan os.Signal, 1)
    signal.Notify(c, ❶os.Interrupt)
  ❷ go func() {
        <-c
        _ = s.Close()
    }()

    fmt.Printf("Listening on %s ...\n", socket)

    for {
        conn, err := ❸s.AcceptUnix()
        if err != nil {
            break
        }
        if ❹auth.Allowed(conn, groups) {
            _, err = conn.Write([]byte("Welcome\n"))
            if err == nil {
                // handle the connection in a goroutine here
                continue
            }
        } else {
            _, err = conn.Write([]byte("Access denied\n"))
        }
        if err != nil {
            log.Println(err)
        }
        _ = conn.Close()
    }
}
```

*Listing 7-16: Authorizing peers based on their credentials (creds/creds.go continued)*

You start by parsing the command line arguments to create the map of allowed group IDs. You then create a listener on the */tmp/creds.sock* socket. The listener accepts connections by using `AcceptUnix` ❸ so a `*net.UnixConn` is returned instead of the usual `net.Conn`, since your `auth.Allowed` function requires a `*net.UnixConn` type as its first argument. You then determine whether the peer's credentials are allowed ❹. Allowed peers stay connected. Disallowed peers are immediately disconnected.

Since you'll execute this service on the command line, you'll stop the service by sending an interrupt signal, usually with the CTRL-C key combination. However, this signal abruptly terminates the service before Go has a chance to clean up the socket file, despite your diligent use of `net.ListenUnix`. Therefore, you need to listen for this signal ❶ and spin off a goroutine in which you gracefully close the listener after receiving the signal ❷. This will make sure Go properly cleans up the socket file.

## Testing the Service with Netcat

Netcat is a popular command line utility that allows you to make TCP, UDP, and Unix domain socket connections. You'll use it to test the service from the command line. You can likely find Netcat in your Linux distribution's package manager. For example, to install the OpenBSD rewrite of Netcat on Debian 10, run the following command:

```
$ sudo apt install netcat-openbsd
```

The command uses the `sudo` command line utility to run `apt install netcat-openbsd` masquerading as the root user. CentOS 8.1 offers Nmap's Netcat replacement. Run this command to install it:

```
$ sudo dnf install nmap-ncat
```

Once it's installed, you should find the *nc* binary in your PATH environment variable.

Before you can connect to your credential-checking service, you need to run the service so that it binds to a socket file:

```
$ cd $GOPATH/src/github.com/awoodbeck/gnp/ch07/creds
$ go run . -- users staff
Listening on /tmp/creds.sock …
```

In this example, you allow connections from any peer in the users or staff groups. The service will deny access to any peers who are not in at least one of these groups. If these groups do not exist in your Linux distribution, choose any group in the */etc/groups* file. The service is listening to the */tmp/creds.sock* socket file, which is the address you give to Netcat.

Next, you need a way of changing your group ID so that you can test whether the service denies access to clients you haven't allowed. Currently, the service is running with your user and group IDs, since you started the service. Therefore, it will accept all your connections, since the service allows its own group (which is our group) to authenticate, per the groups map in Listing 7-15. To change your group when initiating the socket connection with your service, you can use the sudo command line utility.

Since using sudo requires escalated privileges, you are usually prompted for your password when you attempt to do so. I've omitted password prompts from the following examples, but expect to be prompted for your password on sudo's first invocation:

```
$ sudo -g staff -- nc -U /tmp/creds.sock
Welcome
^C
$
```

Using sudo, you modify your group by passing the group name to the -g flag. In this case, you set your group to staff. Then you execute the nc command. The -U flag tells Netcat to make a Unix domain socket connection to the /tmp/creds.sock file.

Since the staff group is one of the allowed groups, you receive the Welcome message upon connecting. You terminate your side of the connection by pressing CTRL-C.

If you repeat the test with a disallowed group, you should receive the opposite result:

```
$ sudo -g nogroup -- nc -U /tmp/creds.sock
Access denied
$
```

This time, you use the group nogroup, which the service doesn't allow. As expected, you immediately receive the Access denied message, and the server side of the socket terminates your connection.

## What You've Learned

You started this chapter with a look at Unix domain sockets. A Unix domain socket is a file-based communication method for processes running on the same node. Two or more processes, such as a local database server and client, can send and receive data through a Unix domain socket. Since Unix domain sockets rely on the filesystem for addressing, you can leverage filesystem ownership and permissions to control access to processes communicating over Unix domain sockets.

You then learned about the types of Unix domain sockets that Go supports: unix, unixgram, and unixpacket. Go makes communication over Unix domain sockets relatively painless and handles many of the details for you, particularly if you stick to the net package's interfaces. For example, code written for use over a stream-based TCP network will also work with little modification over the stream-based unix domain socket, albeit only for local process communication. Likewise, code written for use over a UDP network can be leveraged by the unixgram domain socket. You also touched on the hybrid Unix domain socket type, unixpacket, and learned that its drawbacks don't outweigh its benefits for most applications, particularly with respect to cross-platform support. The other two Unix domain socket types are better options for most use cases.

This chapter introduced peer credentials and showed how you could use them to authenticate client connections. You can go beyond file-based access restrictions to a Unix domain socket and request details about the client on the other side of the Unix domain socket.

You should now be equipped to determine where Unix domain sockets best fit into your network stack.

# PART III

## APPLICATION-LEVEL
## PROGRAMMING

# 8

## WRITING HTTP CLIENTS

The *HyperText Transfer Protocol (HTTP)* is an application layer protocol used by the World Wide Web. In an HTTP communication, a web client sends a *uniform resource locator (URL)* to a web server, and the web server responds with the corresponding media resources. In this context, a *resource* could be an image, a style sheet, an HTML document, a JavaScript file, and so on. For example, if your web browser sent the URL *www.google.com* to Google's web servers, the servers would return Google's main page. Most of us make such web transactions daily, whether they originate from our phones, computers, or Internet of Things (IoT) devices, such as doorbells, thermostats, or toasters (yes, really).

This chapter will introduce you to Go's HTTP client. First, you'll learn the basics of HTTP, including request methods and response codes. Next, you'll explore Go's HTTP client to request resources from web servers, paying attention to potential pitfalls along the way. Then, you'll move into the standard library code and learn the implementations that facilitate the request-response communication between an HTTP client and server. Finally, you'll see common pitfalls to look for when interacting with web servers using Go's HTTP client.

This chapter will give you the basics for interacting with services over HTTP. You'll need this foundation to understand how to handle requests from the server's point of view in the next chapter.

## Understanding the Basics of HTTP

HTTP is a sessionless client-server protocol in which the client initiates a request to the server and the server responds to the client. HTTP is an application layer protocol and serves as the foundation for communication over the web. It uses TCP as its underlying transport layer protocol.

This chapter assumes that you're using HTTP version 1.1 (HTTP/1.1). We'll also cover functionality introduced in HTTP version 2.0 (HTTP/2). Thankfully, Go abstracts many of the differences between these protocols, so we can easily use either protocol with the same bit of code.

### Uniform Resource Locators

A *URL* is an address of sorts used by the client to locate a web server and identify the requested resource. It's composed of five parts: a required *scheme* indicating the protocol to use for the connection, an optional *authority* for the resource, the *path* to the resource, an optional *query*, and an optional *fragment*. A colon (:) followed by two forward slashes (//) separates the scheme from the authority. The authority includes an optional colon-delimited username and password suffixed with an at symbol (@), a hostname, and an optional port number preceded by a colon. The path is a series of segments preceded by a forward slash. A question mark (?) indicates the start of the query, which is conventionally composed of key-value pairs separated by an ampersand (&). A hash mark (#) precedes the fragment, which is an identifier to a subsection of the resource. Taken together, a URL follows this pattern:

```
scheme://user:password@host:port/path?key1=value1&key2=value2#table_of_contents
```

The typical URL you use over the internet includes a scheme and a hostname at minimum. For example, if you felt compelled to look up images of gophers, you could visit Google's image search by entering the following URL in your web browser's address bar, then searching for *gophers* in the image search tab:

```
❶ https://❷ images.google.com❸/
```

The scheme ❶ informs your browser that you want to use HTTPS to connect to the address *images.google.com* ❷ and that you want the default resource ❸. If you specify the web server address without any specific resource, the web server will respond with a default resource. Just as it's helpful for large corporations to send your call to a receptionist when you omit an extension number, it's helpful for web servers to serve up a default resource if you don't specify the resource you want. Google receives your request and responds with the image search page. When you type *gophers* in the search box and submit the form, your browser sends a request using a URL like this, truncated for brevity:

```
https://www.google.com/❶search❷?❸q=gophers&tbm=isch . . .
```

This URL asks Google for a resource named *search* ❶ and includes a *query string*. The query string, indicated by the question mark ❷, contains ampersand-separated parameters defined by, and meaningful to, the web server. In this example, the value of the q parameter ❸ is your search query, gophers. The tbm parameter's value of isch tells Google you're performing an image search. Google defines the parameters and their values. You pass them along to Google's web servers as part of the request. The actual URL in your browser's address bar is quite a bit longer and includes other details Google needs in order to satisfy your request.

If my wife were to send me shopping using HTTP, the URL she would give me might look like this:

```
automobile://the.grocery.store/purchase?butter=irish&eggs=12&coffee=dark_roast
```

This tells me I'm to drive my car to the grocery store and pick up Irish butter, a dozen eggs, and dark roast coffee. It's important to mention that the scheme is relevant only to the context in which it's used. My web browser wouldn't know what to do with the *automobile* scheme, but for the sake of my marriage, I sure do.

## Client Resource Requests

An *HTTP request* is a message sent from a client to a web server that asks the server to respond with a specific resource. The request consists of a method, a target resource, headers, and a body. The *method* tells the server what you want it to do with the target resource. For example, the GET method followed by *robots.txt* tells the server you want it to send you the *robots.txt* file, whereas the DELETE method indicates to the server that you want it to delete that resource.

*Request headers* contain metadata about the content of the request you are sending. The Content-Length header, for example, specifies the size of the request body in bytes. The *request body* is the payload of the request. If you upload a new profile picture to a web server, the request body will contain the image encoded in a format suitable for transport over the network, and the Content-Length header's value will be set to the size in bytes of the image in the request body. Not all request methods require a request body.

Listing 8-1 details a simple GET request for Google's *robots.txt* file over Netcat to Google's web server. "Testing the Service with Netcat" on page 159 walks you through installing Netcat.

```
$ nc www.google.com 80
❶ GET /robots.txt HTTP/1.1

❷ HTTP/1.1 200 OK
❸ Accept-Ranges: none
  Vary: Accept-Encoding
  Content-Type: text/plain
  Date: Mon, 02 Jan 2006 15:04:05 MST
  Expires: Mon, 02 Jan 2006 15:04:05 MST
  Cache-Control: private, max-age=0
  Last-Modified: Mon, 02 Jan 2006 15:04:05 MST
  X-Content-Type-Options: nosniff
  Server: sffe
  X-XSS-Protection: 0
  Transfer-Encoding: chunked

❹ User-agent: *
  Disallow: /search
  Allow: /search/about
  Allow: /search/static
  Allow: /search/howsearchworks
  --snip--
```

*Listing 8-1: Sending a request for Google's* robots.txt *file and receiving a response with its contents*

The GET request ❶ tells Google's web server you want the */robots.txt* file using HTTP/1.1. Following the request, you press the ENTER key twice to send the request followed by an empty line. The web server promptly responds with a status line ❷, a series of headers ❸, an empty line delimiting the headers from the response body, and the contents of the *robots.txt* file in the response body ❹. You'll learn about server responses a bit later in this chapter.

Using Go's net/http package, you can create a request with nothing but an HTTP method and a URL. The net/http package includes constants for the most common RFC 7231 and RFC 5789 request methods. The RFCs contain quite a bit of jargon with respect to request methods. The following descriptions describe how to use these methods in practice:

GET   As in the earlier example, the GET method instructs the server to send you the target resource. The server will deliver the target resource in the response's body. It's important to note that the target resource does not need to be a file; the response could deliver you dynamically generated content, like the *gophers* image search result discussed earlier. The server should never change or remove the resource as the result of a GET request.

**HEAD**   The HEAD method is like GET except it tells the server to exclude the target resource in its response. The server will send only the response code and other various bits of metadata stored in the response headers. You can use this method to retrieve meaningful details about a resource, such as its size, to determine whether you want to retrieve the resource in the first place. (The resource may be larger than you expect.)

**POST**   A POST request is a way for you to upload data included in the request body to a web server. The POST method tells the server that you are sending data to associate with the target resource. For example, you may post a new comment to a news story, in which case the news story would be the target resource. In simple terms, think of the POST method as the method for creating new resources on the server.

**PUT**   Like POST, you can use a PUT request to upload data to a web server. In practice, the PUT method usually updates or completely replaces an existing resource. You could use PUT to edit the comment you POSTed to the news story.

**PATCH**   The PATCH method specifies partial changes to an existing resource, leaving the rest of the resource unmodified. In this way, it's like a *diff*. Let's assume you are buying a Gopher Plush for that someone special in your life, and you've proceeded past the shipping address step of the checkout process when you realize you made a typo in your street address. You jump back to the shipping address form and correct the typo. Now, you could POST the form again and send all its contents to the server. But a PATCH request would be more efficient since you made only a single correction. You'll likely encounter the PATCH method in APIs, rather than HTML forms.

**DELETE**   The DELETE method instructs the server to remove the target resource. Let's say your comment on the news story was too controversial, and now your neighbors avoid making eye contact with you. You can make a DELETE request to the server to remove your comment and restore your social status.

**OPTIONS**   You can ask the server what methods a target resource supports by using the OPTIONS method. For example, you could send an OPTIONS request with your news story comment as the target resource and learn that the DELETE method is not one of the methods the server will support for your comment, meaning your best option now is to find another place to live and meet new neighbors.

**CONNECT**   The client uses CONNECT to request that the web server perform *HTTP tunneling,* or establish a TCP session with a target destination and proxy data between the client and the destination.

**TRACE**   The TRACE method instructs the web server to echo the request back to you instead of processing it. This method allows you to see whether any intermediate nodes modify your request before it reaches the web server.

*Before adding server-side support for the TRACE method, I strongly recommend you read up on its role in cross-site tracing (XST) attacks, whereby an attacker uses a cross-site scripting (XSS) attack to steal authenticated user credentials. The risk of adding a potential attack vector to your web server likely does not outweigh the diagnostic benefits of TRACE support.*

It's important to mention that web servers are under no obligation to implement these request methods. In addition, you may find that some web servers don't correctly implement them. Trust, but verify.

## Server Responses

Whereas the client request always specifies a method and a target resource, the web server's response always includes a status code to inform the client of the status of its request. A successful request results in a response containing a 200-class status code.

If the client makes a request that requires further action on the client's part, the server will return a 300-class status code. For example, if the client requests a resource that has not changed since the client's last request for the resource, the server may return a 304 status code to inform the client that it should instead render the resource from its cache.

If an error occurs because of the client's request, the server will return a 400-class status code in its response. The most common example of this scenario occurs when a client requests a nonexistent target resource, in which case the server responds with a 404 status code to inform the client that it could not find the resource.

The 500-class status codes inform the client that an error has occurred on the server side that prevents the server from fulfilling the request. Let's assume that your request requires the web server to retrieve assets from an upstream server to satisfy your request, but that the upstream server fails to respond. The web server will respond to you with a 504 status code indicating that a time-out occurred during the communication with its upstream server.

A handful of 100-class status codes exist in HTTP/1.1 to give direction to the client. For example, the client can ask for guidance from the server while sending a POST request. To do so, the client would send the POST method, target resource, and request headers to the server, one of which tells the server that the client wants permission to proceed sending the request body. The server can respond with a 100 status code indicating that the client can continue the request and send the body.

The IANA maintains the official list of HTTP status codes, which you can find at *https://www.iana.org/assignments/http-status-codes/http-status-codes .xhtml*. If you encounter a relatively obscure status code, you can typically find a description of it in RFC 7231 at *https://tools.ietf.org/html/rfc7231#section-6*.

Go defines many of these status codes as constants in its net/http package, and I suggest you use the constants in your code. It's much easier to read http.StatusOK than it is to remember what 200 means. The most common HTTP status codes you'll encounter include the following:

**200 OK**  Indicates a successful request. If the request method was GET, the response body contains the target resource.

**201 Created**  Returned when the server has successfully processed a request and added a new resource, as may be the case with a POST request.

**202 Accepted**  Often returned if the request was successful but the server hasn't yet created a new resource. The creation of the resource may still fail despite the successful request.

**204 No Content**  Often returned if the request was successful but the response body is empty.

**304 Not Modified**  Returned when a client requests an unchanged resource. The client should instead use its cached copy of the resource. One method of caching is using an entity tag (ETag) header. When a client requests a resource from the server, the response may include an optional server-derived ETag header, which has meaning to the server. If the client requests the same resource in the future, the client can pass along the cached ETag header and value in its request. The server will check the ETag value in the client's request to determine whether the requested resource has changed. If it is unchanged, the server will likely respond with a 304 status code and an empty response body.

**400 Bad Request**  Returned if the server outright rejects the client's request for some reason. This may be due to a malformed request, like one that includes a request method but no target resource.

**403 Forbidden**  Often returned if the server accepts your request but determines you do not have permission to access the resource, or if the server itself does not have permission to access the requested resource.

**404 Not Found**  Returned if you request a nonexistent resource. You may also find this status code used as a *Glomar response* when a server does not want to confirm or deny your permission to access a resource. In other words, a web server may respond with a 404 status code for a resource you do not have permission to access instead of explicitly responding with a 403 status code confirming your lack of permissions to the resource. Attackers attempting to access sensitive resources on your web server would want to focus their efforts only on existing resources, even if they currently lack permissions to access those resources. Returning a 404 status code for both nonexistent and forbidden resources prevents attackers from differentiating between the two, providing a measure of security. The downside to this approach is you'll have a harder time debugging your permissions on your server, because you won't know whether the resource you're requesting exists or you simply lack permissions. I suggest you articulate the difference in your server logs.

**405 Method Not Allowed**   Returned if you specify a request method for a target resource that the server does not support. Remember the controversial comment you attempted to delete in our discussion of the OPTIONS request method? You would receive a 405 status code in response to that DELETE request.

**426 Upgrade Required**   Returned to instruct the client to first upgrade to TLS before requesting the target resource.

**500 Internal Server Error**   A catchall code of sorts returned when an error occurs on the server that prevents it from satisfying the client's request but that doesn't match the criteria of any other status code. Servers have returned many a 500 error because of some sort of configuration error or syntax error in server-side code. If your server returns this code, check your logs.

**502 Bad Gateway**   Returned when the server proxies data between the client and an upstream service, but the upstream service is unavailable and not accepting requests.

**503 Service Unavailable**   Returned if a web server is unavailable to accept a request. For example, a web server may return a 503 status code for all incoming connections when it's put into maintenance mode.

**504 Gateway Timeout**   Returned by a proxy web server to indicate that the upstream service accepted the request but did not provide a timely reply.

### From Request to Rendered Page

A web page is often composed of various resources, such as images, videos, layout instructions for your web browser, third-party ads, and so on. Accessing each resource requires a separate request to the server. In HTTP version 1.0 (HTTP/1.0), clients must initiate a separate TCP connection for each request. HTTP/1.1 eliminates this requirement, reducing the latency and request-connection overhead associated with multiple HTTP requests to the same web server. Instead, it allows multiple requests and responses over the same TCP connection. (All contemporary web server software and web browsers support HTTP/1.1 at a minimum, so you're unlikely to use HTTP/1.0 at all.)

Table 8-1 demonstrates the retrieval of an HTML document and the subsequent GET calls of all resources specified in that document.

**Table 8-1:** Retrieving Additional Resources After Requesting the Index HTML Document

| Status | Method | Domain | Resource | Type | Bytes transferred | Duration of transfer |
|--------|--------|--------------|--------------|------|-------------------|----------------------|
| 200 | GET | woodbeck.net | / | HTML | 1.83KB | 49 ms |
| 200 | GET | woodbeck.net | main.min.css | CSS | 1.30KB | 20 ms |
| 200 | GET | woodbeck.net | code.css | CSS | 0.99KB | 20 ms |
| 304 | GET | woodbeck.net | avatar.jpeg | JPEG | 0 bytes | 0 ms |
| 404 | GET | woodbeck.net | favicon.ico | IMG | 0 bytes | 0 ms |

The initial GET request for *https://woodbeck.net/* successfully retrieved the HTML document specified by the default resource. This HTML document included links to additional resources necessary to properly render the page, so the web browser requested those too. Since this transfer used HTTP/1.1, the web browser used the same TCP connection to retrieve the remaining resources. The web server instructed the web browser to use its cached copy of *avatar.jpeg*, since that resource hadn't changed since the last time the web browser received it. The web server was unable to find the *favicon.ico* file, so it returned a 404 status code to the web browser.

The latest version of HTTP, HTTP/2, aims to further reduce latency. In addition to reusing the same TCP connection for subsequent requests, the HTTP/2 server can proactively push resources to the client. If the conversation in Table 8-1 occurred over HTTP/2, it may have transpired like this. The client requested the default resource. The server responded with the default resource. But since the server knew that the default resource had dependent resources, it *pushed* those resources to the client without the client's needing to make separate requests for each resource.

The Go HTTP client and server transparently support HTTP/1.0, HTTP/1.1, and HTTP/2, meaning that you can write your code to retrieve and serve resources while letting code in Go's net/http package negotiate the optimal HTTP version. However, while the Go HTTP/2 server implementation can push resources to clients, the Go HTTP/2 client implementation cannot yet consume those server pushes.

## Retrieving Web Resources in Go

Just like your web browser, Go can communicate with web servers by using the net/http package's HTTP client. Unlike your web browser, Go won't directly render an HTML page to your screen. Instead, you could use Go to scrape data from websites (such as financial stock details), submit form data, or interact with APIs that use HTTP for their application protocol, to name a few examples.

Despite the simplicity of making HTTP requests in Go, you'll have to handle some client-side pitfalls. You'll learn about these pitfalls shortly. First, let's look at a simple example request.

### Using Go's Default HTTP Client

The net/http package includes a default client that allows you to make one-off HTTP requests. For example, you can use the http.Get function to send a GET request to a given URL.

Listing 8-2 demonstrates one way you can retrieve the current time from a trusted authority—*time.gov*'s web server—and compare it with the local time on your computer. This will give you a rough idea of how far ahead or behind the local time is on your computer. You certainly wouldn't want to rely on this method for any sort of forensics, but the example serves to demonstrate the Go HTTP client workflow by using a HEAD request and response.

```
package main

import (
    "net/http"
    "testing"
    "time"
)

func TestHeadTime(t *testing.T) {
    resp, err := ❶http.Head("https://www.time.gov/")
    if err != nil {
        t.Fatal(err)
    }
    _ = ❷resp.Body.Close() // Always close this without exception.

    now := time.Now().Round(time.Second)
    date := ❸resp.Header.Get("Date")
    if date == "" {
        t.Fatal("no Date header received from time.gov")
    }

    dt, err := time.Parse(time.RFC1123, date)
    if err != nil {
        t.Fatal(err)
    }

    t.Logf("time.gov: %s (skew %s)", dt, now.Sub(dt))
}
```

*Listing 8-2: Retrieving a timestamp from time.gov (time_test.go)*

The net/http package includes a few helper functions to make GET, HEAD, or POST requests. Here, we use the http.Get function ❶ to *https://www.time.gov/* to retrieve the default resource. Go's HTTP client automatically upgrades to HTTPS for you because that's the protocol indicated by the URL's scheme. Although you don't read the contents of the response body, you must close it ❷. The next section covers why you need to close the response body in every case.

Now that you have a response, you retrieve the Date header ❸, which indicates the time at which the server created the response. You can then use this value to calculate the clock skew of your computer. Granted, you lose accuracy because of latency between the server's generating the header and your code's processing it, as well as the lack of nanosecond resolution of the Date header itself.

## Closing the Response Body

As mentioned earlier, HTTP/1.1 allows the client to maintain a TCP connection with a server for multiple HTTP requests (we call this *keepalive support*). Even so, the client cannot reuse a TCP session when unread bytes from the previous response remain on the wire. Go's HTTP client automatically drains the response body when you close it. This allows your code to reuse the underlying TCP session if you are diligent about closing every response body.

Let's revisit the response from Listing 8-1 to see how Go parses the response (Listing 8-3).

```
❶ HTTP/1.1 200 OK
  Accept-Ranges: none
  Vary: Accept-Encoding
  Content-Type: text/plain
  Date: Mon, 02 Jan 2006 15:04:05 MST
  Expires: Mon, 02 Jan 2006 15:04:05 MST
  Cache-Control: private, max-age=0
  Last-Modified: Mon, 02 Jan 2006 15:04:05 MST
  X-Content-Type-Options: nosniff
  Server: sffe
  X-XSS-Protection: 0
  Transfer-Encoding: chunked

❷ User-agent: *
  Disallow: /search
  Allow: /search/about
  Allow: /search/static
  Allow: /search/howsearchworks
  --snip--
```

*Listing 8-3: Parsing the HTTP response*

Go's HTTP client reads the response status and headers ❶ from the network socket, and this data immediately becomes available to your code as part of the response object. The client doesn't automatically read the response body, however ❷. The body remains unconsumed until your code explicitly reads it or until you close it and Go implicitly drains any unread bytes.

The Go HTTP client's implicit draining of the response body on closing could potentially bite you. For example, let's assume you send a GET request for a file and receive a response from the server. You read the response's Content-Length header and realize the file is much larger than you anticipated. If you close the response body without reading any of its bytes, Go will download the entire file from the server as it drains the body regardless.

A better alternative would be to send a HEAD request to retrieve the Content-Length header. This way, no unread bytes exist in the response body, so closing the response body will not incur any additional overhead while draining it. You properly closed the response body in Listing 8-2, so the Go HTTP client could reuse the TCP session if you made additional calls in the future.

On the rare occasion that you make an HTTP request and want to explicitly drain the response body, the most efficient way is to use the io.Copy function:

```
_, _ = io.Copy(ioutil.Discard, response.Body)
_ = response.Close()
```

The io.Copy function drains the response.Body by reading all bytes from it and writing those bytes to ioutil.Discard. As its name indicates, ioutil.Discard is a special io.Writer that discards all bytes written to it.

You do not have to ignore the return values of io.Copy and response.Close, but doing so lets other developers know you intentionally ignored these values. Some developers may regard this as unnecessary verbosity, and it's true that io.Copy or response.Close will rarely return errors in this context, but it's still a good practice. I've encountered code that implicitly ignores errors, presumably out of habit, when the developer should have otherwise handled the errors.

The bottom line is that you must close the response body no matter whether you read it or not, to avoid resource leaks.

## Implementing Time-outs and Cancellations

Go's default HTTP client and the requests created with the http.Get, http.Head, and http.Post helper functions do not time out. The consequences of this may not be obvious until you get bit by the following fact (after which you'll never forget it): the lack of a time-out or deadline means that a misbehaving or malicious service could cause your code to block indefinitely without producing an error to indicate that anything's wrong. You might not find out that your service is malfunctioning until users start calling you to complain.

For example, Listing 8-4 demonstrates a simple test that causes the HTTP client to block indefinitely.

```
package main

import (
    "context"
    "errors"
    "net/http"
    "net/http/httptest"
    "testing"
    "time"
)

func blockIndefinitely(w http.ResponseWriter, r *http.Request) {
    select {}
}

func TestBlockIndefinitely(t *testing.T) {
    ts := ❶httptest.NewServer(❷http.HandlerFunc(❸blockIndefinitely))
    _, _ = http.Get(❹ts.URL)
    t.Fatal("client did not indefinitely block")
}
```

*Listing 8-4: The test server causes the default HTTP client to block indefinitely (block_test.go).*

The net/http/httptest package includes a useful HTTP test server. The httptest.NewServer ❶ function accepts an http.HandlerFunc ❷, which in turn wraps the blockIndefinitely function ❸. The test server passes any request it receives at its URL ❹ to the `http.HandlerFunc`'s `ServeHTTP` method. This method sends the request and response objects to the `blockIndefinitely` function, where control blocks indefinitely.

Because the helper function `http.Get` uses the default HTTP client, this GET request won't time out. Instead, the go test runner will eventually time out and halt the test, printing the stack trace.

**NOTE** *If you run this test, I recommend you pass the argument `-timeout 5s` to go test to keep from waiting too long.*

To solve this issue, production code should use the technique you learned for timing out network sockets in "Using a Context with a Deadline to Time Out a Connection" on page 57. Create a context and use it to initialize a new request. You can then manually cancel the request by either using the context's cancel function or creating a context with a deadline or time-out.

Let's fix the test in Listing 8-4 by replacing it with the test in Listing 8-5. The new test will time out the request after five seconds without an answer from the server.

```
--snip--

func TestBlockIndefinitelyWithTimeout(t *testing.T) {
    ts := httptest.NewServer(http.HandlerFunc(blockIndefinitely))

    ctx, cancel := context.WithTimeout(context.Background(), 5*time.Second)
    defer cancel()

    req, err := ❶http.NewRequestWithContext(ctx, http.MethodGet, ts.URL, nil)
    if err != nil {
        t.Fatal(err)
    }

    resp, err := http.DefaultClient.Do(req)
    if err != nil {
        if !errors.Is(err, context.DeadlineExceeded) {
            t.Fatal(err)
        }
        return
    }
    _ = resp.Body.Close()
}
```

*Listing 8-5: Adding a time-out to the GET request (block_test.go)*

First, you create a new request ❶ by passing in the context, the request method, the URL, and a `nil` request body, since your request does not have a payload. Keep in mind that the context's timer starts running as soon as you initialize the context. The context controls the entire life cycle of the request. In other words, the client has five seconds to connect to the web server, send the request, read the response headers, and pass the response to your code. You then have the remainder of the five seconds to read the response body. If you are in the middle of reading the response body when the context times out, your next read will immediately return an error. So, use generous time-out values for your specific application.

Alternatively, create a context without a time-out or deadline and control the cancellation of the context exclusively by using a timer and the context's cancel function, like this:

```
ctx, cancel := context.WithCancel(context.Background())
timer := time.AfterFunc(5*time.Second, ❶cancel)
// Make the HTTP request, read the response headers, etc.
// ...
// Add 5 more seconds before reading the response body.
timer.Reset(5*time.Second)
```

This snippet demonstrates how to use a timer that will call the context's cancel function ❶ after it expires. You can reset the timer as needed to push the call to cancel further into the future.

## Disabling Persistent TCP Connections

By default, Go's HTTP client maintains the underlying TCP connection to a web server after reading its response unless explicitly told to disconnect by the server. Although this is desirable behavior for most use cases because it allows you to use the same TCP connection for multiple requests, you may inadvertently deny your computer the ability to open new TCP connections with other web servers.

This is because the number of active TCP connections a computer can maintain is finite. If you write a program that makes one-off requests to numerous web servers, you could find that your program stops working after exhausting all your computer's available TCP connections, leaving it unable to open new ones. In this scenario, TCP session reuse can work against you. Instead of disabling TCP session reuse in the client, a more flexible option is to inform the client what to do with the TCP socket on a per-request basis.

```
--snip--
    req, err := http.NewRequestWithContext(ctx, http.MethodGet, ts.URL, nil)
    if err != nil {
        t.Fatal(err)
    }
  ❶req.Close = true
--snip--
```

Setting the request's Close field ❶ to true tells Go's HTTP client that it should close the underlying TCP connection after reading the web server's response. If you know you're going to send four requests to a web server and no more, you could set the Close field to true on the fourth request. All four requests will use the same TCP session, and the client will terminate the TCP connection after receiving the fourth response.

# Posting Data over HTTP

Sending a POST request and its payload to a web server is like the calls you've made thus far. The difference, of course, is that the request body contains a payload. This payload can be any object that implements the io.Reader interface, including a file handle, standard input, an HTTP response body, or a Unix domain socket, to name a few. But as you'll see, sending data to the web server involves a little more code than a GET request because you must prepare that request body.

## Posting JSON to a Web Server

Before you can send data to a test server, you need to create a handler that can accept it. Listing 8-6 creates a new type named User that you will encode to JavaScript Object Notation (JSON) and post to the handler.

```go
package main

import (
    "bytes"
    "context"
    "encoding/json"
    "fmt"
    "io"
    "io/ioutil"
    "mime/multipart"
    "net/http"
    "net/http/httptest"
    "os"
    "path/filepath"
    "testing"
    "time"
)

type User struct {
    First string
    Last  string
}

❶ func handlePostUser(t *testing.T) func(http.ResponseWriter, *http.Request) {
    return func(w http.ResponseWriter, r *http.Request) {
        defer func(r io.ReadCloser) {
            _, _ = ❷io.Copy(ioutil.Discard, r)
            _ = r.Close()
        }(r.Body)

        if r.Method != ❸http.MethodPost {
          ❹http.Error(w, "", http.StatusMethodNotAllowed)
            return
        }

        var u User
        err := json.NewDecoder(r.Body).Decode(&u)
```

```
            if err != nil {
                t.Error(err)
                http.Error(w, "Decode Failed", http.StatusBadRequest)
                return
            }

        ❺w.WriteHeader(http.StatusAccepted)
        }
}
```

*Listing 8-6: A handler that can decode JSON into a User object (post_test.go)*

The handlePostUser function ❶ returns a function that will handle POST
requests. If the request method is anything other than POST ❸, it returns a
status code indicating that the server disallows the method ❹. The function
then attempts to decode the JSON in the request body to a User object. If
successful, the response's status is set to *Accepted* ❺.

Unlike the Go HTTP client, the Go HTTP server must explicitly drain
the request body ❷ before closing it. We'll discuss this in more detail in
Chapter 9.

The test in Listing 8-7 encodes a User object into JSON and sends it in a
POST request to the test server.

```
--snip--

func TestPostUser(t *testing.T) {
    ts := httptest.NewServer(http.HandlerFunc(handlePostUser(t)))
    defer ts.Close()

    resp, err := http.Get(ts.URL)
    if err != nil {
        t.Fatal(err)
    }
    if ❶resp.StatusCode != http.StatusMethodNotAllowed {
        t.Fatalf("expected status %d; actual status %d",
            http.StatusMethodNotAllowed, resp.StatusCode)
    }

    buf := new(bytes.Buffer)
    u := User{First: "Adam", Last: "Woodbeck"}
❷   err = json.NewEncoder(buf).Encode(&u)
    if err != nil {
        t.Fatal(err)
    }

    resp, err = ❸http.Post(ts.URL, "application/json", buf)
    if err != nil {
        t.Fatal(err)
    }
    if resp.StatusCode != ❹http.StatusAccepted {
        t.Fatalf("expected status %d; actual status %d",
            http.StatusAccepted, resp.StatusCode)
```

```
        }
        _ = resp.Body.Close()
}
```

---

*Listing 8-7: Encoding a User object to JSON and POST to the test server (post_test.go)*

The test first makes sure that the test server's handler properly responds with an error if the client sends the wrong type of request ❶. If the test server receives anything other than a POST request, it will respond with a Method Not Allowed error. Then, the test encodes a User object into JSON and writes the data to a bytes buffer ❷. It makes a POST request to the test server's URL with the content type *application/json* because the bytes buffer, representing the request body, contains JSON ❸. The content type informs the server's handler about the type of data to expect in the request body. If the server's handler properly decoded the request body, the response status code is 202 Accepted ❹.

## Posting a Multipart Form with Attached Files

Posting JSON to a web server is easy. Simply set the appropriate content type and send along the JSON payload in the request body. But how do you handle sending various bits of data to a web server in a single POST request? Answer: use the mime/multipart package.

The mime/multipart package allows you to craft multipart *Multipurpose Internet Mail Extensions (MIME) messages*, which separate each bit of data you want to send from the other bits of data by a string known as a *boundary*. You'll see an example of a boundary a bit later in this section, though it isn't something you typically need to worry about.

Each MIME part includes optional headers that describe the content, as well as a body that contains the content itself. For example, if a web server parsed a MIME part with a Content-Type header set to *text/plain*, it would treat the part's body as plaintext.

Listing 8-8 introduces a new test that walks you through the process of building up a multipart request body using the mime/multipart package.

---

```
--snip--

func TestMultipartPost(t *testing.T) {
    reqBody := ❶new(bytes.Buffer)
    w := ❷multipart.NewWriter(reqBody)

    for k, v := range map[string]string{
        "date":        time.Now().Format(time.RFC3339),
        "description": "Form values with attached files",
    } {
        err := ❸w.WriteField(k, v)
        if err != nil {
            t.Fatal(err)
        }
    }
```

---

*Listing 8-8: Creating a new request body, multipart writer, and write form data (post_test.go)*

First, you create a new buffer ❶ to act as the request body. You then create a new multipart writer ❷ that wraps the buffer. The multipart writer generates a random boundary upon initialization. Finally, you write form fields to the multipart writer ❸. The multipart writer separates each form field into its own part, writing the boundary, appropriate headers, and the form field value to each part's body.

At this point, your request body has two parts, one for the *date* form field and one for the *description* form field. Let's attach a couple of files in Listing 8-9.

```
--snip--

    for i, file := range []string{
        "./files/hello.txt",
        "./files/goodbye.txt",
    } {
        filePart, err := ❶w.CreateFormFile(fmt.Sprintf("file%d", i+1),
            filepath.Base(file))
        if err != nil {
            t.Fatal(err)
        }

        f, err := os.Open(file)
        if err != nil {
            t.Fatal(err)
        }

        _, err = ❷io.Copy(filePart, f)
        _ = f.Close()
        if err != nil {
            t.Fatal(err)
        }
    }

    err := ❸w.Close()
    if err != nil {
        t.Fatal(err)
    }
```

*Listing 8-9: Writing two files to the request body, each in its own MIME part (post_test.go)*

Attaching a field to a request body isn't as straightforward as adding form field data. You have an extra step. First, you need to create a multipart section writer from Listing 8-8's multipart writer ❶. The CreateFormField method accepts a field name and a filename. The server uses this filename when parsing the MIME part. It does not need to match the filename you attach. Now, you just open the file and copy its contents to the MIME part writer ❷.

When you're done adding parts to the request body, you must close the multipart writer ❸, which finalizes the request body by appending the boundary.

Listing 8-10 posts the request to a well-regarded test server, *httpbin.org.*

```
--snip--

    ctx, cancel := context.WithTimeout(context.Background(),
        60*time.Second)
    defer cancel()

    req, err := http.NewRequestWithContext(ctx, http.MethodPost,
      ❶"https://httpbin.org/post", ❷reqBody)
    if err != nil {
        t.Fatal(err)
    }
    req.Header.Set("Content-Type", ❸w.FormDataContentType())

    resp, err := http.DefaultClient.Do(req)
    if err != nil {
        t.Fatal(err)
    }
    defer func() { _ = resp.Body.Close() }()

    b, err := ioutil.ReadAll(resp.Body)
    if err != nil {
        t.Fatal(err)
    }
    if resp.StatusCode != http.StatusOK {
        t.Fatalf("expected status %d; actual status %d",
            http.StatusOK, resp.StatusCode)
    }

    t.Logf("\n%s", b)
}
```

*Listing 8-10: Sending a POST request to* httpbin.org *with Go's default HTTP client (post_test.go)*

First, you create a new request and pass it a context that will time out in 60 seconds. Since you're making this call over the internet, you don't have as much certainty that your request will reach its destination as you do when testing over localhost. The POST request is destined for *https://www.httpbin .org/* ❶ and will send the multipart request body ❷ in its payload.

Before you send the request, you need to set the Content-Type header to inform the web server you're sending multiple parts in this request. The multipart writer's FormDataContentType method ❸ returns the appropriate Content-Type value that includes its boundary. The web server uses the boundary from this header to determine where one part stops and another starts as it reads the request body.

Once you run the test with the -v flag, you should see output like the JSON in Listing 8-11.

```
{
  "args": {},
  "data": "",
❶ "files": {
    "file1": "Hello, world!\n",
    "file2": "Goodbye, world!\n"
  },
❷ "form": {
    "date": "2006-01-02T15:04:05-07:00",
    "description": "Form fields with attached files"
  },
  "headers": {
    "Accept-Encoding": "gzip",
    "Content-Length": "739",
❸   "Content-Type": "multipart/form-data; boundary=e9ad4b62e0dfc8d7dc57ccfa8ba
62244342f1884608e6d88018f9de8abcb",
    "Host": "httpbin.org",
    "User-Agent": "Go-http-client/1.1"
  },
  "json": null,
  "origin": "192.168.0.1",
  "url": "https://httpbin.org/post"
}
```

*Listing 8-11: Response body from the multipart POST request*

This is *httpbin.org*'s standard POST response and includes some fields irrelevant to the request you sent. But if you have a look, you'll see the contents of each text file you attached ❶ and the form fields you submitted ❷. You can also see the Content-Type header ❸ added by the multipart writer. Notice the boundary is a random string. With your code as is, the boundary will randomly change with each request. But you can set a boundary by using the multipart writer's SetBoundary method if you so choose.

## What You've Learned

HTTP allows clients to send requests to, and receive resources from, servers over the World Wide Web. This chapter showed you how to use Go to craft HTTP requests. Target resources can take the form of web pages, images, videos, documents, files, games, and so on. To retrieve a resource, the HTTP client sends a GET request with a URL to the web server. The web server uses the URL to locate the correct resource and send it along to the client in the server's response. The client always initiates this HTTP request-response workflow.

The client can send diverse types of resource requests to the server. The most used request methods are GET, HEAD, POST, PUT, and DELETE. A GET request asks the server to retrieve the specified resource. The client may send a HEAD request to retrieve the response headers without the requested payload. This can be useful for determining whether a resource exists and inspecting response headers before retrieving the resource. A POST request allows the client to send a resource to the server, whereas you typically use a PUT request to update an existing resource on the server. The client can request a resource's deletion from the server by sending a DELETE request.

The net/http package provides all necessary types and functions to interact with servers over HTTP. It includes a default HTTP client that allows you to make a quick, one-off HTTP request and receive the response. However, you must diligently close the response body to prevent resource leaks, no matter whether you read the body's contents or not. It's also important to note that the default HTTP client and the requests sent using helper functions such as http.Get, http.Head, and http.Post do not time out. This means that a misbehaving or malicious service could cause your code to block indefinitely. Therefore, it's important to manage request cancellation yourself by using a context.

The mime/multipart package allows you to easily add multiple MIME parts to a request body. You can efficiently craft requests that upload files and form content to a web server.

# 9

## BUILDING HTTP SERVICES

Now that you've written client code to send HTTP requests, let's build a server that can process these requests and send resources to the client. The net/http package handles most of the implementation details for you, so you can focus on instantiating and configuring a server, creating resources, and handling each client request.

In Go, an HTTP server relies on several interacting components: handlers, middleware, and a multiplexer. When it includes all these parts, we call this server a *web service*. We'll begin by looking at a simple HTTP web service and then explore each of its components over the course of the chapter. The big picture should help you understand topics that beginners often find abstract.

You'll also learn more advanced uses of the net/http package, such as adding TLS support and pushing data to HTTP/2 clients. By the end, you should feel comfortable configuring a Go-based HTTP server, writing middleware, and responding to requests with handlers.

# The Anatomy of a Go HTTP Server

Figure 9-1 illustrates the path a request takes in a typical net/http-based server.

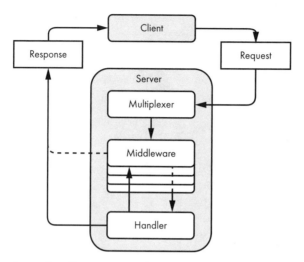

*Figure 9-1: Client request culminating in a server response in the handler*

First, the server's *multiplexer* (*router,* in computer-networking parlance) receives the client's request. The multiplexer determines the destination for the request, then passes it along to the object capable of handling it. We call this object a *handler.* (The multiplexer itself is a handler that routes requests to the most appropriate handler.) Before the handler receives the request, the request may pass through one or more functions called *middleware.* Middleware changes the handlers' behavior or performs auxiliary tasks, such as logging, authentication, or access control.

Listing 9-1 creates an HTTP server that follows this basic structure. If you have trouble following along, don't worry; you'll spend the rest of the chapter learning how these parts work.

```
package main

import (
    "bytes"
    "fmt"
    "io"
    "io/ioutil"
    "net"
    "net/http"
    "testing"
    "time"

    "github.com/awoodbeck/gnp/ch09/handlers"
)
```

```
func TestSimpleHTTPServer(t *testing.T) {
    srv := &http.Server{
        Addr: "127.0.0.1:8081",
        Handler: ❶http.TimeoutHandler(
            handlers.DefaultHandler(), 2*time.Minute, ""),
        IdleTimeout:       5 * time.Minute,
        ReadHeaderTimeout: time.Minute,
    }

    l, err := ❷net.Listen("tcp", srv.Addr)
    if err != nil {
        t.Fatal(err)
    }

    go func() {
        err := ❸srv.Serve(l)
        if err != http.ErrServerClosed {
            t.Error(err)
        }
    }()
}()
```

*Listing 9-1: Instantiating a multiplexer and an HTTP server (server_test.go)*

Requests sent to the server's handler first pass through middleware named http.TimeoutHandler ❶, then to the handler returned by the handlers .DefaultHandler function. In this very simple example, you specify only a single handler for all requests instead of relying on a multiplexer.

The server has a few fields. The Handler field accepts a multiplexer or other object capable of handling client requests. The Address field should look familiar to you by now. In this example, you want the server to listen to port 8081 on IP address 127.0.0.1. I'll explain the IdleTimeout and ReadHeaderTimeout fields in the next section. Suffice it to say now, you should always define these two fields.

Finally, you create a new net.Listener bound to the server's address ❷ and instruct the server to Serve ❸ requests from this listener. The Serve method returns http.ErrServerClosed when it closes normally.

Now let's test this server. Listing 9-2 picks up where Listing 9-1 leaves off. It details a few test requests and their expected results.

```
--snip--

    testCases := []struct {
        method   string
        body     io.Reader
        code     int
        response string
    }{
        ❶{http.MethodGet, nil, http.StatusOK, "Hello, friend!"},
        ❷{http.MethodPost, bytes.NewBufferString("<world>"), http.StatusOK,
            "Hello, &lt;world&gt;!"},
        ❸{http.MethodHead, nil, http.StatusMethodNotAllowed, ""},
    }
```

```
client := new(http.Client)
path := fmt.Sprintf("http://%s/", srv.Addr)
```

*Listing 9-2: Request test cases for the HTTP server (server_test.go)*

First, you send a GET request ❶, which results in a 200 OK status code. The response body has the Hello, friend! string.

In the second test case ❷, you send a POST request with the string <world> in its body. The angle brackets are intentional, and they show an often-overlooked aspect of handling client input in the handler: always escape client input. You'll learn about escaping client input in "Handlers" on page 193. This test case results in the string Hello, &lt;world&gt;! in the response body. The response looks a bit silly, but your web browser renders it as Hello, <world>!.

The third test case ❸ a sends a HEAD request to the HTTP server. The handler returned by the handlers.DefaultHandler function, which you'll explore shortly, does not handle the HEAD method. Therefore, it returns a 405 Method Not Allowed status code and an empty response body.

Listing 9-3 continues the code in Listing 9-2 and runs through each test case.

```
--snip--

for i, c := range testCases {
    r, err := ❶http.NewRequest(c.method, path, c.body)
    if err != nil {
        t.Errorf("%d: %v", i, err)
        continue
    }

    resp, err := ❷client.Do(r)
    if err != nil {
        t.Errorf("%d: %v", i, err)
        continue
    }

    if resp.StatusCode != c.code {
        t.Errorf("%d: unexpected status code: %q", i, resp.Status)
    }

    b, err := ❸ioutil.ReadAll(resp.Body)
    if err != nil {
        t.Errorf("%d: %v", i, err)
        continue
    }
    _ = ❹resp.Body.Close()

    if c.response != string(b) {
        t.Errorf("%d: expected %q; actual %q", i, c.response, b)
    }
}
```

```
    if err := ❺srv.Close(); err != nil {
        t.Fatal(err)
    }
}
```

*Listing 9-3: Sending test requests to the HTTP server (server_test.go)*

First, you create a new request, passing the parameters from the test case ❶. Next, you pass the request to the client's Do method ❷, which returns the server's response. You then check the status code and read in the entire response body ❸. You should be in the habit of consistently closing the response body if the client did not return an error ❹, even if the response body is empty or you ignore it entirely. Failure to do so may prevent the client from reusing the underlying TCP connection.

Once all tests complete, you call the server's Close method ❺. This causes its Serve method in Listing 9-1 to return, stopping the server. The Close method abruptly closes client connections. You'll see an example of the HTTP server's graceful shutdown support when we discuss HTTP/2 pushes later in this chapter.

Go's HTTP server supports a few other features, which we'll explore in the following sections. It can proactively serve, or push, resources to clients. It also offers graceful shutdown support. Abruptly shutting down your web server may leave some clients in an awkward state if they were waiting for a response when you stopped the server, because those clients will never receive a response. Graceful shutdowns allow for all pending responses to reach each client before the server is stopped.

## Clients Don't Respect Your Time

Just as I recommended setting the client's time-out values, I recommend that you manage the various server time-out values, for the simple reason that clients won't otherwise respect your server's time. A client can take its sweet time sending a request to your server. Meanwhile, your server uses resources waiting to receive the request in its entirety. Likewise, your server is at the client's mercy when it sends the response because it can send data only as fast as the client reads it (or can send only as much as there is TCP buffer space available). Avoid letting the client dictate the duration of a request-response life cycle.

Listing 9-1 includes a server instance with two of its time-out values specified: the length of time clients can remain idle between requests and how long the server should wait to read a request header:

```
srv := &http.Server{
    Addr:              "127.0.0.1:8081",
    Handler:           mux,
    IdleTimeout:       5 * time.Minute,
    ReadHeaderTimeout: time.Minute,
}
```

Although several time-out fields on the http.Server are available to you, I recommend setting only the IdleTimeout and ReadHeaderTimeout fields. The IdleTimeout field dictates how long the server will keep its side of the TCP socket open while waiting for the next client request when the communication uses keepalives. The ReadHeaderTimeout value determines how long the server will wait to finish reading the request headers. Keep in mind that this duration has no bearing on the time it takes to read the request body.

If you want to enforce a time limit for reading an incoming request across all handlers, you could manage the request deadline by using the ReadTimeout field. If the client hasn't sent the complete request (the headers and body) by the time the ReadTimeout duration elapses, the server ends the TCP connection. Likewise, you could give the client a finite duration in which to send the request and read the response by using the WriteTimeout field. The ReadTimeout and WriteTimeout values apply to all requests and responses because they dictate the ReadDeadline and WriteDeadline values of the TCP socket, as discussed in Chapter 4.

These blanket time-out values may be inappropriate for handlers that expect clients to send large files in a request body or handlers that indefinitely stream data to the client. In these two examples, the request or response may abruptly time out even if everything went ahead as expected. Instead, a good practice is to rely on the ReadHeaderTimeout value. You can separately manage the time it takes to read the request body and send the response using middleware or handlers. This gives you the greatest control over request and response durations per resource. You'll learn how to manage the request-response duration by using middleware in "Middleware" on page 202.

## Adding TLS Support

HTTP traffic is plaintext by default, but web clients and servers can use HTTP over an encrypted TLS connection, a combination known as *HTTPS*. Go's HTTP server enables HTTP/2 support over TLS connections only, but enabling TLS is a simple matter. You need to modify only two lines from Listing 9-1's server implementation: the port number and the Serve method:

```
srv := &http.Server{
    Addr:              ❶"127.0.0.1:8443",
    Handler:           mux,
    IdleTimeout:       5 * time.Minute,
    ReadHeaderTimeout: time.Minute,
}

l, err := net.Listen("tcp", srv.Addr)
if err != nil {
    t.Fatal(err)
}

go func() {
    ❷ err := srv.ServeTLS(l, "cert.pem", "key.pem")
    if err != http.ErrServerClosed {
```

```
            t.Error(err)
        }
    }()
```

Technically, you don't need to change the port number ❶, but the convention is to serve HTTPS over port 443, or an augmentation of port 443, like 8443. Using the server's ServeTLS method, you instruct the server to use TLS over HTTP ❷. The ServeTLS method requires the path to both a certificate and a corresponding private key. I recommend you check out the mkcert project at *https://github.com/FiloSottile/mkcert/* to get a key pair. You can use mkcert to create locally trusted key pairs for development purposes only. For production use, you should consider using and supporting Let's Encrypt at *https://letsencrypt.org/*.

# Handlers

When a client sends a request to an HTTP server, the server needs to figure out what to do with it. The server may need to retrieve various resources or perform an action, depending on what the client requests. A common design pattern is to specify bits of code to handle these requests, known as *handlers*. You may have a handler that knows how to retrieve an image and another handler that knows how to retrieve information from a database. We'll discuss how the server figures out which handler is most apt for each request in "Multiplexers" on page 207.

In Go, handlers are objects that implement the http.Handler interface. They read client requests and write responses. The http.Handler interface consists of a single method to receive both the response and the request:

```
type Handler interface {
    ServeHTTP(http.ResponseWriter, *http.Request)
}
```

Any object that implements the http.Handler interface may handle client requests, as far as the Go HTTP server is concerned. We often define handlers as functions, as in this common pattern:

```
handler := http.HandlerFunc(
    func(w http.ResponseWriter, r *http.Request) {
        _, _ = w.Write([]byte("Hello, world!"))
    },
)
```

Here, you wrap a function that accepts an http.ResponseWriter and an http.Request pointer in the http.HandlerFunc type, which implements the Handler interface. This results in an http.HandlerFunc object that calls the wrapped func(w http.ResponseWriter, r *http.Request) function when the server calls its ServeHTTP method. This handler responds to the client with the string Hello, world! in the response body.

Notice that you ignore the number of written bytes and any potential write error. In the wild, writes to a client can fail for any number of reasons.

It isn't worth logging these errors. Instead, one option is to keep track of the write error frequency and have your server send you an alert should the number of errors exceed an appropriate threshold. You'll learn about instrumenting your code in Chapter 13.

Now that you're familiar with the structure of a handler, let's have a look at the handler returned by the handlers.DefaultHandler function in Listing 9-4.

```go
package handlers

import (
    "html/template"
    "io"
    "io/ioutil"
    "net/http"
)

var t = ❶template.Must(template.New("hello").Parse("Hello, {{.}}!"))

func DefaultHandler() http.Handler {
    return http.HandlerFunc(
        func(w http.ResponseWriter, r *http.Request) {
            ❷ defer func(r io.ReadCloser) {
                _, _ = io.Copy(ioutil.Discard, r)
                _ = r.Close()
            }(r.Body)

            var b []byte

            ❸ switch r.Method {
            case http.MethodGet:
                b = []byte("friend")
            case http.MethodPost:
                var err error
                b, err = ioutil.ReadAll(r.Body)
                if err != nil {
                    ❹ http.Error(w, "Internal server error",
                        http.StatusInternalServerError)
                    return
                }
            default:
                // not RFC-compliant due to lack of "Allow" header
                ❺ http.Error(w, "Method not allowed",
                    http.StatusMethodNotAllowed)
                return
            }

            _ = ❻t.Execute(w, string(b))
        },
    )
}
```

*Listing 9-4: The default handler implementation (handlers/default.go)*

The handlers.DefaultHandler function returns a function converted to the http.HandlerFunc type. The http.HandlerFunc type implements the http.Handler interface. Go programmers commonly convert a function with the signature func(w http.ResponseWriter, r *http.Request) to the http.HandlerFunc type so the function implements the http.Handler interface.

The first bit of code you see is a deferred function that drains and closes the request body ❷. Just as it's important for the client to drain and close the response body to reuse the TCP session, it's important for the server to do the same with the request body. But unlike the Go HTTP client, closing the request body does not implicitly drain it. Granted, the http.Server will close the request body for you, but it won't drain it. To make sure you can reuse the TCP session, I recommend you drain the request body at a minimum. Closing it is optional.

The handler responds differently depending on the request method ❸. If the client sent a GET request, the handler writes Hello, friend! to the response writer. If the request method is a POST, the handler first reads the entire request body. If an error occurs while reading the request body, the handler uses the http.Error function ❹ to succinctly write the message Internal server error to the response body and set the response status code to 500. Otherwise, the handler returns a greeting using the request body contents. If the handler receives any other request method, it responds with a 405 Method Not Allowed status ❺. The 405 response is technically not RFC-compliant without an Allow header showing which methods the handler accepts. We'll shore up this deficiency in "Any Type Can Be a Handler" on page 198. Finally, the handler writes the response body.

This code could have a security vulnerability since part of the response body might come from the request body. A malicious client can send a request payload that includes JavaScript, which could run on a client's computer. This behavior can lead to an XSS attack. To prevent these attacks, you must properly escape all client-supplied content before sending it in a response. Here, you use the html/template package to create a simple template ❶ that reads Hello, {{.}}!, where {{.}} is a placeholder for part of your response. Templates derived from the html/template package automatically escape HTML characters when you populate them and write the results to the response writer ❻. HTML-escaping explains the funky characters in Listing 9-2's second test case. The client's browser will properly display the characters instead of interpreting them as part of the HTML and JavaScript in the response body. The bottom line is to always use the html/template package when writing untrusted data to a response writer.

## Test Your Handlers with httptest

Saying "make sure you test your code" is the developer's equivalent of my mother telling me to clean my bedroom. It's good advice, but I'd much rather continue hacking away than write test code. But my mother was correct, and writing test code now will serve me well in the future. The Go standard library architects—motivated by clean bedrooms, no doubt— made sure to give us the net/http/httptest package. This package makes unit-testing handlers painless.

The net/http/httptest package exports a NewRequest function that accepts an HTTP method, a target resource, and a request body io.Reader. It returns a pointer to an http.Request ready for use in an http.Handler:

```
func NewRequest(method, target string, body io.Reader) *http.Request
```

Unlike its http.NewRequest equivalent, httptest.NewRequest will panic instead of returning an error. This is preferable in tests but not in production code.

The httptest.NewRecorder function returns a pointer to an httptest .ResponseRecorder, which implements the http.ResponseWriter interface. Although the httptest.ResponseRecorder exports fields that look tempting to use (I don't want to tempt you by mentioning them), I recommend you call its Result method instead. The Result method returns a pointer to an http.Response object, just like the one we used in the last chapter. As the method's name implies, it waits until the handler returns before retrieving the httptest.ResponseRecorder's results.

If you're interested in performing integration tests, the net/http/httptest package includes a test server implementation. For the purposes of this chapter, we'll use httptest.NewRequest and httptest.NewRecorder.

## How You Write the Response Matters

Here's one potential pitfall: the order in which you write to the response body and set the response status code matters. The client receives the response status code first, followed by the response body from the server. If you write the response body first, Go infers that the response status code is 200 OK and sends it along to the client before sending the response body. To see this in action, look at Listing 9-5.

```
package handlers

import (
    "net/http"
    "net/http/httptest"
    "testing"
)

func TestHandlerWriteHeader(t *testing.T) {
    handler := func(w http.ResponseWriter, r *http.Request) {
        _, _ = ❶w.Write([]byte("Bad request"))
      ❷w.WriteHeader(http.StatusBadRequest)
    }
    r := httptest.NewRequest(http.MethodGet, "http://test", nil)
    w := httptest.NewRecorder()
    handler(w, r)
    t.Logf("Response status: %q", ❸w.Result().Status)

    handler = func(w http.ResponseWriter, r *http.Request) {
      ❹w.WriteHeader(http.StatusB)
        _, _ = ❺w.Write([]byte("Bad request"))
    }
```

```
    r = httptest.NewRequest(http.MethodGet, "http://test", nil)
    w = httptest.NewRecorder()
    handler(w, r)
    t.Logf("Response status: %q", ❻w.Result().Status)
}
```

*Listing 9-5: Writing the status first and the response body second for expected results (handlers/pitfall_test.go)*

At first glance, it may seem like the first handler function generates a response status code of 400 Bad Request and the string `Bad request` in the response body. But this isn't what happens. Calling the ResponseWriter's Write method causes Go to make an implicit call to the response's WriteHeader method with http.StatusOK for you. Once the response's status code is set with an explicit or implicit call to WriteHeader, you cannot change it.

The Go authors made this design choice because they reasoned you'd need to call WriteHeader only for adverse conditions, and in that case, you should do so before you write anything to the response body. Remember, the server sends the response status code before the response body. Once the response's status code is set with an explicit or implicit call to WriteHeader, you cannot change it because it's likely on its way to the client.

In this example, however, you make a call to the Write method ❶, which implicitly calls WriteHeader(http.StatusOK). Since the status code is not yet set, the response code is now 200 OK. The next call to WriteHeader ❷ is effectively a no-op because the status code is already set. The response code 200 OK persists ❸.

Now, if you switch the order of the calls so you set the status code ❹ before you write to the response body ❺, the response has the proper status code ❻.

Let's have a look at the test output to confirm that this is the case:

```
=== RUN   TestHandlerWriteHeader
    TestHandlerWriteHeader: pitfall_test.go:17: Response status: "200 OK"
    TestHandlerWriteHeader: pitfall_test.go:26: Response status: "400 Bad
Request"
--- PASS: TestHandlerWriteHeader (0.00s)
PASS
```

As you can see from the test output, any writes to the response body before you call the WriteHeader method result in a 200 OK status code. The only way to dictate the response status code is to call the WriteHeader method before any writes to the response body.

You can improve this code even further by using the http.Error function, which simplifies the process of writing a response status code and response body. For example, you could replace your handlers with this single line of code:

```
http.Error(w, "Bad request", http.StatusBadRequest)
```

This function sets the content type to *text/plain*, sets the status code to 400 Bad Request, and writes the error message to the response body.

## Any Type Can Be a Handler

Because http.Handler is an interface, you can use it to write powerful constructs for handling client requests. Let's improve upon the default handler from Listing 9-4 by defining a new type that implements the http.Handler interface in Listing 9-6. This type will allow you to appropriately respond to specific HTTP methods and will automatically implement the OPTIONS method for you.

```
package handlers

import (
    "fmt"
    "html"
    "io"
    "io/ioutil"
    "net/http"
    "sort"
    "strings"
)

❶ type Methods map[string]http.Handler

func (h Methods) ❷ServeHTTP(w http.ResponseWriter, r *http.Request) {
    ❸ defer func(r io.ReadCloser) {
        _, _ = io.Copy(ioutil.Discard, r)
        _ = r.Close()
    }(r.Body)

    if handler, ok := h[r.Method]; ok {
        if handler == nil {
        ❹ http.Error(w, "Internal server error",
                http.StatusInternalServerError)
        } else {
        ❺ handler.ServeHTTP(w, r)
        }

        return
    }

    ❻ w.Header().Add("Allow", h.allowedMethods())
    if r.Method != ❼http.MethodOptions {
        http.Error(w, "Method not allowed", http.StatusMethodNotAllowed)
    }
}

func (h Methods) allowedMethods() string {
    a := make([]string, 0, len(h))

    for k := range h {
        a = append(a, k)
```

```
        }
        sort.Strings(a)

        return strings.Join(a, ", ")
    }
```

*Listing 9-6: Methods map that dynamically routes requests to the right handler
(handlers/methods.go)*

The new type, named Methods, is a map ❶ whose key is an HTTP
method and whose value is an http.Handler. It has a ServeHTTP method ❷
to implement the http.Handler interface, so you can use Methods as a handler
itself. The ServeHTTP method first defers a function to drain and close the
request body ❸, saving the map's handlers from having to do so.

The ServeHTTP method looks up the request method in the map and
retrieves the handler. To protect us from panics, the ServeHTTP method
makes sure the corresponding handler is not nil, responding with 500
Internal Server Error ❹ if it is. Otherwise, you call the corresponding
handler's ServeHTTP method ❺. The Methods type is a multiplexer (router)
since it routes requests to the appropriate handler.

If the request method isn't in the map, ServeHTTP responds with the Allow
header ❻ and a list of supported methods in the map. All that's left do now
is determine whether the client explicitly requested the OPTIONS ❼ method. If
so, the ServeHTTP method returns, resulting in a 200 OK response to the client. If not, the client receives a 405 Method Not Allowed response.

Listing 9-7 uses the Methods handler to implement a better default handler than the one found in Listing 9-4. The old default handler did not
automatically add the Allow header and support the OPTIONS method. This
one will, which makes your job a bit easier. All you need to determine is
which methods your Methods handler should support, then implement them.

```
--snip--

func DefaultMethodsHandler() http.Handler {
    return Methods{
  ❶     http.MethodGet: http.HandlerFunc(
            func(w http.ResponseWriter, r *http.Request) {
                _, _ = w.Write([]byte("Hello, friend!"))
            },
        ),
  ❷     http.MethodPost: http.HandlerFunc(
            func(w http.ResponseWriter, r *http.Request) {
                b, err := ioutil.ReadAll(r.Body)
                if err != nil {
                    http.Error(w, "Internal server error",
                        http.StatusInternalServerError)
                    return
                }

                _, _ = fmt.Fprintf(w, "Hello, %s!",
                    html.EscapeString(string(b)))
```

```
                },
            ),
        }
}
```

*Listing 9-7: Default implementation of the Methods handler (methods.go)*

Now, the handler returned by the `handlers.DefaultMethodsHandler` func-tion supports the `GET`, `POST`, and `OPTIONS` methods. The `GET` method simply writes the `Hello,  friend!` message to the response body ❶. The `POST` method greets the client with the HTML-escaped request body contents ❷. The remaining functionality to support the `OPTIONS` method and properly set the Allow header are inherent to the `Methods` type's `ServeHTTP` method.

The handler returned by the `handlers.DefaultMethodsHandler` function is a drop-in replacement for the handler returned by the `handlers.DefaultHandler` function. You can exchange the following snippet of code from Listing 9-1:

```
Handler: http.TimeoutHandler(handlers.DefaultHandler(), 2*time.Minute, ""),
```

for this code:

```
Handler: http.TimeoutHandler(handlers.DefaultMethodsHandler(), 2*time.Minute, ""),
```

to take advantage of the added functionality provided by the `Methods` handler.

## Injecting Dependencies into Handlers

The `http.Handler` interface gives you access to the request and response objects. But it's likely you'll require access to additional functionality like a logger, metrics, cache, or database to handle a request. For example, you may want to inject a logger to record request errors or inject a database object to retrieve data used to create the response. The easiest way to inject an object into a handler is by using a closure.

Listing 9-8 demonstrates how to inject a SQL database object into an `http.Handler`.

```
dbHandler := func(❶db *sql.DB) http.Handler {
    return http.HandlerFunc(
        func(w http.ResponseWriter, r *http.Request) {
            err := ❷db.Ping()
            // do something with the database here…
        },
    )
}

http.Handle("/three", ❸dbHandler(db))
```

*Listing 9-8: Injecting a dependency into a handler using a closure*

You create a function that accepts a pointer to a SQL database object ❶ and returns a handler, then assign it to a variable named `dbHandler`. Since this function closes over the returned handler, you have access to the db variable in the handler's scope ❷. Instantiating the handler is as simple as calling dbHandler and passing in a pointer to a SQL database object ❸.

This approach can get a bit cumbersome if you have multiple handlers that require access to the same database object or your design is evolving and you're likely to require access to additional objects in the future. A more extensible approach is to use a struct whose fields represent objects and data you want to access in your handler and to define your handlers as struct methods (see Listing 9-9). Injecting dependencies involves adding struct fields instead of modifying a bunch of closure definitions.

```
type Handlers struct {
    db *sql.DB
  ❶log *log.Logger
}

func (h *Handlers) Handler1() http.Handler {
    return http.HandlerFunc(
        func(w http.ResponseWriter, r *http.Request) {
            err := h.db.Ping()
            if err != nil {
              ❷h.log.Printf("db ping: %v", err)
            }
            // do something with the database here
        },
    )
}

func (h *Handlers) Handler2() http.Handler {
    return http.HandlerFunc(
        func(w http.ResponseWriter, r *http.Request) {
            // ...
        },
    )
}
```

Listing 9-9: Injecting dependencies into multiple handlers defined as struct methods

You define a struct that contains pointers to a database object and a logger ❶. Any method you define on the handler now has access to these objects ❷. If your handlers require access to additional resources, you simply add fields to the struct.

Listing 9-10 illustrates how to use the Handlers struct.

```
h := &Handlers{
    db: ❶db,
    log: log.New(os.Stderr, "handlers: ", log.Lshortfile),
}
http.Handle("/one", h.Handler1())
http.Handle("/two", h.Handler2())
```

Listing 9-10: Initializing the Handlers struct and using its handlers

Assuming db ❶ is a pointer to a `sql.DB` object, you initialize a `Handlers` object and use its methods with `http.Handle`, for example.

## Middleware

Middleware comprises reusable functions that accept an `http.Handler` and return an `http.Handler`:

```
func(http.Handler) http.Handler
```

You can use middleware to inspect the request and make decisions based on its content before passing it along to the next handler. Or you might use the request content to set headers in the response. For example, the middleware could respond to the client with an error if the handler requires authentication and an unauthenticated client sent the request. Middleware can also collect metrics, log requests, or control access to resources, to name a few uses. Best of all, you can reuse them on multiple handlers. If you find yourself writing the same handler code over and over, ask yourself if you can put the functionality into middleware and reuse it across your handlers.

Listing 9-11 shows just a few uses of middleware, such as enforcing which methods the handler allows, adding headers to the response, or performing ancillary functions like logging.

```
func Middleware(next http.Handler) http.Handler {
    return ❶http.HandlerFunc(
      ❷ func(w http.ResponseWriter, r *http.Request) {
            if r.Method == http.MethodTrace {
                ❸http.Error(w, "Method not allowed",
                    http.StatusMethodNotAllowed)
            }

          ❹w.Header().Set("X-Content-Type-Options", "nosniff")

            start := time.Now()
          ❺next.ServeHTTP(w, r)
          ❻log.Printf("Next handler duration %v", time.Now().Sub(start))
        },
    )
}
```

*Listing 9-11: Example middleware function*

The `Middleware` function uses a common pattern you first saw in Listing 9-4: it defines a function that accepts an `http.ResponseWriter` and a pointer to an `http.Request` ❷ and wraps it with an `http.HandlerFunc` ❶.

In most cases, middleware calls the given handler ❺. But in some cases that may not be proper, and the middleware should block the next handler and respond to the client itself ❸. Likewise, you may want to use middleware to collect metrics, ensure specific headers are set on the response ❹, or write to a log file ❻.

Listing 9-11 is a contrived example. I don't recommend performing so many tasks in a single middleware function. Instead, it's best to follow the Unix philosophy and write minimalist middleware, with each function doing one thing very well. Ideally, you would split the middleware in Listing 9-11 into three middleware functions to check the request method and respond to the client ❸, enforce response headers ❹, and collect metrics ❻.

The net/http package includes useful middleware to serve static files, redirect requests, and manage request time-outs. Let's dig into their source code to see how you might use them. In addition to these standard library functions, check out the middleware at *https://go.dev/*.

## Timing Out Slow Clients

As I mentioned earlier, it's important not to let clients dictate the duration of a request-response life cycle. Malicious clients could use this leniency to their ends and exhaust your server's resources, effectively denying service to legit clients. Yet at the same time, setting read and write time-outs server-wide makes it hard for the server to stream data or use different time-out durations for each handler.

Instead, you should manage time-outs in middleware or individual handlers. The net/http package includes a middleware function that allows you to control the duration of a request and response on a per-handler basis. The http.TimeoutHandler accepts an http.Handler, a duration, and a string to write to the response body. It sets an internal timer to the given duration. If the http.Handler does not return before the timer expires, the http.TimeoutHandler blocks the http.Handler and responds to the client with a 503 Service Unavailable status.

Listing 9-12 uses the http.TimeoutHandler to wrap an http.Handler that mimics a slow client.

```
package middleware

import (
    "io/ioutil"
    "net/http"
    "net/http/httptest"
    "testing"
    "time"
)

func TestTimeoutMiddleware(t *testing.T) {
    handler := ❶http.TimeoutHandler(
        http.HandlerFunc(func(w http.ResponseWriter, r *http.Request) {
            w.WriteHeader(http.StatusNoContent)
          ❷time.Sleep(time.Minute)
        }),
        time.Second,
        "Timed out while reading response",
    )

    r := httptest.NewRequest(http.MethodGet, "http://test/", nil)
    w := httptest.NewRecorder()
```

```
    handler.ServeHTTP(w, r)

    resp := w.Result()
    if resp.StatusCode != ❸http.StatusServiceUnavailable {
        t.Fatalf("unexpected status code: %q", resp.Status)
    }

    b, err := ❹ioutil.ReadAll(resp.Body)
    if err != nil {
        t.Fatal(err)
    }
    _ = resp.Body.Close()

❺  if actual := string(b); actual != "Timed out while reading response" {
        t.Logf("unexpected body: %q", actual)
    }
}
```

*Listing 9-12: Giving clients a finite time to read the response (middleware/timeout_test.go)*

Despite its name, `http.TimeoutHandler` is middleware that accepts an `http.Handler` and returns an `http.Handler` ❶. The wrapped `http.Handler` purposefully sleeps for a minute ❷ to simulate a client's taking its time to read the response, preventing the `http.Handler` from returning. When the handler doesn't return within one second, `http.TimeoutHandler` sets the response status code to 503 Service Unavailable ❸. The test reads the entire response body ❹, properly closes it, and makes sure the response body has the string written by the middleware ❺.

## Protecting Sensitive Files

Middleware can also keep clients from accessing information you'd like to keep private. For example, the `http.FileServer` function simplifies the process of serving static files to clients, accepting an `http.FileSystem` interface, and returning an `http.Handler`. The problem is, it won't protect against serving up potentially sensitive files. Any file in the target directory is fair game. By convention, many operating systems store configuration files or other sensitive information in files and directories prefixed with a period and then hide these dot-prefixed files and directories by default. (This is particularly true in Unix-compatible systems.) But the `http.FileServer` will gladly serve dot-prefixed files or traverse dot-prefixed directories.

The net/http package documentation includes an example of an `http` `.FileSystem` that prevents the `http.FileServer` from serving dot-prefixed files and directories. Listing 9-13 takes a different approach by using middleware to offer the same protection.

```
package middleware

import (
    "net/http"
    "path"
```

```
    "strings"
)

func RestrictPrefix(prefix string, next http.Handler) http.Handler {
    return ❶http.HandlerFunc(
        func(w http.ResponseWriter, r *http.Request) {
          ❷ for _, p := range strings.Split(path.Clean(r.URL.Path), "/") {
                if strings.HasPrefix(p, prefix) {
                  ❸ http.Error(w, "Not Found", http.StatusNotFound)
                    return
                }
            }
            next.ServeHTTP(w, r)
        },
    )
}
```

*Listing 9-13: Protecting any file or directory with a given prefix (middleware/ restrict_prefix.go).*

The RestrictPrefix middleware ❶ examines the URL path ❷ to look for any elements that start with a given prefix. If the middleware finds an element in the URL path with the given prefix, it preempts the http.Handler and responds with a 404 Not Found status ❸.

Listing 9-14 uses the RestrictPrefix middleware with a series of test cases.

```
package middleware

import (
    "net/http"
    "net/http/httptest"
    "testing"
)

func TestRestrictPrefix(t *testing.T) {
    handler := ❶http.StripPrefix("/static/",
        ❷RestrictPrefix(".", ❸http.FileServer(http.Dir("../files/"))),
    )

    testCases := []struct {
        path string
        code int
    }{
      ❹{"http://test/static/sage.svg", http.StatusOK},
        {"http://test/static/.secret", http.StatusNotFound},
        {"http://test/static/.dir/secret", http.StatusNotFound},
    }

    for i, c := range testCases {
        r := httptest.NewRequest(http.MethodGet, c.path, nil)
        w := httptest.NewRecorder()
        handler.ServeHTTP(w, r)
```

```
        actual := w.Result().StatusCode
        if c.code != actual {
            t.Errorf("%d: expected %d; actual %d", i, c.code, actual)
        }
    }
}
```

*Listing 9-14: Using the* RestrictPrefix *middleware (middleware/restrict_prefix_test.go)*

It's important to realize the server first passes the request to the http.StripPrefix middleware ❶, then the RestrictPrefix middleware ❷, and if the RestrictPrefix middleware approves the resource path, the http.FileServer ❸. The RestrictPrefix middleware evaluates the request's resource path to determine whether the client is requesting a restricted path, no matter whether the path exists or not. If so, the RestrictPrefix middleware responds to the client with an error without ever passing the request onto the http.FileServer.

The static files served by this test's http.FileServer exist in a directory named *files* in the *restrict_prefix_test.go* file's parent directory. Files in the *../files* directory are in the root of the filesystem passed to the http.FileServer. For example, the *../files/sage.svg* file on the operating system's filesystem is at */sage.svg* in the http.FileSystem passed to the http.FileServer. If a client wanted to retrieve the *sage.svg* file from the http.FileServer, the request path should be */sage.svg*.

But the URL path for each of our test cases ❹ includes the */static/* prefix followed by the static filename. This means that the test requests *static/ sage.svg* from the http.FileServer, which doesn't exist. The test uses another bit of middleware from the net/http package to solve this path discrepancy. The http.StripPrefix middleware strips the given prefix from the URL path before passing along the request to the http.Handler, the http.FileServer in this test.

Next, you block access to sensitive files by wrapping the http.FileServer with the RestrictPrefix middleware to prevent the handler from serving any file or directory prefixed with a period. The first test case results in a 200 OK status, because no element in the URL path has a period prefix. The http.StripPrefix middleware removes the */static/* prefix from the test case's URL, changing it from */static/sage.svg* to *sage.svg*. It then passes this path to the http.FileServer, which finds the corresponding file in its http .FileSystem. The http.FileServer writes the file contents to the response body.

The second test case results in a 404 Not Found status because the *.secret* filename has a period as its first character. The third case also results in a 404 Not Found status due to the *.dir* element in the URL path, because your RestrictPrefix middleware considers the prefix of each segment in the path, not just the file.

A better approach to restricting access to resources would be to block all resources by default and explicitly allow select resources. As an exercise, try implementing the inverse of the RestrictPrefix middleware by creating middleware that permits requests for only an allowed list of resources.

# Multiplexers

One afternoon, I walked into the University of Michigan's library, the fourth largest library in the United States. I was looking for a well-worn copy of Kurt Vonnegut's *Cat's Cradle* and had no idea where to start my search. I found the nearest librarian and asked for help finding the book. When we arrived at the correct location, the book was 404 Not Found.

A *multiplexer*, like the friendly librarian routing me to the proper bookshelf, is a general handler that routes a request to a specific handler. The http.ServeMux multiplexer is an http.Handler that routes an incoming request to the proper handler for the requested resource. By default, http.ServeMux responds with a 404 Not Found status for all incoming requests, but you can use it to register your own patterns and corresponding handlers. It will then compare the request's URL path with its registered patterns, passing the request and response writer to the handler that corresponds to the longest matching pattern.

Listing 9-1 used a multiplexer to send all requests to a single endpoint. Listing 9-15 introduces a slightly more complex multiplexer that has three endpoints. This one evaluates the requested resource and routes the request to the right endpoint.

```
package main

import (
    "fmt"
    "io"
    "io/ioutil"
    "net/http"
    "net/http/httptest"
    "testing"
)

❶ func drainAndClose(next http.Handler) http.Handler {
    return http.HandlerFunc(
        func(w http.ResponseWriter, r *http.Request) {
          ❷ next.ServeHTTP(w, r)
            _, _ = io.Copy(ioutil.Discard, r.Body)
            _ = r.Body.Close()
        },
    )
}

func TestSimpleMux(t *testing.T) {
    serveMux := http.NewServeMux()
  ❸ serveMux.HandleFunc("/", func(w http.ResponseWriter, r *http.Request) {
        w.WriteHeader(http.StatusNoContent)
    })
    serveMux.HandleFunc(❹"/hello", func(w http.ResponseWriter,
        r *http.Request) {
        _, _ = fmt.Fprint(w, "Hello friend.")
    })
    serveMux.HandleFunc(❺"/hello/there/", func(w http.ResponseWriter,
```

```
        r *http.Request) {
        _, _ = fmt.Fprint(w, "Why, hello there.")
    })
    mux := drainAndClose(serveMux)
```

*Listing 9-15: Registering patterns to a multiplexer and wrapping the entire multiplexer with middleware (mux_test.go).*

The test creates a new multiplexer and registers three routes using the multiplexer's HandleFunc method ❸. The first route is simply a forward slash, showing the default or empty URL path, and a function that sets the 204 No Content status in the response. This route will match all URL paths if no other route matches. The second is */hello* ❹, which writes the string Hello friend. to the response. The final path is */hello/there/* ❺, which writes the string Why, hello there. to the response.

Notice that the third route ends in a forward slash, making it a subtree, while the earlier route ❹ did not end in a forward slash, making it an absolute path. This distinction tends to be a bit confusing for unaccustomed users. Go's multiplexer treats absolute paths as exact matches: either the request's URL path matches, or it doesn't. By contrast, it treats subtrees as prefix matches. In other words, the multiplexer will look for the longest registered pattern that comes at the beginning of the request's URL path. For example, */hello/there/* is a prefix of */hello/there/you* but not of */hello/you*.

Go's multiplexer can also redirect a URL path that doesn't end in a forward slash, such as */hello/there*. In those cases, the http.ServeMux first attempts to find a matching absolute path. If that fails, the multiplexer appends a forward slash, making the path */hello/there/*, for example, and responds to the client with it. This new path becomes a permanent redirect. You'll see an example of this in Listing 9-16.

Now that you've defined routes for the multiplexer, it's ready to use. But there's one issue with the handlers: none of them drain and close the request body. This isn't a big concern in a test like this, but you should stick to best practices, nonetheless. If you don't do so in a real scenario, you may cause increased overhead and potential memory leaks. Here, you use middleware ❶ to drain and close the request body. In the drainAndClose middleware, you call the next handler first ❷ and then drain and close the request body. There is no harm in draining and closing a previously drained and closed request body.

Listing 9-16 tests a series of requests against Listing 9-15's multiplexer.

```
--snip--

    testCases := []struct {
        path     string
        response string
        code     int
    }{
 ❶   {"http://test/", "", http.StatusNoContent},
      {"http://test/hello", "Hello friend.", http.StatusOK},
      {"http://test/hello/there/", "Why, hello there.", http.StatusOK},
 ❷   {"http://test/hello/there",
```

```
               "<a href=\"/hello/there/\">Moved Permanently</a>.\n\n",
               http.StatusMovedPermanently},
  ❸ {"http://test/hello/there/you", "Why, hello there.", http.StatusOK},
  ❹ {"http://test/hello/and/goodbye", "", http.StatusNoContent},
     {"http://test/something/else/entirely", "", http.StatusNoContent},
     {"http://test/hello/you", "", http.StatusNoContent},
    }

    for i, c := range testCases {
        r := httptest.NewRequest(http.MethodGet, c.path, nil)
        w := httptest.NewRecorder()
        mux.ServeHTTP(w, r)
        resp := w.Result()

        if actual := resp.StatusCode; c.code != actual {
            t.Errorf("%d: expected code %d; actual %d", i, c.code, actual)
        }

        b, err := ❺ioutil.ReadAll(resp.Body)
        if err != nil {
            t.Fatal(err)
        }
        _ = ❻resp.Body.Close()

        if actual := string(b); c.response != actual {
            t.Errorf("%d: expected response %q; actual %q", i,
                c.response, actual)
        }
    }
}
```

*Listing 9-16: Running through a series of test cases and verifying the response status code and body (mux_test.go).*

The first three test cases ❶, including the request for the */hello/there/* path, match exact patterns registered with the multiplexer. But the fourth test case ❷ is different. It doesn't have an exact match. When the multiplexer appends a forward slash to it, however, it discovers that it exactly matches a registered pattern. Therefore, the multiplexer responds with a 301 Moved Permanently status and a link to the new path in the response body. The fifth test case ❸ matches the */hello/there/* subtree and receives the Why, hello there. response. The last three test cases ❹ match the default path of / and receive the 204 No Content status.

Just as the test relies on middleware to drain and close the request body, it drains ❺ and closes ❻ the response body.

## HTTP/2 Server Pushes

The Go HTTP server can push resources to clients over HTTP/2, a feature that has the potential to improve efficiency. For example, a client may request the home page from a web server, but the client won't know it needs the associated style sheet and images to properly render the home page until it receives the HTML in the response. An HTTP/2 server can proactively send the style sheet and images along with the HTML in the response, saving the client from having to make subsequent calls for those resources. But server pushes have the potential for abuse. This section shows you how to use server pushes and then discusses cases when you should avoid doing so.

## Pushing Resources to the Client

Let's retrieve the HTML page in Listing 9-17 over HTTP/1.1, then retrieve the same page over HTTP/2 and compare the differences.

```
<!DOCTYPE html>
<html lang="en">
<head>
    <meta charset="UTF-8">
    <title>H2 Server Push</title>
 ❶ <link href="/static/style.css" rel="stylesheet">
</head>
<body>
    ❷ <img src="/static/hiking.svg" alt="hiking gopher">
</body>
</html>
```

Listing 9-17: Simple index file having links to two resources (files/index.html)

This HTML file requires the browser to retrieve two more resources, a style sheet ❶ and an SVG image ❷, to properly show the entire page. Figure 9-2 shows Google Chrome's request accounting for the HTML when served using HTTP/1.1.

| Name | Status | Type | Initiator | Size | Time | Waterfall |
|---|---|---|---|---|---|---|
| localhost | 200 | document | Other | 434 B | 315 ... | |
| style.css | 200 | stylesheet | (index) | 390 B | 3 ms | |
| hiking.svg | 200 | svg+xml | (index) | 93.3 KB | 3 ms | |
| favicon.ico | 200 | text/html | Other | 434 B | 2 ms | |

Figure 9-2: Downloaded index page and associated resources over HTTP/1.1

Aside from the *favicon.ico* file, which Chrome retrieves on its own, the browser made three requests to retrieve all required resources—one for the HTML file, one for the style sheet, and one for the SVG image. Any web browser requesting the *index.html* file (*localhost* in Figure 9-2) will also request the *style.css* and *hiking.svg* files to properly render the *index.html* file. The web server could improve efficiency and proactively push these two files to the web browser, since it knows the web browser will inevitably request them. This proactive approach by the web server would save the web browser from the overhead of having to make two more requests.

Figure 9-3 shows the same retrieval using HTTP/2. In this case, the server pushes the *style.css* and *hiking.svg* files.

| Name | Status | Type | Initiator | Size | Time | Waterfall |
|------|--------|------|-----------|------|------|-----------|
| localhost | 200 | document | Other | 296 B | 7 ms | □▮ |
| style.css | 200 | stylesheet | Push / (index) | 230 B | 2 ms | |
| hiking.svg | 200 | svg+xml | Push / (index) | 93.2 KB | 2 ms | |
| favicon.ico | 200 | text/html | Other | 307 B | 3 ms | |

*Figure 9-3: Downloaded index page with resources pushed by the server side*

The client receives all three resources after a single request to the server for the *index.html* file. The Initiator column in Figure 9-3 shows that Chrome retrieved the resources from its dedicated push cache.

Let's write a command line executable that can push resources to clients. Listing 9-18 shows the first part of the program.

```
package main

import (
    "context"
    "flag"
    "log"
    "net/http"
    "os"
    "os/signal"
    "path/filepath"
    "time"

    "github.com/awoodbeck/gnp/ch09/handlers"
    "github.com/awoodbeck/gnp/ch09/middleware"
)

var (
    addr  = flag.String("listen", "127.0.0.1:8080", "listen address")
❶   cert  = flag.String("cert", "", "certificate")
❷   pkey  = flag.String("key", "", "private key")
    files = flag.String("files", "./files", "static file directory")
)

func main() {
    flag.Parse()

    err := ❸run(*addr, *files, *cert, *pkey)
    if err != nil {
        log.Fatal(err)
    }

    log.Println("Server gracefully shutdown")
}
```

*Listing 9-18: Command line arguments for the HTTP/2 server (server.go)*

The server needs the path to a certificate ❶ and a corresponding private key ❷ to enable TLS support and allow clients to negotiate HTTP/2 with the server. If either value is empty, the server will listen for plain HTTP connections. Next, pass the command line flag values to a run function ❸.

The run function, defined in Listing 9-19, has the bulk of your server's logic and ultimately runs the web server. Breaking this functionality into a separate function eases unit testing later.

```
--snip--

func run(addr, files, cert, pkey string) error {
    mux := http.NewServeMux()
❶  mux.Handle("/static/",
        http.StripPrefix("/static/",
            middleware.RestrictPrefix(
                ".", http.FileServer(http.Dir(files)),
            ),
        ),
    )
❷  mux.Handle("/",
        handlers.Methods{
            http.MethodGet: http.HandlerFunc(
                func(w http.ResponseWriter, r *http.Request) {
❸                  if pusher, ok := w.(http.Pusher); ok {
                        targets := []string{
❹                          "/static/style.css",
                            "/static/hiking.svg",
                        }
                        for _, target := range targets {
                            if err := ❺pusher.Push(target, nil); err != nil {
                                log.Printf("%s push failed: %v", target, err)
                            }
                        }
                    }

❻                  http.ServeFile(w, r, filepath.Join(files, "index.html"))
                },
            ),
        },
    )
❼  mux.Handle("/2",
        handlers.Methods{
            http.MethodGet: http.HandlerFunc(
                func(w http.ResponseWriter, r *http.Request) {
                    http.ServeFile(w, r, filepath.Join(files, "index2.html"))
                },
            ),
        },
    )
```

*Listing 9-19: Multiplexer, middleware, and handlers for the HTTP/2 server (server.go)*

The server's multiplexer has three routes: one for static files ❶, one for the default route ❷, and one for the /2 absolute path ❼. If the http .ResponseWriter is an http.Pusher ❸, it can push resources to the client ❺ without a corresponding request. You specify the path to the resource from the client's perspective ❹, not the file path on the server's filesystem because the server treats the request as if the client originated it to facilitate the server push. After you've pushed the resources, you serve the response for the handler ❻. If, instead, you sent the *index.html* file before pushing the associated resources, the client's browser may send requests for the associated resources before it handles the pushes.

Web browsers cache HTTP/2-pushed resources for the life of the connection and make it available across routes. Therefore, if the *index2.html* file served by the /2 route ❼ references the same resources pushed by the default route, and the client first visits the default route, the client's web browser may use the pushed resources when rendering the /2 route.

You have one more task to complete: instantiate an HTTP server to serve your resources. Listing 9-20 does this by making use of the multiplexer.

```
--snip--

srv := &http.Server{
        Addr:              addr,
        Handler:           mux,
        IdleTimeout:       time.Minute,
        ReadHeaderTimeout: 30 * time.Second,
}

done := make(chan struct{})
go func() {
        c := make(chan os.Signal, 1)
        signal.Notify(c, os.Interrupt)

        for {
        ❶    if <-c == os.Interrupt {
                ❷    if err := srv.Shutdown(context.Background()); err != nil {
                            log.Printf("shutdown: %v", err)
                    }
                    close(done)
                    return
            }
        }
}()

log.Printf("Serving files in %q over %s\n", files, srv.Addr)

var err error
if cert != "" && pkey != "" {
        log.Println("TLS enabled")
    ❸    err = srv.ListenAndServeTLS(cert, pkey)
```

```
    } else {
❹     err = srv.ListenAndServe()
    }

    if err == http.ErrServerClosed {
        err = nil
    }

    <-done

    return err
}
```

*Listing 9-20: HTTP/2-capable server implementation (server.go)*

When the server receives an os.Interrupt signal ❶, it triggers a call to the server's Shutdown method ❷. Unlike the server's Close method, which abruptly closes the server's listener and all active connections, Shutdown gracefully shuts down the server. It instructs the server to stop listening for incoming connections and blocks until all client connections end. This gives the server the opportunity to finish sending responses before stopping the server.

If the server receives a path to both a certificate and a corresponding private key, the server will enable TLS support by calling its ListenAndServeTLS method ❸. If it cannot find or parse either the certificate or private key, this method returns an error. In the absence of these paths, the server uses its ListenAndServe method ❹.

Go ahead and test this server. As mentioned in Chapter 8, Go doesn't include the support needed to test the server's push functionality with code, but you can interact with this program by using your web browser.

### Don't Be Too Pushy

Although HTTP/2 server pushing can improve the efficiency of your communications, it can do just the opposite if you aren't careful. Remember that web browsers store pushed resources in a separate cache for the lifetime of the connection. If you're serving resources that don't change often, the web browser will likely already have them in its regular cache, so you shouldn't push them. Once it caches them, the browser can use them for future requests spanning many connections. You probably shouldn't push the resources in Listing 9-19, for instance, because they're unlikely to change often.

My advice is to be conservative with server pushes. Use your handlers and rely on metrics to figure out when you should push a resource. If you do push resources, do so before writing the response.

# What You've Learned

Go's net/http package includes a capable server implementation. In this chapter, you used its handlers, middleware, multiplexer, and HTTP/2 support to process client requests intelligently and efficiently.

Go's http.Handler is an interface that describes an object capable of accepting a request and responding with a status code and payload. A special handler, known as a *multiplexer*, can parse a request and pass it along to the most proper handler, effectively functioning as a request router. *Middleware* is code that augments the behavior of handlers or performs auxiliary tasks. It might change the request, add headers to the response, collect metrics, or preempt the handler, to name a few use cases. Finally, Go's server supports HTTP/2 over TLS. When it uses HTTP/2, the server can push resources to clients, potentially making the communication more efficient.

By putting these features together, you can build comprehensive, useful HTTP-based applications with surprisingly little code.

# 10

## CADDY: A CONTEMPORARY WEB SERVER

Chapter 9 focused on the web service building blocks available to you in Go's standard library. You learned how to create a simple web server with relatively little code by using handlers, middleware, and multiplexers. Although you can build a capable web server with those tools alone, writing your own server from scratch may not always be the quickest approach. Adding support for logging, metrics, authentication, access control, and encryption, to name a few features, can be daunting and hard to get right. Instead, you may find it more convenient to use an existing, comprehensive web server to host your web services.

This chapter will introduce you to the Caddy web server and show you how to focus your time on writing web services while relying on Caddy to serve your application. You'll get Caddy up and running and then take a dive into its real-time configuration API. Next, you'll learn how to extend Caddy's functionality by using custom modules and configuration adapters. You'll then use Caddy to serve your application's static files and proxy requests to your web services. Finally, you'll learn about Caddy's automatic TLS support by using free certificates from Let's Encrypt and automated key management.

After reading this chapter, you should feel comfortable choosing the best solution for your web applications: either a simple net/http-based web server or a comprehensive solution like Caddy.

# What Is Caddy?

*Caddy* is a contemporary web server that focuses on security, performance, and ease of use. Among its hallmark features, it offers automatic TLS certificate management, allowing you to easily implement HTTPS. Caddy also takes advantage of Go's concurrency primitives to serve a considerable amount of all web traffic. It's one of the few open source projects with enterprise-grade support.

## Let's Encrypt Integration

*Let's Encrypt* is a nonprofit certificate authority that supplies digital certificates free of charge for the public to facilitate HTTPS communication. Let's Encrypt certificates run on more than half of all websites on the internet, and they're trusted by all popular web browsers. You can retrieve certificates for your website by using Let's Encrypt's automated issuance and renewal protocol, known as *Automated Certificate Management Environment (ACME)*.

Typically, getting a certificate requires three steps: a certificate request, domain validation, and certificate issuance. First, you request a certificate for your domain from Let's Encrypt. Let's Encrypt then confirms your domain to make sure you administer it. Once Let's Encrypt has ensured that you're the domain's rightful owner, it issues you a certificate, which your web server can use for HTTPS support. Each certificate is good for 90 days, though you should renew it every 60 days to prevent service interruption.

Caddy has inherent support for the ACME protocol and will automatically request, validate, and install Let's Encrypt certificates if Caddy can properly derive the domain names it hosts. We'll discuss how best to do this in "Adding Automatic HTTPS" on page 237. Caddy also handles automatic renewals, eliminating the need for you to keep track of certificate expiration dates.

### How Does Caddy Fit into the Equation?

Caddy works just like other popular web servers, such as NGINX and Apache. It's best positioned on the edge of your network, between web clients and your web services, as shown in Figure 10-1.

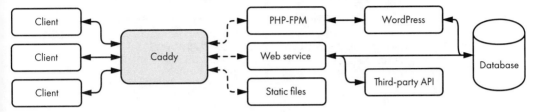

Figure 10-1: Caddy reverse-proxying client requests to web services

Caddy can serve static files and forward requests between clients and backend services, a process known as *reverse proxying*. In this example, you can see Caddy serving a WordPress blog through PHP's FastCGI Process Manager (PHP-FPM), static files, and a Go-based web service. We'll replicate a similar setup later in the chapter, sans WordPress blog.

Caddy helps abstract web services from clients in much the same way we use abstraction in our code. If you use Caddy's automatic TLS, static file server, data compression, access control, and logging features, you won't have to add that functionality to each web service. In addition, using Caddy has the benefit of allowing you to abstract your network topography from clients. As the services increase in popularity and the capacity on web services starts to negatively affect clients, you can add web services to Caddy and instruct Caddy to balance the load among them all, without interruption to your clients.

## Retrieving Caddy

In this chapter, we'll use version 2 of Caddy. You have a few options for installation, described in this section.

### Downloading Caddy

You can install Caddy by using a static binary, built by the Caddy team. This binary is available through the download link at *https://caddyserver.com/*.

Caddy is also available as a Docker image; a DigitalOcean droplet; an Advanced Package Tool (APT) source for Debian derivatives; and in the Fedora Copr build system for use in Fedora, CentOS, or Red Hat Enterprise Linux. You can find details in the Install documentation at *https://caddyserver.com/docs/download*.

### Building Caddy from Source Code

If you do not find a suitable static binary for your operating system and architecture, or if you wish to customize Caddy, you can also compile Caddy from source code.

Caddy relies heavily on Go's support for modules. Therefore, you need to use at least Go 1.14 before running the following commands:

```
$ git clone "https://github.com/caddyserver/caddy.git"
Cloning into 'caddy'...
$ cd caddy/cmd/caddy
$ go build
```

Clone the Caddy Git repository and change to the *caddy/cmd/caddy* subdirectory, where you'll find the main package. Run go build to create a binary named *caddy* in the current directory for your operating system and architecture. To simplify commands, the rest of this chapter assumes that the *caddy* binary is in your PATH.

While you're in this subdirectory, make note of the *main.go* file. You'll revisit it later in this chapter when you learn how to customize Caddy by adding modules.

## Running and Configuring Caddy

For configuration purposes, Caddy exposes an administration endpoint on TCP port 2019, over which you can interact with Caddy's configuration in real time. You can configure Caddy by posting JSON to this endpoint, and you can read the configuration with a GET request. Caddy's full JSON API documentation is available at *https://caddyserver.com/docs/json/*.

Before you can configure Caddy, you need to start it. Running this command starts Caddy as a background process:

```
$ caddy start
2006/01/02 15:04:05.000 INFO    admin   endpoint started
{"address": "tcp/localhost:2019", "enforce_origin": false,
"origins": ["localhost:2019", "[::1]:2019", "127.0.0.1:2019"]}
2006/01/02 15:04:05.000 INFO    serving initial configuration
Successfully started Caddy (pid=24587) - Caddy is running in the background
```

You'll see log entries showing that the admin endpoint started and Caddy is using the initial configuration. You'll also see log entries printed to standard output as you interact with the admin endpoint.

Caddy's configuration is empty by default. Let's send meaningful configuration data to Caddy. Listing 10-1 uses the curl command to post JSON to the load resource on Caddy's admin endpoint.

```
$ curl localhost:2019/load \
❶ -X POST -H "Content-Type: application/json" \
-d '
```

```
{
  "apps": {
    "http": {
      "servers": {
        "hello": {
          "listen": ["localhost:2020"],
      ❷ "routes": [{
            "handle": [{
          ❸ "handler": "static_response",
              "body": "Hello, world!"
          }]
        }]
      }
    }
  }
}
}'
```

*Listing 10-1: Posting configuration to Caddy's admin endpoint*

You send a POST request containing JSON in the request body ❶ to the load resource of the Caddy instance listening on port 2019. The top-level apps namespace lists the applications Caddy will load at runtime. In this case, you're telling Caddy to load the http application. The http application configuration consists of one or more servers. This example sets up a single server named hello listening on localhost port 2020. Feel free to name your server whatever you'd like.

Since the listen value is an array of addresses, you can configure this server to listen to more than one socket address. Caddy passes these address values to net.Listen, just as you did in Chapter 3. You also have the option of specifying a port range, such as *localhost:2020-2025*. Caddy will recognize that you used a range and properly extrapolate the range into separate socket addresses. Caddy allows you to restrict listeners to specific network types by prefixing the socket address. For example, *udp/localhost:2020* tells the server to bind to UDP port 2020 on localhost. The forward slash is not part of the address but rather a separator. If you want the server to bind to a Unix socket */tmp/caddy.sock*, specify the address *unix//tmp/caddy.sock*.

The hello server's routes value ❷ is an array of routes, like the multiplexer from the preceding chapter, which dictates how the server will handle incoming requests. If a route matches the request, Caddy passes the request onto each handler in the handle array. Since handle is an array, you can specify more than one handler per route. Caddy will pass the request to each successive handler in the same way you chained middleware together in the preceding chapter. In this example, you specify a single route to match all requests and add a single handler to this route. You're using the built-in static_response handler ❸, which will write the value of the body (Hello, world! in this example) in the response body.

Provided there are no errors in the configuration, Caddy will at once start using the new configuration. Let's confirm Caddy is now listening on both the administrative port 2019 and your hello server port 2020:

```
$ lsof -Pi :2019-2025
COMMAND   PID USER   FD   TYPE DEVICE SIZE/OFF NODE NAME
caddy   24587 user    3u  IPv4 811511      0t0  TCP localhost:2019 (LISTEN)
caddy   24587 user    9u  IPv4 915742      0t0  TCP localhost:2020 (LISTEN)
```

Looks good. This command won't work on Windows. Instead, you can see similar output by running the netstat -b command in an Administrator command prompt. Now, you can ask Caddy for its configuration by sending a GET request:

```
$ curl localhost:2019/config/
{"apps":{"http":{"servers":{"hello":{"listen":["localhost:2020"],
"routes":[{"handle":[{"body":"Hello, world!","handler":"static_
response"}]}]}}}}}
```

Caddy returns its JSON-formatted configuration in the response body. Note that you need to write the trailing slash on the /config/ resource, because /config/ is the resource prefix under which Caddy exposes its configuration. You are asking Caddy for all resources found under the /config/ prefix. If you accidentally omit the trailing slash, Caddy thinks you're asking for an absolute resource named /config, which doesn't exist in Caddy's admin API on port 2019.

Caddy supports *configuration traversal*. Configuration traversal lets you request a subset of the configuration by treating each JSON key in the configuration data as a resource address. For example, you can request the listen value for the hello server from our example configuration by issuing a GET request, like this:

```
$ curl localhost:2019/config/apps/http/servers/hello/listen
["localhost:2020"]
```

Caddy returns a JSON array containing *localhost:2020,* just as you'd expect. Let's send a GET request to this socket address:

```
$ curl localhost:2020
Hello, world!
```

You see the Hello, world! string returned from the static_response handler.

## Modifying Caddy's Configuration in Real Time

You can use the other HTTP verbs you learned in Chapter 8 to modify your server's configuration. Any changes you make will take immediate effect, so long as Caddy can parse the JSON you send. If Caddy fails to parse the JSON, or if a fundamental error exists in the new configuration, Caddy will log an error with an explanation of what went wrong and continue to use its existing configuration.

Let's say you want to make your hello server listen on port 2021 as well. You can append another listen value by using a POST request and immediately check that the change took effect:

```
$ curl localhost:2019/config/apps/http/servers/hello/listen \
-X POST -H "Content-Type: application/json" -d '"localhost:2021"'
$ lsof -Pi :2019-2025
COMMAND   PID USER    FD   TYPE  DEVICE SIZE/OFF NODE NAME
caddy   24587 user    3u   IPv4  811511      0t0 TCP localhost:2019 (LISTEN)
caddy   24587 user    9u   IPv4  915742      0t0 TCP localhost:2020 (LISTEN)
❶ caddy 24587 user   11u   IPv4 1148212      0t0 TCP localhost:2021 (LISTEN)
```

You can see that Caddy is now listening on port 2021 ❶ in addition to ports 2019 and 2020.

Suppose you want to replace the listening addresses and use a range instead. For that, you can send a PATCH request with the new listen array value you want Caddy to use:

```
$ curl localhost:2019/config/apps/http/servers/hello/listen \
-X PATCH -H "Content-Type: application/json" -d '["localhost:2020-2025"]'
$ lsof -Pi :2019-2025
COMMAND   PID USER    FD   TYPE  DEVICE SIZE/OFF NODE NAME
caddy   24587 user    3u   IPv4  811511      0t0 TCP localhost:2019 (LISTEN)
❶ caddy 24587 user    9u   IPv4  915742      0t0 TCP localhost:2020 (LISTEN)
caddy   24587 user   10u   IPv4 1149557      0t0 TCP localhost:2021 (LISTEN)
caddy   24587 user   11u   IPv4 1166333      0t0 TCP localhost:2022 (LISTEN)
caddy   24587 user   12u   IPv4 1169409      0t0 TCP localhost:2023 (LISTEN)
caddy   24587 user   13u   IPv4 1169413      0t0 TCP localhost:2024 (LISTEN)
❷ caddy 24587 user   14u   IPv4 1169417      0t0 TCP localhost:2025 (LISTEN)
```

In addition to the admin port 2019, Caddy is now listening on ports 2020 ❶ through 2025 ❷.

Although you may not find yourself changing Caddy's configuration on the fly very often, it's a handy feature for development, because it lets you quickly spin up a new server to add functionality. Let's add a new server to Caddy while it's running. You'll name this new server test and configure it to listen on port 2030. Listing 10-2 adds the new test server to Caddy in real time.

```
$ curl localhost:2019/config/apps/http/servers/test \
-X POST -H "Content-Type: application/json" \
-d '{
  "listen": ["localhost:2030"],
  "routes": [{
    "handle": [{
      "handler": "static_response",
      "body": "Welcome to my temporary test server."
    }]
  }]
}'
```

*Listing 10-2: Adding a new server to Caddy in real time*

The name of the new server, test, is part of the resource you POST to. You can think of test as the key and the JSON in the request body as the value, if you defined this server in the original configuration from Listing 10-1. At this point, Caddy has two servers: hello listening on ports 2020 to 2025 and test listening on port 2030. To confirm Caddy is serving test, you can check the new endpoint on port 2030:

```
$ curl localhost:2030
Welcome to my temporary test server.
```

The static_response handler properly responds with the expected message. If you want to remove the test server, it's as simple as issuing a DELETE request:

```
$ curl localhost:2019/config/apps/http/servers/test -X DELETE
```

Here again, you specify the test server in the resource. Caddy is no longer listening on localhost port 2030, and the test server no longer exists. You were able to stand up a new server to handle entirely different requests without interrupting the functionality of your hello server. Changing the configuration in real time opens possibilities. Do you want a server or route to be accessible only certain times of the day? No problem. Do you want to temporarily redirect traffic without having to bounce your entire web server, interrupting existing web traffic? Sure, go ahead.

### Storing the Configuration in a File

We typically provide Caddy with its configuration as part of the startup process. Write the JSON configuration from Listing 10-1 to a file named *caddy.json*. Then start Caddy by using the following command:

```
$ caddy start --config caddy.json
Successfully started Caddy (pid=46112) - Caddy is running in the background
$ curl localhost:2019/config/
{"apps":{"http":{"servers":{"hello":{"listen":["localhost:2020"],
"routes":[{"handle":[{"body":"Hello, world!","handler":"static_
response"}]}]}}}}}
```

Caddy starts in the background, as in Listing 10-1—but this time, it populates its configuration from the *caddy.json* file during initialization.

## Extending Caddy with Modules and Adapters

Caddy uses a modular architecture to organize its functionality. This modular approach allows you to extend Caddy's capabilities by writing your own modules and configuration adapters. In this section, we'll walk through the process of writing a configuration adapter that will allow you to store your Caddy configuration in a Tom's Obvious, Minimal Language (TOML) file. We'll also replicate the restrict_prefix middleware from the preceding chapter in a proper Caddy module.

## Writing a Configuration Adapter

Although JSON is a perfectly good format for configuration files, it isn't as well suited for human consumption as other formats. JSON lacks support for comments and multiline strings, two characteristics that make configuration files easier for people to read. Caddy supports the use of *configuration adapters* that adapt one format, such as TOML, to Caddy's native JSON format. TOML is a configuration file format that is easy for humans to read. It supports both comments and multiline strings. You can find more details at *https://github.com/toml-lang/toml/tree/v0.5.0/*.

Caddy version 1 supported a custom configuration file format named *Caddyfile*, which was also the name of the configuration file by convention. If you want to use Caddyfile with Caddy v2, you must rely on a configuration adapter so Caddy can ingest it. Caddy is smart enough to know it needs to use the caddyfile adapter when you specify a filename that starts with *Caddyfile*. But to specify an adapter from the command line, you explicitly tell Caddy which adapter to use:

```
$ caddy start --config Caddyfile --adapter caddyfile
```

The adapter flag tells Caddy which adapter it should use. Caddy will invoke the adapter to adapt the configuration file to JSON and then parse the JSON returned by the adapter as if you had presented the configuration in JSON format in the first place.

But Caddy doesn't ship with an official configuration adapter for TOML, so let's take a crack at writing one. You need to first create a Go module for your TOML configuration adapter:

```
$ mkdir caddy-toml-adapter
$ cd caddy-toml-adapter
❶ $ go mod init github.com/awoodbeck/caddy-toml-adapter
go: creating new go.mod: module github.com/awoodbeck/caddy-toml-adapter
```

You should use a fully qualified module name ❶ different from the one used here. I created this module on GitHub under my *awoodbeck* account. The fully qualified name for your module will differ depending on where, and under what account, it's hosted.

Now that you've created a module, you can write the code. Create a file in the current directory named *toml.go* and add the code in Listing 10-3.

```
package tomladapter

import (
    "encoding/json"

    "github.com/caddyserver/caddy/v2/caddyconfig"
    "github.com/pelletier/go-toml"
)

func init() {
    caddyconfig.RegisterAdapter(❶"toml", ❷Adapter{})
```

```
}

// Adapter converts a TOML Caddy configuration to JSON.
type Adapter struct{}

// Adapt the TOML body to JSON.
func (a Adapter) Adapt(body []byte, _ map[string]interface{}) (
    []byte, []caddyconfig.Warning, error) {
    tree, err := ❸toml.LoadBytes(body)
    if err != nil {
        return nil, nil, err
    }

    b, err := json.Marshal(❹tree.ToMap())

    return b, nil, err
}
```

*Listing 10-3: Creating a TOML configuration adapter and registering it with Caddy*

You use Thomas Pelletier's *go-toml* library to parse the configuration file contents ❸. This saves a considerable amount of code. You then convert the parsed TOML into a map ❹ and marshal the map to JSON.

The last bit of accounting is to register your configuration adapter with Caddy. For this, you include a call to caddyconfig.RegisterAdapter in the init function and pass it the adapter's type ❶ and an Adapter object ❷ implementing the caddyconfig.Adapter interface. When you import this module from Caddy's *main.go* file, the configuration adapter registers itself with Caddy, adding support for parsing the TOML configuration file. You'll look at a concrete example of importing this module from Caddy in "Injecting Your Module into Caddy" on page 231.

Now that you've created the *toml.go* file, tidy up the module:

```
$ go mod tidy
go: finding module for package github.com/caddyserver/caddy/v2/caddyconfig
go: found github.com/caddyserver/caddy/v2/caddyconfig in
github.com/caddyserver/caddy/v2 v2.0.0
```

This command adds the Caddy dependency to the *go.mod* file. All that's left to do is to publish your module to GitHub, as in this example, or another suitable version-control system supported by go get.

## Writing a Restrict Prefix Middleware Module

Chapter 9 introduced the concept of middleware, a design pattern that allows your code to manipulate a request and a response and to perform ancillary tasks when the server receives a request, such as logging request details. Let's explore how to use middleware with Caddy.

In Go, middleware is a function that accepts an http.Handler and returns an http.Handler:

```
func(http.Handler) http.Handler
```

An http.Handler describes an object with a ServeHTTP method that accepts an http.RequestWriter and an http.Request:

```
type Handler interface {
    ServeHTTP(http.ResponseWriter, *http.Request)
}
```

The handler reads from the request and writes to the response. Assuming myHandler is an object that implements the http.Handler interface, and middleware1, middleware2, and middleware3 all accept an http.Handler and return an http.Handler, you can apply the middleware functions to myHandler in Listing 10-4.

```
h := middleware1(middleware2(middleware3(myHandler)))
```

*Listing 10-4: Multiple middleware functions wrapping a handler*

You can replace any of the middleware functions with the RestrictPrefix middleware you wrote in the preceding chapter, since it's a function that accepts an http.Handler and returns an http.Handler.

Unfortunately for us, Caddy's middleware does not use this design pattern, so it cannot use RestrictPrefix. Caddy includes interfaces for both handlers and middleware, unlike net/http, which describes only handlers. Caddy's equivalent of the http.Handler interface is caddyhttp.Handler:

```
type Handler interface {
    ServeHTTP(http.ResponseWriter, *http.Request) error
}
```

The only difference between caddyhttp.Handler and http.Handler is that the former's ServeHTTP method returns an error interface.

Caddy middleware is a special type of handler that implements the caddyhttp.MiddlewareHandler interface:

```
type MiddlewareHandler interface {
    ServeHTTP(http.ResponseWriter, *http.Request, Handler) error
}
```

Like caddyhttp.Handler, Caddy's middleware accepts both an http .ResponseWriter and an http.Request, and it returns an error interface. But it accepts an additional argument: the caddyhttp.Handler, downstream from the middleware in the same way that myHandler is downstream from middleware3 in Listing 10-4. Instead of accepting an http.Handler and returning an http .Handler, Caddy expects its middleware to act as handlers, with access to the caddyhttp.Handler that should receive the request and response after the middleware is done with them.

Let's create a new Caddy module that replicates the functionality of your RestrictPrefix middleware:

```
$ mkdir caddy-restrict-prefix
$ cd caddy-restrict-prefix
```

```
$ go mod init github.com/awoodbeck/caddy-restrict-prefix
go: creating new go.mod: module github.com/awoodbeck/caddy-restrict-prefix
```

As before, your fully qualified module name will differ from mine.
Create a new file named *restrict_prefix.go* and add the code from Listing 10-5
to the file.

```
package restrictprefix

import (
    "fmt"
    "net/http"
    "strings"

    "github.com/caddyserver/caddy/v2"
    "github.com/caddyserver/caddy/v2/modules/caddyhttp"
    "go.uber.org/zap"
)

func init() {
  ❶ caddy.RegisterModule(RestrictPrefix{})
}

// RestrictPrefix is middleware that restricts requests where any portion
// of the URI matches a given prefix.
type RestrictPrefix struct {
  ❷ Prefix string `json:"prefix,omitempty"`
  ❸ logger *zap.Logger
}

// CaddyModule returns the Caddy module information.
func (RestrictPrefix) ❹ CaddyModule() caddy.ModuleInfo {
    return caddy.ModuleInfo{
      ❺ ID:  "http.handlers.restrict_prefix",
      ❻ New: func() caddy.Module { return new(RestrictPrefix) },
    }
}
```

*Listing 10-5: Defining and registering a new Caddy module*

The RestrictPrefix middleware implementation from the preceding
chapter expected the prefix of a URL path as a string. Here, you're storing the prefix in the RestrictPrefix struct ❷ and assigning it a struct tag
to use the json.Unmarshal behavior of matching incoming keys to struct tags.
The struct tag tells json.Unmarshal which JSON key corresponds to this field.
In this example, you're telling json.Unmarshal that it should take the value
associated with the prefix key in the JSON configuration and assign it to
the struct's Prefix field. The RestrictPrefix struct also has a logger field ❸
so you can log events, as necessary.

Your module needs to register itself with Caddy upon initialization ❶.
The caddy.RegisterModule function accepts any object that implements the
caddy.Module interface. For that, you add the CaddyModule method ❹ to return

information to Caddy about your module. Caddy requires an ID ❺ for each module. Since you're creating an HTTP middleware handler, you'll use the ID `http.handler.restrict_prefix`, where `restrict_prefix` is the unique name of your module. Caddy also expects a function ❻ that can create a new instance of your module.

Now that you can register your module with Caddy, let's add more functionality so you can retrieve the logger from Caddy and validate your module's settings. Listing 10-6 picks up where we left off.

```
--snip--

// Provision a Zap logger to RestrictPrefix.
func (p *RestrictPrefix) ❶Provision(ctx caddy.Context) error {
    p.logger = ❷ctx.Logger(p)
    return nil
}

// Validate the prefix from the module's configuration, setting the
// default prefix "." if necessary.
func (p *RestrictPrefix) ❸Validate() error {
    if p.Prefix == "" {
        p.Prefix = "."
    }
    return nil
}
```

*Listing 10-6: Implementing various Caddy interfaces*

You add the `Provision` method ❶ to your struct. Caddy will recognize that your module implements the `caddy.Provisioner` interface and call this method. You can then retrieve the logger from the given `caddy.Context` ❷. Likewise, Caddy will call your module's `Validate` method ❸ since it implements the `caddy.Validator` interface. You can use this method to make sure all required settings have been unmarshaled from the configuration into your module. If anything goes wrong, you can return an error and Caddy will complain on your behalf. In this example, you're using this method to set the default prefix if one was not provided in the configuration.

You're almost done. The last piece of the puzzle is the middleware implementation itself. Listing 10-7 rounds out your module's implementation by adding support for the `caddyhttp.MiddlewareHandler` interface.

```
--snip--

// ServeHTTP implements the caddyhttp.MiddlewareHandler interface.
func (p RestrictPrefix) ServeHTTP(w http.ResponseWriter, r *http.Request,
    next caddyhttp.Handler) error {
❶ for _, part := range strings.Split(r.URL.Path, "/") {
        if strings.HasPrefix(part, p.Prefix) {
            ❷http.Error(w, "Not Found", http.StatusNotFound)
            if p.logger != nil {
                ❸p.logger.Debug(fmt.Sprintf(
                    "restricted prefix: %q in %s", part, r.URL.Path))
```

```
            }
            return nil
        }
    }
    return ❹next.ServeHTTP(w, r)
}

var (
    ❺ _ caddy.Provisioner            = (*RestrictPrefix)(nil)
      _ caddy.Validator              = (*RestrictPrefix)(nil)
      _ caddyhttp.MiddlewareHandler = (*RestrictPrefix)(nil)
)
```

Listing 10-7: Implementing the `MiddlewareHandler` interface

The logic is almost identical to the middleware from the preceding
chapter. You loop through the URL path components, checking each one
for the prefix ❶. If you find a match, you respond with a 404 Not Found
status ❷ and log the occurrence for debugging purposes ❸. If everything
checks out, you pass control onto the next handler in the chain ❹.

It's a good practice to guard against interface changes by explicitly
making sure your module implements the expected interfaces ❺. If one of
these interfaces happens to change in the future (for example, if you add a
new method), these interface guards will cause compilation to fail, giving
you an early warning that you need to adapt your code.

The final steps are to tidy up your module's dependencies and publish it:

```
$ go mod tidy
go: finding module for package github.com/caddyserver/caddy/v2
go: finding module for package github.com/caddyserver/caddy/v2/modules/
caddyhttp
go: finding module for package go.uber.org/zap
go: found github.com/caddyserver/caddy/v2 in github.com/caddyserver/caddy/v2
v2.0.0
go: found go.uber.org/zap in go.uber.org/zap v1.15.0
go: downloading github.com/golang/mock v1.4.1
go: downloading github.com/onsi/gomega v1.8.1
go: downloading github.com/smallstep/assert v0.0.0-20200103212524-b99dc1097b15
go: downloading github.com/onsi/ginkgo v1.11.0
go: downloading github.com/imdario/mergo v0.3.7
go: downloading github.com/chzyer/test v0.0.0-20180213035817-a1ea475d72b1
go: downloading github.com/golang/glog v0.0.0-20160126235308-23def4e6c14b
go: downloading github.com/alangpierce/go-forceexport v0.0.0-20160317203124-
8f1d6941cd75
go: downloading github.com/chzyer/logex v1.1.10
go: downloading github.com/hpcloud/tail v1.0.0
go: downloading gopkg.in/tomb.v1 v1.0.0-20141024135613-dd632973f1e7
go: downloading gopkg.in/fsnotify.v1 v1.4.7
```

Publish your module to GitHub or a similar version-control system supported by go get.

## Injecting Your Module into Caddy

The module and adapter you wrote are both self-registering. All you need to do to include their functionality in Caddy is to import them at build time. To do that, you need to compile Caddy from source. Start by making a directory for your build:

```
$ mkdir caddy
$ cd caddy
```

Building Caddy from source code requires a small amount of boilerplate code, to which you'll include your modules. Your modules register themselves with Caddy as a side effect of the import. Create a new file named *main.go* and add the code from Listing 10-8 into it.

```
package main

import (
❶ cmd "github.com/caddyserver/caddy/v2/cmd"
❷ _ "github.com/caddyserver/caddy/v2/modules/standard"

    // Injecting custom modules into Caddy
❸ _ "github.com/awoodbeck/caddy-restrict-prefix"
❹ _ "github.com/awoodbeck/caddy-toml-adapter"
)

func main() {
    cmd.Main()
}
```

*Listing 10-8: Injecting custom modules into Caddy*

First, you import the Caddy command module ❶ into your build. This has the Main function that starts the caddy server. Then, you import the standard modules ❷ that you'll find in Caddy's binary distribution. Finally, you include your restrict prefix module ❸ and your TOML configuration adapter ❹.

All that's left to do now is initialize the caddy module and build it:

```
$ go mod init caddy
$ go build
```

At this point, you should have a binary named caddy in the current directory. You can verify that it has your custom imports by looking for them in the caddy binary's list of modules. The following command is specific to Linux and macOS:

```
$ ./caddy list-modules | grep "toml\|restrict_prefix"
caddy.adapters.toml
http.handlers.restrict_prefix
```

For my Windows friends, run this command instead:

```
> caddy list-modules | findstr "toml restrict_prefix"
caddy.adapters.toml
http.handlers.restrict_prefix
```

The caddy binary you built can read its configuration from TOML files and deny clients access to resources whose path includes a given prefix.

## Reverse-Proxying Requests to a Backend Web Service

You now have all the building blocks to create something meaningful in Caddy. Let's put everything you've learned together by configuring Caddy to reverse-proxy requests to a backend web service and serve up static files on behalf of the backend web service. You'll create two endpoints in Caddy. The first endpoint will serve up only static content from Caddy's file server, showing Caddy's static file-serving abilities. The second endpoint will reverse-proxy requests to a backend web service. This backend service will send the client HTML that will prompt the client to retrieve static files from Caddy, which will show how your web services can lean on Caddy to serve static content on their behalf.

Before you start building, you need to set up the proper directory structure. If you're following along, you're currently in the *caddy* directory, which has a caddy binary built from the code in Listing 10-8. Create two subdirectories, *files* and *backend*:

```
$ mkdir files backend
```

You can retrieve the contents of the *files* subdirectory from *https://github .com/awoodbeck/gnp/tree/master/ch10/files/*. The *backend* subdirectory will store a simple backend service created in the next section.

### Creating a Simple Backend Web Service

You need a backend web service for Caddy to reverse-proxy requests to, as illustrated in Figure 10-1. This service will respond to all requests with an HTML document that includes the static files Caddy serves on the service's behalf.

Listing 10-9 is the initial code for the backend web service.

```
package main

import (
    "flag"
    "fmt"
    "log"
    "net/http"
    "os"
    "os/signal"
    "time"
)
```

```
var addr = flag.String("listen", ❶"localhost:8080", "listen address")

func main() {
    flag.Parse()

    c := make(chan os.Signal, 1)
    signal.Notify(c, os.Interrupt)

    err := ❷run(*addr, c)
    if err != nil {
        log.Fatal(err)
    }

    log.Println("Server stopped")
}
```

*Listing 10-9: Creating a backend service (backend/main.go)*

This bit of code should be familiar since it's a simplified version of what you wrote in the preceding chapter. You're setting up a web service that listens on port 8080 of localhost ❶. Caddy will direct requests to this socket address. Listing 10-10 implements the run function ❷.

```
--snip--

func run(addr string, c chan os.Signal) error {
    mux := http.NewServeMux()
    mux.Handle("/",
        http.HandlerFunc(func(w http.ResponseWriter, r *http.Request) {
            clientAddr := r.Header.Get(❶"X-Forwarded-For")
            log.Printf("%s -> %s -> %s", clientAddr, r.RemoteAddr, r.URL)
            _, _ = w.Write(❷index)
        }),
    )

    srv := &http.Server{
        Addr:              addr,
        Handler:           mux,
        IdleTimeout:       time.Minute,
        ReadHeaderTimeout: 30 * time.Second,
    }

    go func() {
        for {
            if <-c == os.Interrupt {
                _ = srv.Close()
                return
            }
        }
    }()

    fmt.Printf("Listening on %s ...\n", srv.Addr)
    err := srv.ListenAndServe()
```

```
        if err == http.ErrServerClosed {
            err = nil
        }

        return err
}
```

*Listing 10-10: The main logic of the backend service (backend/main.go)*

The web service receives all requests from Caddy, no matter which client originated the request. Likewise, it sends all responses back to Caddy, which then routes the response to the right client. Conveniently, Caddy adds an X-Forwarded-For header ❶ to each request with the originating client's IP address. Although you don't do anything other than log this information, your backend service could use this IP address to differentiate between client requests. The service could deny requests based on client IP address, for example.

The handler writes a slice of bytes ❷ to the response that has HTML defined in Listing 10-11.

```
--snip--

var index = []byte(`<!DOCTYPE html>
<html lang="en">
<head>
    <meta charset="UTF-8">
    <title>Caddy Backend Test</title>
    <link href=❶"/style.css" rel="stylesheet">
</head>
<body>
    <p><img src=❷"/hiking.svg" alt="hiking gopher"></p>
</body>
</html>`)
```

*Listing 10-11: The index HTML served by the backend service (backend/main.go)*

The /style.css ❶ and /hiking.svg ❷ resources do not include a full URL (such as *http://localhost:2020/style.css*) because the backend web service does not know anything about Caddy or how clients access Caddy. When you exclude the scheme, hostname, and port number in the resource address, the client's web browser should encounter /style.css in the HTML and prepend the scheme, hostname, and port number it used for the initial request before sending the request to Caddy. For that all to work, you need to configure Caddy in the next section to send some requests to the backend web service and serve static files for the rest of the requests.

## Setting Up Caddy's Configuration

As mentioned earlier in the chapter, Caddy uses JSON as its native configuration format. You could certainly write your configuration in JSON, but you've already written a perfectly good configuration adapter that allows you to use TOML, so you'll implement that instead.

You want to configure Caddy to reverse-proxy requests to your back-end web service and serve static files from the *files* subdirectory. You'll need two routes: one to the backend web service and one for static files. Let's start by defining your server configuration in a file named *caddy.toml* (Listing 10-12).

❶ [apps.http.servers.test_server]
listen = [
    'localhost:2020',
]

*Listing 10-12: Caddy test server configuration (caddy.toml)*

Your TOML adapter directly converts TOML to JSON. Therefore, you need to make sure you're using the same namespaces Caddy expects. The namespace for your server is apps.http.servers.test_server ❶. (For simplicity, you'll refer to this namespace simply as test_server from here on out.) It listens for incoming connections on port 2020 of localhost.

## Adding a Reverse-Proxy to Your Service

Caddy includes a powerful reverse-proxy handler that makes quick work of sending incoming requests to your backend web service. Just as in the server implementation in the preceding chapter, Caddy matches an incoming request to a route and then passes the request onto the associated handler.

Listing 10-13 adds a route and a reverse-proxy handler to the *caddy.toml* file.

```
--snip--

❶ [[apps.http.servers.test_server.routes]]
❷ [[apps.http.servers.test_server.routes.match]]
path = [
    '/backend',
  ❸ '/backend/*',
]
❹ [[apps.http.servers.test_server.routes.handle]]
handler = 'reverse_proxy'
❺ [[apps.http.servers.test_server.routes.handle.upstreams]]
dial = ❻'localhost:8080'
```

*Listing 10-13: Adding a reverse proxy to the backend service (caddy.toml)*

The test_server configuration includes a routes array ❶, and each route in the array has zero or more matchers ❷. A *matcher* is a special module that allows you to specify matching criteria for incoming requests, like the http .ServeMux.Handle method's pattern matching discussed in the preceding chapter. Caddy includes matcher modules that allow you to consider each part of a request.

For this route, you add a single matcher that matches any request for the absolute path */backend* or any path starting with */backend/* ❸. The * character is a wildcard that tells Caddy you want to match on the */backend/* prefix. For example, a request for the resource */backend/this/is/a/test* will also match.

The route may have one or more handlers **❹**. Here, you tell Caddy you want to send all matching requests to the reverse-proxy handler. The reverse-proxy handler needs to know where to send the requests. You specify an upstream entry **❺** with its dial property set to the backend server's socket address **❻**.

## Serving Static Files

You relied on the http.FileServer to serve static files for you in the preceding chapter. Caddy exposes similar functionality with its file_server handler. Listing 10-14 adds a second route to your *caddy.toml* file for serving static files.

```
--snip--
❶ [[apps.http.servers.test_server.routes]]
❷ [[apps.http.servers.test_server.routes.handle]]
handler = 'restrict_prefix'
prefix = '.'
❸ [[apps.http.servers.test_server.routes.handle]]
handler = 'file_server'
root = ❹'./files'
index_names = [
  ❺'index.html',
]
```

*Listing 10-14: Adding a default route to serve static files (caddy.toml)*

Unlike the route you added in Listing 10-13, this route **❶** does not include any matchers. As such, Caddy would send every request to this route's handler if the request didn't match previous routes. In other words, this route is your default route, and so its position in the file matters. If you moved this route before the reverse-proxy route, all requests would match it, and no requests would ever make their way to the reverse proxy. Whenever you specify a route with no matches, make sure you put it at the end of your routes array, as you do here.

As with the file server in the preceding chapter, you want to protect against accidentally serving sensitive files prefixed with a period. Therefore, you include your restrict_prefix middleware **❷** in the array of handlers before the file_server handler **❸**. You add more configuration options to serve files found in the *files* subdirectory **❹** and return the *index.html* file **❺** if the request didn't specify a file.

## Checking Your Work

Everything is in place. Start Caddy and verify that your configuration works as expected. Since some of the static files are images, I recommend you use a web browser to interact with Caddy while it runs on your computer.

Start Caddy by using the *caddy.toml* file and the *toml* adapter:

```
$ ./caddy start --config caddy.toml --adapter toml
```

On Windows, the command looks like this:

```
> caddy start --config caddy.toml --adapter toml
```

Now, run the backend web service:

```
$ cd backend
$ go run backend.go
Listening on localhost:8080 ...
```

Open your web browser and visit *http://localhost:2020/*. Caddy will send your request to the file server handler, which in turn will respond with the *index.html* file, since you didn't indicate a specific file in the request. Your browser then asks Caddy for the *style.css* and *sage.svg* files to finish rendering the page. If everything succeeds, you should now be looking at a sage gopher.

Now, let's test the reverse proxy to the backend web service. Visit *http://localhost:2020/backend*. This request matches the reverse-proxy route's matcher, so the reverse-proxy handler should handle it, sending the request onto the backend service. The backend web service responds with HTML that instructs your browser to retrieve the *style.css* and *hiking.svg* files from Caddy, where the file server handler happily serves them up. You should now be looking at a hiking gopher rendered using HTML from the backend web service and static files from Caddy.

If you copied the *files* subdirectory from this book's source code repository, it should contain *./files/.secret* and *./files/.dir/secret* files. Your middleware should block access to both files. In other words, both *http://localhost:2020/files/.secret* and *http://localhost:2020/files/.dir/secret* will return a 404 Not Found status if you try to request them.

### Adding Automatic HTTPS

Now let's add Caddy's key feature to your web server: automatic HTTPS.

I once used Caddy to stand up a website with full HTTPS support, using certificates trusted by all contemporary web browsers, in a matter of minutes. The server has been rock-solid ever since, happily rotating Let's Encrypt keys every few months with no intervention on my part. This isn't to say I couldn't replicate this functionality in my own Go-based web server; my time was simply best spent building services and leaving the web serving to Caddy. If Caddy lacked any functionality, I could add it as a module.

Caddy automatically enables TLS when it can determine what domain names you've configured it to serve. The *caddy.toml* configuration created in this chapter didn't give Caddy enough information to determine which domain it was serving. Therefore, Caddy didn't enable HTTPS for you. You told Caddy to bind to localhost, but that tells Caddy only what it's listening to, not what domains it's serving.

The most common way to enable automatic HTTPS is by adding a host matcher to one of Caddy's routes. Here's an example matcher:

```
[[apps.http.servers.server.routes.match]]
host = [
    'example.com',
]
```

This host matcher supplies enough information for Caddy to determine that it is serving the *example.com* domain. If Caddy doesn't already have a valid certificate for *example.com* to enable HTTPS, it will go through the process of validating the domain with Let's Encrypt and retrieving a certificate. Caddy will manage your certificate, automatically renewing it, as necessary.

Caddy's file-server subcommand tells Caddy you want it to exclusively serve files over HTTP. The file-server's --domain flag is enough information for Caddy to invoke its automatic HTTPS and allow you to serve files over HTTPS as well.

Caddy's reverse-proxy subcommand allows you to put Caddy into a reverse-proxy-only mode, where it will send all incoming requests onto the socket address specified by the --to flag. Caddy will retrieve a TLS certificate and enable automatic HTTPS if you specify a hostname with the --from flag.

I encourage you to read more about Caddy's automatic HTTPS in production environments at *https://caddyserver.com/docs/automatic-https*.

**NOTE** *Caddy defaults to using Let's Encrypt as its certificate authority for non-localhost names and IP addresses. But Caddy supports its own internal certificate authority for enabling HTTPS over localhost, which you may want to do for testing purposes. If you specify* localhost *as your hostname in the earlier settings to enable automatic HTTPS, Caddy will use its internal certificate authority for its TLS certificate. It will also try to install its root certificate in your operating system's root certificate trust store, which is where your operating system keeps track of all root certificates it inherently trusts.*

## What You've Learned

Caddy is a contemporary web server written in Go that offers security, performance, and extensibility through modules and configuration adapters. Caddy can automatically use HTTPS through its integration with Let's Encrypt, a nonprofit certificate authority that supplies free digital certificates. Together, Caddy and Let's Encrypt allow you to stand up a web server with seamless HTTPS support.

Caddy uses JSON as its native configuration format, and it exposes an API on localhost port 2019 that allows you to post JSON to change its configuration. The configuration changes take immediate effect. But since JSON isn't an ideal configuration format, Caddy makes use of configuration adapters. Configuration adapters translate configuration files from more configuration-friendly formats, like TOML, to JSON. If you don't want to use JSON for your Caddy configuration or if you don't find a configuration adapter that meets your needs, you can also write your own, as you did in this chapter.

You can also extend Caddy's functionality with the use of modules. This chapter shows how to write a middleware module, compile it into Caddy, configure the module, and put it to effective use.

Finally, this chapter showed you how to integrate Caddy into your network architecture. You'll often make Caddy the first server in your network, using it to receive client requests before sending the requests onto their final destinations. In this chapter, you configured an instance of Caddy to reverse-proxy client requests to your backend web service and serve static files on behalf of the backend web service. As a result, you kept your backend web service as simple as possible and saved it from having to manage its static content. Your backend web service can use Caddy for HTTPS support, caching, and file serving.

Now that you have some experience with Caddy, you should be able to determine whether your web services would do better when served by a comprehensive web server solution or a comparatively minimal net/http web server implementation. If you expect to make your web service available to the public, using a proven web server like Caddy at the edge of your application will free up time you can better spend on your backend web service.

# 11

## SECURING COMMUNICATIONS WITH TLS

Five years before whistleblower Edward Snowden showed us how much we took our electronic privacy for granted, author and activist Cory Doctorow wrote, "We should treat personal electronic data with the same care and respect as weapons-grade plutonium—it is dangerous, long-lasting, and once it has leaked, there's no getting it back."

Prior to 2013, most people communicated on the internet by using plaintext. Social Security numbers, credit card details, passwords, sensitive emails, and other potentially embarrassing information traveled over the internet, ripe for interception by malicious actors. Most popular websites defaulted to HTTP; Google was one of the only major tech companies supporting HTTPS.

Today, it's unusual to find a website that doesn't support HTTPS, particularly now that Let's Encrypt offers free TLS certificates for your domain. We're treating information in transit more like weapons-grade plutonium, helping ensure the privacy and integrity of the information we share. Our network applications should be no different. We should strive to authenticate our communication and use encryption where appropriate, particularly when that information has the potential to leak over insecure networks.

Up to this point, we've used TLS only as an afterthought in our code. This is partly because Go's net/http library makes its use relatively effortless, but it's also because we haven't adequately explored the TLS protocol and the infrastructure that makes it possible. To write secure software, you should carefully plan for security before development starts and then use good security practices as you write code. TLS is a terrific way to improve the security posture of your software by protecting data in transit.

This chapter will introduce you to the basics of TLS from a programmer's perspective. You'll learn about the client-server handshake process and the inherent trust that makes that process work. Then we'll discuss how things can (and do) go wrong even when you use TLS. Finally, we'll look at practical examples of how to incorporate TLS into your applications, including mutual client-server authentication.

# A Closer Look at Transport Layer Security

The TLS protocol supplies secure communication between a client and a server. It allows the client to authenticate the server and optionally permits the server to authenticate clients. The client uses TLS to encrypt its communication with the server, preventing third-party interception and manipulation.

TLS uses a handshake process to establish certain criteria for the stateful TLS session. If the client initiated a TLS 1.3 handshake with the server, it would go something like this:

> **Client** Hello *google.com*. I'd like to communicate with you using TLS version 1.3. Here is a list of ciphers I'd like to use to encrypt our messages, in order of my preference. I generated a public- and private-key pair specifically for this conversation. Here's my public key.

> **Server** Greetings, client. TLS version 1.3 suits me fine. Based on your cipher list, I've decided we'll use the Advanced Encryption Standard with Galois/Counter Mode (AES-GCM) cipher. I, too, created a new key pair for this conversation. Here is my public key and my certificate so you can prove that I truly am *google.com*. I'm also sending along a 32-byte value that corresponds to the TLS version you asked me to use. Finally, I'm including both a signature and a *message authentication code (MAC)* derived using your public key of everything we've discussed so far so you can verify the integrity of my reply when you receive it.

> **Client (to self)** An authority I trust signed the server's certificate, so I'm confident I'm speaking to *google.com*. I've derived this conversation's symmetric key from the server's signature by using my private key. Using this symmetric key, I've verified the MAC and made sure no one has tampered with the server's reply. The 32 bytes in the reply

corresponds to TLS version 1.3, so no one is attempting to trick the server into using an older, weaker version of TLS. I now have everything I need to securely communicate with the server.

**Client (to server)**   *Here is some encrypted data.*

The 32-byte value in the server's hello message prevents *downgrade attacks*, in which an attacker intercepts the client's hello message and modifies it to request an older, weaker version of TLS. If the client asked for TLS v1.3, but an attacker changed the client's hello message to ask for TLS v1.1, the 32-byte value in the server's hello message would correspond to TLS v1.1. When the client received the server's hello message, it would notice that the value indicated the wrong TLS version and abort the handshake.

From this point forward, the client and server communicate using AES-GCM symmetric-key cryptography (in this hypothetical example). Both the client and the server encapsulate application layer payloads in TLS records before passing the payloads onto the transport layer.

Despite its name, TLS is not a transport layer protocol. Instead, it's situated between the transport and application layers of the TCP/IP stack. TLS encrypts an application layer protocol's payload before passing the payload onto the transport layer. Once the payload reaches its destination, TLS receives the payload from the transport layer, decrypts it, and passes the payload along to the application layer protocol.

## Forward Secrecy

The handshake method in our hypothetical conversation is an example of the Diffie-Hellman (DH) key exchange used in TLS v1.3. The *DH key exchange* calls for the creation of new client and server key pairs, and a new symmetric key, all of which should exist for only the duration of the session. Once a session ends, the client and server shall discard the session keys.

The use of per-session keys means that TLS v1.3 gives you *forward secrecy*; an attacker who compromises your session keys can compromise only the data exchanged during that session. An attacker cannot use those keys to decrypt data exchanged during any other session.

## In Certificate Authorities We Trust

My father and I took a trip to Ireland shortly before I started authoring this book. In preparation for our adventure, I needed to obtain a new passport, since my old one had long since expired. The process was easy. I filled out an application, collected my vital records, took a picture of the bad side of my head, and presented everything, along with an application fee, to my local US Post Office branch. I also attested I was myself to the notary. A few weeks later, I received a newly minted US passport in the mail.

When we arrived in Ireland, a lovely customs agent greeted us and requested our passports. She asked questions about our holiday as her computer authenticated our identities. After no more than three minutes, she returned our passports and welcomed us to Ireland.

My passport represents the US government's attestation that I am Adam Woodbeck. But it's only as good as Ireland's trust in the US government's ability to verify my identity. If Ireland doesn't trust the United States, it will not take the United States' word that I am me and will most likely refuse to let me enter the country. (If I'm being honest, I'm not charming enough to convince the customs agent to let me in on my word alone.)

TLS's certificates work in much the same way as my passport. If I wanted a new TLS certificate for *woodbeck.net*, I would send a request to a certificate authority, such as Let's Encrypt. The certificate authority would then verify I am the proper owner of *woodbeck.net*. Once satisfied, the certificate authority would issue a new certificate for *woodbeck.net* and cryptographically sign it with its certificate. My server can present this certificate to clients so they can authenticate my server by confirming the certificate authority's signature, giving them the confidence that they're communicating with the real *woodbeck.net*, not an impostor.

A certificate authority issuing a signed certificate for *woodbeck.net* is analogous to the US government issuing my passport. They are both issued by trusted institutions that attest to their subject's authenticity. Like Ireland's trust of the United States, clients are inclined to trust the *woodbeck.net* certificate only if they trust the certificate authority that signed it. I could create my own certificate authority and self-sign certificates as easy as I could create a document claiming to be my passport. But Ireland would sooner admit that Jack Daniel's Tennessee Whiskey is superior to Jameson Irish Whiskey than trust my self-issued passport, and no operating system or web browser in the world would trust my self-signed certificate.

## How to Compromise TLS

On December 24, 2013, Google learned that the Turktrust certificate authority in Turkey had mistakenly issued a certificate that allowed a malicious actor to masquerade as *google.com*. This meant that attackers could fool your web browser into thinking it was talking to Google over a TLS connection and trick you into divulging your credentials. Google quickly noticed the mistake and took steps to remedy the situation.

Turktrust's mess-up undermined its authority and compromised our trust. But even if the certificate authorities operate correctly, attackers can narrow their focus and target individuals instead. If an attacker were able to install his own CA certificate in your operating system's trusted certificate storage, your computer would trust any certificate he signs. This means an attacker could compromise all your TLS traffic.

Most people don't get this kind of special attention. Instead, an attacker is more likely to compromise a server. Once compromised, the attacker could capture all TLS traffic and the corresponding session keys from memory.

You're unlikely to encounter any of these scenarios, but it's important to be aware that they are possible. Overall, TLS 1.3 offers excellent security and is tough to compromise because of its full handshake signature, downgrade protection, forward secrecy, and strong encryption.

## Protecting Data in Transit

Ensuring the integrity of the data you transmit over a network should be your primary focus, no matter whether it's your own data or the data of others. Go makes using TLS so easy that you would have a tough time justifying not using it. In this section, you'll learn how to add TLS support to both the client and the server. You'll also see how TLS works over TCP and how to mitigate the threat of malicious certificates with certificate pinning.

### Client-side TLS

The client's primary concern during the handshake process is to authenticate the server by using its certificate. If the client cannot trust the server, it cannot consider its communication with the server secure. The net/http/httptest package provides constructs that easily demonstrate Go's HTTP-over-TLS support (see Listing 11-1).

```
package ch11

import (
    "crypto/tls"
    "net"
    "net/http"
    "net/http/httptest"
    "strings"
    "testing"
    "time"

    "golang.org/x/net/http2"
)

func TestClientTLS(t *testing.T) {
    ts := ❶httptest.NewTLSServer(
        http.HandlerFunc(
            func(w http.ResponseWriter, r *http.Request) {
                if ❷r.TLS == nil {
                    u := "https://" + r.Host + r.RequestURI
                    http.Redirect(w, r, u, http.StatusMovedPermanently)
                    return
                }

                w.WriteHeader(http.StatusOK)
            },
        ),
    )
    defer ts.Close()

    resp, err := ❸ts.Client().Get(ts.URL)
    if err != nil {
        t.Fatal(err)
    }
```

```
    if resp.StatusCode != http.StatusOK {
        t.Errorf("expected status %d; actual status %d",
            http.StatusOK, resp.StatusCode)
    }
}
```

*Listing 11-1: Testing HTTPS client and server support (tls_client_test.go)*

The httptest.NewTLSServer function returns an HTTPS server ❶. Aside from the function name, this bit of code looks identical to our use of httptest in Chapter 8. Here, the httptest.NewTLSServer function handles the HTTPS server's TLS configuration details, including the creation of a new certificate. No trusted authority signed this certificate, so no discerning HTTPS client would trust it. You'll see how to work around this detail in just a moment by using a preconfigured client.

If the server receives the client's request over HTTP, the request's TLS field will be nil. You can check for this case ❷ and redirect the client to the HTTPS endpoint accordingly.

For testing purposes, the server's Client method ❸ returns a new *http .Client that inherently trusts the server's certificate. You can use this client to test TLS-specific code within your handlers.

Let's see what happens in Listing 11-2 when you attempt to communicate with the same server by using a new client without inherent trust for the server's certificate.

```
--snip--

    tp := &http.Transport{
        TLSClientConfig: &tls.Config{
            CurvePreferences: []tls.CurveID{❶tls.CurveP256},
            MinVersion:       tls.VersionTLS12,
        },
    }

    err = ❷http2.ConfigureTransport(tp)
    if err != nil {
        t.Fatal(err)
    }

    client2 := &http.Client{Transport: tp}

    _, err = client2.Get(ts.URL)
    if err == nil || !strings.Contains(err.Error(),
        "certificate signed by unknown authority") {
        t.Fatalf("expected unknown authority error; actual: %q", err)
    }

❸ tp.TLSClientConfig.InsecureSkipVerify = true

    resp, err = client2.Get(ts.URL)
    if err != nil {
        t.Fatal(err)
    }
```

```
        if resp.StatusCode != http.StatusOK {
            t.Errorf("expected status %d; actual status %d",
                http.StatusOK, resp.StatusCode)
        }
    }
}
```

*Listing 11-2: Testing the HTTPS server with a discerning client (tls_client_test.go)*

You override the default TLS configuration in your client's transport by creating a new transport, defining its TLS configuration, and configuring http2 to use this transport. It's good practice to restrict your client's curve preference to the P-256 curve ❶ and avoid the use of P-384 and P-521. P-256 is immune to timing attacks, whereas P-384 and P-521 are not. Also, your client will negotiate a minimum of TLS 1.2.

An *elliptic curve* is a plane curve in which all points along the curve satisfy the same polynomial equation. Whereas first-generation cryptography like RSA uses large prime numbers to derive keys, elliptic curve cryptography uses points along an elliptic curve for key generation. P-256, P-384, and P-521 are specific elliptic curves defined in the National Institute of Standards and Technology's Digital Signature Standard. You can find more details in the Federal Information Processing Standards (FIPS) publication 186-4 (*https://nvlpubs.nist.gov/nistpubs/FIPS/NIST.FIPS.186-4.pdf*).

Since your transport no longer relies on the default TLS configuration, the client no longer has inherent HTTP/2 support. You need to explicitly bless your transport with HTTP/2 support ❷ if you want to use it. Of course, this test doesn't rely on HTTP/2, but this implementation detail can trip you up if you're unaware that overriding the transport's TLS configuration removes HTTP/2 support.

Your client uses the operating system's trusted certificate store because you don't explicitly tell it which certificates to trust. The first call to the test server results in an error because your client doesn't trust the server certificate's signatory. You could work around this and configure your client's transport to skip verification of the server's certificate by setting its InsecureSkipVerify field to true ❸. I don't recommend you entertain enabling InsecureSkipVerify for anything other than debugging. Shipping code with this enabled is a code smell in my opinion. You'll learn a better alternative later in this chapter when we discuss a concept known as *certificate pinning.* As the field name implies, enabling it makes your client inherently insecure and susceptible to man-in-the-middle attacks, since it now blindly trusts any certificate a server offers up. If you make the same call with your newly naive client, you'll see that it happily negotiates TLS with the server.

## TLS over TCP

TLS is stateful; a client and a server negotiate session parameters during the initial handshake only, and once they've agreed, they exchange encrypted TLS records for the duration of the session. Since TCP is also stateful, it's the ideal transport layer protocol with which to implement TLS, because you can leverage TCP's reliability guarantees to maintain your TLS sessions.

Let's take the application protocol out of the picture for a moment and learn how to establish a TLS connection over TCP. Listing 11-3 demonstrates how to use the crypto/tls package to initiate a TLS connection with a few lines of code.

```
--snip--

func TestClientTLSGoogle(t *testing.T) {
    conn, err := ❶tls.DialWithDialer(
        &net.Dialer{Timeout: 30 * time.Second},
        "tcp",
        "www.google.com:443",
        &tls.Config{
            CurvePreferences: []tls.CurveID{tls.CurveP256},
            MinVersion:       tls.VersionTLS12,
        },
    )
    if err != nil {
        t.Fatal(err)
    }

    state := ❷conn.ConnectionState()
    t.Logf("TLS 1.%d", state.Version-tls.VersionTLS10)
    t.Log(tls.CipherSuiteName(state.CipherSuite))
    t.Log(state.VerifiedChains[0][0].Issuer.Organization[0])

    _ = conn.Close()
}
```

Listing 11-3: Starting a TLS connection with www.google.com (tls_client_test.go)

The tls.DialWithDialer function ❶ accepts a *net.Dialer, a network, an address, and a *tls.Config. Here, you give your dialer a time-out of 30 seconds and specify recommended TLS settings. If successful, you can inspect the connection's state ❷ to glean details about your TLS connection.

Listing 11-4 shows the output of Listing 11-3's test.

```
$ go test -race -run TestClientTLSGoogle -v ./...
=== RUN   TestClientTLSGoogle
    TestClientTLSGoogle: tls_client_test.go:89: TLS 1.3
    TestClientTLSGoogle: tls_client_test.go:90: TLS_AES_128_GCM_SHA256
    TestClientTLSGoogle: tls_client_test.go:91: Google Trust Services
--- PASS: TestClientTLSGoogle (0.31s)
PASS
```

Listing 11-4: Running the TestClientTLSGoogle test

Your TLS client is using the TLS_AES_128_GCM_SHA256 cipher suite over TLS version 1.3. Notice that tls.DialWithDialer did not object to the server's certificate. The underlying TLS client used the operating system's trusted certificate storage and confirmed that *www.google.com*'s certificate is signed by a trusted CA—Google Trust Services, in this example.

## Server-side TLS

The server-side code isn't much different from what you've learned thus far. The main difference is that the server needs to present a certificate to the client as part of the handshake process. You can create one with the *generate_cert.go* file found in Go's *src/crypto/tls* subdirectory. For production use, you're better off using certificates from Let's Encrypt or another certificate authority. You can use the LEGO library (*https://github.com/go-acme/lego/*) to add certificate management to your services. Generate a new cert and private key, like so:

```
$ go run $GOROOT/src/crypto/tls/generate_cert.go -host localhost -ecdsa-curve P256
```

This command creates a certificate named *cert.pem* with the hostname *localhost* and a private key named *key.pem*. The rest of the code in this section assumes that both files exist in the current directory.

Keeping with the tradition of earlier chapters, Listing 11-5 includes the first bit of code for a TLS-only echo server.

```
package ch11

import (
    "context"
    "crypto/tls"
    "fmt"
    "net"
    "time"
)

func NewTLSServer(ctx context.Context, address string,
    maxIdle time.Duration, tlsConfig *tls.Config) *Server {
    return &Server{
        ctx:       ctx,
        ready:     make(chan struct{}),
        addr:      address,
        maxIdle:   maxIdle,
        tlsConfig: tlsConfig,
    }
}

type Server struct {
    ctx   context.Context
    ready chan struct{}

    addr      string
    maxIdle   time.Duration
    tlsConfig *tls.Config
}

func (s *Server) ❶Ready() {
    if s.ready != nil {
        <-s.ready
    }
}
```

*Listing 11-5: Server struct type and constructor function (tls_echo.go)*

The Server struct has a few fields used to record its settings, its TLS configuration, and a channel to signal when the server is ready for incoming connections. You'll write a test case and use the Ready method ❶ a little later in this section to block until the server is ready to accept connections.

The NewTLSServer function accepts a context for stopping the server, an address, the maximum duration the server should allow connections to idle, and a TLS configuration. Although controlling for idling clients isn't related to TLS, you'll use the maximum idle duration to push the socket deadline forward, as in Chapter 3.

Servers you used in earlier chapters rely on the separate concepts of listening and serving. Often, you'll invoke a helper function that will do both for you, such as the net/http server's ListenAndServe method. Listing 11-6 adds a similar method to the echo server.

```
--snip--

func (s *Server) ListenAndServeTLS(certFn, keyFn string) error {
    if s.addr == "" {
        s.addr = "localhost:443"
    }

    l, err := net.Listen("tcp", s.addr)
    if err != nil {
        return fmt.Errorf("binding to tcp %s: %w", s.addr, err)
    }

    if s.ctx != nil {
        go func() {
            <-s.ctx.Done()
            _ = l.Close()
        }()
    }

    return s.ServeTLS(l, certFn, keyFn)
}
```

*Listing 11-6: Adding methods to listen and serve and signal the server's readiness for connections (tls_echo.go)*

The ListenAndServe method accepts full paths to a certificate and a private key and returns an error. It creates a new net.Listener bound to the server's address and then spins off a goroutine to close the listener when you cancel the context. Finally, the method passes the listener, the certificate path, and the key path onto the server's ServeTLS method.

Listing 11-7 rounds out the echo server's implementation with its ServeTLS method.

```
--snip--

func (s Server) ServeTLS(l net.Listener, certFn, keyFn string) error {
    if s.tlsConfig == nil {
        s.tlsConfig = &tls.Config{
```

```
        CurvePreferences:      []tls.CurveID{tls.CurveP256},
        MinVersion:            tls.VersionTLS12,
      ❶ PreferServerCipherSuites: true,
    }
}

if len(s.tlsConfig.Certificates) == 0 &&
    s.tlsConfig.GetCertificate == nil {
    cert, err := ❷tls.LoadX509KeyPair(certFn, keyFn)
    if err != nil {
        return fmt.Errorf("loading key pair: %v", err)
    }

    s.tlsConfig.Certificates = []tls.Certificate{cert}
}

tlsListener := ❸tls.NewListener(l, s.tlsConfig)
if s.ready != nil {
    close(s.ready)
}
```

*Listing 11-7: Adding TLS support to a net.Listener (tls_echo.go)*

The ServeTLS method first checks the server's TLS configuration. If it's nil, it adds a default configuration with PreferServerCipherSuites set to true ❶. PreferServerCipherSuites is meaningful to the server only, and it makes the server use its preferred cipher suite instead of deferring to the client's preference.

If the server's TLS configuration does not have at least one certificate, or if its GetCertificate method is nil, you create a new tls.Certificate by reading in the certificate and private-key files from the filesystem ❷.

At this point in the code, the server has a TLS configuration with at least one certificate ready to present to clients. All that's left is to add TLS support to the net.Listener by passing it and the server's TLS configuration to the tls.NewListener function ❸. The tls.NewListener function acts like middleware, in that it augments the listener to return TLS-aware connection objects from its Accept method.

Listing 11-8 finishes up the ServeTLS method by accepting connections from the listener and handling them in separate goroutines.

```
--snip--

    for {
        conn, err := ❶tlsListener.Accept()
        if err != nil {
            return fmt.Errorf("accept: %v", err)
        }

        go func() {
            defer func() { _ = ❷conn.Close() }()

            for {
                if s.maxIdle > 0 {
```

```
                    err := ❸conn.SetDeadline(time.Now().Add(s.maxIdle))
                    if err != nil {
                        return
                    }
                }

                buf := make([]byte, 1024)
                n, err := ❹conn.Read(buf)
                if err != nil {
                    return
                }

                _, err = conn.Write(buf[:n])
                if err != nil {
                    return
                }
            }
        }()
    }
}
```

*Listing 11-8: Accepting TLS-aware connections from the listener (tls_echo.go)*

This pattern is like the one you've seen in earlier chapters. You use an endless for loop to continually block on the listener's Accept method ❶, which returns a new net.Conn object when a client successfully connects. Since you're using a TLS-aware listener, it returns connection objects with underlying TLS support. You interact with these connection objects the same as you always do. Go abstracts the TLS details away from you at this point. You then spin off this connection into its own goroutine to handle the connection from that point forward.

The server handles each connection the same way. It first conditionally sets the socket deadline to the server's maximum idle duration ❸, then waits for the client to send data. If the server doesn't read anything from the socket before it reaches the deadline, the connection's Read method ❹ returns an *I/O time-out* error, ultimately causing the connection to close ❷.

If, instead, the server reads data from the connection, it writes that same payload back to the client. Control loops back around to reset the deadline and then wait for the next payload from the client.

## Certificate Pinning

Earlier in the chapter, we discussed ways to compromise the trust that TLS relies on, whether by a certificate authority issuing fraudulent certificates or an attacker injecting a malicious certificate into your computer's trusted certificate storage. You can mitigate both attacks by using certificate pinning.

*Certificate pinning* is the process of scrapping the use of the operating system's trusted certificate storage and explicitly defining one or more trusted certificates in your application. Your application will trust connections only from hosts presenting a pinned certificate or a certificate signed by a pinned certificate. If you plan on deploying clients in zero-trust environments that must securely communicate with your server, consider pinning your server's certificate to each client.

Assuming the server introduced in the preceding section uses the *cert.pem* and the *key.pem* you generated for the hostname *localhost*, all clients will abort the TLS connection as soon as the server presents its certificate. Clients won't trust the server's certificate because no trusted certificate authority signed it.

You could set the tls.Config's InsecureSkipVerify field to true, but as this method is insecure, I don't recommend you consider it a practical choice. Instead, let's explicitly tell our client it can trust the server's certificate by pinning the server's certificate to the client. Listing 11-9 has the beginnings of a test to show that process.

```
package ch11

import (
    "bytes"
    "context"
    "crypto/tls"
    "crypto/x509"
    "io"
    "io/ioutil"
    "strings"
    "testing"
    "time"
)

func TestEchoServerTLS(t *testing.T) {
    ctx, cancel := context.WithCancel(context.Background())
    defer cancel()

    serverAddress := "localhost:34443"
    maxIdle := time.Second
    server := NewTLSServer(ctx, serverAddress, maxIdle, nil)
    done := make(chan struct{})

    go func() {
        err := ❶ server.ListenAndServeTLS("cert.pem", "key.pem")
        if err != nil && !strings.Contains(err.Error(),
            "use of closed network connection") {
            t.Error(err)
            return
        }
        done <- struct{}{}
    }()
❷   server.Ready()
```

*Listing 11-9: Creating a new TLS echo server and starting it in the background (tls_echo_test.go)*

Since the hostname in *cert.pem* is *localhost*, you create a new TLS echo server listening on *localhost* port 34443. The port isn't important here, but clients expect the server to be reachable by the same hostname as the one in the certificate it presents. You spin up the server in the background by using the *cert.pem* and *key.pem* files ❶ and block until it's ready for incoming connections ❷.

Listing 11-10 picks up where we left off by creating a client TLS configuration with explicit trust for the server's certificate.

```
--snip--

    cert, err := ioutil.ReadFile("cert.pem")
    if err != nil {
        t.Fatal(err)
    }

    certPool := ❶x509.NewCertPool()
    if ok := certPool.AppendCertsFromPEM(cert); !ok {
        t.Fatal("failed to append certificate to pool")
    }

    tlsConfig := &tls.Config{
        CurvePreferences: []tls.CurveID{tls.CurveP256},
        MinVersion:       tls.VersionTLS12,
      ❷ RootCAs:          certPool,
    }
```

*Listing 11-10: Pinning the server certificate to the client (tls_echo_test.go)*

Pinning a server certificate to the client is straightforward. First, you read in the *cert.pem* file. Then, you create a new certificate pool ❶ and append the certificate to it. Finally, you add the certificate pool to the tls.Config's RootCAs field ❷. As the name suggests, you can add more than one trusted certificate to the certificate pool. This can be useful when you are migrating to a new certificate but have yet to completely phase out the old certificate.

The client, using this configuration, will authenticate only servers that present the *cert.pem* certificate or any certificate signed by it. Let's confirm this behavior in the rest of the test (see Listing 11-11).

```
--snip--

    conn, err := ❶tls.Dial("tcp", serverAddress, tlsConfig)
    if err != nil {
        t.Fatal(err)
    }

    hello := []byte("hello")
    _, err = conn.Write(hello)
    if err != nil {
        t.Fatal(err)
    }

    b := make([]byte, 1024)
    n, err := conn.Read(b)
    if err != nil {
```

```
        t.Fatal(err)
    }

    if actual := b[:n]; !bytes.Equal(hello, actual) {
        t.Fatalf("expected %q; actual %q", hello, actual)
    }

❷ time.Sleep(2 * maxIdle)
    _, err = conn.Read(b)
    if err != ❸io.EOF {
        t.Fatal(err)
    }

    err = conn.Close()
    if err != nil {
        t.Fatal(err)
    }

    cancel()
    <-done
}
```

*Listing 11-11: Authenticating the server by using a pinned certificate (tls_echo_test.go)*

You pass tls.Dial the tls.Config with the pinned server certificate ❶.
Your TLS client authenticates the server's certificate without having
to resort to using InsecureSkipVerify and all the insecurity that option
introduces.

Now that you've set up a trusted connection with a server, even though
the server presented an unsigned certificate, let's make sure the server
works as expected. It should echo back any message you send it. If you idle
long enough ❷, you find that your next interaction with the socket results
in an error ❸, showing the server closed the socket.

## Mutual TLS Authentication

In the preceding section, you learned how clients authenticate servers
by using the server's certificate and a trusted third-party certificate or by
configuring the client to explicitly trust the server's certificate. Servers can
authenticate clients in the same manner. This is particularly useful in zero-
trust network infrastructures, where clients and servers must each prove
their identities. For example, you may have a client outside your network
that must present a certificate to a proxy before the proxy will allow the
client to access your trusted network resources. Likewise, the client authenticates the certificate presented by your proxy to make sure it's talking to
your proxy and not one controlled by a malicious actor.

You can instruct your server to set up TLS sessions with only authenticated clients. Those clients would have to present a certificate signed by a
trusted certificate authority or pinned to the server. Before you can look at
example code, the client needs a certificate it can present to the server for

authentication. However, clients cannot use the certificates generated with *$GOROOT/src/crypto/tls/generate_cert.go* for client authentication. Instead, you need to create your own certificate and private key.

## Generating Certificates for Authentication

Go's standard library contains everything you need to generate your own certificates using the elliptic curve digital signature algorithm (ECDSA) and the P-256 elliptic curve. Listing 11-12 shows the beginnings of a command line utility for doing exactly that. As you go through it, keep in mind that it may not entirely fit your use case. For example, it creates 10-year certificates and uses my name as the certificate's subject, which you likely don't want to use in your code (though if you do, I'm flattered). Tweak, as necessary.

```go
package main

import (
    "crypto/ecdsa"
    "crypto/elliptic"
    "crypto/rand"
    "crypto/x509"
    "crypto/x509/pkix"
    "encoding/pem"
    "flag"
    "log"
    "math/big"
    "net"
    "os"
    "strings"
    "time"
)

var (
    host = flag.String("host", "localhost",
        "Certificate's comma-separated host names and IPs")
    certFn = flag.String("cert", "cert.pem", "certificate file name")
    keyFn  = flag.String("key", "key.pem", "private key file name")
)

func main() {
    flag.Parse()

    serial, err := ❶rand.Int(rand.Reader, new(big.Int).Lsh(big.NewInt(1),
        128))
    if err != nil {
        log.Fatal(err)
    }

    notBefore := time.Now()
    template := x509.Certificate{
        SerialNumber: serial,
```

```
        Subject: pkix.Name{
            Organization: []string{"Adam Woodbeck"},
        },
        NotBefore: notBefore,
        NotAfter:  notBefore.Add(10 * 356 * 24 * time.Hour),
        KeyUsage: x509.KeyUsageKeyEncipherment |
            x509.KeyUsageDigitalSignature |
            x509.KeyUsageCertSign,
        ExtKeyUsage: []x509.ExtKeyUsage{
            x509.ExtKeyUsageServerAuth,
          ❷x509.ExtKeyUsageClientAuth,
        },
        BasicConstraintsValid: true,
        IsCA:                  true,
    }
```

*Listing 11-12: Creating an X.509 certificate template (cert/generate.go)*

The command line utility accepts a comma-separated list of hostnames and IP addresses that will use the certificate. It also allows you to specify the certificate and private-key filenames, but it defaults to our familiar *cert.pem* and *key.pem* filenames.

The process of generating a certificate and a private key involves building a template in your code that you then encode to the X.509 format. Each certificate needs a serial number, which a certificate authority typically assigns. Since you're generating your own self-signed certificate, you generate your own serial number using a cryptographically random, unsigned 128-bit integer ❶. You then create an x509.Certificate object that represents an X.509-formatted certificate and set various values, such as the serial number, the certificate's subject, the validity lifetime, and various usages for this certificate. Since you want to use this certificate for client authentication, you must include the x509.ExtKeyUsageClientAuth value ❷. If you omit this value, the server won't be able to verify the certificate when presented by the client.

The template is almost ready. You just need to add the hostnames and IP addresses before generating the certificate (see Listing 11-13).

```
--snip--

    for _, h := range ❶strings.Split(*host, ",") {
        if ip := net.ParseIP(h); ip != nil {
          ❷ template.IPAddresses = append(template.IPAddresses, ip)
        } else {
          ❸ template.DNSNames = append(template.DNSNames, h)
        }
    }

    priv, err := ❹ecdsa.GenerateKey(elliptic.P256(), rand.Reader)
    if err != nil {
        log.Fatal(err)
    }
```

```
der, err := ❺x509.CreateCertificate(rand.Reader, &template,
    &template, &priv.PublicKey, priv)
if err != nil {
    log.Fatal(err)
}

cert, err := os.Create(*certFn)
if err != nil {
    log.Fatal(err)
}

err = ❻pem.Encode(cert, &pem.Block{Type: "CERTIFICATE", Bytes: der})
if err != nil {
    log.Fatal(err)
}

if err := cert.Close(); err != nil {
    log.Fatal(err)
}
log.Println("wrote", *certFn)
```

*Listing 11-13: Writing the Privacy-Enhanced Mail (PEM)–encoded certificate (cert/generate.go)*

You loop through the comma-separated list of hostnames and IP addresses ❶, assigning each to its appropriate slice in the template. If the hostname is an IP address, you assign it to the IPAddresses slice ❷. Otherwise, you assign the hostname to the DNSNames slice ❸. Go's TLS client uses these values to authenticate a server. For example, if the client connects to *https://www.google.com* but the common name or alternative names in the server's certificate do not match *www.google.com*'s hostname or resolved IP address, the client fails to authenticate the server.

Next you generate a new ECDSA private key ❹ using the P-256 elliptic curve. At this point, you have everything you need to generate the certificate. The x509.CreateCertificate function ❺ accepts a source of entropy (crypto/rand's Reader is ideal), the template for the new certificate, a parent certificate, a public key, and a corresponding private key. It then returns a slice of bytes containing the Distinguished Encoding Rules (DER)–encoded certificate. You use your template for the parent certificate since the resulting certificate signs itself. All that's left to do is create a new file, generate a new pem.Block with the DER-encoded byte slice, and PEM-encode everything to the new file ❻. You don't have to concern yourself with the various encodings. Go is quite happy with using PEM-encoded certificates on disk.

Now that you have a new certificate on disk, let's write the corresponding private key in Listing 11-14.

```
--snip--

key, err := os.OpenFile(*keyFn, os.O_WRONLY|os.O_CREATE|os.O_TRUNC,
    ❶0600)
if err != nil {
    log.Fatal(err)
```

```
    }

    privKey, err := ❷x509.MarshalPKCS8PrivateKey(priv)
    if err != nil {
        log.Fatal(err)
    }

    err = ❸pem.Encode(key, &pem.Block{Type: "EC PRIVATE KEY",
    Bytes: privKey})
    if err != nil {
        log.Fatal(err)
    }

    if err := key.Close(); err != nil {
        log.Fatal(err)
    }
    log.Println("wrote", *keyFn)
}
```

*Listing 11-14: Writing the PEM-encoded private key (cert/generate.go)*

Whereas the certificate is meant to be publicly shared, the private key is just that: private. You should take care to assign it minimal permissions. Here, you're giving only the user read-write access to the private-key file ❶ and removing access for everyone else. We marshal the private key into a byte slice ❷ and, similarly, assign it to a new pem.Block before writing the PEM-encoded output to the private-key file ❸.

Listing 11-15 uses the preceding code to generate certificate and key pairs for the server and the client.

```
$ go run cert/generate.go -cert serverCert.pem -key serverKey.pem -host
localhost
2006/01/02 15:04:05 wrote serverCert.pem
2006/01/02 15:04:05 wrote serverKey.pem
$ go run cert/generate.go -cert clientCert.pem -key clientKey.pem -host
localhost
2006/01/02 15:04:05 wrote clientCert.pem
2006/01/02 15:04:05 wrote clientKey.pem
```

*Listing 11-15: Generating a certificate and private-key pair for the server and the client*

Since the server binds to *localhost* and the client connects to the server from *localhost*, this value is appropriate for both the client and server certificates. If you want to move the client to a different hostname or bind the server to an IP address, for example, you'll need to change the *host* flag accordingly.

## Implementing Mutual TLS

Now that you've generated certificate and private-key pairs for both the server and the client, you can start writing their code. Let's write a test that implements mutual TLS authentication between our echo server and a client, starting in Listing 11-16.

```
package ch11

import (
    "bytes"
    "context"
    "crypto/tls"
    "crypto/x509"
    "errors"
    "io/ioutil"
    "strings"
    "testing"
)

func caCertPool(caCertFn string) (*x509.CertPool, error) {
    caCert, err := ❶ioutil.ReadFile(caCertFn)
    if err != nil {
        return nil, err
    }

    certPool := x509.NewCertPool()
    if ok := ❷certPool.AppendCertsFromPEM(caCert); !ok {
        return nil, errors.New("failed to add certificate to pool")
    }

    return certPool, nil
}
```

*Listing 11-16: Creating a certificate pool to serve CA certificates (tls_mutual_test.go)*

Both the client and server use the caCertPool function to create a new X.509 certificate pool. The function accepts the file path to a PEM-encoded certificate, which you read in ❶ and append to the new certificate pool ❷. The certificate pool serves as a source of trusted certificates. The client puts the server's certificate in its certificate pool, and vice versa.

Listing 11-17 details the initial test code to demonstrate mutual TLS authentication between a client and a server.

```
--snip--

func TestMutualTLSAuthentication(t *testing.T) {
    ctx, cancel := context.WithCancel(context.Background())
    defer cancel()

    serverPool, err := caCertPool(❶"clientCert.pem")
    if err != nil {
        t.Fatal(err)
    }

    cert, err := ❷tls.LoadX509KeyPair("serverCert.pem", "serverKey.pem")
    if err != nil {
        t.Fatalf("loading key pair: %v", err)
    }
```

*Listing 11-17: Instantiating a CA cert pool and a server certificate (tls_mutual_test.go)*

Before creating the server, you need to first populate a new CA certificate pool with the client's certificate ❶. You also need to load the server's certificate at this point ❷ instead of relying on the server's ServeTLS method to do it for you, as you have in previous listings. Why you need the server's certificate now will be clear when you see the TLS configuration changes in Listing 11-18.

```
--snip--

    serverConfig := &tls.Config{
        Certificates: []tls.Certificate{cert},
    ❶ GetConfigForClient: func(hello *tls.ClientHelloInfo) (*tls.Config,
            error) {
            return &tls.Config{
                Certificates:           []tls.Certificate{❷cert},
            ❸ ClientAuth:              tls.RequireAndVerifyClientCert,
            ❹ ClientCAs:               serverPool,
                CurvePreferences:       []tls.CurveID{tls.CurveP256},
                MinVersion:             ❺tls.VersionTLS13,
                PreferServerCipherSuites: true,
```

Listing 11-18: Accessing the client's hello information using GetConfigForClient (tls_mutual_test.go)

Remember that in Listing 11-13, you defined the IPAddresses and DNSNames slices of the template used to generate your client's certificate. These values populate the common name and alternative names portions of the client's certificate. You learned that Go's TLS client uses these values to authenticate the server. But the server does not use these values from the client's certificate to authenticate the client.

Since you're implementing mutual TLS authentication, you need to make some changes to the server's certificate verification process so that it authenticates the client's IP address or hostnames against the client certificate's common name and alternative names. To do that, the server at the very least needs to know the client's IP address. The only way you can get client connection information before certificate verification is by defining the tls.Config's GetConfigForClient method ❶. This method allows you to define a function that receives the *tls.ClientHelloInfo object created as part of the TLS handshake process with the client. From this, you can retrieve the client's IP address. But first, you need to return a proper TLS configuration.

You add the server's certificate to the TLS configuration ❷ and the server pool to the TLS configuration's ClientCAs field ❹. This field is the server's equivalent to the TLS configuration's RootCAs field on the client. You also need to tell the server that every client must present a valid certificate before completing the TLS handshake process ❸. Since you control both the client and the server, specify a minimum TLS protocol version of 1.3 ❺.

This function returns the same TLS configuration for every client connection. As mentioned, the only reason you're using the GetConfigForClient method is so you can retrieve the client's IP from its hello information.

Listing 11-19 implements the verification process that authenticates the client by using its IP address and its certificate's common name and alternative names.

```
--snip--
❶ VerifyPeerCertificate: func(rawCerts [][]byte,
        verifiedChains [][]*x509.Certificate) error {

    opts := x509.VerifyOptions{
        KeyUsages: []x509.ExtKeyUsage{
          ❷x509.ExtKeyUsageClientAuth,
        },
        Roots: ❸serverPool,
    }

    ip := strings.Split(hello.Conn.RemoteAddr().String(),
        ":")[0]
    hostnames, err := ❹net.LookupAddr(ip)
    if err != nil {
        t.Errorf("PTR lookup: %v", err)
    }
    hostnames = append(hostnames, ip)

    for _, chain := range verifiedChains {
        opts.Intermediates = x509.NewCertPool()
        for _, cert := range ❺chain[1:] {
            opts.Intermediates.AddCert(cert)
        }

        for _, hostname := range hostnames {
            opts.DNSName = ❻hostname
            _, err = chain[0].Verify(opts)
            if err == nil {
                return nil
            }
        }
    }

    return errors.New("client authentication failed")
    },
}, nil
},
}
```

*Listing 11-19: Making the server authenticate the client's IP and hostnames (tls_mutual_test.go)*

Since you want to augment the usual certificate verification process on the server, you define an appropriate function and assign it to the TLS configuration's VerifyPeerCertificate method ❶. The server calls this method after the normal certificate verification checks. The only check you're performing above and beyond the normal checks is to verify the client's hostname with the leaf certificate.

The *leaf certificate* is the last certificate in the certificate chain given to the server by the client. The leaf certificate contains the client's public key. All other certificates in the chain are intermediate certificates used to verify the authenticity of the leaf certificate and culminate with the certificate authority's certificate. You'll find each leaf certificate at index 0 in each verifiedChains slice. In other words, you can find the leaf certificate of the first chain at verifiedChains[0][0]. If the server calls your function assigned to the VerifyPeerCertificate method, the leaf certificate in the first chain exists at a minimum.

Create a new x509.VerifyOptions object and modify the KeyUsages method to indicate you want to perform client authentication ❷. Then, assign the server pool to the Roots method ❸. The server uses this pool as its trusted certificate source during verification.

Now, extract the client's IP address from the connection object in the *tls.ClientHelloInfo object named hello passed into Listing 11-18's GetConfigForClient method. Use the IP address to perform a reverse DNS lookup ❹ to consider any hostnames assigned to the client's IP address. If this lookup fails or returns an empty slice, the way you handle that situation is up to you. If you're relying on the client's hostname for authentication and the reverse lookup fails, you cannot authenticate the client. But if you're using the client's IP address only in the certificate's common name or alternative names, then a reverse lookup failure is inconsequential. For demonstration purposes, we'll consider a failed reverse lookup to equate to a failed test. At minimum, you append the client's IP address to the hostnames slice.

All that's left to do is loop through each verified chain, assign a new intermediate certificate pool to opts.Intermediates, add all certificates but the leaf certificate to the intermediate certificate pool ❺, and attempt to verify the client ❻. If verification returns a nil error, you authenticated the client. If you fail to verify each hostname with each leaf certificate, return an error to indicate that client authentication failed. The client will receive an error, and the server will terminate the connection.

Now that the server's TLS configuration properly authenticates client certificates, continue with the server implementation in Listing 11-20.

```
--snip--

    serverAddress := "localhost:44443"
    server := NewTLSServer(ctx, serverAddress, 0, ❶serverConfig)
    done := make(chan struct{})

    go func() {
        err := server.ListenAndServeTLS("serverCert.pem", "serverKey.pem")
        if err != nil &&!strings.Contains(err.Error(),
            "use of closed network connection") {
            t.Error(err)
            return
    }
```

```
        done <- struct{}{}
    }()
 ❷ server.Ready()
```

*Listing 11-20: Starting the TLS server (tls_mutual_test.go)*

Create a new TLS server instance, making sure to pass in the TLS configuration you just created ❶. Call its `ListenAndServeTLS` method in a goroutine and make sure to wait until the server is ready for connections ❷ before proceeding.

Now that the server implementation is ready, let's move on to the client portion of the test. Listing 11-21 implements a TLS client that can present *clientCert.pem* upon request by the server.

```
--snip--

    clientPool, err := caCertPool(❶"serverCert.pem")
    if err != nil {
        t.Fatal(err)
    }

    clientCert, err := tls.LoadX509KeyPair("clientCert.pem", "clientKey.pem")
    if err != nil {
        t.Fatal(err)
    }

    conn, err := tls.Dial("tcp", serverAddress, &tls.Config{
     ❷ Certificates:    []tls.Certificate{clientCert},
        CurvePreferences: []tls.CurveID{tls.CurveP256},
        MinVersion:      tls.VersionTLS13,
     ❸ RootCAs:         clientPool,
    })
    if err != nil {
        t.Fatal(err)
    }
```

*Listing 11-21: Pinning the server certificate to the client (tls_mutual_test.go)*

The client retrieves a new certificate pool populated with the server's certificate ❶. The client then uses the certificate pool in the `RootCAs` field of its TLS configuration ❸, meaning the client will trust only server certificates signed by *serverCert.pem*. You also configure the client with its own certificate ❷ to present to the server upon request.

It's worth noting that the client and server have not initialized a TLS session yet. They haven't completed the TLS handshake. If `tls.Dial` returns an error, it isn't because of an authentication issue but more likely a TCP connection issue. Let's continue with the client code to initiate the handshake (see Listing 11-22).

```
--snip--

    hello := []byte("hello")
    _, err = conn.Write(hello)
```

```
if err != nil {
    t.Fatal(err)
}

b := make([]byte, 1024)
n, err := ❶conn.Read(b)
if err != nil {
    t.Fatal(err)
}

if actual := b[:n]; !bytes.Equal(hello, actual) {
    t.Fatalf("expected %q; actual %q", hello, actual)
}

err = conn.Close()
if err != nil {
    t.Fatal(err)
}

cancel()
<-done
}
```

*Listing 11-22: TLS handshake completes as you interact with the connection (tls_mutual_test.go)*

The first read from, or write to, the socket connection automatically initiates the handshake process between the client and the server. If the server rejects the client certificate, the read call ❶ will return a *bad certificate* error. But if you created appropriate certificates and properly pinned them, both the client and the server are happy, and this test passes.

# What You've Learned

Transport Layer Security provides both authentication and encrypted communication between a client and a server. The server presents a certificate, signed by certificate authority, to a client as part of the TLS handshake process. The client verifies the certificate's signatory. If a third party, trusted by the client, signed the server's certificate, the server is authentic in the eyes of the client. From that point forward, the client and server communicate using symmetric-key cryptography.

By default, Go's TLS configuration uses the operating system's trusted certificate storage. This storage typically consists of certificates from the world's foremost trusted certificate authorities. However, we can modify the TLS configuration to trust specific keys, a process known as key pinning.

We can also modify a server's TLS configuration to require a certificate from the client. The server would then use this certificate to authenticate the client in the same manner the client authenticates the server. This process is known as mutual TLS authentication.

TLS 1.3 provides forward secrecy for all communication between a client and server. This means that compromising one session does not compromise any other session. Both the client and server generate per-session public- and private-key pairs. They also exchange an ephemeral shared secret as part of the handshake process. Once the session ends, the client and server shall purge the shared secret and their temporary key pairs. An attacker who was able to capture the shared secret and session traffic would be able to decrypt only that session's traffic. An attacker could not use the shared secret from one session to decrypt traffic from any other session.

Even though TLS is ubiquitous and secures much of the world's digital communication, attackers can compromise it. Part of a certificate authority's job is to verify that the entity requesting a certificate for a specific domain name owns the domain name. If attackers dupe a certificate authority, or the certificate authority otherwise makes a mistake and issues a fraudulent certificate, the owner of the fraudulent certificate could masquerade as Google, for example, and trick people into divulging sensitive information.

Another attack vector includes fooling a client into adding the attacker's certificate into the client's trusted certificate storage. The attacker could then issue and sign any certificate they want, and the client would inherently trust that the attacker is who their certificate claims them to be.

An attacker could also compromise a server and intercept TLS session keys and secrets, or even capture traffic at the application later after the server has decrypted it.

Overall, however, these attacks are rare, and TLS succeeds at achieving its goals of authentication and encrypted communication.

# PART IV

## SERVICE ARCHITECTURE

# 12

## DATA SERIALIZATION

A sizable portion of our work as developers involves integrating our network services with existing services, including legacy or third-party ones implemented in languages other than Go. These services must communicate by exchanging bytes of data in a way that is meaningful to both the sender and receiver, despite the different programming languages they're using. To do this, the sender converts data into bytes using a standard format and transfers the bytes over the network to the receiver. If the receiver understands the format used by the sender, it can convert the bytes back into structured data. This process of transforming structured data into successive bytes is known as *data serialization*.

Services can use data serialization to convert structured data to a series of bytes suitable for transport over a network or for persistence to storage. No matter whether the serialized data came from a network or disk, any code that understands the serialization format should be able to deserialize it to reconstruct a clone of the original object.

While writing this chapter, I initially struggled to explain the concept of data serialization. Then I realized we serialize data as we speak. Electrical impulses in my brain form words. My brain instructs my voice box to *serialize* these words into sound waves, which travel through the air and reach your ear. The sound waves vibrate your eardrum, which in turn transmits the vibrations to your inner ear. Hair-like structures in your inner ear deserialize these vibrations into electrical signals that your brain interprets as the original words I formed in my brain. We've just communicated using the serialization format of English, since it's a format we both understand.

You already have a bit of experience serializing data in your Go code too. The type-length-value binary encoding you learned in Chapter 4 and the JavaScript Object Notation (JSON) you posted over HTTP in Chapter 8 are examples of translating objects into well-known data serialization formats. We also PEM-encoded the certificates and private keys in Chapter 11 for persistence to disk.

This chapter will take a deeper dive into using data serialization for the purposes of storing data or sending between systems, which can make it accessible to services written in other languages. We could cover many data serialization formats, but we'll focus on the three that get the most use in Go network programming: JSON, protocol buffers, and Gob. We'll also spend some time on how to execute code on remote machines using a framework named gRPC. By the end of this chapter, you will know how to serialize data for storage or transmission and decode that data into meaningful data structures. You should be able to use techniques in this chapter to build services that can exchange complex data over a network or write code to communicate with existing network services.

## Serializing Objects

Objects or structured data cannot traverse a network connection as is. In other words, you cannot pass in an object to net.Conn's Write method, since it accepts only a byte slice. Therefore, you need to serialize the object to a byte slice, which you can then pass to the Write method. Thankfully, Go makes this easy.

Go's standard library includes excellent support for popular data serialization formats in its encoding package. You've already used encoding/binary to serialize numbers into byte sequences, encoding/json to serialize objects into JSON for submission over HTTP, and encoding/pem to serialize TLS certificates and private keys to files. (Anytime you encounter a function or method whose name includes *encode* or *marshal*, it likely serializes data. Likewise, *decode* and *unmarshal* are synonymous with deserializing data.)

This section will build an application that serializes data into three binary encoding formats: JSON, protocol buffers, and Gob. Since I often have trouble keeping track of housework, the application will document chores to do around the house. The application's state will persist between executions because you don't want it to forget the chores when it exits. You'll serialize each task to a file and use your app to update it as needed.

To keep this program simple, you need a description of the chore and a way to determine whether it's complete. Listing 12-1 defines a new package with a type that represents a household chore.

```
package housework

type Chore struct {
    Complete    bool
    Description string
}
```

*Listing 12-1: A type to represent a household chore (housework/housework.go)*

Go's JSON and Gob encoding packages can serialize exported struct fields only, so you define Chore as a struct, making sure to export its fields. The Complete field's value will be true if you've completed the chore. The Description field is the human-readable description of the chore.

You could use struct tags to instruct the encoders on how to treat each field, if necessary. For example, you could place the struct tag `` `json:"-"` `` on the Complete field to tell Go's JSON encoder to ignore this field instead of encoding it. Since you're perfectly happy to pass along all field values, you omit struct tags.

Once you've defined a chore structure, you can use it in an application that tracks chores on the command line. This application should show a list of chores and their status, allow you to add chores to the list, and mark chores as complete. Listing 12-2 includes the initial code for this housework application, including its command line usage details.

```
package main

import (
    "flag"
    "fmt"
    "log"
    "os"
    "path/filepath"
    "strconv"
    "strings"

    "github.com/awoodbeck/gnp/ch12/housework"
❶   storage "github.com/awoodbeck/gnp/ch12/json"
    // storage "github.com/awoodbeck/gnp/ch12/gob"
    // storage "github.com/awoodbeck/gnp/ch12/protobuf"
)
```

```
var dataFile string

func init() {
    flag.StringVar(&dataFile, "file", "housework.db", "data file")

    flag.Usage = func() {
        fmt.Fprintf(flag.CommandLine.Output(),
          ❷ `Usage: %s [flags] [add chore, ...|complete #]
        add            add comma-separated chores
        complete       complete designated chore

Flags:
`, filepath.Base(os.Args[0]))
        flag.PrintDefaults()
    }
}
```

*Listing 12-2: Initial housework application code (cmd/housework.go)*

This bit of code sets up the command line arguments and their usage ❷:
you can specify the add argument, followed by a comma-separated list of
chores to add to the list, or you can pass the argument complete and a chore
number to mark the chore as complete. In the absence of command line
options, the app will display the current list of chores.

Since the ultimate purpose of this application is to demonstrate data
serialization, you'll use multiple serialization formats to store the data. This
should show you how easy it is to switch between various formats. To prepare for that, you include import statements for those formats ❶. This will
make it easier for you to switch between the formats later.

Let's write the code to load chores from storage (see Listing 12-3).

```
--snip--

func load() ([]*housework.Chore, error) {
    if _, err := os.Stat(dataFile); ❶os.IsNotExist(err) {
        return make([]*housework.Chore, 0), nil
    }

    df, err := ❷os.Open(dataFile)
    if err != nil {
        return nil, err
    }
    defer func() {
        if err := df.Close(); err != nil {
            fmt.Printf("closing data file: %v", err)
        }
    }()

    return ❸storage.Load(df)
}
```

*Listing 12-3: Deserializing chores from a file (cmd/housework.go)*

This function returns a slice of pointers to housework.Chore structs from Listing 12-1. If the data file does not exist ❶, you exit early, returning an empty slice. This default case will occur when you first run the application.

If the app finds a data file, you open it ❷ and pass it along to the storage's Load function ❸, which expects an io.Reader. You used the same pattern of accepting an interface and returning a concrete type in previous chapters.

Listing 12-4 defines a function that flushes the chores in memory to your storage for persistence.

```
--snip--

func flush(chores []*housework.Chore) error {
    df, err := ❶os.Create(dataFile)
    if err != nil {
        return err
    }
    defer func() {
        if err := df.Close(); err != nil {
            fmt.Printf("closing data file: %v", err)
        }
    }()

    return ❷storage.Flush(df, chores)
}
```

*Listing 12-4: Flushing chores to the storage (cmd/housework.go)*

Here, you create a new file or truncate the existing file ❶ and pass the file pointer and slice of chores to the storage's Flush function ❷. This function accepts an io.Writer and your slice. There's certainly room for improvement in the way you handle the existing serialized file. But for the purposes of demonstration, this will suffice.

You need a way to display the chores on the command line. Listing 12-5 adds such a function to your application.

```
--snip--

func list() error {
    chores, err := ❶load()
    if err != nil {
        return err
    }

    if len(chores) == 0 {
        fmt.Println("You're all caught up!")
        return nil
    }

    fmt.Println("#\t[X]\tDescription")
    for i, chore := range chores {
        c := " "
```

```
            if chore.Complete {
                c = "X"
            }
            fmt.Printf("%d\t[%s]\t%s\n", i+1, c, chore.Description)
        }

        return nil
    }
```

*Listing 12-5: Printing the list of chores to standard output (cmd/housework.go)*

First, you load the list of chores from storage ❶. If there are no chores in your list, you simply print as much to standard output. Otherwise, you print a header and the list of chores, which looks something like this (see Listing 12-6).

```
#       [X]      Description
1       [ ]      Mop floors
2       [ ]      Clean dishes
3       [ ]      Mow the lawn
```

*Listing 12-6: Example output of the list function with three chores in the list*

The first column represents the chore number. You can reference this number to mark the chore complete, which will add an X between its brackets in the second column. The third column describes the chore.

Listing 12-7 implements the add function, which allows you to add chores to the list.

```
--snip--

func add(s string) error {
    chores, err := ❶load()
    if err != nil {
        return err
    }

    for _, chore := range ❷strings.Split(s, ",") {
        if desc := strings.TrimSpace(chore); desc != "" {
            chores = append(chores, &housework.Chore{
                Description: desc,
            })
        }
    }

    return ❸flush(chores)
}
```

*Listing 12-7: Adding chores to the list (cmd/housework.go)*

Unlike a long-running service, this application's lifetime starts when you execute it on the command line and ends when it completes whatever task you ask it to perform. Therefore, because you want your list of chores to persist between executions of the application, you need to store the chore state on disk. In other words, you retrieve the chores from storage ❶, modify them, and flush the changes to storage ❸. The changes persist until the next time you run the app.

You want the option to add more than one chore at a time, so you split the incoming chore description by commas ❷ and append each chore to the slice. Granted, this keeps you from using commas in individual chore descriptions, so the members of your household will have to keep their requests short (which isn't all bad, in my opinion). As an exercise, figure out a way around this limitation. One approach may be to use a different delimiter, but keep in mind, whatever you choose as a delimiter may have significance on the command line. Another approach may be to add support for quoted strings containing commas.

The last piece of this puzzle is my favorite part about working on chores: marking them as complete (see Listing 12-8).

```
--snip--

func complete(s string) error {
    i, err := strconv.Atoi(s)
    if err != nil {
        return err
    }

    chores, err := load()
    if err != nil {
        return err
    }

    if i < 1 || i > len(chores) {
        return fmt.Errorf("chore %d not found", i)
    }

❶  chores[i-1].Complete = true

    return flush(chores)
}
```

*Listing 12-8: Marking a chore as complete (cmd/housework.go)*

The complete function accepts the command line argument representing the chore you want to complete and converts it to an integer. I find I'm more efficient if I perform tasks one by one, so I'll have you mark only one complete at a time. You then load the chores from storage and make sure the integer is within range. If so, you mark the chore complete. Since you're numbering chores starting with 1 when displaying the list, you need to account for placement in the slice by subtracting 1 ❶. Finally, you flush the chores to storage.

Now, let's tie everything together by implementing the app's main function in Listing 12-9.

```
--snip--

func main() {
    flag.Parse()

    var err error

    switch strings.ToLower(flag.Arg(0)) {
    case "add":
        err = add(strings.Join(flag.Args()[1:], " "))
    case "complete":
        err = complete(flag.Arg(1))
    }

    if err != nil {
        log.Fatal(err)
    }

    err = list()
    if err != nil {
        log.Fatal(err)
    }
}
```

Listing 12-9: The main logic of the housework application (cmd/housework.go)

You've put as much logic in the previous functions as possible, so this main function is quite minimal. You check the first argument to determine whether it's an expected subcommand. If so, you call the appropriate function. You call the list function if err is still nil after accounting for the optional subcommand and its arguments.

All that's left to do now is implement the storage Load and Flush functions for JSON, Gob, and protocol buffers.

## JSON

JSON is a common, human-readable, text-based data serialization format that uses key-value pairs and arrays to represent complex data structures. Most contemporary languages offer official library support for JSON, which is one reason it's the customary encoding format for RESTful APIs.

JSON's types include strings, Booleans, numbers, arrays, key-value objects, and nil values specified by the keyword *null*. JSON numbers do not differentiate between floating-points and integers. You can read more about Go's JSON implementation at *https://blog.golang.org/json*.

Let's look at what the contents of the *housework.db* file would be if we JSON-encoded the chores from Listing 12-6. I've formatted the JSON for easier reading in Listing 12-10, though you could use the encoder's SetIndent method to do it for you.

```
❶ [
❷   {
       "Complete": false,
       "Description": "Mop floors"
     },
     {
       "Complete": false,
       "Description": "Clean dishes"
     },
     {
       "Complete": false,
       "Description": "Mow the lawn"
     }
  ]
```

*Listing 12-10: Formatted contents of the* housework.db *file after serializing the chores to JSON*

As you can see, the JSON is an array of objects ❶, and each object ❷ includes Complete and Description fields and corresponding values.

Listing 12-11 details the JSON storage implementation using Go's encoding/json package.

```
package json

import (
    "encoding/json"
    "io"

    "github.com/awoodbeck/gnp/ch12/housework"
)

func Load(r io.Reader) ([]*housework.Chore, error) {
    var chores []*housework.Chore

    return chores, ❶ json.NewDecoder(r).Decode(&chores)
}

func Flush(w io.Writer, chores []*housework.Chore) error {
    return ❷ json.NewEncoder(w).Encode(chores)
}
```

*Listing 12-11: JSON storage implementation (*json/housework.go*)*

The Load function passes the io.Reader to the json.NewDecoder function ❶ and returns a decoder. You then call the decoder's Decode method, passing it a pointer to the chores slice. The decoder reads JSON from the io.Reader, deserializes it, and populates the chores slice.

The `Flush` function accepts an `io.Writer` and a chores slice. It then passes the `io.Writer` to the `json.NewEncoder` function ❷, which returns an encoder. You pass the chores slice to the encoder's `Encode` function, which serializes the chores slice into JSON and writes it to the `io.Writer`.

Now that you've implemented a JSON package that can serve as storage for your application, let's try it out in Listing 12-12.

```
$ go run cmd/housework.go
You're all caught up!
$ go run cmd/housework.go add Mop floors, Clean dishes, Mow the lawn
#       [X]      Description
1       [ ]      Mop floors
2       [ ]      Clean dishes
3       [ ]      Mow the lawn
$ go run cmd/housework.go complete 2
#       [X]      Description
1       [ ]      Mop floors
2       [X]      Clean dishes
3       [ ]      Mow the lawn
$ cat housework.db
[{"Complete":false,"Description":"Mop floors"},
{"Complete":true,"Description":"Clean dishes"},
{"Complete":false,"Description":"Mow the lawn"}]
```

*Listing 12-12: Testing the housework application with JSON storage on the command line*

Your first execution of the app lets you know you have nothing in your list of chores. You then add three comma-separated chores and complete the second one. Looks good. Notice also that the *housework.db* file contains readable JSON (to see this on Windows, use the `type` command instead of `cat`). Let's modify this application to use a binary encoding format native to Go.

## Gob

*Gob*, as in "gobs of binary data," is a binary serialization format native to Go. Engineers on the Go team developed Gob to combine the efficiency of protocol buffers, arguably the most popular binary serialization format, with JSON's ease of use. For example, protocol buffers don't let us simply instantiate a new encoder and throw data structures at it, as you did in the JSON example in Listing 12-11. On the other hand, Gob functions much the same way as the JSON encoder, in that Gob can intelligently infer an object's structure and serialize it.

If you're interested in exploring the motivation and finer points of Gob, give Rob Pike's "Gobs of Data" blog post a read (*https://blog.golang.org/gob*). In the meantime, let's implement our storage backend in Gob (see Listing 12-13).

```
package gob

import (
    "encoding/gob"
    "io"
```

```
        "github.com/awoodbeck/gnp/ch12/housework"
)

func Load(r io.Reader) ([]*housework.Chore, error) {
    var chores []*housework.Chore

    return chores, gob.NewDecoder(r).Decode(&chores)
}

func Flush(w io.Writer, chores []*housework.Chore) error {
    return gob.NewEncoder(w).Encode(chores)
}
```

*Listing 12-13: Gob storage implementation (gob/housework.go)*

If you're looking at this code and observing that it replaces all occurrences of json from Listing 12-11 with gob, you're not wrong. In Go, Gob is as easy to use as JSON, since it infers what it needs to encode from the object itself. You'll see how this differs from protocol buffers in the next section.

All that's left to do is swap out the JSON storage implementation for the Gob one by modifying the imports from Listing 12-2 (Listing 12-14).

```
--snip--
        "github.com/awoodbeck/gnp/ch12/housework"
❶   // storage "github.com/awoodbeck/gnp/ch12/json"
❷   storage "github.com/awoodbeck/gnp/ch12/gob"
    // storage "github.com/awoodbeck/gnp/ch12/protobuf"
--snip--
```

*Listing 12-14: Swapping the JSON storage package for the Gob storage package (cmd/ housework.go)*

Comment out the JSON storage package import ❶ in Listing 12-2 and uncomment the Gob storage package one ❷.

Since your current *housework.db* file contains JSON, it isn't compatible with Gob. Therefore, the housework application will throw an error when attempting to decode it using Gob. Remove the *housework.db* file and retest the application (see Listing 12-15).

```
$ rm housework.db
$ go run cmd/housework.go
You're all caught up!
$ go run cmd/housework.go add Mop floors, Clean dishes, Mow the lawn
#       [X]     Description
1       [ ]     Mop floors
2       [ ]     Clean dishes
3       [ ]     Mow the lawn
$ go run cmd/housework.go complete 2
#       [X]     Description
1       [ ]     Mop floors
2       [X]     Clean dishes
3       [ ]     Mow the lawn
$ hexdump -c housework.db
0000000  \r 377 203 002 001 002 377 204  \0 001 377 202  \0  \0   ) 377
```

```
0000010 201 003 001 002 377 202  \0 001 002 001  \b   C   o   m   p   l
0000020   e   t   e 001 002  \0 001  \v   D   e   s   c   r   i   p   t
0000030   i   o   n 001  \f  \0  \0  \0   1 377 204  \0 003 002  \n   M
0000040   o   p       f   l   o   o   r   s  \0 001 001 001  \f   C   l
0000050   e   a   n       d   i   s   h   e   s  \0 002  \f   M   o   w
0000060       t   h   e       l   a   w   n  \0
000006a
```

*Listing 12-15: Testing the housework application with Gob storage on the command line*

Everything still works as expected. Using the hexdump tool, you can see that the *housework.db* file now includes binary data. It's certainly not human-readable as JSON was in Listing 12-12, but Go happily deserializes the Gob-encoded data, even though it's harder for us to make sense of it. (My Windows friends can find a hexdump binary at *https://www.di-mgt.com.au/hexdump-for-windows.html*, though you'll have to use the -C flag to get the same effect.)

If you are communicating with other Go services that support Gob, I recommend you use Gob over JSON. Go's encoding/gob is more performant than encoding/json. Gob encoding is also more succinct, in that Gob uses less data to represent objects than JSON does. This can make a difference when storing or transmitting serialized data

Now that you have a taste for serializing data using encoding/json and encoding/gob, let's add protocol buffer support to your storage backend.

## Protocol Buffers

Like Gob, *protocol buffers* use binary encoding to store or exchange information across various platforms. It's faster and more succinct than Go's JSON encoding. Unlike Gob and like JSON, protocol buffers are language neutral and enjoy wide support among popular programming languages. This makes them ideally suited for using in Go-based services that you hope to integrate with services written in other programming languages. This chapter assumes you're using the *proto3* version of the format.

Protocol buffers use a definition file, conventionally suffixed with *.proto*, to define messages. *Messages* describe the structured data you want to serialize for storage or transmission. For example, a protocol buffer message representing the Chore type looks like the definition in Listing 12-16.

```
message Chore {
  bool complete = 1;
  string description = 2;
}
```

*Listing 12-16: Protocol buffer message definition representing a Chore type*

You define a new message by using the message keyword, followed by the unique name of the message. Convention dictates you use Pascal case. (*Pascal casing* is a style of code formatting in which you concatenate capitalized words: *ThisIsPascalCasing*.) You then add fields to the Chore message. Each field definition includes a type, a snake-cased name, and a field number unique to the message. (*Snake casing* is like Pascal casing except the first word is lowercase: *thisIsSnakeCasing*.) The field's type and number identify the field in the binary payload, so these must not change once used or you'll break backward compatibility. However, it's fine to add new messages and message fields to an existing *.proto* file.

Speaking of backward compatibility, it's a good practice to treat your protocol buffer definitions as you would an API. If third parties use your protocol buffer definition to communicate with your service, consider versioning your definition; this allows you to create new versions anytime you need to break backward compatibility. Your development can move forward with the latest version while clients continue to use the previous version until they're ready to target the latest version. You'll see one method of versioning the protocol buffer definitions later in this section.

You'll have to compile the *.proto* file to generate Go code from it. This code allows you to serialize and deserialize the messages defined in the *.proto* file. Third parties that want to exchange messages with you can use the same *.proto* file to generate code for their target programming language. The resulting code can exchange messages with you too. Therefore, before you can start using protocol buffers in earnest, you must install the protocol buffer compiler and its Go generation module. Your operating system's package manager may allow you to easily install the protocol buffer compiler. For example, on Debian 10, run the following:

```
$ sudo apt install protobuf-compiler
```

On macOS with Homebrew, run this:

```
$ brew install protobuf
```

On Windows, download the latest protocol buffer compiler ZIP file from *https://github.com/protocolbuffers/protobuf/releases/*, extract it, and add its *bin* subdirectory to your PATH. You should now be able to run the *protoc* binary on your command line.

A simple go get will install the protocol buffer's Go generator on your system. Make sure you have the resulting *protoc-gen-go* binary in your PATH or *protoc* won't recognize the plug-in:

```
$ GO111MODULE=on go get -u github.com/golang/protobuf/protoc-gen-go
```

Now that you've installed the protocol buffer compiler and Go generation module, let's create a new *.proto* file for your housework application (see Listing 12-17). You'll create this file in *housework/v1/housework.proto*. The v1 in the path stands for *version 1* and allows you to introduce future versions of this package.

❶ syntax = "proto3";
❷ package housework;

❸ option go_package = "github.com/awoodbeck/gnp/ch12/housework/v1/housework";

```
message Chore {
  bool complete = 1;
  string description = 2;
}

message Chores {
❹ repeated Chore chores = 1;
}
```

*Listing 12-17: Protocol buffer definition for your housework application (housework/v1/housework.proto)*

First, you specify that you're using the proto3 syntax ❶ and that you want any generated code to have the package name housework ❷. Next, you add a go_package option ❸ with the full import path of the generated module. Then you define the Chore message and a second message named Chores that represents a collection of Chore messages based on the repeated field type ❹.

Now, let's compile the *.proto* file to Go code:

```
$ protoc ❶--go_out=. ❷--go_opt=paths=source_relative housework/v1/housework.proto
```

You call *protoc* with flags indicating you want to generate Go code ❶ from the *housework/v1/housework.proto* file you created in Listing 12-17 and output the generated code to the *.proto* file's current directory, with relative paths ❷.

If you receive the following error indicating *protoc* cannot find the *protoc-gen-go* binary, make sure *protoc-gen-go*'s location (likely *$GOPATH/bin*) is in your PATH environment variable:

```
protoc-gen-go: program not found or is not executable
--go_out: protoc-gen-go: Plugin failed with status code 1.
```

If *protoc* is happy with the *.proto* file and successfully generated the Go code, you'll find that a new file named *housework/v1/housework.pb.go* exists with these first few lines, though the version numbers may differ. I'll use the head command on Linux/macOS to print the first seven lines:

```
$ head -n 7 housework/v1/housework.pb.go
// Code generated by protoc-gen-go. DO NOT EDIT.
// versions:
//      protoc-gen-go v1.25.0
//      protoc        v3.6.1
// source: housework/v1/housework.proto

package housework
```

As the comments indicate, you shouldn't edit this module. Instead, make any necessary changes to the *.proto* file and recompile it.

Now that you've generated a Go module from the *.proto* file, you can put it to effective use in Listing 12-18 by implementing your storage backend with protocol buffers.

```
package protobuf

import (
    "io"
    "io/ioutil"

    "google.golang.org/protobuf/proto"

 ❶ "github.com/awoodbeck/gnp/ch12/housework/v1"
)

func Load(r io.Reader) ([]*housework.Chore, error) {
    b, err := ioutil.ReadAll(r)
    if err != nil {
        return nil, err
    }

    var chores housework.Chores

    return chores.Chores, proto.Unmarshal(b, &chores)
}

func Flush(w io.Writer, chores []*housework.Chore) error {
    b, err := proto.Marshal(❷&housework.Chores{Chores: chores})
    if err != nil {
        return err
    }

    _, err = w.Write(b)

    return err
}
```

*Listing 12-18: Protocol buffers storage implementation (protobuf/housework.go)*

Instead of relying on the housework package from Listing 12-1, as you did when working with JSON and Gob, you import version 1 of the *protoc*-generated package, which you also named housework ❶. The generated Chores type ❷ is a struct with a Chores field, which itself is a slice of Chore pointers. Also, Go's protocol buffers package doesn't implement encoders and decoders. Therefore, you must marshal objects to bytes, write them to the io.Writer, and unmarshal bytes from the io.Reader yourself.

Revisit the code in Listing 12-2 and plug in the protocol buffers implementation with the two simple changes shown in Listing 12-19.

```
--snip--
 ❶ "github.com/awoodbeck/gnp/ch12/housework/v1"
    // storage "github.com/awoodbeck/gnp/ch12/json"
```

```
   // storage "github.com/awoodbeck/gnp/ch12/gob"
❷ storage "github.com/awoodbeck/gnp/ch12/protobuf"
--snip--
```

Listing 12-19: Swapping the JSON storage package for the protobuf storage package (cmd/housework.go)

You replace the housework package from Listing 12-1 with your generated package ❶, make sure to comment out the json and gob imports, and uncomment the protobuf storage import ❷. The actual functionality of the housework application remains unchanged.

## Transmitting Serialized Objects

Although you may sometimes need to serialize and store objects locally, you're more likely to build a network service that serializes data. For example, an online store may have a web service that communicates with inventory, user accounting, billing, shipping, and notification services to facilitate customer orders. If these services ran on the same server, you'd have to buy a larger server to scale the online store as business grows. Another approach would be to run each service on its own server and increase the number of servers. But then you'd have a new problem: how can you share data among services when they no longer reside on a single server and so can't access the same memory?

Large technology companies facilitate this with *remote procedure calls (RPCs)*, a technique by which a client can transparently call a subroutine on a server as if the call were local. From your application's perspective, RPC services take code that appears to run locally and distribute it over a network. Your code may call a function that transparently relays a message to a server. The server would locally execute the function, then respond with the results, which your code receives as the function's return value. As far as your code is concerned, the function call is local, despite RPC's transparent interaction with the server. This approach allows you to scale services across servers while abstracting the details away from your code. In other words, your code functions the same no matter whether the function call runs on the same computer or on one over the network.

Most companies now implement RPC with *gRPC*, a cross-platform framework that leverages HTTP/2 and protocol buffers. Let's use it here to build something more sophisticated than an app to keep track of the housework you have yet to do. You'll write a service that can send tasks to Rosie, the robotic maid from the classic animated series *The Jetsons*, who can take over your domestic responsibilities. Granted, she won't be available until the year 2062, but you can get a head start on the code.

### Connecting Services with gRPC

The gRPC framework is a collection of libraries that abstracts many of the RPC implementation details. It is platform neutral and programming-language agnostic; you can use it to integrate a Go service running on

Windows with a Rust service running on Linux, for example. Now that you know how to work with protocol buffers, you have the foundation needed to add gRPC support to your application. You'll reuse the *.proto* file from the previous section.

First, make sure your gRPC package is up-to-date:

```
$ go get -u google.golang.org/grpc
```

Next, get the appropriate module for generating gRPC Go code:

```
$ go get -u google.golang.org/grpc/cmd/protoc-gen-go-grpc
```

The protocol buffer compiler includes a gRPC module. This module will output Go code that lets you easily add gRPC support. First, you need to add definitions to the *.proto* file. Listing 12-20 defines a new service and two additional messages.

```
--snip--

service RobotMaid {
❶   rpc Add (Chores) returns (Response);
    rpc Complete (CompleteRequest) returns (Response);
    rpc List (Empty) returns (Chores);
}

message CompleteRequest {
    int32 ❷ chore_number = 1;
}

❸ message Empty {}

message Response {
    string message = 1;
}
```

*Listing 12-20: Additional definitions to support a gRPC RobotMaid service (housework/v1/housework.proto)*

The service needs to support the same three calls you used on the command line: add, complete, and list. You define a new service named RobotMaid, then add three RPC methods to it. These RPC methods correspond to the functions defined in Listings 12-5, 12-7, and 12-8 for use on the command line: the list, add, and complete functions, respectively. Instead of calling these functions locally, you'll call the corresponding method on the RobotMaid to execute these commands via RPC. You prefix each method with the rpc keyword and follow this with the Pascal-cased method name. Next, you write the request message type in parentheses, the returns keyword, and the return message type in parentheses ❶.

The List method doesn't require any user input, but as in the command line application, you still must provide a request message type for it, even if it's nil. In gRPC, the message type equivalent to nil is an empty message, which you call Empty ❸.

Until you've had the opportunity to add proper artificial intelligence (AI) to the robot, you'll need to tell Rosie when her current chore is complete so she can move on to the next one. For this, you add a new message that informs her of the completed chore number ❷. Since you expect feedback from Rosie, you also add a response message that contains a string.

Now compile the *.proto* file to use the new service and messages. Tell *protoc* to use the *protoc-gen-go-grpc* binary, which must also be in your PATH environment variable, like this:

```
$ protoc ❶--go-grpc_out=. ❷--go-grpc_opt=paths=source_relative \
housework/v1/housework.proto
```

The --go-grpc_out flag ❶ invokes the *protoc-gen-go-grpc* binary to add gRPC support to the generated code. This binary generates the relevant gRPC service code for you and writes gRPC-specific code to the *housework/v1/housework_grpc.pb.go* file since you told *protoc-gen-go-grpc* to use relative paths ❷. You can now use the generated code to build a gRPC server and client.

### Creating a TLS-Enabled gRPC Server

Now let's implement a gRPC client and server. By default, gRPC requires a secure connection, so you'll add TLS support to your server. You'll use the server's *cert.pem* and *key.pem* files created in the preceding chapter for your gRPC server and pin the server's certificate to your client. See the "Generating Certificates for Authentication" section on page 256 for details.

You'll leverage the Go code generated by your *.proto* file to define a new RobotMaid client and server and use the client to communicate with the server over the network using gRPC. First, let's create the server portion of your robot maid. The RobotMaidServer interface generated from your *.proto* file looks like this:

```
type RobotMaidServer interface {
    Add(context.Context, *Chores) (*Response, error)
    Complete(context.Context, *CompleteRequest) (*Response, error)
    List(context.Context, *empty.Empty) (*Chores, error)
    mustEmbedUnimplementedRobotMaidServer()
}
```

You'll implement this interface in Listing 12-21 by creating a new type named Rosie.

```
package main

import (
    "context"
    "fmt"
    "sync"

    "github.com/awoodbeck/gnp/ch12/housework/v1"
)
```

```
type Rosie struct {
    mu sync.Mutex
 ❶ chores []*housework.Chore
}

func (r *Rosie) Add(_ context.Context, chores *housework.Chores) (
    *housework.Response, error) {
    r.mu.Lock()
    r.chores = append(r.chores, chores.Chores...)
    r.mu.Unlock()

    return ❷&housework.Response{Message: "ok"}, nil
}

func (r *Rosie) Complete(_ context.Context,
    req *housework.CompleteRequest) (*housework.Response, error) {
    r.mu.Lock()
    defer r.mu.Unlock()

    if r.chores == nil || req.ChoreNumber < 1 ||
        int(req.ChoreNumber) > len(r.chores) {
        return nil, fmt.Errorf("chore %d not found", req.ChoreNumber)
    }

    r.chores[req.ChoreNumber-1].Complete = true

    return &housework.Response{Message: "ok"}, nil
}

func (r *Rosie) List(_ context.Context, _ *housework.Empty) (
    *housework.Chores, error) {
    r.mu.Lock()
    defer r.mu.Unlock()

    if r.chores == nil {
        r.chores = make([]*housework.Chore, 0)
    }

    return &housework.Chores{Chores: r.chores}, nil
}

func (r *Rosie) Service() *housework.RobotMaidService {
    return ❸&housework.RobotMaidService{
        Add:      r.Add,
        Complete: r.Complete,
        List:     r.List,
    }
}
```

*Listing 12-21: Building a RobotMaid-compatible type named Rosie (server/rosie.go)*

The new Rosie struct keeps its list of chores in memory ❶, guarded by a mutex, since more than one client can concurrently use the service. The Add, Complete, and List methods all return either a response message type ❷ or an error, both of which ultimately make their way back to the client.

The Service method returns a pointer to a new housework.RobotMaidService instance ❸ where Rosie's Add, Complete, and List methods map to their corresponding method on the new instance.

Now, let's set up a new gRPC server instance by using the Rosie struct (Listing 12-22).

```go
package main

import (
    "crypto/tls"
    "flag"
    "fmt"
    "log"
    "net"

    "google.golang.org/grpc"

    "github.com/awoodbeck/gnp/ch12/housework/v1"
)

var addr, certFn, keyFn string

func init() {
    flag.StringVar(&addr, "address", "localhost:34443", "listen address")
    flag.StringVar(&certFn, "cert", "cert.pem", "certificate file")
    flag.StringVar(&keyFn, "key", "key.pem", "private key file")
}

func main() {
    flag.Parse()

    server := ❶grpc.NewServer()
    rosie := new(Rosie)
  ❷housework.RegisterRobotMaidServer(server, ❸rosie.Service())

    cert, err := tls.LoadX509KeyPair(certFn, keyFn)
    if err != nil {
        log.Fatal(err)
    }

    listener, err := net.Listen("tcp", addr)
    if err != nil {
        log.Fatal(err)
    }

    fmt.Printf("Listening for TLS connections on %s ...", addr)
    log.Fatal(
      ❹ server.Serve(
          ❺ tls.NewListener(
                listener,
                &tls.Config{
                    Certificates:       []tls.Certificate{cert},
                    CurvePreferences:   []tls.CurveID{tls.CurveP256},
                    MinVersion:         tls.VersionTLS12,
```

```
                    PreferServerCipherSuites: true,
            },
        ),
    ),
)
}
```

*Listing 12-22: Creating a new gRPC server using Rosie (server/server.go)*

First, you retrieve a new server instance ❶. You pass it and a
new *housework.RobotMaidService from Rosie's Service ❸ method to the
RegisterRobotMaidServer function ❷ in the generated gRPC code. This
registers Rosie's RobotMaidService implementation with the gRPC server.
You must do this before you call the server's Serve method ❹. You then
load the server's key pair and create a new TLS listener ❺, which you
pass to the server when calling Serve.

Now that you have a gRPC server implementation, let's work on the
client.

### Creating a gRPC Client to Test the Server

The client-side code isn't much different from what you wrote in the
"Serializing Objects" section on page 270. The main difference is that
you need to instantiate a new gRPC client and modify the add, complete,
and list functions to use it. Remember, you can implement the client
portion in a separate programming language if the programming language offers protobuf support. You can generate code for your target
language from your *.proto* file with the expectation it will work seamlessly
with your server in Listing 12-22.

Listing 12-23 details the changes to Listing 12-2 necessary to add gRPC
support to the housework application.

```
package main

import (
❶   "context"
❷   "crypto/tls"
❸   "crypto/x509"
    "flag"
    "fmt"
❹   "io/ioutil"
    "log"
    "os"
    "path/filepath"
    "strconv"
    "strings"

    "google.golang.org/grpc"
    "google.golang.org/grpc/credentials"

    "github.com/awoodbeck/gnp/ch12/housework/v1"
)
```

```
var addr, caCertFn string

func init() {
❺  flag.StringVar(&addr, "address", "localhost:34443", "server address")
❻  flag.StringVar(&caCertFn, "ca-cert", "cert.pem", "CA certificate")

    flag.Usage = func() {
        fmt.Fprintf(flag.CommandLine.Output(),
            `Usage: %s [flags] [add chore, ...|complete #]
    add             add comma-separated chores
    complete        complete designated chore

Flags:
`, filepath.Base(os.Args[0]))
            flag.PrintDefaults()
    }
}
```

*Listing 12-23: Initial gRPC client code for our housework application (client/client.go)*

Aside from all the new imports ❶ ❷ ❸ ❹, you add flags for the gRPC server address ❺ and its certificate ❻.

Listing 12-24 uses the gRPC client to list the current chores.

```
--snip--

func list(ctx context.Context, client housework.RobotMaidClient) error {
    chores, err := client.List(ctx, ❶new(housework.Empty))
    if err != nil {
        return err
    }

    if len(chores.Chores) == 0 {
        fmt.Println("You have nothing to do!")
        return nil
    }

    fmt.Println("#\t[X]\tDescription")
    for i, chore := range chores.Chores {
        c := " "
        if chore.Complete {
            c = "X"
        }
        fmt.Printf("%d\t[%s]\t%s\n", i+1, c, chore.Description)
    }

    return nil
}
```

*Listing 12-24: Using the gRPC client to list the current chores (client/client.go)*

This code is quite like Listing 12-5, except you're asking the gRPC client for the list of chores, which retrieves them from the server. You need to pass along an empty message to make gRPC happy ❶.

Listing 12-25 uses the gRPC client to add new chores to the gRPC server's chores.

```
--snip--

func add(ctx context.Context, client housework.RobotMaidClient,
    s string) error {
    chores := new(housework.Chores)

    for _, chore := range strings.Split(s, ",") {
        if desc := strings.TrimSpace(chore); desc != "" {
            chores.Chores = append(chores.Chores, &housework.Chore{
                Description: desc,
            })
        }
    }

    var err error
    if len(chores.Chores) > 0 {
        _, ❶err = client.Add(ctx, chores)
    }

    return err
}
```

*Listing 12-25: Adding new chores using the gRPC client (client/client.go)*

As you did in the previous section, you parse the comma-separated list of chores. Instead of flushing these chores to disk, you pass them along to the gRPC client. The gRPC client transparently sends them to the gRPC server and returns the response to you. Since you know Rosie returns a non-nil error when the Add call fails, you return the error ❶ as the result of the add function.

In Listing 12-26, you write the code to mark chores complete. Doing this over gRPC requires a bit less code than Listing 12-8 since most of the logic is in the server.

```
--snip--

func complete(ctx context.Context, client housework.RobotMaidClient,
    s string) error {
    i, err := strconv.Atoi(s)
    if err == nil {
        _, err = client.Complete(ctx,
            &housework.CompleteRequest{❶ChoreNumber: int32(i)})
    }

    return err
}
```

*Listing 12-26: Marking chores complete by using the gRPC client (client/client.go)*

Notice the *protoc-gen-go* module, which converts the snake-cased chore_number field in Listing 12-20 to Pascal case in the generated Go code ❶. You must also convert the int returned by strconv.Atoi to an int32 before assigning it to the complete request message's chore number since ChoreNumber is an int32.

Listing 12-27 creates a new gRPC connection and pins the server's certificate to its TLS configuration.

```
--snip--

func main() {
    flag.Parse()

    caCert, err := ioutil.ReadFile(caCertFn)
    if err != nil {
        log.Fatal(err)
    }
    certPool := x509.NewCertPool()
    if ok := certPool.AppendCertsFromPEM(caCert); !ok {
        log.Fatal("failed to add certificate to pool")
    }

    conn, err := ❶grpc.Dial(
        addr,
      ❷ grpc.WithTransportCredentials(
          ❸ credentials.NewTLS(
                &tls.Config{
                    CurvePreferences: []tls.CurveID{tls.CurveP256},
                    MinVersion:       tls.VersionTLS12,
                    RootCAs:          certPool,
                },
            ),
        ),
    )
    if err != nil {
        log.Fatal(err)
    }
}
```

*Listing 12-27: Creating a new gRPC connection using TLS and certificate pinning (client/client.go)*

On the client side, you first create a new gRPC network connection ❶ and then use the network connection to instantiate a new gRPC client. For most use cases, you can simply pass the address to grpc.Dial. But you want to pin the server's certificate to the client connection. Therefore, you need to explicitly pass in a grpc.DialOption with the appropriate TLS credentials. This involves using the grpc.WithTransportCredentials function ❷ to return the grpc.DialOption and the credentials.NewTLS function ❸ to create the transport credentials from your TLS configuration. The result is a gRPC network connection that speaks TLS with the server and authenticates the server by using the pinned certificate.

You use this gRPC network connection to instantiate a new gRPC client in Listing 12-28.

```
--snip--

    rosie := ❶housework.NewRobotMaidClient(conn)
    ctx := context.Background()

    switch strings.ToLower(flag.Arg(0)) {
    case "add":
        err = add(ctx, rosie, strings.Join(flag.Args()[1:], " "))
    case "complete":
        err = complete(ctx, rosie, flag.Arg(1))
    }

    if err != nil {
        log.Fatal(err)
    }

    err = list(ctx, rosie)
    if err != nil {
        log.Fatal(err)
    }
}
```

Listing 12-28: Instantiating a new gRPC client and making calls (client/client.go)

Aside from instantiating a new gRPC client from the gRPC network connection ❶, this bit of code doesn't vary much from Listing 12-9. The difference, of course, lies in the fact that any interaction with the list of chores transparently takes place over a TLS connection to the gRPC server.

Give it a try. In one terminal, start the server:

```
$ go run server/server.go server/rosie.go -cert server/cert.pem -key server/
key.pem
Listening for TLS connections on localhost:34443 ...
```

And in another terminal, run the client:

```
$ go run client/client.go -ca-cert server/cert.pem
You have nothing to do!
$ go run client/client.go -ca-cert server/cert.pem add Mop floors, Wash dishes
#       [X]     Description
1       [ ]     Mop floors
2       [ ]     Wash dishes
$ go run client/client.go -ca-cert server/cert.pem complete 2
#       [X]     Description
1       [ ]     Mop floors
2       [X]     Wash dishes
```

Of course, restarting the server wipes out the list of chores. I'll leave it as an exercise for you to implement persistence on the server. One approach is to have the server load the chores from and flush chores to disk as you did earlier in this chapter.

## What You've Learned

Data serialization allows you to exchange data in a platform-neutral and language-neutral way. You can also serialize data for long-term storage, retrieve and deserialize the data, and pick up where your application left off.

JSON is arguably the most popular text-based data serialization format. Contemporary programming languages offer good support for JSON, which is one reason for its ubiquity in RESTful APIs. Go offers good support for binary-based data serialization formats as well, including Gob, which is nearly a drop-in replacement for JSON. Gob is Go's native binary data serialization format, and it's designed to be efficient and easy to use.

If you're looking for a binary data serialization format with wider support, consider protocol buffers. Google designed protocol buffers to facilitate the exchange of serialized binary data across its supported platforms and programming languages. Many contemporary programming languages currently offer support for protocol buffers. Although protocol buffers aren't the same drop-in replacement in Go as Gob is for JSON, Go has excellent protocol buffer support, nonetheless. You first need to add definitions that define the data structures you intend to serialize in a *.proto* file. You then use the protocol buffer compiler and its Go module to generate Go code that corresponds to your defined data structures. Finally, you use the generated code to serialize your data structures into protocol buffer-formatted binary data and deserialize that binary data back into your data structures.

The gRPC framework is a high-performance, platform-neutral standard for making distributed function calls across a network. The *RPC* in *gRPC* stands for *remote procedure call*, which is a technique for transparently calling a function on a remote system and receiving the result as if you had executed the function on your local system. gRPC uses protocol buffers as its underlying data serialization format. Go's protocol buffer module allows you to easily add gRPC support by defining services in your *.proto* file and leveraging the generated code. This lets you quickly and efficiently stand up distributed services or integrate with existing gRPC services.

# 13

## LOGGING AND METRICS

In an ideal world, our code would be free of bugs from the outset. Our network services would exceed our expectations for performance and capacity, and they would be robust enough to adapt to unexpected input without our intervention. But in the real world, we need to worry about unexpected and potentially malicious input, hardware degradation, network outages, and outright bugs in our code.

Monitoring our applications, no matter whether they are on premises or in the cloud, is vital to providing resilient, functional services to our users. Comprehensive logging allows us to receive timely details about errors, anomalies, or other actionable events, and metrics give us insight into the current state of our services, as well as help us identify bottlenecks. Taken together, logging and metrics allow us to manage service issues and focus our development efforts to avoid future failures.

You've used Go's `log` and `fmt` packages to give you feedback in previous chapters, but this chapter will take a deeper dive into logging and instrumenting your services. You will learn how to use log levels to increase or decrease the verbosity of your logs and when to use each log level. You'll learn how to add structure to your log entries so software can help you make better sense of log entries and zero in on relevant logs. I'll introduce you to the concept of wide event logging, which will help you maintain a handle on the amount of data you log as your services scale. You'll learn techniques for dynamically enabling debug logging and managing log file rotation from your code.

This chapter will also introduce you to Go kit's `metrics` package. Per Go kit's documentation, the `metrics` package "provides a set of uniform interfaces for service instrumentation." You'll learn how to instrument your services by using counters, gauges, and histograms.

By the end of this chapter, you should have a handle on how to approach logging, how to manage log files to prevent them from consuming too much hard drive space, and how to instrument your services to gain insight into their current state.

## Event Logging

Logging is hard. Even experienced developers struggle to get it right. It's tough to anticipate what questions you'll need your logs to answer in the future, when your service fails—yet you should resist the urge to log everything just in case. You need to strike a balance in order to log the right information to answer those questions without overwhelming yourself with irrelevant log lines. Overzealous logging may suit you fine in development, where you control the scale of testing and overall entropy of your service, but it will quickly degrade your ability to find the needle in the haystack when you need to diagnose production failures.

In addition to figuring out what to log, you need to consider that logging isn't free. It consumes CPU and I/O time your application could otherwise use. A log entry added to a busy `for` loop while in development may help you understand what your service is doing. But it may become a bottleneck in production, insidiously adding latency to your service.

Instead, sampling these log entries, or logging on demand, may provide suitable compromises between log output and overhead. You might find it helpful to use *wide event* log entries, which summarize a transaction. For example, a service in development may log half a dozen entries about a request, any intermediate steps, and a response. In production, a single wide event log entry providing these details scales better. You'll learn more about wide event log entries in "Scaling Up with Wide Event Logging" on page 312.

Lastly, logging is subjective. An anomaly may be inconsequential in my application but indicative of a larger issue in your application. Whereas I could ignore the anomaly, you'd likely want to know about it. For this reason, it's best if we discuss logging in terms of best practices. These practices are a good baseline approach, but you should tailor them to each application.

## The log Package

You have superficial experience using Go's log package, in earlier chapters, for basic logging needs, like timestamping log entries and optionally exiting your application with log.Fatal. But it has a few more features we have yet to explore. These require us to go beyond the package-level logger and instantiate our own *log.Logger instance. You can do this using the log.New function:

```
func New(out io.Writer, prefix string, flag int) *Logger
```

The log.New function accepts an io.Writer, a string prefix to use on each log line, and a set of flags that modify the logger's output. Accepting an io.Writer means the logger can write to anything that satisfies that interface, including an in-memory buffer or a network socket.

The default logger writes its output to os.Stderr, standard error. Let's look at an example logger in Listing 13-1 that writes to os.Stdout, standard output.

```
func Example_log() {
    l := log.New(❶os.Stdout, ❷"example: ", ❸log.Lshortfile)
    l.Print("logging to standard output")

    // Output:
    // example: ❹log_test.go:12: logging to standard output
}
```

Listing 13-1: Writing a log entry to standard output (log_test.go)

You create a new *log.Logger instance that writes to standard output ❶. The logger prefixes each line with the string *example:* ❷. The flags of the default logger are log.Ldate and log.Ltime, collectively log.LstdFlags, which print the timestamp of each log entry. Since you want to simplify the output for testing purposes when you run the example on the command line, you omit the timestamp and configure the logger to write the source code filename and line of each log entry ❸. The l.Print function on line 12 of the *log_test.go* file results in the output of those values ❹. This behavior can help with development and debugging, allowing you to zero in on the exact file and line of an interesting log entry.

Recognizing that the logger accepts an io.Writer, you may realize this allows you to use multiple writers, such as a log file and standard output or an in-memory ring buffer and a centralized logging server over a network. Unfortunately, the io.MultiWriter is not ideal for use in logging. An io.MultiWriter writes to each of its writers in sequence, aborting if it receives an error from any Write call. This means that if you configure your io.MultiWriter to write to a log file and standard output in that order, standard output will never receive the log entry if an error occurred when writing to the log file.

Fear not. It's an easy problem to solve. Let's create our own io.MultiWriter implementation, starting in Listing 13-2, that sustains writes across its writers and accumulates any errors it encounters.

```
package ch13

import (
    "io"

    "go.uber.org/multierr"
)

type sustainedMultiWriter struct {
    writers []io.Writer
}

func (s *sustainedMultiWriter) ❶Write(p []byte) (n int, err error) {
    for _, w := range s.writers {
        i, wErr := ❷w.Write(p)
        n += i
        err = ❸multierr.Append(err, wErr)
    }

    return n, err
}
```

*Listing 13-2: A multiwriter that sustains writing even after receiving an error (writer.go)*

As with io.MultiWriter, you'll use a struct that contains a slice of io.Writer instances for your sustained multiwriter. Your multiwriter implements the io.Writer interface ❶, so you can pass it into your logger. It calls each writer's Write method ❷, accumulating any errors with the help of Uber's multierr package ❸, before ultimately returning the total written bytes and cumulative error.

Listing 13-3 adds a function to initialize a new sustained multiwriter from one or more writers.

```
--snip--

func SustainedMultiWriter(writers ...io.Writer) io.Writer {
    mw := &sustainedMultiWriter{writers: ❶make([]io.Writer, 0, len(writers))}

    for _, w := range writers {
        if m, ok := ❷w.(*sustainedMultiWriter); ok {
            mw.writers = ❸append(mw.writers, m.writers...)
            continue
        }

        mw.writers = ❹append(mw.writers, w)
```

```
    }

    return mw
}
```

*Listing 13-3: Creating a sustained multiwriter (writer.go)*

First, you instantiate a new *sustainedMultiWriter, initialize its writers slice ❶, and cap it to the expected length of writers. You then loop through the given writers and append them to the slice ❹. If a given writer is itself a *sustainedMultiWriter ❷, you instead append its writers ❸. Finally, you return the pointer to the initialized sustainedMultiWriter.

You can now put your sustained multiwriter to good use in Listing 13-4.

```
package ch13

import (
    "bytes"
    "fmt"
    "log"
    "os"
)

func Example_logMultiWriter() {
    logFile := new(bytes.Buffer)
    w := ❶ SustainedMultiWriter(os.Stdout, logFile)
    l := log.New(w, "example: ", ❷ log.Lshortfile|log.Lmsgprefix)

    fmt.Println("standard output:")
    l.Print("Canada is south of Detroit")

    fmt.Print("\nlog file contents:\n", logFile.String())

    // Output:
    // standard output:
    // log_test.go:24: example: Canada is south of Detroit
    //
    // log file contents:
    // log_test.go:24: example: Canada is south of Detroit
}
```

*Listing 13-4: Logging simultaneously to a log file and standard output (log_test.go)*

You create a new sustained multiwriter ❶, writing to standard output, and a bytes.Buffer meant to act as a log file in this example. Next, you create a new logger using your sustained multiwriter, the prefix example:, and two flags ❷ to modify the logger's behavior. The addition of the log.Lmsgprefix flag (first available in Go 1.14) tells the logger to locate the prefix just before the log message. You can see the effect this has on the log entries in the example output. When you run this example, you see that the logger writes the log entry to the sustained multiwriter, which in turn writes the log entry to both standard output and the log file.

## Leveled Log Entries

I wrote earlier in the chapter that verbose logging may be inefficient in production and can overwhelm you with the sheer number of log entries as your service scales up. One way to avoid this is by instituting *logging levels*, which assign a priority to each kind of event, enabling you to always log high-priority errors but conditionally log low-priority entries more suited for debugging and development purposes. For example, you'd always want to know if your service is unable to connect to its database, but you may care to log only details about individual connections while in development or when diagnosing a failure.

I recommend you create just a few log levels to begin with. In my experience, you can address most use cases with just an *error* level and a *debug* level, maybe even an *info* level on occasion. Error log entries should accompany some sort of alert, since these entries indicate a condition that needs your attention. Info log entries typically log non-error information. For example, it may be appropriate for your use case to log a successful database connection or to add a log entry when a listener is ready for incoming connections on a network socket. Debug log entries should be verbose and serve to help you diagnose failures, as well as aid development by helping you reason about the workflow.

Go's ecosystem offers several logging packages, most of which support numerous log levels. Although Go's log package does not have inherent support for leveled log entries, you can add similar functionality by creating separate loggers for each log level you need. Listing 13-5 does this: it writes log entries to a log file, but it also writes debug logs to standard output.

```
--snip--

func Example_logLevels() {
    lDebug := log.New(os.Stdout, ❶"DEBUG: ", log.Lshortfile)
    logFile := new(bytes.Buffer)
    w := SustainedMultiWriter(logFile, ❷lDebug.Writer())
    lError := log.New(w, ❸"ERROR: ", log.Lshortfile)

    fmt.Println("standard output:")
    lError.Print("cannot communicate with the database")
    lDebug.Print("you cannot hum while holding your nose")

    fmt.Print("\nlog file contents:\n", logFile.String())

    // Output:
    // standard output:
    // ERROR: log_test.go:43: cannot communicate with the database
    // DEBUG: log_test.go:44: you cannot hum while holding your nose
    //
    // log file contents:
    // ERROR: log_test.go:43: cannot communicate with the database
}
```

*Listing 13-5: Writing debug entries to standard output and errors to both the log file and standard output (log_test.go)*

First, you create a debug logger that writes to standard output and uses the DEBUG: prefix ❶. Next, you create a *bytes.Buffer to masquerade as a log file for this example and instantiate a sustained multiwriter. The sustained multiwriter writes to both the log file and the debug logger's io.Writer ❷. Then, you create an error logger that writes to the sustained multiwriter by using the prefix ERROR: ❸ to differentiate its log entries from the debug logger. Finally, you use each logger and verify that they output what you expect. Standard output should display log entries from both loggers, whereas the log file should contain only error log entries.

As an exercise, figure out how to make the debug logger conditional without wrapping its Print call in a conditional. If you need a hint, you'll find a suitable writer in the io/ioutil package that will let you discard its output.

This section is meant to demonstrate additional uses of the log package beyond what you've used so far in this book. Although it's possible to use this technique to log at different levels, you'd be better served by a logger with inherent support for log levels, like the Zap logger described in the next section.

## Structured Logging

The log entries made by the code you've written so far are meant for human consumption. They are easy for you to read, since each log entry is little more than a message. This means that finding log lines relevant to an issue involves liberal use of the grep command or, at worst, manually skimming log entries. But this could become more challenging if the number of log entries increases. You may find yourself looking for a needle in a haystack. Remember, logging is useful only if you can quickly find the information you need.

A common approach to solving this problem is to add metadata to your log entries and then parse the metadata with software to help you organize them. This type of logging is called *structured logging*. Creating structured log entries involves adding key-value pairs to each log entry. In these, you may include the time at which you logged the entry, the part of your application that made the log entry, the log level, the hostname or IP address of the node that created the log entry, and other bits of metadata that you can use for indexing and filtering. Most structured loggers encode log entries as JSON before writing them to log files or shipping them to centralized logging servers. Structured logging makes the whole process of collecting logs in a centralized server easy, since the additional metadata associated with each log entry allows the server to organize and collate log entries across services. Once they're indexed, you can query the log server for specific log entries to better find timely answers to your questions.

### Using the Zap Logger

Discussing specific centralized logging solutions is beyond the scope of this book. If you're interested in learning more, I suggest you initially investigate

Elasticsearch or Apache Solr. Instead, this section focuses on implementing the logger itself. You'll use the Zap logger from Uber, found at *https://pkg.go .dev/go.uber.org/zap/*, which allows you to integrate log file rotation.

*Log file rotation* is the process of closing the current log file, renaming it, and then opening a new log file after the current log file reaches a specific age or size threshold. Rotating log files is a good practice to prevent them from filling up your available hard drive space. Plus, searching through smaller, date-delimited log files is more efficient than searching through a single, monolithic log file. For example, you may want to rotate your log files every week and keep only eight weeks' worth of rotated log files. If you wanted to look at log entries for an event that occurred last week, you could limit your search to a single log file. Also, you can compress the rotated log files to further save hard drive space.

I've used other structured loggers on large projects, and in my experience, Zap causes the least overhead; I can use it in busy bits of code without a noticeable performance hit, unlike other heavyweight structured loggers. But your mileage may vary, so I encourage you to find what works best for you. You can apply the structured logging principles and log file management techniques described here to other structured loggers.

The Zap logger includes zap.Core and its options. The zap.Core has three components: a log-level threshold, an output, and an encoder. The *log-level threshold* sets the minimum log level that Zap will log; Zap will simply ignore any log entry below that level, allowing you to leave debug logging in your code and configure Zap to conditionally ignore it. Zap's *output* is a zapcore .WriteSyncer, which is an io.Writer with an additional Sync method. Zap can write log entries to any object that implements this interface. And the *encoder* can encode the log entry before writing it to the output.

### Writing the Encoder

Although Zap provides a few helper functions, such as zap.NewProduction or zap.NewDevelopment, to quickly create production and development loggers, you'll create one from scratch, starting with the encoder configuration in Listing 13-6.

```
package ch13

import (
    "bytes"
    "fmt"
    "io/ioutil"
    "log"
    "os"
    "path/filepath"
    "runtime"
    "testing"
    "time"

    "go.uber.org/zap"
    "go.uber.org/zap/zapcore"
    "gopkg.in/fsnotify.v1"
```

```
        "gopkg.in/natefinch/lumberjack.v2"
)

var encoderCfg = zapcore.EncoderConfig{
    MessageKey:  ❶"msg",
    NameKey:     ❷"name",

    LevelKey:    "level",
    EncodeLevel: ❸zapcore.LowercaseLevelEncoder,

    CallerKey:    "caller",
    EncodeCaller: ❹zapcore.ShortCallerEncoder,

❺ // TimeKey:    "time",
   // EncodeTime: zapcore.ISO8601TimeEncoder,
}
```

*Listing 13-6: The encoder configuration for your Zap logger (zap_test.go)*

The encoder configuration is independent of the encoder itself in that you can use the same encoder configuration no matter whether you're passing it to a JSON encoder or a console encoder. The encoder will use your configuration to dictate its output format. Here, your encoder configuration dictates that the encoder use the key msg ❶ for the log message and the key name ❷ for the logger's name in the log entry. Likewise, the encoder configuration tells the encoder to use the key level for the logging level and encode the level name using all lowercase characters ❸. If the logger is configured to add caller details, you want the encoder to associate these details with the caller key and encode the details in an abbreviated format ❹.

Since you need to keep the output of the following examples consistent, you'll omit the time key ❺ so it won't show up in the output. In practice, you'd want to uncomment these two fields.

### Creating the Logger and Its Options

Now that you've defined the encoder configuration, let's use it in Listing 13-7 by instantiating a Zap logger.

```
--snip--

func Example_zapJSON() {
    zl := zap.New(
     ❶ zapcore.NewCore(
         ❷ zapcore.NewJSONEncoder(encoderCfg),
         ❸ zapcore.Lock(os.Stdout),
         ❹ zapcore.DebugLevel,
        ),
     ❺ zap.AddCaller(),
        zap.Fields(
         ❻ zap.String("version", runtime.Version()),
        ),
    )
    defer func() { _ = ❼zl.Sync() }()
```

```
    example := ❽zl.Named("example")
    example.Debug("test debug message")
    example.Info("test info message")

    // Output:
  ❾ // {"level":"debug","name":"example","caller":"ch13/zap_test.go:49",
    "msg":"test debug message","version":"❿go1.15.5"}
    // {"level":"info","name":"example","caller":"ch13/zap_test.go:50",
    "msg":"test info message","version":"go1.15.5"}
}
```

*Listing 13-7: Instantiating a new logger from the encoder configuration and logging to JSON (zap_test.go)*

The zap.New function accepts a zap.Core ❶ and zero or more zap.Options. In this example, you're passing the zap.AddCaller option ❺, which instructs the logger to include the caller information in each log entry, and a field ❻ named version that inserts the runtime version in each log entry.

The zap.Core consists of a JSON encoder using your encoder configuration ❷, a zapcore.WriteSyncer ❸, and the logging threshold ❹. If the zapcore .WriteSyncer isn't safe for concurrent use, you can use zapcore.Lock to make it concurrency safe, as in this example.

The Zap logger includes seven log levels, in increasing severity: DebugLevel, InfoLevel, WarnLevel, ErrorLevel, DPanicLevel, PanicLevel, and FatalLevel. The InfoLevel is the default. DPanicLevel and PanicLevel entries will cause Zap to log the entry and then panic. An entry logged at the FatalLevel will cause Zap to call os.Exit(1) after writing the log entry. Since your logger is using DebugLevel, it will log all entries.

I recommend you restrict the use of DPanicLevel and PanicLevel to development and FatalLevel to production, and only then for catastrophic startup errors, such as a failure to connect to the database. Otherwise, you're asking for trouble. As mentioned earlier, you can get a lot of mileage out of DebugLevel, ErrorLevel, and on occasion, InfoLevel.

Before you start using the logger, you want to make sure you defer a call to its Sync method ❼ to ensure all buffered data is written to the output.

You can also assign the logger a name by calling its Named method ❽ and using the returned logger. By default, a logger has no name. A named logger will include a name key in the log entry, provided you defined one in the encoder configuration.

The log entries ❾ now include metadata around the log message, so much so that the log line output exceeds the width of this book. It's also important to mention that the Go version ❿ in the example output is dependent on the version of Go you're using to test this example. Although you're encoding each log entry in JSON, you can still read the additional metadata you're including in the logs. You could ingest this JSON into something like Elasticsearch and run queries on it, letting Elasticsearch do the heavy lifting of returning only those log lines that are relevant to your query.

## Using the Console Encoder

The preceding example included a bunch of functionality in relatively little code. Let's instead assume you want to log something a bit more human-readable, yet that has structure. Zap includes a console encoder that's essentially a drop-in replacement for its JSON encoder. Listing 13-8 uses the console encoder to write structured log entries to standard output.

```
--snip--

func Example_zapConsole() {
    zl := zap.New(
        zapcore.NewCore(
          ❶ zapcore.NewConsoleEncoder(encoderCfg),
            zapcore.Lock(os.Stdout),
          ❷ zapcore.InfoLevel,
        ),
    )
    defer func() { _ = zl.Sync() }()

    console := ❸ zl.Named("[console]")
    console.Info("this is logged by the logger")
  ❹ console.Debug("this is below the logger's threshold and won't log")
    console.Error("this is also logged by the logger")

    // Output:
  ❺ // info    [console]   this is logged by the logger
    // error   [console]   this is also logged by the logger
}
```

*Listing 13-8: Writing structured logs using console encoding (zap_test.go)*

The console encoder ❶ uses tabs to separate fields. It takes instruction from your encoder configuration to determine which fields to include and how to format each.

Notice you don't pass the zap.AddCaller and zap.Fields options to the logger in this example. As a result, the log entries won't have caller and version fields. Log entries will include the caller field only if the logger has the zap.AddCaller option and the encoder configuration defines its CallerKey, as in Listing 13-6.

You name the logger ❸ and write three log entries, each with a different log level. Since the logger's threshold is the info level ❷, the debug log entry ❹ does not appear in the output because debug is below the info threshold.

The output ❺ lacks key names but includes the field values delimited by a tab character. Although not obvious in print, there's a tab character between the log level, the log name, and the log message. If you type this into your editor, be mindful to add tab characters between those elements lest the example fail when you run it.

### Logging with Different Outputs and Encodings

Zap includes useful functions that allow you to concurrently log to different outputs, using different encodings, at different log levels. Listing 13-9 creates a logger that writes JSON to a log file and console encoding to standard output. The logger writes only the debug log entries to the console.

```
--snip--

func Example_zapInfoFileDebugConsole() {
    logFile := ❶new(bytes.Buffer)
    zl := zap.New(
        zapcore.NewCore(
            zapcore.NewJSONEncoder(encoderCfg),
            zapcore.Lock(❷zapcore.AddSync(logFile)),
            zapcore.InfoLevel,
        ),
    )
    defer func() { _ = zl.Sync() }()

❸  zl.Debug("this is below the logger's threshold and won't log")
    zl.Error("this is logged by the logger")
```

*Listing 13-9: Using *bytes.Buffer as the log output and logging JSON to it (zap_test.go)*

You're using *bytes.Buffer ❶ to act as a mock log file. The only problem with this is that *bytes.Buffer does not have a Sync method and does not implement the zapcore.WriteSyncer interface. Thankfully, Zap includes a helper function named zapcore.AddSync ❷ that intelligently adds a no-op Sync method to an io.Writer. Aside from the use of this function, the rest of the logger implementation should be familiar to you. It's logging JSON to the log file and excluding any log entries below the info level. As a result, the first log entry ❸ should not appear in the log file at all.

Now that you have a logger writing JSON to a log file, let's experiment with Zap and create a new logger in Listing 13-10 that can simultaneously write JSON log entries to a log file and console log entries to standard output.

```
--snip--

    zl = ❶zl.WithOptions(
    ❷  zap.WrapCore(
            func(c zapcore.Core) zapcore.Core {
                ucEncoderCfg := encoderCfg
            ❸  ucEncoderCfg.EncodeLevel = zapcore.CapitalLevelEncoder
                return ❹zapcore.NewTee(
                    c,
                ❺  zapcore.NewCore(
                        zapcore.NewConsoleEncoder(ucEncoderCfg),
                        zapcore.Lock(os.Stdout),
                        zapcore.DebugLevel,
                    ),
                )
            },
        ),
```

```
    )

    fmt.Println("standard output:")
❻ zl.Debug("this is only logged as console encoding")
    zl.Info("this is logged as console encoding and JSON")

    fmt.Print("\nlog file contents:\n", logFile.String())

    // Output:
    // standard output:
    // DEBUG   this is only logged as console encoding
    // INFO    this is logged as console encoding and JSON
    //
    // log file contents:
    // {"level":"error","msg":"this is logged by the logger"}
    // {"level":"info","msg":"this is logged as console encoding and JSON"}
}
```

*Listing 13-10: Extending the logger to log to multiple outputs (zap_test.go)*

Zap's WithOptions method ❶ clones the existing logger and configures
the clone with the given options. You can use the zap.WrapCore function ❷
to modify the underlying zap.Core of the cloned logger. To mix things up,
you make a copy of the encoder configuration and tweak it to instruct the
encoder to output the level using all capital letters ❸. Lastly, you use the
zapcore.NewTee function, which is like the io.MultiWriter function, to return
a zap.Core that writes to multiple cores ❹. In this example, you're passing
in the existing core and a new core ❺ that writes debug-level log entries to
standard output.

When you use the cloned logger, both the log file and standard output
receive any log entry at the info level or above, whereas only standard output receives debugging log entries ❻.

### Sampling Log Entries

One of my warnings to you with regard to logging is to consider how it
impacts your application from a CPU and I/O perspective. You don't want
logging to become your application's bottleneck. This normally means
taking special care when logging in the busy parts of your application.

One method to mitigate the logging overhead in critical code paths,
such as a loop, is to sample log entries. It may not be necessary to log each
entry, especially if your logger is outputting many duplicate log entries.
Instead, try logging every *n*th occurrence of a duplicate entry.

Conveniently, Zap has a logger that does just that. Listing 13-11 creates
a logger that will constrain its CPU and I/O overhead by logging a subset of
log entries.

```
--snip--

func Example_zapSampling() {
    zl := zap.New(
❶     zapcore.NewSamplerWithOptions(
```

```
                zapcore.NewCore(
                    zapcore.NewJSONEncoder(encoderCfg),
                    zapcore.Lock(os.Stdout),
                    zapcore.DebugLevel,
                ),
                ❷time.Second, ❸1, ❹3,
            ),
        )
        defer func() { _ = zl.Sync() }()

        for i := 0; i < 10; i++ {
            if i == 5 {
                ❺ time.Sleep(time.Second)
            }
            ❻ zl.Debug(fmt.Sprintf("%d", i))
            ❼ zl.Debug("debug message")
        }

        // ❽ Output:
        // {"level":"debug","msg":"0"}
        // {"level":"debug","msg":"debug message"}
        // {"level":"debug","msg":"1"}
        // {"level":"debug","msg":"2"}
        // {"level":"debug","msg":"3"}
        // {"level":"debug","msg":"debug message"}
        // {"level":"debug","msg":"4"}
        // {"level":"debug","msg":"5"}
        // {"level":"debug","msg":"debug message"}
        // {"level":"debug","msg":"6"}
        // {"level":"debug","msg":"7"}
        // {"level":"debug","msg":"8"}
        // {"level":"debug","msg":"debug message"}
        // {"level":"debug","msg":"9"}
}
```

*Listing 13-11: Logging a subset of log entries to limit CPU and I/O overhead (zap_test.go)*

The NewSamplerWithOptions function ❶ wraps zap.Core with sampling functionality. It requires three additional arguments: a sampling interval ❷, the number of initial duplicate log entries to record ❸, and an integer ❹ representing the *n*th duplicate log entry to record after that point. In this example, you are logging the first log entry, and then every third duplicate log entry that the logger receives in a one-second interval. Once the interval elapses, the logger starts over and logs the first entry, then every third duplicate for the remainder of the one-second interval.

Let's look at this in action. You make 10 iterations around a loop. Each iteration logs both the counter ❻ and a generic debug message ❼, which stays the same for each iteration. On the sixth iteration, the example sleeps for one second ❺ to ensure that the sample logger starts logging anew during the next one-second interval.

Examining the output ❽, you see that the debug message prints during the first iteration and not again until the logger encounters the third duplicate debug message during the fourth loop iteration. But on the sixth iteration, the example sleeps, and the sample logger ticks over to the next one-second interval, starting the logging over. It logs the first debug message of the interval in the sixth loop iteration and the third duplicate debug message in the ninth iteration of the loop.

Granted, this is a contrived example, but one that illustrates how to use this log-sampling technique as a compromise in CPU- and I/O-sensitive portions of your code. One place this technique may be applicable is when sending work to worker goroutines. Although you may send work as fast as the workers can handle it, you might want periodic updates on each worker's progress without having to incur too much logging overhead. The sample logger allows you to temper the log output and strike a balance between timely updates and minimal overhead.

### Performing On-Demand Debug Logging

If debug logging introduces an unacceptable burden on your application under normal operation, or if the sheer amount of debug log data overwhelms your available storage space, you might want the ability to enable debug logging on demand. One technique is to use a semaphore file to enable debug logging. A *semaphore file* is an empty file whose existence is meant as a signal to the logger to change its behavior. If the semaphore file is present, the logger outputs debug-level logs. Once you remove the semaphore file, the logger reverts to its previous log level.

Let's use the fsnotify package to allow your application to watch for filesystem notifications. In addition to the standard library, the fsnotify package uses the x/sys package. Before you start writing code, let's make sure our x/sys package is current:

```
$ go get -u golang.org/x/sys/...
```

Not all logging packages provide safe methods to asynchronously modify log levels. Be aware that you may introduce a race condition if you attempt to modify a logger's level at the same time that the logger is reading the log level. The Zap logger allows you to retrieve a sync/atomic-based leveler to dynamically modify a logger's level while avoiding race conditions. You'll pass the atomic leveler to the zapcore.NewCore function in place of a log level, as you've previously done.

The zap.AtomicLevel struct implements the http.Handler interface. You can integrate it into an API and dynamically change the log level over HTTP instead of using a semaphore.

Listing 13-12 begins an example of dynamic logging using a semaphore file. You'll implement this example over the next few listings.

```
--snip--

func Example_zapDynamicDebugging() {
    tempDir, err := ioutil.TempDir("", "")
    if err != nil {
        log.Fatal(err)
    }
```

```
    defer func() { _ = os.RemoveAll(tempDir) }()

    debugLevelFile := ❶filepath.Join(tempDir, "level.debug")
    atomicLevel := ❷zap.NewAtomicLevel()

    zl := zap.New(
        zapcore.NewCore(
            zapcore.NewJSONEncoder(encoderCfg),
            zapcore.Lock(os.Stdout),
          ❸ atomicLevel,
        ),
    )
    defer func() { _ = zl.Sync() }()
```

*Listing 13-12: Creating a new logger using an atomic leveler (zap_test.go)*

Your code will watch for the *level.debug* file ❶ in the temporary directory. When the file is present, you'll dynamically change the logger's level to debug. To do that, you need a new atomic leveler ❷. By default, the atomic leveler uses the info level, which suits this example just fine. You pass in the atomic leveler ❸ when creating the core as opposed to specifying a log level itself.

Now that you have an atomic leveler and a place to store your semaphore file, let's write the code that will watch for semaphore file changes in Listing 13-13.

```
--snip--

    watcher, err := ❶fsnotify.NewWatcher()
    if err != nil {
        log.Fatal(err)
    }
    defer func() { _ = watcher.Close() }()

    err = ❷watcher.Add(tempDir)
    if err != nil {
        log.Fatal(err)
    }

    ready := make(chan struct{})
    go func() {
        defer close(ready)

        originalLevel := ❸atomicLevel.Level()

        for {
            select {
            case event, ok := ❹<-watcher.Events:
                if !ok {
                    return
                }
                if event.Name == ❺debugLevelFile {
                    switch {
                    case event.Op&fsnotify.Create == ❻fsnotify.Create:
                        atomicLevel.SetLevel(zapcore.DebugLevel)
```

```
                    ready <- struct{}{}
                case event.Op&fsnotify.Remove == ❼fsnotify.Remove:
                    atomicLevel.SetLevel(originalLevel)
                    ready <- struct{}{}
                }
            }
        case err, ok := ❽<-watcher.Errors:
            if !ok {
                return
            }
            zl.Error(err.Error())
        }
    }
}()
```

*Listing 13-13: Watching for any changes to the semaphore file (zap_test.go)*

First, you create a filesystem watcher ❶, which you'll use to watch the temporary directory ❷. The watcher will notify you of any changes to or within that directory. You also want to capture the current log level ❸ so that you can revert to it when you remove the semaphore file.

Next, you listen for events from the watcher ❹. Since you're watching a directory, you filter out any event unrelated to the semaphore file ❺ itself. Even then, you're interested in only the creation of the semaphore file or its removal. If the event indicates the creation of the semaphore file ❻, you change the atomic leveler's level to debug. If you receive a semaphore file removal event ❼, you set the atomic leveler's level back to its original level.

If you receive an error from the watcher ❽ at any point, you log it at the error level.

Let's see how this works in practice. Listing 13-14 tests the logger with and without the semaphore file present.

```
--snip--

❶ zl.Debug("this is below the logger's threshold")

    df, err := ❷os.Create(debugLevelFile)
    if err != nil {
        log.Fatal(err)
    }
    err = df.Close()
    if err != nil {
        log.Fatal(err)
    }
    <-ready

❸ zl.Debug("this is now at the logger's threshold")

    err = ❹os.Remove(debugLevelFile)
    if err != nil {
        log.Fatal(err)
    }
    <-ready
```

```
❺ zl.Debug("this is below the logger's threshold again")
❻ zl.Info("this is at the logger's current threshold")

    // Output:
    // {"level":"debug","msg":"this is now at the logger's threshold"}
    // {"level":"info","msg":"this is at the logger's current threshold"}
}
```

*Listing 13-14: Testing the logger's use of the semaphore file (zap_test.go)*

The logger's current log level via the atomic leveler is info. Therefore, the logger does not write the initial debug log entry ❶ to standard output. But if you create the semaphore file ❷, the code in Listing 13-13 should dynamically change the logger's level to debug. If you add another debug log entry ❸, the logger should write it to standard output. You then remove the semaphore file ❹ and write both a debug log entry ❺ and an info log entry ❻. Since the semaphore file no longer exists, the logger should write only the info log entry to standard output.

## Scaling Up with Wide Event Logging

*Wide event logging* is a technique that creates a single, structured log entry per event to summarize the transaction, instead of logging numerous entries as the transaction progresses. This technique is most applicable to request-response loops, such as API calls, but it can be adapted to other use cases. When you summarize transactions in a structured log entry, you reduce the logging overhead while conserving the ability to index and search for transaction details.

One approach to wide event logging is to wrap an API handler in middleware. But first, since the http.ResponseWriter is a bit stingy with its output, you need to create your own response writer type (Listing 13-15) to collect and log the response code and length.

```
package ch13

import (
    "io"
    "io/ioutil"
    "net"
    "net/http"
    "net/http/httptest"
    "os"

    "go.uber.org/zap"
    "go.uber.org/zap/zapcore"
)

type wideResponseWriter struct {
❶   http.ResponseWriter
    length, status int
}
```

```go
func (w *wideResponseWriter) ❷WriteHeader(status int) {
    w.ResponseWriter.WriteHeader(status)
    w.status = status
}

func (w *wideResponseWriter) ❸Write(b []byte) (int, error) {
    n, err := w.ResponseWriter.Write(b)
    w.length += n

    if w.status == 0 {
        w.status = ❹http.StatusOK
    }

    return n, err
}
```

*Listing 13-15: Creating a ResponseWriter to capture the response status code and length (wide_test.go)*

The new type embeds an object that implements the http.ResponseWriter interface ❶. In addition, you add length and status fields, since those values are ultimately what you want to log from the response. You override the WriteHeader method ❷ to easily capture the status code. Likewise, you override the Write method ❸ to keep an accurate accounting of the number of written bytes and optionally set the status code ❹ should the caller execute Write before WriteHeader.

Listing 13-16 uses your new type in wide event logging middleware.

```go
--snip--

func WideEventLog(logger *zap.Logger, next http.Handler) http.Handler {
    return http.HandlerFunc(
        func(w http.ResponseWriter, r *http.Request) {
            wideWriter := ❶&wideResponseWriter{ResponseWriter: w}

          ❷ next.ServeHTTP(wideWriter, r)

            addr, _, _ := net.SplitHostPort(r.RemoteAddr)
          ❸ logger.Info("example wide event",
                zap.Int("status_code", wideWriter.status),
                zap.Int("response_length", wideWriter.length),
                zap.Int64("content_length", r.ContentLength),
                zap.String("method", r.Method),
                zap.String("proto", r.Proto),
                zap.String("remote_addr", addr),
                zap.String("uri", r.RequestURI),
                zap.String("user_agent", r.UserAgent()),
            )
        },
    )
}
```

*Listing 13-16: Implementing wide event logging middleware (wide_test.go)*

The wide event logging middleware accepts both a *zap.Logger and an http.Handler and returns an http.Handler. If this pattern is unfamiliar to you, please read "Handlers" on page 193.

First, you embed the http.ResponseWriter in a new instance of your wide event logging–aware response writer ❶. Then, you call the ServeHTTP method of the next http.Handler ❷, passing in your response writer. Finally, you make a single log entry ❸ with various bits of data about the request and response.

Keep in mind that I'm taking care here to omit values that would change with each execution and break the example output, like call duration. You would likely have to write code to deal with these in a real implementation.

Listing 13-17 puts the middleware into action and demonstrates the expected output.

```
--snip--

func Example_wideLogEntry() {
    zl := zap.New(
        zapcore.NewCore(
            zapcore.NewJSONEncoder(encoderCfg),
            zapcore.Lock(os.Stdout),
            zapcore.DebugLevel,
        ),
    )
    defer func() { _ = zl.Sync() }()

    ts := httptest.NewServer(
      ❶ WideEventLog(zl, http.HandlerFunc(
            func(w http.ResponseWriter, r *http.Request) {
                defer func(r io.ReadCloser) {
                    _, _ = io.Copy(ioutil.Discard, r)
                    _ = r.Close()
                }(r.Body)
                _, _ = ❷w.Write([]byte("Hello!"))
            },
        )),
    )
    defer ts.Close()

    resp, err := ❸http.Get(ts.URL + "/test")
    if err != nil {
      ❹ zl.Fatal(err.Error())
    }
    _ = resp.Body.Close()

    // ❺Output:
    // {"level":"info","msg":"example wide event","status_code":200,
    "response_length":6,"content_length":0,"method":"GET","proto":"HTTP/1.1",
    "remote_addr":"127.0.0.1","uri":"/test","user_agent":"Go-http-client/1.1"}
}
```

*Listing 13-17: Using the wide event logging middleware to log the details of a GET call (wide_test.go)*

As in Chapter 9, you use the httptest server with your WideEventLog middleware ❶. You pass *zap.Logger into the middleware as the first argument and http.Handler as the second argument. The handler writes a simple *Hello!* to the response ❷ so the response length is nonzero. That way, you can prove that your response writer works. The logger writes the log entry immediately before you receive the response to your GET request ❸. As before, I must wrap the JSON output ❺ for printing in this book, but it consumes a single line otherwise.

Since this is just an example, I elected to use the logger's Fatal method ❹, which writes the error message to the log file and calls os.Exit(1) to terminate the application. You shouldn't use this in code that is supposed to keep running in the event of an error.

## Log Rotation with Lumberjack

If you elect to output log entries to a file, you could leverage an application like *logrotate* to keep them from consuming all available hard drive space. The downside to using a third-party application to manage log files is that the third-party application will need to signal to your application to reopen its log file handle lest your application keep writing to the rotated log file.

A less invasive and more reliable option is to add log file management directly to your logger by using a library like *Lumberjack*. Lumberjack handles log rotation in a way that is transparent to the logger, because your logger treats Lumberjack as any other io.Writer. Meanwhile, Lumberjack keeps track of the log entry accounting and file rotation for you.

Listing 13-18 adds log rotation to a typical Zap logger implementation.

```
--snip--

func TestZapLogRotation(t *testing.T) {
    tempDir, err := ioutil.TempDir("", "")
    if err != nil {
        t.Fatal(err)
    }
    defer func() { _ = os.RemoveAll(tempDir) }()

    zl := zap.New(
        zapcore.NewCore(
            zapcore.NewJSONEncoder(encoderCfg),
          ❶ zapcore.AddSync(
              ❷ &lumberjack.Logger{
                    Filename:   ❸filepath.Join(tempDir, "debug.log"),
                    Compress:   ❹true,
                    LocalTime:  ❺true,
                    MaxAge:     ❻7,
                    MaxBackups: ❼5,
                    MaxSize:    ❽100,
                },
            ),
            zapcore.DebugLevel,
        ),
    )
```

```
    defer func() { _ = zl.Sync() }()

    zl.Debug("debug message written to the log file")
}
```

*Listing 13-18: Adding log rotation to the Zap logger using Lumberjack (zap_test.go)*

Like the *bytes.Buffer in Listing 13-9, *lumberjack.Logger ❷ does not implement the zapcore.WriteSyncer. It, too, lacks a Sync method. Therefore, you need to wrap it in a call to zapcore.AddSync ❶.

Lumberjack includes several fields to configure its behavior, though its defaults are sensible. It uses a log filename in the format *<processname>-lumberjack.log*, saved in the temporary directory, unless you explicitly give it a log filename ❸. You can also elect to save hard drive space and have Lumberjack compress ❹ rotated log files. Each rotated log file is time-stamped using UTC by default, but you can instruct Lumberjack to use local time ❺ instead. Finally, you can configure the maximum log file age before it should be rotated ❻, the maximum number of rotated log files to keep ❼, and the maximum size in megabytes ❽ of a log file before it should be rotated.

You can continue using the logger as if it were writing directly to standard output or *os.File. The difference is that Lumberjack will intelligently handle the log file management for you.

## Instrumenting Your Code

*Instrumenting* your code is the process of collecting metrics for the purpose of making inferences about the current state of your service—such as the duration of each request-response loop, the size of each response, the number of connected clients, the latency between your service and a third-party API, and so on. Whereas logs provide a record of how your service got into a certain state, metrics give you insight into that state itself.

Instrumentation is easy, so much so that I'm going to give you the opposite advice I did for logging: instrument everything (initially). Fine-grained instrumentation involves hardly any overhead, it's efficient to ship, and it's inexpensive to store. Plus, instrumentation can solve one of the challenges of logging I mentioned earlier: that you won't initially know all the questions you'll want to ask, particularly for complex systems. An insidious problem may be ready to ruin your weekend because you lack critical metrics to give you an early warning that something is wrong.

This section will introduce you to metric types and show you the basics for using those types in your services. You will learn about Go kit's metrics package, which is an abstraction layer that provides useful interfaces for popular metrics platforms. You'll round out the instrumentation by using Prometheus as your target metrics platform and set up an endpoint for Prometheus to scrape. If you elect to use a different platform in the future, you will need to swap out only the Prometheus bits of this code; you could leave the Go kit code as is. If you're just getting started with instrumentation, one option is to use Grafana Cloud at *https://grafana.com/products/cloud/* to scrape and visualize your metrics. Its free tier is adequate for experimenting with instrumentation.

## Setup

To abstract the implementation of your metrics and the packages they depend on, let's begin by putting them in their own package (Listing 13-19).

```
package metrics

import (
    "flag"

❶    "github.com/go-kit/kit/metrics"
❷    "github.com/go-kit/kit/metrics/prometheus"
❸    prom "github.com/prometheus/client_golang/prometheus"
)

var (
    Namespace = ❹flag.String("namespace", "web", "metrics namespace")
    Subsystem = ❺flag.String("subsystem", "server1", "metrics subsystem")
```

*Listing 13-19: Imports and command line flags for the metrics example (instrumentation/ metrics/metrics.go)*

You import Go kit's metrics package ❶, which provides the interfaces your code will use, its prometheus adapter ❷ so you can use Prometheus as your metrics platform, and Go's Prometheus client package ❸ itself. All Prometheus-related imports reside in this package. The rest of your code will use Go kit's interfaces. This allows you to swap out the underlying metrics platform without the need to change your code's instrumentation.

Prometheus prefixes its metrics with a namespace and a subsystem. You could use the service name for the namespace and the node or hostname for the subsystem, for example. In this example, you'll use web for the namespace ❹ and server1 for the subsystem ❺ by default. As a result, your metrics will use the web_server1_ prefix. You'll see this prefix in Listing 13-30's command line output.

Now let's explore the various metric types, starting with counters.

## Counters

*Counters* are used for tracking values that only increase, such as request counts, error counts, or completed task counts. You can use a counter to calculate the rate of increase for a given interval, such as the number of connections per minute.

Listing 13-20 defines two counters: one to track the number of requests and another to account for the number of write errors.

```
--snip--

    Requests ❶metrics.Counter = ❷prometheus.NewCounterFrom(
        ❸ prom.CounterOpts{
            Namespace: *Namespace,
            Subsystem: *Subsystem,
            Name:      ❹"request_count",
            Help:      ❺"Total requests",
        },
        []string{},
    )

    WriteErrors metrics.Counter = prometheus.NewCounterFrom(
        prom.CounterOpts{
            Namespace: *Namespace,
            Subsystem: *Subsystem,
            Name:      "write_errors_count",
            Help:      "Total write errors",
        },
        []string{},
    )
```

*Listing 13-20: Creating counters as Go kit interfaces (instrumentation/metrics/metrics.go)*

Each counter implements Go kit's `metrics.Counter` interface ❶. The concrete type for each counter comes from Go kit's prometheus adapter ❷ and relies on a `CounterOpts` struct ❸ from the Prometheus client package for configuration. Aside from the namespace and subsystem values we covered, the other important values you set are the metric name ❹ and its help string ❺, which describes the metric.

### Gauges

*Gauges* allow you to track values that increase or decrease, such as the current memory usage, in-flight requests, queue sizes, fan speed, or the number of ThinkPads on my desk. Gauges do not support rate calculations, such as the number of connections per minute or megabits transferred per second, while counters do.

Listing 13-21 creates a gauge to track open connections.

```
--snip--

    OpenConnections ❶metrics.Gauge = ❷prometheus.NewGaugeFrom(
        ❸ prom.GaugeOpts{
            Namespace: *Namespace,
            Subsystem: *Subsystem,
            Name:      "open_connections",
            Help:      "Current open connections",
        },
        []string{},
    )
```

*Listing 13-21: Creating a gauge as a Go kit interface (instrumentation/metrics/metrics.go)*

Creating a gauge is much like creating a counter. You create a new variable of Go kit's `metrics.Gauge` interface ❶ and use the `NewGaugeFrom` function ❷ from Go kit's prometheus adapter to create the underlying type. The Prometheus client's `GaugeOpts` struct ❸ provides the settings for your new gauge.

## Histograms and Summaries

A *histogram* places values into predefined buckets. Each bucket is associated with a range of values and named after its maximum one. When a value is observed, the histogram increments the maximum value of the smallest bucket into which the value fits. In this way, a histogram tracks the frequency of observed values for each bucket.

Let's look at a quick example. Assuming you have three buckets valued at 0.5, 1.0, and 1.5, if a histogram observes the value 0.42, it will increment the counter associated with bucket 0.5, because 0.5 is the smallest bucket that can contain 0.42. It covers the range of 0.5 and smaller values. If the histogram observes the value 1.23, it will increment the counter associated with the bucket 1.5, which covers values in the range of above 1.0 through 1.5. Naturally, the 1.0 bucket covers the range of above 0.5 through 1.0.

You can use a histogram's distribution of observed values to estimate a percentage or an average of all values. For example, you could use a histogram to calculate the average request sizes or response sizes observed by your service.

A *summary* is a histogram with a few differences. First, a histogram requires predefined buckets, whereas a summary calculates its own buckets. Second, the metrics server calculates averages or percentages from histograms, whereas your service calculates the averages or percentages from summaries. As a result, you can aggregate histograms across services on the metrics server, but you cannot do the same for summaries.

The general advice is to use summaries when you don't know the range of expected values, but I'd advise you to use histograms whenever possible so that you can aggregate histograms on the metrics server. Let's use a histogram to observe request duration (see Listing 13-22).

```
--snip--

RequestDuration ❶metrics.Histogram = ❷prometheus.NewHistogramFrom(
    ❸ prom.HistogramOpts{
        Namespace: *Namespace,
        Subsystem: *Subsystem,
        Buckets: ❹[]float64{
            0.0000001, 0.0000002, 0.0000003, 0.0000004, 0.0000005,
            0.000001, 0.0000025, 0.000005, 0.0000075, 0.00001,
            0.0001, 0.001, 0.01,
        },
        Name: "request_duration_histogram_seconds",
        Help: "Total duration of all requests",
    },
    []string{},
)
)
```

*Listing 13-22: Creating a histogram metric (instrumentation/metrics/metrics.go)*

Both the summary and histogram metric types implement Go kit's `metrics.Histogram` interface ❶ from its `prometheus` adapter. Here, you're using a histogram metric type ❷, using the Prometheus client's `HistogramOpts` struct ❸ for configuration. Since Prometheus's default bucket sizes are too large for the expected request duration range when communicating over localhost, you define custom bucket sizes ❹. I encourage you to experiment with the number of buckets and bucket sizes.

If you'd rather implement `RequestDuration` as a summary metric, you can substitute the code in Listing 13-22 for the code in Listing 13-23.

```
--snip--

    RequestDuration ❶metrics.Histogram = prometheus.NewSummaryFrom(
        prom.SummaryOpts{
            Namespace: *Namespace,
            Subsystem: *Subsystem,
            Name: "request_duration_summary_seconds",
            Help: "Total duration of all requests",
        },
        []string{},
    )
)
```

Listing 13-23: Optionally creating a summary metric

As you can see, this looks a lot like a histogram, minus the `Bucket` method. Notice that you still use the `metrics.Histogram` interface ❶ with a Prometheus summary metric. This is because Go kit does not distinguish between histograms and summaries; only your implementation of the interface does.

## Instrumenting a Basic HTTP Server

Let's combine these metric types in a practical example: instrumenting a Go HTTP server. The biggest challenges here are determining what you want to instrument, where best to instrument it, and what metric type is most appropriate for each value you want to track. If you use Prometheus for your metrics platform, as you'll do here, you'll also need to add an HTTP endpoint for the Prometheus server to scrape.

Listing 13-24 details the initial code needed for an application that comprises an HTTP server to serve the metrics endpoint and another HTTP server to pass all requests to an instrumented handler.

```
package main

import (
    "bytes"
    "flag"
    "fmt"
```

```
    "io"
    "io/ioutil"
    "log"
    "math/rand"
    "net"
    "net/http"
    "sync"
    "time"

❶  "github.com/prometheus/client_golang/prometheus/promhttp"

❷  "github.com/awoodbeck/gnp/ch13/instrumentation/metrics"
)

var (
    metricsAddr = ❸flag.String("metrics", "127.0.0.1:8081",
        "metrics listen address")
    webAddr = ❹flag.String("web", "127.0.0.1:8082", "web listen address")
)
```

*Listing 13-24: Imports and command line flags for the metrics example (instrumentation/ main.go)*

The only imports your code needs are the promhttp package for the metrics endpoint and your metrics package to instrument your code. The promhttp package ❶ includes an http.Handler that a Prometheus server can use to scrape metrics from your application. This handler serves not only your metrics but also metrics related to the runtime, such as the Go version, number of cores, and so on. At a minimum, you can use the metrics provided by the Prometheus handler to gain insight into your service's memory utilization, open file descriptors, heap and stack details, and more.

All variables exported by your metrics package ❷ are Go kit interfaces. Your code doesn't need to concern itself with the underlying metrics platform or its implementation, only how these metrics are made available to the metrics server. In a real-world application, you could further abstract the Prometheus handler to fully remove any dependency other than your metrics package from the rest of your code. But in the interest of keeping this example succinct, I've included the Prometheus handler in the main package.

Now, onto the code you want to instrument. Listing 13-25 adds the function your web server will use to handle all incoming requests.

```
--snip--

func helloHandler(w http.ResponseWriter, _ *http.Request) {
❶  metrics.Requests.Add(1)
    defer func(start time.Time) {
❷    metrics.RequestDuration.Observe(time.Since(start).Seconds())
    }(time.Now())
```

```
    _, err := w.Write([]byte("Hello!"))
    if err != nil {
        ❸ metrics.WriteErrors.Add(1)
    }
}
```

*Listing 13-25: An instrumented handler that responds with random latency
(instrumentation/main.go)*

Even in such a simple handler, you're able to make three meaningful
measurements. You increment the requests counter upon entering the handler ❶ since it's the most logical place to account for it. You also immediately
defer a function that calculates the request duration and uses the request
duration summary metric to observe it ❷. Lastly, you account for any errors
writing the response ❸.

Now, you need to put the handler to use. But first, you need a helper
function that will allow you to spin up a couple of HTTP servers: one to
serve the metrics endpoint and one to serve this handler. Listing 13-26
details such a function.

```
--snip--

func newHTTPServer(addr string, mux http.Handler,
    stateFunc ❶func(net.Conn, http.ConnState)) error {
    l, err := net.Listen("tcp", addr)
    if err != nil {
        return err
    }

    srv := &http.Server{
        Addr:              addr,
        Handler:           mux,
        IdleTimeout:       time.Minute,
        ReadHeaderTimeout: 30 * time.Second,
        ConnState:         stateFunc,
    }

    go func() { log.Fatal(srv.Serve(l)) }()

    return nil
}

func ❷connStateMetrics(_ net.Conn, state http.ConnState) {
    switch state {
    case http.StateNew:
        ❸ metrics.OpenConnections.Add(1)
    case http.StateClosed:
        ❹ metrics.OpenConnections.Add(-1)
    }
}
```

*Listing 13-26: Functions to create an HTTP server and instrument connection states
(instrumentation/main.go)*

This HTTP server code resembles that of Chapter 9. The exception here is you're defining the server's ConnState field, accepting it as an argument ❶ to the newHTTPServer function.

The HTTP server calls its ConnState field anytime a network connection changes. You can leverage this functionality to instrument the number of open connections the server has at any one time. You can pass the connStateMetrics function ❷ to the newHTTPServer function anytime you want to initialize a new HTTP server and track its open connections. If the server establishes a new connection, you increment the open connections gauge ❸ by 1. If a connection closes, you decrement the gauge ❹ by 1. Go kit's gauge interface provides an Add method, so decrementing a value involves adding a negative number.

Let's create an example that puts all these pieces together. Listing 13-27 creates an HTTP server to serve up the Prometheus endpoint and another HTTP server to serve your instrumented handler.

```
--snip--

func main() {
    flag.Parse()
    rand.Seed(time.Now().UnixNano())

    mux := http.NewServeMux()
❶ mux.Handle("/metrics/", promhttp.Handler())
    if err := newHTTPServer(*metricsAddr, mux, ❷nil); err != nil {
        log.Fatal(err)
    }
    fmt.Printf("Metrics listening on %q ...\n", *metricsAddr)

    if err := newHTTPServer(*webAddr, ❸http.HandlerFunc(helloHandler),
      ❹connStateMetrics); err != nil {
        log.Fatal(err)
    }
    fmt.Printf("Web listening on %q ...\n\n", *webAddr)
```

Listing 13-27: Starting two HTTP servers to serve metrics and the helloHandler (instrumentation/main.go)

First, you spawn an HTTP server with the sole purpose of serving the Prometheus handler ❶ at the /metrics/ endpoint where Prometheus scrapes metrics from by default. Since you do not pass in a function for the third argument ❷, this HTTP server won't have a function assigned to its ConnState field to call on each connection state change. Then, you spin up another HTTP server to handle each request with the helloHandler ❸. But this time, you pass in the connStateMetrics function ❹. As a result, this HTTP server will gauge open connections.

Now, you can spin up many HTTP clients to make a bunch of requests to affect your metrics (see Listing 13-28).

```
    clients := ❶500
    gets := ❷100
    wg := new(sync.WaitGroup)

    fmt.Printf("Spawning %d connections to make %d requests each ...",
        clients, gets)
    for i := 0; i < clients; i++ {
        wg.Add(1)
        go func() {
            defer wg.Done()

            c := &http.Client{
                Transport: ❸http.DefaultTransport.(*http.Transport).Clone(),
            }

            for j := 0; j < gets; j++ {
                resp, err := ❹c.Get(fmt.Sprintf("http://%s/", *webAddr))
                if err != nil {
                    log.Fatal(err)
                }
                _, _ = ❺io.Copy(ioutil.Discard, resp.Body)
                _ = ❻resp.Body.Close()
            }
        }()
    }
❼ wg.Wait()
    fmt.Print(" done.\n\n")
```

*Listing 13-28: Instructing 500 HTTP clients to each make 100 GET calls (instrumentation/main.go)*

You start by spawning 500 HTTP clients ❶ to each make 100 GET calls ❷. But first, you need to address a problem. The http.Client uses the http.DefaultTransport if its Transport method is nil. The http.DefaultTransport does an outstanding job of caching TCP connections. If all 500 HTTP clients use the same transport, they'll all make calls over about two TCP sockets. Our open connections gauge would reflect the two idle connections when you're done with this example, which isn't really the goal.

Instead, you must make sure to give each HTTP client its own transport. Cloning the default transport ❸ is good enough for our purposes.

Now that each client has its own transport and you're assured each client will make its own TCP connection, you iterate through a GET call ❹ 100 times with each client. You must also be diligent about draining ❺ and closing ❻ the response body so each client can reuse its TCP connection.

Once all 500 HTTP clients complete their 100 calls ❼, you can move on to Listing 13-29 and check the current state of the metrics.

```
--snip--
    resp, err := ❶http.Get(fmt.Sprintf("http://%s/metrics", *metricsAddr))
    if err != nil {
        log.Fatal(err)
    }

    b, err := ioutil.ReadAll(resp.Body)
    if err != nil {
        log.Fatal(err)
    }
    _ = resp.Body.Close()

    metricsPrefix := ❷fmt.Sprintf("%s_%s", *metrics.Namespace,
        *metrics.Subsystem)
    fmt.Println("Current Metrics:")
    for _, line := range bytes.Split(b, []byte("\n")) {
        if ❸bytes.HasPrefix(line, []byte(metricsPrefix)) {
            fmt.Printf("%s\n", line)
        }
    }
}
```

Listing 13-29: Displaying the current metrics matching your namespace and subsystem (instrumentation/main.go)

You retrieve all the metrics from the metrics endpoint ❶. This will cause the metrics web server to return all metrics stored by the Prometheus client, in addition to details about each metric it tracks, which includes the metrics you added. Since you're interested in only your metrics, you can check each line starting with your namespace, an underscore, and your subsystem ❷. If the line matches this prefix ❸, you print it to standard output. Otherwise, you ignore the line and move on.

Let's run this example on the command line and examine the resulting metrics in Listing 13-30.

```
$ go run instrumentation/main.go
Metrics listening on "127.0.0.1:8081" ...
Web listening on "127.0.0.1:8082" ...

Spawning 500 connections to make 100 requests each ... done.

Current Metrics:
web_server1_open_connections ❶500
web_server1_request_count ❷50000
web_server1_request_duration_histogram_seconds_bucket{le="1e-07"} ❸0
web_server1_request_duration_histogram_seconds_bucket{le="2e-07"} 1
web_server1_request_duration_histogram_seconds_bucket{le="3e-07"} 613
web_server1_request_duration_histogram_seconds_bucket{le="4e-07"} 13591
web_server1_request_duration_histogram_seconds_bucket{le="5e-07"} 33216
web_server1_request_duration_histogram_seconds_bucket{le="1e-06"} 40183
```

```
web_server1_request_duration_histogram_seconds_bucket{le="2.5e-06"} 49876
web_server1_request_duration_histogram_seconds_bucket{le="5e-06"} 49963
web_server1_request_duration_histogram_seconds_bucket{le="7.5e-06"} 49973
web_server1_request_duration_histogram_seconds_bucket{le="1e-05"} 49979
web_server1_request_duration_histogram_seconds_bucket{le="0.0001"} 49994
web_server1_request_duration_histogram_seconds_bucket{le="0.001"} 49997
web_server1_request_duration_histogram_seconds_bucket{le="0.01"} ❹50000
web_server1_request_duration_histogram_seconds_bucket{le="+Inf"} 50000
web_server1_request_duration_histogram_seconds_sum ❺0.04102166899999979
web_server1_request_duration_histogram_seconds_count ❻50000
```

*Listing 13-30: Web server output and resulting metrics*

As expected, 500 connections were open ❶ at the time you queried the metrics. These connections are idle. You can experiment with the HTTP client by invoking its CloseIdleConnections method after it's done making 100 GET calls; see how that change affects the open connections gauge. Likewise, see what happens to the open connections when you don't define their Transport field.

The request count is 50,000 ❷, so all requests succeeded.

Do you notice what's missing? The write errors counter. Since no write errors occur, the write errors counter never increments. As a result, it doesn't show up in the metrics output. You could make a call to metrics.WriteErrors .Add(0) to make the metric show up without changing its value, but its absence probably bothers you more than it bothers Prometheus. Just be aware that the metrics output may not include all instrumented metrics, just the ones that have changed since initialization.

The underlying Prometheus histogram is a *cumulative* histogram: any value that increments a bucket's counter also increments the counters for all buckets less than the value. Therefore, you see increasing values in each bucket until you reach the 0.01 bucket ❹. Even though you define a range of buckets, Prometheus adds an infinite bucket for you. In this example, you defined a bucket smaller than all observed values ❸, so its counter is still zero.

A histogram and a summary maintain two additional counters: the sum of all observed values ❺ and the total number of observed values ❻. If you use a summary, the Prometheus endpoint will present only these two counters. It will not detail the summary's buckets as it does with a histogram. Therefore, the Prometheus server can aggregate histogram buckets but cannot do the same for summaries.

## What You've Learned

Logging is hard. Instrumentation, not so much. Be frugal with your logging and generous with your instrumentation. Logging isn't free and can quickly add latency if you aren't mindful of where and how much you log. You cannot go wrong by logging actionable items, particularly ones that should trigger an alert. On the other hand, instrumentation is very efficient. You should instrument everything, at least initially. Metrics detail the current state of your service and provide insight into potential problems, whereas logs provide an immutable audit trail of sorts that explains the current state of your service and helps you diagnose failures.

Go's log package provides enough functionality to satisfy basic log requirements. But it becomes cumbersome when you need to log to more than one output or at varying levels of verbosity. At that point, you're better off with a comprehensive solution such as Uber's Zap logger. No matter what logger you use, consider adding structure to your log entries by including additional metadata. Structured logging allows you to leverage software to quickly filter and search log entries, particularly if you centralize logs across your infrastructure.

On-demand debug logging and wide event logging are two methods you can use to collect important information while minimizing logging's impact on the performance of your service. You can use the creation of a semaphore file to signal your logger to enable debug logging. When you remove the semaphore file, the logger immediately disables debug logging. Wide event logs summarize events in a request-response loop. You can replace numerous log entries with a single wide event log without hindering your ability to diagnose failures.

One approach to instrumentation is to use Go kit's metrics package, which provides interfaces for common metric types and adapters for popular metrics platforms. It allows you to abstract the details of each metrics platform away from your instrumented code.

The metrics package supports counters, gauges, histograms, and summaries. Counters monotonically increase and can be used to calculate rates of change. Use counters to track values like request counts, error counts, or completed tasks. Gauges track values that can increase and decrease, such as current memory usage, in-flight requests, and queue sizes. Histograms and summaries place observed values in buckets and allow you to estimate averages or percentages of all values. You could use a histogram or summary to approximate the average request duration or response size.

Taken together, logging and metrics give you necessary insight into your service, allowing you to proactively address potential problems and recover from failures.

# 14

## MOVING TO THE CLOUD

In August of 2006, Amazon Web Services (AWS) brought public cloud infrastructure to the mainstream when it introduced its virtual computer, Elastic Compute Cloud (EC2). EC2 removed barriers to providing services over the internet; you no longer needed to purchase servers and software licenses, sign support contracts, rent office space, or hire IT professionals to maintain your infrastructure. Instead, you paid AWS as needed for the use of EC2 instances, allowing you to scale your business while AWS handled the maintenance, redundancy, and standards compliance details for you. In the following years, both Google and Microsoft released public cloud offerings to compete with AWS. Now all three cloud providers offer comprehensive services that cover everything from analytics to storage.

The goal of this chapter is to give you an apples-to-apples comparison of Amazon Web Services, Google Cloud, and Microsoft Azure. You'll create and deploy an application to illustrate the differences in each provider's tooling, authentication, and deployment experience. Your application will follow the *platform-as-a-service (PaaS)* model, in which you create the application and deploy it on the cloud provider's platform. Specifically, you'll create a function and deploy it to AWS Lambda, Google Cloud Functions, and Microsoft Azure Functions. We'll stick to the command line as much as possible to keep the comparisons relative and introduce you to each provider's tooling.

All three service providers offer a trial period, so you shouldn't incur any costs. If you've exhausted your trial, please keep potential costs in mind as you work through the following sections.

You'll create a simple function that retrieves the URL of the latest XKCD comic, or optionally the previous comic. This will demonstrate how to retrieve data from within the function to fulfill the client's request and persist function state between executions.

By the end of this chapter, you should feel comfortable writing an application, deploying it, and testing it to leverage the PaaS offerings of AWS, Google Cloud, and Microsoft Azure. You should have a better idea of which provider's workflow best fits your use case if you choose to make the jump to the cloud.

## Laying Some Groundwork

The XKCD website offers a Real Simple Syndication (RSS) feed at *https:// xkcd.com/rss.xml*. As its file extension indicates, the feed uses XML. You can use Go's *encoding/xml* package to parse the feed.

Before you deploy a function to the cloud that can retrieve the URL of the latest XKCD comic, you need to write some code that will allow you to make sense of the RSS feed. Listing 14-1 creates two types for parsing the feed.

```
package feed

import (
    "context"
    "encoding/xml"
    "fmt"
    "io/ioutil"
    "net/http"
)

type Item struct {
    Title     string `xml:"title"`
    URL       string `xml:"link"`
    Published string ❶`xml:"pubDate"`
}
```

```
type RSS struct {
    Channel struct {
        Items []Item `xml:"item"`
    } `xml:"channel"`
    entityTag ❷string
}
```

*Listing 14-1: Structure that represents the XKCD RSS feed (feed/rss.go)*

The RSS struct represents the RSS feed, and the Item struct represents each item (comic) in the feed. Like Go's *encoding/json* package you used in earlier chapters, its *encoding/xml* package can use struct tags to map XML tags to their corresponding struct fields. For example, the Published field's tag ❶ instructs the *encoding/xml* package to assign it the item's pubDate value.

It's important to be a good internet neighbor and keep track of the feed's entity tag ❷. Web servers often derive entity tags for content that may not change from one request to another. Clients can track these entity tags and present them with future requests. If the server determines that the requested content has the same entity tag, it can forgo returning the entire payload and return a 304 Not Modified status code so the client knows to use its cached copy instead. You'll use this value in Listing 14-2 to conditionally update the RSS struct when the feed changes.

```
--snip--
func (r RSS) Items() []Item {
    items := ❶make([]Item, len(r.Channel.Items))
    copy(items, r.Channel.Items)

    return items
}

func (r *RSS) ParseURL(ctx context.Context, u string) error {
    req, err := http.NewRequestWithContext(ctx, http.MethodGet, u, nil)
    if err != nil {
        return err
    }

    if r.entityTag != "" {
      ❷ req.Header.Add("ETag", r.entityTag)
    }

    resp, err := http.DefaultClient.Do(req)
    if err != nil {
        return err
    }

    switch resp.StatusCode {
    case ❷http.StatusNotModified: // no-op
    case ❸http.StatusOK:
        b, err := ioutil.ReadAll(resp.Body)
        if err != nil {
```

```
            return err
        }
        _ = resp.Body.Close()

        err = xml.Unmarshal(b, r)
        if err != nil {
            return err
        }

        r.entityTag = ❹resp.Header.Get("ETag")
    default:
        return fmt.Errorf("unexpected status code: %v", resp.StatusCode)
    }

    return nil
}
```

*Listing 14-2: Methods to parse the XKCD RSS feed and return a slice of items (feed/rss.go)*

There are three things to note here. First, the RSS struct and its methods are not safe for concurrent use. This isn't a concern for your use case, but it's best that you're aware of this fact. Second, the Items method returns a slice of the items in the RSS struct, which is empty until your code calls the ParseURL method to populate the RSS struct. Third, the Items method makes a copy of the Items slice ❶ and returns the copy to prevent possible corruption of the original Items slice. This is also a bit of overkill for your use case, but it's best to be aware that you're returning a reference type that the receiver can modify. If the receiver modifies the copy, it won't affect your original.

Parsing the RSS feed is straightforward and should look familiar. The ParseURL method retrieves the RSS feed by using a GET call. If the feed is new, the method reads the XML from the response body and invokes the xml .Unmarshal function to populate the RSS struct with the XML in the server.

Notice you conditionally set the request's ETag header ❷ so the XKCD server can determine whether it needs to send the feed contents or you currently have the latest version. If the server responds with a 304 Not Modified status code, the RSS struct remains unchanged. If you receive a 200 OK ❸, you received a new version of the feed and unmarshal the response body's XML into the RSS struct. If successful, you update the entity tag ❹.

With this logic in place, the RSS struct should update itself only if its entity tag is empty, as it would be on initialization of the struct, or if a new feed is available.

The last task is to create a *go.mod* file by using the following commands:

```
$ cd feed
feed$ go mod init github.com/awoodbeck/gnp/ch14/feed
go: creating new go.mod: module github.com/awoodbeck/gnp/ch14/feed
feed$ cd -
```

These commands initialize a new module named *github.com/awoodbeck/gnp/ch14/feed*, which will be used by code later in this chapter.

# AWS Lambda

*AWS Lambda* is a serverless platform that offers first-class support for Go. You can create Go applications, deploy them, and let Lambda handle the implementation details. It will scale your code to meet demand. Before you can get started with Lambda, please make sure you create a trial account at *https://aws.amazon.com/*.

## Installing the AWS Command Line Interface

AWS offers version 2 of its command line interface (CLI) tools for Windows, macOS, and Linux. You can find detailed instructions for installing them at *https://docs.aws.amazon.com/cli/latest/userguide/cli-chap-install.html*. Use the following commands to install the AWS CLI tools on Linux:

```
$ curl "https://awscli.amazonaws.com/awscli-exe-linux-x86_64.zip" \
-o "awscliv2.zip"
  % Total    % Received % Xferd  Average Speed   Time    Time     Time
Current
                                 Dload  Upload   Total   Spent    Left  Speed
100 32.3M  100 32.3M    0     0  31.1M      0  0:00:01  0:00:01 --:--:-- 31.1M
$ unzip -q awscliv2.zip
$ sudo ./aws/install
[sudo] password for user:
You can now run: /usr/local/bin/aws --version
$ aws --version
aws-cli/2.0.56 Python/3.7.3 Linux/5.4.0-7642-generic exe/x86_64.pop.20
```

Download the AWS CLI version 2 archive. Use curl to download the ZIP file from the command line. Then unzip the archive and use sudo to run the *./aws/install* executable. Once it's complete, run aws --version to verify that the AWS binary is in your path and that you're running version 2.

## Configuring the CLI

Now that you have the AWS CLI installed, you need to configure it with credentials so it can interact with AWS on your account's behalf. This section walks you through that process. If you get confused, review the AWS CLI configuration quick-start guide at *https://docs.aws.amazon.com/cli/latest/userguide/cli-configure-quickstart.html*.

First, access the AWS Console at *https://console.aws.amazon.com*. Log into the AWS Console to access the drop-down menu shown in Figure 14-1.

Figure 14-1: Accessing your AWS
account security credentials

Click your account name in the upper-right corner of the AWS Console
(**Personal** in Figure 14-1). Then, select **My Security Credentials** from the
drop-down menu. This link should take you to the Your Security Credentials
page, shown in Figure 14-2.

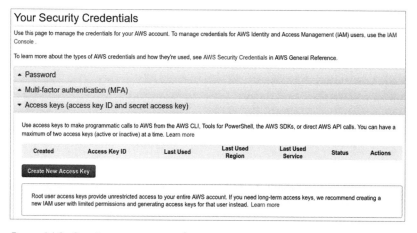

Figure 14-2: Creating a new access key

Select the **Access keys** section heading to expand the section. Then
click the **Create New Access Key** button to create credentials to use on
the command line. This will display the credentials (Figure 14-3).

Figure 14-3: Retrieving the new access Key ID and secret access key

You'll need both the access Key ID and secret access key values to authenticate your commands on the command line with AWS. Make sure you download the key file and keep it in a secure place in case you need to retrieve it in the future. For now, you'll use them to configure your AWS command line interface:

```
$ aws configure
AWS Access Key ID [None]: AIDA1111111111EXAMPLE
AWS Secret Access Key [None]: YxMCBWETtZjZhW6VpLwPDY5KqH8hsDG45EXAMPLE
Default region name [None]: us-east-2
Default output format [None]: yaml
```

On the command line, invoke the `aws configure` command. You'll be prompted to enter the access key ID and secret access key from Figure 14-3.

You can also specify a default region and the default output format. The *region* is the geographic endpoint for your services. In this example, I'm telling AWS I want my services to use the us-east-2 endpoint by default, which is in Ohio. You can find a general list of regional endpoints at *https:// docs.aws.amazon.com/general/latest/gr/rande.html*.

## Creating a Role

Your code requires a specific identity to run in AWS. This identity is called a *role*. You can have multiple roles under your AWS account and assign various permissions to each role. You can then assign roles to AWS services, which gives services permissions to access your resources without you having to assign credentials (such as your access key ID and secret access key) to each service. In this chapter, you'll use a role to give AWS Lambda permission to access the Lambda function you'll write.

For now, you'll create just one role and give AWS Lambda permission to assume that role so it can invoke your code. Listing 14-3 details a simple trust policy document that assigns the proper access. The trust policy document outlines a set of permissions, which you'll assign to a new role.

```
{
  "Version": ❶"2012-10-17",
  "Statement": [
    {
      "Effect": ❷"Allow",
      "Principal": {
        "Service": ❸"lambda.amazonaws.com"
      },
      "Action": ❹"sts:AssumeRole"
    }
  ]
}
```

*Listing 14-3: Defining a trust policy for your new role (aws/trust-policy.json)*

This trust policy tells AWS that you want to allow ❷ the Lambda service ❸ to assume the role ❹. The trust policy version ❶ is the current version of the trust policy language, not an arbitrary date.

Next, create the role to which you'll assign this trust policy:

```
$ aws iam create-role --role-name "lambda-xkcd" \
--assume-role-policy-document file://aws/trust-policy.json
Role:
❶ Arn: arn:aws:iam::123456789012:role/lambda-xkcd
❷ AssumeRolePolicyDocument:
    Statement:
    - Action: sts:AssumeRole
      Effect: Allow
      Principal:
        Service: lambda.amazonaws.com
    Version: '2012-10-17'
  CreateDate: '2006-01-02T15:04:05+00:00'
  Path: /
  RoleId: AROA1111111111EXAMPLE
  RoleName: lambda-xkcd
```

Create a new role with the AWS Identity and Access Management (IAM) service using the role name *lambda-xkcd* and the *aws/trust-policy.json* document you created in Listing 14-3. If successful, this creates a new role using your trust policy ❷. IAM assigns the role an Amazon Resource Name (ARN). The ARN ❶ is a unique identifier for this role that you'll use when invoking your code.

### *Defining an AWS Lambda Function*

AWS Lambda's Go library gives you some flexibility when it comes to your Lambda function's signature. Your function must conform to one of these formats:

```
func()

func() error

func(TypeIn) error

func() (TypeOut, error)

func(context.Context) error

func(context.Context, TypeIn) error

func(context.Context) (TypeOut, error)

func(context.Context, TypeIn) (TypeOut, error)
```

TypeIn and TypeOut correspond to *encoding/json*-compatible types, in that JSON input sent to your Lambda function will be unmarshaled into TypeIn. Likewise, the TypeOut your function returns will be marshaled to JSON before reaching its destination. You'll use the last function signature in this section.

The function you'll write should give you a taste for what you can do with serverless environments. It will accept input from the client, retrieve resources over the internet, maintain its state between function calls, and respond to the client. If you've read Chapter 9, you know that you could write an http.Handler that performs these actions, but AWS Lambda requires a slightly different approach. You won't work with an http.Request or an http.ResponseWriter. Instead, you'll use types you create or import from other modules. AWS Lambda handles the decoding and encoding of the data to and from your function for you.

Let's get started writing your first bit of serverless code (Listing 14-4).

```
package main

import (
    "context"

    "github.com/awoodbeck/gnp/ch14/feed"
    "github.com/aws/aws-lambda-go/lambda"
)

var (
    rssFeed ❶ feed.RSS
    feedURL = ❷ "https://xkcd.com/rss.xml"
)

type EventRequest struct {
    Previous bool `json:"previous"`
}

type EventResponse struct {
    Title     string `json:"title"`
    URL       string `json:"url"`
    Published string `json:"published"`
}
```

*Listing 14-4: Creating persistent variables and request and response types (aws/xkcd.go)*

You can specify variables at the package level that will persist between function calls while the function persists in memory. In this example, you define a feed object ❶ and the URL of the RSS feed ❷. Creating and populating a new feed.RSS object involves a bit of overhead. You can avoid that overhead on subsequent function calls if you store the object in a variable at the package level so it lives beyond each function call. This also allows you to take advantage of the entity tag support in feed.RSS.

The EventRequest and EventResponse types define the format of a client request and the function's response. AWS Lambda unmarshals the JSON from the client's HTTP request body into the EventRequest object and marshals the function's EventResponse to JSON to the HTTP response body before returning it to the client.

Listing 14-5 defines the `main` function and begins to define the AWS Lambda-compatible function.

```
--snip--
func main() {
❶ lambda.Start(LatestXKCD)
}

func LatestXKCD(ctx context.Context, req EventRequest) (
    EventResponse, error) {
    resp := ❷EventResponse{Title: "xkcd.com", URL: "https://xkcd.com/"}

    if err := ❸rssFeed.ParseURL(ctx, feedURL); err != nil {
        return resp, err
    }
```

*Listing 14-5: Main function and first part of the Lambda function named LatestXKCD (aws/xkcd.go)*

Hook your function into Lambda by passing it to the `lambda.Start` method ❶. You're welcome to instantiate dependencies in an init function, or before this statement, if your function requires it.

The `LatestXKCD` function accepts a context and an `EventRequest` and returns an `EventResponse` and an error interface. It defines a response object ❷ with default `Title` and `URL` values. The function returns the response as is in the event of an error or an empty feed.

Parsing the feed URL ❸ from Listing 14-4 populates the `rssFeed` object with the latest feed details. Listing 14-6 uses these details to formulate the response.

```
--snip--
    switch items := rssFeed.Items(); {
    case ❶req.Previous && len(items) > 1:
        resp.Title = items[1].Title
        resp.URL = items[1].URL
        resp.Published = items[1].Published
    case len(items) > 0:
        resp.Title = items[0].Title
        resp.URL = items[0].URL
        resp.Published = items[0].Published
    }

    return resp, nil
}
```

*Listing 14-6: Populating the response with the feed results (aws/xkcd.go)*

If the client requests the previous XKCD comic ❶ and there are at least two feed items, the function populates the response with details of the previous XKCD comic. Otherwise, the function populates the response with the most recent XKCD comic details, provided there's at least one feed item. If neither of those cases is true, the client receives the response with its default values from Listing 14-5.

## Compiling, Packaging, and Deploying Your Function

AWS Lambda expects you to compile your code and zip the resulting binary before deploying the archive, using the AWS CLI tools. To do this, use the following commands in Linux, macOS, or WSL:

```
$ GOOS=linux go build aws/xkcd.go
$ zip xkcd.zip xkcd
  adding: xkcd (deflated 50%)
$ aws lambda create-function --function-name "xkcd" --runtime "go1.x" \
--handler "xkcd" --role "arn:aws:iam::123456789012:role/lambda-xkcd" \
--zip-file "fileb://xkcd.zip"
CodeSha256: M36I7oiS8+S9AryIthcizsjdLDKXMaJKvZvsZzZDNHO=
CodeSize: 6597490
Description: ''
FunctionArn: arn:aws:lambda:us-east-2:123456789012:function:xkcd
FunctionName: ❶xkcd
Handler: ❷xkcd
LastModified: 2006-01-02T15:04:05.000+0000
LastUpdateStatus: Successful
MemorySize: 128
RevisionId: b094a881-9c49-4b86-86d5-eb4335507eb0
Role: arn:aws:iam::123456789012:role/lambda-xkcd
Runtime: go1.x
State: Active
Timeout: 3
TracingConfig:
  Mode: PassThrough
Version: $LATEST
```

Compile *aws/xkcd.go* and add the resulting *xkcd* binary to a ZIP file. Then, use the AWS CLI to create a new function named xkcd, a handler named xkcd, the go1.x runtime, the role ARN you created earlier, and the ZIP file containing the *xkcd* binary. Notice the *fileb://xkcd.zip* URL in the command line. This tells the AWS CLI that it can find a binary file (*fileb*) in the current directory named *xkcd.zip*.

If successful, the AWS CLI outputs the details of the new Lambda function: the function name ❶ in AWS, which you'll use on the command line to manage your function, and the filename of the binary in the zip file ❷.

Compilation of the binary and packing it is a bit different on Windows. I recommend you do this in PowerShell since you can compress the cross-compiled binary on the command line without the need to install a specific archiver.

```
PS C:\Users\User\dev\gnp\ch14> setx GOOS linux

SUCCESS: Specified value was saved.
PS C:\Users\User\dev\gnp\ch14> \Go\bin\go.exe build -o xkcd .\aws\xkcd.go
go: downloading github.com/aws/aws-lambda-go v1.19.1
--snip--
PS C:\Users\User\dev\gnp\ch14> Compress-Archive xkcd xkcd.zip
```

At this point, use the AWS CLI tools to deploy the ZIP file as in the previous listing.

If you need to update your function code, recompile the binary and archive it again. Then use the following command to update the existing Lambda function:

```
$ aws lambda update-function-code --function-name "xkcd" \
--zip-file "fileb://xkcd.zip"
```

Since you're updating an existing function, the only values you need to provide are the names of the function and ZIP file. AWS takes care of the rest.

As an exercise, update the code to allow the client to request a forced refresh of the XKCD RSS feed. Then, update the function with those changes and move on to the next section to test those changes.

## Testing Your AWS Lambda Function

The AWS CLI tools make it easy to test your Lambda function. You can use them to send a JSON payload and capture the JSON response. Invoke the function by providing the function name and the path to a file in the AWS CLI. The AWS CLI will populate this with the response body:

```
$ aws lambda invoke --function-name "xkcd" response.json
ExecutedVersion: $LATEST
StatusCode: 200
```

If the invocation is successful, you can verify that your function provided the XKCD comic name and URL by reviewing the *response.json* contents:

```
$ cat response.json
{"title":"Election Screen Time","url":"https://xkcd.com/2371/",
"published":"Mon, 12 Oct 2020 04:00:00 -0000"}
```

You can also invoke the function with a custom request body by adding a few additional command line arguments. You can pass a payload string if you specify its format as raw-in-base64-out. This tells the AWS CLI to take the string you provide and Base64-encode it before assigning it to the request body and passing it along to the function:

```
$ aws lambda invoke --cli-binary-format "raw-in-base64-out" \
--payload '{"previous":true}' --function-name "xkcd" response.json
ExecutedVersion: $LATEST
StatusCode: 200
$ cat response.json
{"title":"Chemist Eggs","url":"https://xkcd.com/2373/",
"published":"Fri, 16 Oct 2020 04:00:00 -0000"}
```

# Google Cloud Functions

Like AWS Lambda, Google Cloud Functions allows you to deploy code in a serverless environment, offloading the implementation details to Google. Not surprisingly, Go enjoys first-class support in Cloud Functions.

You'll need a Google Cloud account before proceeding with this section. Visit *https://cloud.google.com* to get started with a trial account.

## Installing the Google Cloud Software Development Kit

The Google Cloud Software Development Kit (SDK) requires Python 2.7.9 or 3.5+. You'll need to make sure a suitable version of Python is installed on your operating system before proceeding. You can follow Google's comprehensive installation guide at *https://cloud.google.com/sdk/docs/install/*, where you'll find specific installation instructions for Windows, macOS, and various flavors of Linux.

Here are the generic Linux installation steps:

```
$ curl -O https://dl.google.com/dl/cloudsdk/channels/rapid/downloads/\
google-cloud-sdk-319.0.1-linux-x86_64.tar.gz
  % Total    % Received % Xferd  Average Speed   Time    Time     Time
Current
                                 Dload  Upload   Total   Spent    Left  Speed
100 81.9M  100 81.9M    0     0  34.1M      0  0:00:02  0:00:02 --:--:-- 34.1M
$ tar xf google-cloud-sdk-319.0.1-linux-x86_64.tar.gz
$ ./google-cloud-sdk/install.sh
Welcome to the Google Cloud SDK!
--snip--
```

Download the current Google Cloud SDK tarball (the version changes frequently!) and extract it. Then, run the *./google-cloud-sdk/install.sh* script. The installation process asks you questions that pertain to your environment. I snipped them from the output for brevity.

## Initializing the Google Cloud SDK

You need to authorize the Google Cloud SDK before you're able to use it to deploy your code. Google makes this process simple compared to AWS. There's no need to create credentials and then copy and paste them to the command line. Instead, Google Cloud uses your web browser for authentication and authorization.

The gcloud init command is equivalent to the aws configure command, in that it will walk you through the configuration of your Google Cloud command line environment:

```
$ ./google-cloud-sdk/bin/gcloud init
Welcome! This command will take you through the configuration of gcloud.
--snip--
Pick cloud project to use:
```

```
❶ [1] Create a new project
Please enter numeric choice or text value (must exactly match list
item): 1

Enter a Project ID. Note that a Project ID CANNOT be changed later.
Project IDs must be 6-30 characters (lowercase ASCII, digits, or
hyphens) in length and start with a lowercase letter. goxkcd
--snip--
$ gcloud projects list
PROJECT_ID                      NAME                    PROJECT_NUMBER
goxkcd                          goxkcd                  123456789012
```

The first step in the process will open a page in your web browser to authenticate your Google Cloud SDK with your Google Cloud account. Your command line output may look a little different from the output here if your Google Cloud account has existing projects. For the purposes of this chapter, elect to create a new project ❶ and give it a project ID—goxkcd in this example. Your project ID must be unique across Google Cloud. Once you've completed this step, you're ready to interact with Google Cloud from the command line, just as you did with AWS.

## Enable Billing and Cloud Functions

You need to make sure billing is enabled for your project before it can use Cloud Functions. Visit *https://cloud.google.com/billing/docs/how-to/modify-project/* to learn how to modify the billing details of an existing project. Once enabled, you can then enable your project's Cloud Functions access. At this point, you can start writing code.

## Defining a Cloud Function

Cloud Functions uses Go's module support instead of requiring you to write a stand-alone application as you did for AWS Lambda. This simplifies your code a bit since you don't need to import any libraries specific to Cloud Functions or define a main function as the entry point of execution.

Listing 14-7 provides the initial code for a Cloud Functions–compatible module.

```
package gcp

import (
    "encoding/json"
    "log"
    "net/http"

    "github.com/awoodbeck/gnp/ch14/feed"
)

var (
    rssFeed feed.RSS
    feedURL = "https://xkcd.com/rss.xml"
)
```

```
type EventRequest struct {
    Previous bool `json:"previous"`
}

type EventResponse struct {
    Title       string `json:"title"`
    URL         string `json:"url"`
    Published   string `json:"published"`
}
```

*Listing 14-7: Creating persistent variables and request and response types (gcp/xkcd.go)*

The types are identical to the code we wrote for AWS Lambda. Unlike AWS Lambda, Cloud Functions won't unmarshal the request body into an EventRequest for you. Therefore, you'll have to handle the unmarshaling and marshaling of the request and response payloads on your own.

Whereas AWS Lambda accepted a range of function signatures, Cloud Functions uses the familiar net/http handler function signature: func(http .ResponseWriter, *http.Request), as shown in Listing 14-8.

```
--snip--
func LatestXKCD(w http.ResponseWriter, r *http.Request) {
    var req EventRequest
    resp := EventResponse{Title: "xkcd.com", URL: "https://xkcd.com/"}

    defer ❶func() {
        w.Header().Set("Content-Type", "application/json")
        out, _ := json.Marshal(&resp)
        _, _ = w.Write(out)
    }()

    if err := ❷json.NewDecoder(r.Body).Decode(&req); err != nil {
        log.Printf("decoding request: %v", err)
        return
    }

    if err := rssFeed.ParseURL(❸r.Context(), feedURL); err != nil {
        log.Printf("parsing feed: %v:", err)
        return
    }
}
```

*Listing 14-8: Handling the request and response and optionally updating the RSS feed (gcp/xkcd.go)*

Like the AWS code, this LatestXKCD function refreshes the RSS feed by using the ParseURL method. But unlike the equivalent AWS code, you need to JSON-unmarshal the request body ❷ and marshal the response to JSON ❶ before sending it to the client. Even though LatestXKCD doesn't receive a context in its function parameters, you can use the request's context ❸ to cancel the parser if the socket connection with the client terminates before the parser returns.

Listing 14-9 implements the remainder of the LatestXKCD function.

```
--snip--
    switch items := rssFeed.Items(); {
    case req.Previous && len(items) > 1:
        resp.Title = items[1].Title
        resp.URL = items[1].URL
        resp.Published = items[1].Published
    case len(items) > 0:
        resp.Title = items[0].Title
        resp.URL = items[0].URL
        resp.Published = items[0].Published
    }
}
```

Listing 14-9: Populating the response with the feed results (gcp/xkcd.go)

Like Listing 14-6, this code populates the response fields with the appropriate feed item. The deferred function in Listing 14-8 handles writing the response to the http.ResponseWriter, so there's nothing further to do here.

### Deploying Your Cloud Function

You need to address one bit of module accounting before you deploy your code; you need to create a *go.mod* file so Google can find dependencies, because unlike with AWS Lambda, you don't compile and package the binary yourself. Instead, the code is ultimately compiled on Cloud Functions.

Use the following commands to create the *go.mod* file:

```
$ cd gcp
gcp$ go mod init github.com/awoodbeck/gnp/ch14/gcp
go: creating new go.mod: module github.com/awoodbeck/gnp/ch14/gcp
gcp$ go mod tidy
--snip--
gcp$ cd -
```

These commands initialize a new module named *github.com/awoodbeck/gnp/ch14/gcp* and tidy the module requirements in the *go.mod* file.

Your module is ready for deployment. Use the gcloud functions deploy command, which accepts your code's function name, the source location, and the Go runtime version:

```
$ gcloud functions deploy LatestXKCD --source ./gcp/ --runtime go113 \
--trigger-http --allow-unauthenticated
Deploying function (may take a while - up to 2 minutes)...
For Cloud Build Stackdriver Logs, visit:
https://console.cloud.google.com/logs/viewer--snip--
Deploying function (may take a while - up to 2 minutes)...done.
availableMemoryMb: 256
buildId: 5d7fee9b-7468-4b04-badc-81015aa62e59
entryPoint: ❶LatestXKCD
httpsTrigger:
  url: ❷https://us-central1-goxkcd.cloudfunctions.net/LatestXKCD
ingressSettings: ❸ALLOW_ALL
```

```
labels:
  deployment-tool: cli-gcloud
name: projects/goxkcd/locations/us-central1/functions/LatestXKCD
runtime: ❹go113
serviceAccountEmail: goxkcd@appspot.gserviceaccount.com
sourceUploadUrl: https://storage.googleapis.com/--snip--
status: ACTIVE
timeout: 60s
updateTime: '2006-01-02T15:04:05.000Z'
versionId: '1'
```

The addition of the `--trigger-http` and `--allow-unauthenticated` flags tells Google you want to trigger a call to your function by an incoming HTTP request and that no authentication is required for the HTTP endpoint.

Once created, the SDK output shows the function name ❶, the HTTP endpoint ❷ for your function, the permissions for the endpoint ❸, and the Go runtime version ❹.

Although the Cloud Functions deployment workflow is simpler than the AWS Lambda workflow, there's a limitation: you're restricted to the Go runtime version that Cloud Functions supports, which may not be the latest version. Therefore, you need to make sure the code you write doesn't use newer features added since Go 1.13. You don't have a similar limitation when deploying to AWS Lambda, since you locally compile the binary before deployment.

### Testing Your Google Cloud Function

The Google Cloud SDK doesn't include a way to invoke your function from the command line, as you did using the AWS CLI. But your function's HTTP endpoint is publicly accessible, so you can directly send HTTP requests to it.

Use curl to send HTTP requests to your function's HTTP endpoint:

```
$ curl -X POST -H "Content-Type: application/json" --data '{}' \
https://us-central1-goxkcd.cloudfunctions.net/LatestXKCD
{"title":"Chemist Eggs","url":"https://xkcd.com/2373/",
"published":"Fri, 16 Oct 2020 04:00:00 -0000"}
$ curl -X POST -H "Content-Type: application/json" \
--data '{"previous":true}' \
https://us-central1-goxkcd.cloudfunctions.net/LatestXKCD
{"title":"Chemist Eggs","url":"https://xkcd.com/2373/",
"published":"Fri, 16 Oct 2020 04:00:00 -0000"}
```

Here, you send `POST` requests with the `Content-Type` header indicating that the request body contains JSON. The first request sends an empty object, so you correctly receive the current XKCD comic title and URL. The second request asks for the previous comic, which the function correctly returns in its response.

Keep in mind that, unlike with AWS, the only security your function's HTTP endpoint has with the use of the `--allow-unauthenticated` flag is obscurity, as anyone can send requests to your Google Clouds function. Since you aren't returning sensitive information, the main risk you face is the potential cost you may incur if you neglect to delete or secure your function after you're done with it.

Once you're satisfied that the function works as expected, go ahead and delete it. I'll sleep better at night if you do. You can remove the function from the command line like this:

```
$ gcloud functions delete LatestXKCD
```

You'll be prompted to confirm the deletion.

# Azure Functions

Unlike AWS Lambda and Google Cloud Functions, Microsoft Azure Functions doesn't offer first-class support for Go. But all is not lost. We can define a custom handler that exposes an HTTP server. Azure Functions will proxy requests and responses between clients and your custom handler's HTTP server. You can read more details about the Azure Functions custom handlers at *https://docs.microsoft.com/en-us/azure/azure-functions/functions-custom -handlers#http-only-function*. In addition, your code runs in a Windows environment as opposed to Linux, which is an important distinction when compiling your code for deployment on Azure Functions.

You'll need a Microsoft Azure account before proceeding. Visit *https:// azure.microsoft.com* to create one.

## Installing the Azure Command Line Interface

The Azure CLI has installation packages for Windows, macOS, and several popular Linux distributions. You can find details for your operating system at *https://docs.microsoft.com/en-us/cli/azure/install-azure-cli/*.

The following commands install the Azure CLI on a Debian-compatible Linux system:

```
$ curl -sL https://aka.ms/InstallAzureCLIDeb | sudo bash
[sudo] password for user:
export DEBIAN_FRONTEND=noninteractive
apt-get update
--snip--
$ az version
{
  "azure-cli": "2.15.0",
  "azure-cli-core": "2.15.0",
  "azure-cli-telemetry": "1.0.6",
  "extensions": {}
}
```

The first command downloads the `InstallAzureCLIDeb` shell script and pipes it to `sudo bash`. After authenticating, the script installs an Apt repository, updates Apt, and installs the *azure-cli* package.

Once installed, the `az version` command displays the current Azure CLI component versions.

## Configuring the Azure CLI

Whereas the AWS CLI required you to provide its credentials during configuration, and the Google Cloud SDK opened a web page to authorize itself during configuration, the Azure CLI separates configuration and authentication into separate steps. First, issue the `az configure` command and follow the instructions for configuring the Azure CLI. Then, run the `az login` command to authenticate your Azure CLI using your web browser:

```
$ az configure
Welcome to the Azure CLI! This command will guide you through logging in and
setting some default values.

Your settings can be found at /home/user/.azure/config
Your current configuration is as follows:
--snip--
$ az login
❶ You have logged in. Now let us find all the subscriptions to which you have
access...
[
  {
    "cloudName": "AzureCloud",
--snip--
  }
]
```

The Azure CLI supports several configuration options not covered in the `az configure` process. You can use the Azure CLI to set these values instead of directly editing the *$HOME/.azure/config* file. For example, you can disable telemetry by setting the `core.collect_telemetry` variable to off:

```
$ az config set core.collect_telemetry=off
Command group 'config' is experimental and not covered by customer support.
Please use with discretion.
```

## Installing Azure Functions Core Tools

Unlike the other cloud services covered in this chapter, the Azure CLI tools do not directly support Azure Functions. You need to install another set of tools specific to Azure Functions.

The "Install the Azure Functions Core Tools" section of *https://docs .microsoft.com/en-us/azure/azure-functions/functions-run-local/* details the process of installing version 3 of the tools on Windows, macOS, and Linux.

## Creating a Custom Handler

You can use the Azure Functions core tools to initialize a new custom handler. Simply run the func init command, setting the --worker-runtime flag to custom:

```
$ cd azure
$ func init --worker-runtime custom
Writing .gitignore
Writing host.json
Writing local.settings.json
Writing /home/user/dev/gnp/ch14/azure/.vscode/extensions.json
```

The core tools then create a few project files, the most relevant to us being the *host.json* file.

You need to complete a few more tasks before you start writing code. First, create a subdirectory named after your desired function name in Azure Functions:

```
$ mkdir LatestXKCDFunction
```

This example names the Azure Function LatestXKCDFunction by creating a subdirectory with the same name. This name will be part of your function's endpoint URL.

Second, create a file named *function.json* in the subdirectory with the contents in Listing 14-10.

```
{
  "bindings": [
    {
      "type": ❶"httpTrigger",
      "direction": ❷"in",
      "name": "req",
    ❸ "methods": [ "post" ]
    },
    {
      "type": ❹"http",
      "direction": ❺"out",
      "name": "res"
    }
  ]
}
```

Listing 14-10: Binds incoming HTTP trigger and outgoing HTTP (azure/LatestXKCDFunction/function.json)

The Azure Functions Core Tools will use this *function.json* file to configure Azure Functions to use your custom handler. This JSON instructs Azure Functions to bind an incoming HTTP trigger to your custom handler and expect HTTP output from it. Here, you're telling Azure Functions that incoming ❷ POST requests ❸ shall trigger ❶ your custom handler, and your custom handler returns ❹ HTTP responses ❺.

Lastly, the generated *host.json* file needs some tweaking (Listing 14-11).

```
{
  "version": "2.0",
  "logging": {
    "applicationInsights": {
      "samplingSettings": {
        "isEnabled": true,
        "excludedTypes": "Request"
      }
    }
  },
  "extensionBundle": {
    "id": "Microsoft.Azure.Functions.ExtensionBundle",
    "version": "[1.*, 2.0.0)"
  },
  "customHandler": {
❶  "enableForwardingHttpRequest": true,
    "description": {
      "defaultExecutablePath": ❷"xkcd.exe",
      "workingDirectory": "",
      "arguments": []
    }
  }
}
```

*Listing 14-11: Tweaking the host.json file (azure/host.json)*

Make sure to enable the forwarding of HTTP requests from Azure Functions to your custom handler ❶. This instructs Azure Functions to act as a proxy between clients and your custom handler. Also, set the default executable path to the name of your Go binary ❷. Since your code will run on Windows, make sure to include the *.exe* file extension.

## Defining a Custom Handler

Your custom handler needs to instantiate its own HTTP server, but you can leverage code you've already written for Google Cloud Functions. Listing 14-12 is the entire custom handler implementation.

```
package main

import (
    "log"
    "net/http"
    "os"
    "time"

    "github.com/awoodbeck/gnp/ch14/gcp"
)

func main() {
    port, exists := ❶os.LookupEnv("FUNCTIONS_CUSTOMHANDLER_PORT")
    if !exists {
        log.Fatal("FUNCTIONS_CUSTOMHANDLER_PORT environment variable not set")
    }
```

```
    srv := &http.Server{
        Addr:              ":" + port,
        Handler:           http.HandlerFunc(❷gcp.LatestXKCD),
        IdleTimeout:       time.Minute,
        ReadHeaderTimeout: 30 * time.Second,
    }

    log.Printf("Listening on %q ...\n", srv.Addr)
    log.Fatal(srv.ListenAndServe())
}
```

*Listing 14-12: Using the Google Cloud Functions code to handle requests (azure/xkcd.go)*

Azure Functions expects your HTTP server to listen to the port number it assigns to the FUNCTIONS_CUSTOMHANDLER_PORT environment variable ❶. Since the LatestXKCD function you wrote for Cloud Functions can be cast as an http.HandlerFunc, you can save a bunch of keystrokes by importing its module and using the function as your HTTP server's handler ❷.

## Locally Testing the Custom Handler

The Azure Functions Core Tools allow you to locally test your code before deployment. Let's walk through the process of building and running the Azure Functions code on your computer. First, change into the directory with your Azure Functions code:

```
$ cd azure
```

Next, build your code, making sure that the resulting binary name matches the one you defined in your host file—*xkcd.exe*, in this example:

```
azure$ go build -o xkcd.exe xkcd.go
```

Since your code will run locally, you do not need to explicitly compile your binary for Windows.

Finally, run func start, which will read the *host.json* file and execute the *xkcd.exe* binary:

```
azure$ func start
Azure Functions Core Tools (3.0.2931 Commit hash:
d552c6741a37422684f0efab41d541ebad2b2bd2)
Function Runtime Version: 3.0.14492.0
[2020-10-18T16:07:21.857] Worker process started and initialized.
[2020-10-18T16:07:21.915] 2020/10/18 12:07:21 Listening on ❶":44687" ...
[2020-10-18T16:07:21.915] 2020/10/18 12:07:21 decoding request: EOF
Hosting environment: Production
Content root path: /home/user/dev/gnp/ch14/azure
Now listening on: ❷http://0.0.0.0:7071
Application started. Press Ctrl+C to shut down.
```

```
Functions:

    LatestXKCDFunction: [POST] ❸http://localhost:7071/api/LatestXKCDFunction

For detailed output, run func with –verbose flag.
```

Here, the Azure Functions code set the FUNCTIONS_CUSTOMHANDLER_PORT environment variable to 44687 ❶ before executing the *xkcd.exe* binary. Azure Functions also exposes an HTTP endpoint on port 7071 ❷. Any requests sent to the *LatestXKCDFunction* endpoint ❸ are forwarded onto the *xkcd.exe* HTTP server, and responses are forwarded to the client.

Now that the *LatestXKCDFunction* endpoint is active, you can send HTTP requests to it as you did with your Google Cloud Functions code:

```
$ curl -X POST -H "Content-Type: application/json" --data '{}' \
http://localhost:7071/api/LatestXKCDFunction
{"title":"Chemist Eggs","url":"https://xkcd.com/2373/",
"published":"Fri, 16 Oct 2020 04:00:00 -0000"}
$ curl -X POST -H "Content-Type: application/json" –data \
'{"previous":true}' http://localhost:7071/api/LatestXKCDFunction
{"title":"Dialect Quiz","url":"https://xkcd.com/2372/",
"published":"Wed, 14 Oct 2020 04:00:00 -0000"}
```

As with Google Cloud, sending a POST request with empty JSON in the request body causes the custom handler to return the current XKCD comic title and URL. Requesting the previous comic accurately returns the previous comic's title and URL.

## Deploying the Custom Handler

Since you're using a custom handler, the deployment process is slightly more complicated than that for Lambda or Cloud Functions. This section walks you through the steps on Linux. You can find the entire process detailed at *https://docs.microsoft.com/en-us/azure/azure-functions/functions-create-first-azure-function-azure-cli/*.

Start by issuing the az login command to make sure your Azure CLI's authorization is current:

```
$ az login
You have logged in.
```

Next, create a resource group and specify the location you'd like to use. You can get a list of locations using az account list-locations. This example uses NetworkProgrammingWithGo for the resource group name and eastus for the location:

```
$ az group create --name NetworkProgrammingWithGo --location eastus
{
  "id": "/subscriptions/--snip--/resourceGroups/NetworkProgrammingWithGo",
  "location": "eastus",
```

```
  "managedBy": null,
  "name": "NetworkProgrammingWithGo",
  "properties": {
    "provisioningState": "Succeeded"
  },
  "tags": null,
  "type": "Microsoft.Resources/resourceGroups"
}
```

Then, create a unique storage account, specifying its name, location, the resource group name you just created, and the Standard_LRS SKU:

```
$ az storage account create --name npwgstorage --location eastus \
--resource-group NetworkProgrammingWithGo --sku Standard_LRS
 - Finished ..
--snip--
```

Finally, create a function application with a unique name, making sure to specify you're using Functions 3.0 and a custom runtime:

```
$ az functionapp create --resource-group NetworkProgrammingWithGo \
--consumption-plan-location eastus --runtime custom \
--functions-version 3 --storage-account npwgstorage --name latestxkcd
Application Insights "latestxkcd" was created for this Function App.
--snip--
```

At this point, you're ready to compile your code and deploy it. Since your code will run on Windows, it's necessary to build your binary for Windows. Then, publish your custom handler.

```
$ cd azure
azure$ GOOS=windows go build -o xkcd.exe xkcd.go
azure$ func azure functionapp publish latestxkcd --no-build
Getting site publishing info...
Creating archive for current directory…
Skipping build event for functions project (--no-build).
Uploading 6.12 MB [#######################################################]
Upload completed successfully.
Deployment completed successfully.
Syncing triggers...
Functions in latestxkcd:
    LatestXKCDFunction - [httpTrigger]
        Invoke url: ❶https://latestxkcd.azurewebsites.net/api/
latestxkcdfunction
```

Once the code is deployed, you can send POST requests to your custom handler's URL ❶. The actual URL is a bit longer than this one, and it includes URI parameters relevant to Azure Functions. I've snipped it for brevity.

### Testing the Custom Handler

Assuming you're using your custom handler's full URL, it should return results like those seen here:

```
$ curl -X POST -H "Content-Type: application/json" --data '{}' \
https://latestxkcd.azurewebsites.net/api/latestxkcdfunction?--snip--
{"title":"Chemist Eggs","url":"https://xkcd.com/2373/",
"published":"Fri, 16 Oct 2020 04:00:00 -0000"}
$ curl -X POST -H "Content-Type: application/json" \
--data '{"previous":true}' \
https://latestxkcd.azurewebsites.net/api/latestxkcdfunction?--snip--
{"title":"Chemist Eggs","url":"https://xkcd.com/2373/",
"published":"Fri, 16 Oct 2020 04:00:00 -0000"}
```

Use `curl` to query your Azure Functions custom handler. As expected, empty JSON results in the current XKCD comic's title and URL, whereas a request for the previous comic properly returns the previous comic's details.

## What You've Learned

When you use cloud offerings, you can focus on application development and avoid the costs of acquiring a server infrastructure, software licensing, and the human resources required to maintain it all. This chapter explored Amazon Web Services, Google Cloud, and Microsoft Azure, all of which offer comprehensive solutions that allow you to scale your business and pay as you go. We used AWS Lambda, Google Cloud Functions, and Microsoft Azure Functions, which are all PaaS offerings that allow you to deploy an application while letting the platform handle the implementation details.

As you saw, developing and deploying an application on the three cloud environments follow the same general process. First, you install the platform's command line tools. Next, you authorize the command line tools to act on behalf of your account. You then develop your application for the target platform and deploy it. Finally, you make sure your application works as expected.

Both AWS Lambda and Cloud Functions have first-class support for Go, making the development and deployment workflow easy. Although Azure Functions doesn't explicitly support Go, you can write a custom handler to use with the service. But despite the small variations in the development, deployment, and testing workflows, all three cloud platforms can generate the same result. Which one you should use comes down to your use case and budget.

# INDEX

*Network Programming with Go* is set in New Baskerville, Futura, Dogma, and TheSansMono Condensed. The book was printed and bound by Sheridan Books, Inc. in Chelsea, Michigan. The paper is 60# Finch Offset, which is certified by the Forest Stewardship Council (FSC).

The book uses a layflat binding, in which the pages are bound together with a cold-set, flexible glue and the first and last pages of the resulting book block are attached to the cover. The cover is not actually glued to the book's spine, and when open, the book lies flat and the spine doesn't crack.

# RESOURCES

Visit *https://nostarch.com/networkprogrammingwithgo/* for errata and more information.

Never before has the world relied so heavily on the Internet to stay connected and informed. That makes the Electronic Frontier Foundation's mission—to ensure that technology supports freedom, justice, and innovation for all people—more urgent than ever.

For over 30 years, EFF has fought for tech users through activism, in the courts, and by developing software to overcome obstacles to your privacy, security, and free expression. This dedication empowers all of us through darkness. With your help we can navigate toward a brighter digital future.